FRUCTOSE

GLUTEN DIABETES LACTOSE

HELPFUL DIETARY RECIPES FOR MOST INTOLERANCES

INTERNATIONAL CUISINE

SALICYLATES AND OXALATES

IRRITABLE BOWEL SYNDROME

BY JOAN MAGUIRE

COPYRIGHT PAGE

National Library of Australia Cataloguing-in-Publication entry : (paperback)

Creator: Maguire, Joan, author.

Title: Helpful dietary recipes for most intolerances international cuisine cookbook. Book 2 / Joan Maguire.

ISBN: 9780994543127 (paperback)

Notes: Includes index.

Subjects: International cooking.
 Malabsorption syndromes--Diet therapy--Recipes.
 Gluten-free diet--Recipes.
 Lactose intolerance--Diet therapy--Recipes.
 Diabetes--Diet therapy--Recipes.
 Irritable colon--Diet therapy--Recipes.

TABLE OF CONTENTS

Title Page	
Copyright Page	2
Table Of Contents	3
Acknowledgements	4
Introduction	5
Chapter One: Gluten Free Flour Mixes	13
Chapter Two: Sugars and Sweeteners	14
Chapter Three: Herbs and Spices	25
Chapter Four: Lactose Free Hard Cheeses Chart, Homemade Ricotta Cheese, Farmer's Cheese, and Yogurt Cheese Recipes	34
Chapter Five: Indigenous Recipes (Mainland Aborigines and Torres Strait Islanders)	38
Chapter Six: Special Salicylate and Oxalate Recipes	51
Chapter Seven: Vegetarian	63
Chapter Eight: Chile	76
Chapter Nine: Poland	87
Chapter Ten: France	99
Chapter Eleven: Philippine	105
Chapter Twelve: Jewish	116
Chapter Thirteen: Creole	136
Chapter Fourteen: Holland	145
Chapter Fifteen: Eastern Europe	156
Chapter Sixteen: Tonga	162
Chapter Seventeen: Hungary	166
Chapter Eighteen: Jamaica	174
Chapter Nineteen: Switzerland	185
Chapter Twenty: Turkey	200
Chapter Twenty One: Ireland	211
Chapter Twenty Two: Ethiopia	223
Chapter Twenty Three: Italy	236
Chapter Twenty Four: Southern Africa	254
Nigeria	255
Zimbabwe	258
Congo	262
Kenya	265
Ghana	268
Chapter Twenty Five: Japan	272
Chapter Twenty Six: Colombia	289
Chapter Twenty Seven: Cyprus	300

ACKNOWLEDGEMENTS

I would like to thank everyone who created and recreated some of the recipes that are in this book and that have been taken from my first book. I am hoping that with their help we can make a difference to someone's life.

I would like to thank the many people from the different cultures here in Brisbane who has kindly donated recipes to make this book possible. Some recipes were sent to me from organisation headquarters interstate; however, the initial contact was made to the organisation or people here in Brisbane.

I would like to thank my children and grandchildren for their constant support and keeping me grounded each time I write a new book, especially as this book is a follow up on my last cook book which was completely different to all my other books.

I would like to thank the many people who have answered many of my questions and have shared their wealth of knowledge with me so that I can relate as much correct information to you as possible.

I would like to thank my two special friends who have brought the Salicylate and Oxalates issues to my attention and inspired me to add these medical conditions to this book.

I would like to thank all my taste testers who tried some of the recipes for me and kept coming back for more.

INTRODUCTION

This cookbook is a continuation of the first "Helpful Dietary Recipes For Most Intolerances"; however, whilst it has the same dietary theme, it has an International Cuisine flavour.

Many people have kindly donated at least six everyday cultural recipes that they would have at home using ingredients that would be in their pantries and refrigerators. There are recipes that don't have amounts beside the ingredients because these cultures cook to the amount of people they are cooking for, so you will have to use the amounts that you feel will suit your family. Some people have given me permission to use the recipes; however, they didn't want their names mentioned but instead to state that they came from their community.

Some have even kindly donated their time to make sure that I have given you the most suitable substitution for the dishes and I would like to thank each and every one of them for their help and knowledge. Please remember that by adapting the original recipe it will change the taste and the composition of the recipes. You may have to alter the fluid measurements when using or changing from Gluten Free flour to another flour because the Gluten Free flour uses extra liquid. Spices and herbs will alter the taste and so you will need to adapt these to your liking.

Cookbooks are the imagination and the invention of recipes that someone has thought up. They are new ways of introducing different foods into your life in creative ways and some everyday foods in different, new and enjoyable ways. As the years roll by, another person, like me, takes recipes and changes them to keep up with the times and different life styles and then another cook book is created. And as the years have gone by, the medical profession with the aid of researchers and scientists have been able to put names to many illnesses that people have had to live with. Diets have been changed, so preparing food for people with special needs has become, in many ways, a very difficult and expensive road to travel.

Back in the early 1970s I was diagnosed with Irritable Bowel Syndrome (IBS) and was told that it was brought on by stress and there was nothing that could be done for it. I have lived most of my life being bloated due to excess wind. I have also been accused of being obese and lazy and fat. Okay, so I am carrying a bit of extra weight; however, being vertically challenged with a bloating issue, can make me look worse than what I am and I never know how bloated I will be at any time of the day or night. I know that there are other people out there who are like me as I have read some of their stories and I have personally spoken to them, so hopefully this cook book may even help them as well.

In 2013, my doctor sent me for a special breath test because of my bloating and the results came back stating that I was a Type 2 Diabetic. My diet had hardly changed over the years. I rarely ate fast foods, sweet things nor did I eat many fatty foods and I don't drink alcohol, fruit juices or gassy drinks. I cooked all my own meals from fresh vegetables and using only the occasional frozen vegetables but my wind/gas issue became worse.

Two years later my doctor arranged for an Endoscopy to be done and just before I was taken into the theatre, the surgeon who was doing the procedure asked me a few questions then stated that it sounded like I had Fructose Malabsorption (FM) and I may have had it all my life. Fructose Malabsorption has only been identified within the last 10 years; however, it was always known as IBS. Fructose Malabsorption is a complicated dietary condition. It means that I, personally, can't tolerate Fructose, Fructans, Polyols and Galactans (GOS) very well and they are in just about all fruit, veggies, herbs, spices and to a small extent, eggs.

I will attempt to put better explanations of Fructose Malabsorption and Salicylates and Oxalates at the end of the Introduction.

The breath test that I had done two years prior is the same test that is done for a few other medical issues as well. Everybody who has a medical issue is unique because their symptoms are different from everybody else. With me, my Fructose Malabsorption can play up severely with my glucose levels so I have to be a "fussy" eater both at home and when I'm out. I am also allergic to seafood, so that cuts out another food group for me. I had to find food that would not activate the IBS or cause my glucose levels to go sky high or give me the wind issues on top of what I already have. I had very little choice because just about everything has Fructose, Fructans, Polyols and Galactans (GOS) in it, especially the vegetables that my diet was based around.

After a year of eating only meat and dairy with the occasional vegetable gracing my plate, I was missing my vegetables and my body was also telling me that they wanted them too. I started researching different foods and diets to find something that was right for me and this is where my first cookbook came in. I enjoyed writing the first book and then I came up with the idea of getting more recipes to try from different countries. It was not an easy process; however, I was able to persuade quite a few people once I told them my idea for the book to assist me. Other people jumped at the chance of giving me recipes and I am very grateful to them.

I have tried to get as many different cultural recipes from every part of the world and I haven't excluded any creed, religious groups or countries unless they declined to give me some recipes or there wasn't anybody for me to contact from that country. I have not used any recipes from the net for the main recipes; however, some homemade recipes have been taken from my last book and these were from the net. The recipes in this book have been given to me freely.

I have left the original ingredients in; and have suggested other ingredients to use and to the best of my ability have made all the recipes, that can be made, into Gluten Free, Lactose Free or Lactose Friendly, Dairy Free, Fructose Free or Fructose Friendly, Diabetic Friendly and ISB Friendly; and have also added more information in the "Notes" so that you have a bigger choice of what you can use. Please read these; they are important.

Due to conflicting information on the net, I may have stated that a particular ingredient has Fructose instead of Fructans and/or Polyols. Galactans can come as part as Fructans but not all Fructans can cause "gas/wind" issues so I have mentioned them separately. Even though many of the herbs and spices are used in very small amounts and shouldn't bother many people, I have still stated where possible if they have any Fructose, Fructans, Polyols or Galactans in them so that you will know. You know your intolerances and you will know if you can use and digest these ingredients. Don't forget that if you are not using Gluten Free flour, then you have to use less liquid and I will leave that choice up to you as to which liquid you decrease.

I have also become aware of Oxalates and Salicylic Acid. Salicylates can have a dis-abilitating effect on some people who have a sensitivity to these ingredients; like Reyes Syndrome and again Fibromyalgia, so I have also tried to include a rating against the ingredients. These ratings will be done in a code form which will be stated at the beginning of every chapter. This cookbook is meant for 'most intolerances' and these are just a couple more. There will be many more intolerances out there that I don't know of, so you will have to be the judge of what ingredients you eat.

Yes, I have had many failures in making the recipes but I have also had many successes and that is what learning new things is all about. I suppose I can say that I am the worst person to follow a recipe so please consider each recipe as a basic one and make it your own by changing and using your own ingredients and what is best for you. I am not very fond of spicy or herby foods so if you like a bit of spice and can enjoy them; then by all means "spice" up the recipes or add your favourite herbs that you enjoy.

I live in Brisbane Australia, so when I say butter, I use Nuttelex Original that is made from all vegetable sources. It is like a margarine or soft spreadable butter and it is Free from milk and Lactose, Gluten Free, Free from Artificial Additives, Free from Nut oils, Free from Soy and it is Vegetarian and Vegan friendly. It is great to cook with.

I also use Liddell's Lactose Free dairy products when available and I buy some of my ingredients from a place called Simply Good here in Brisbane as they sell their products in bulk and you can buy just the amounts you need. They cater for just about everybody and have a good range of Gluten Free products and is the only place where I buy my Cacao Butter. (Now that I've told you, I had better go and replenish my stock just in case you go and buy what they have left). Remember, your choice of ingredients is what works for you.

I have begun this book with information gathered from many people and sources from the net. All this information is what I had to find out for myself and I must say that it can be contradictory from one site to another, and from what source, but I found out what I needed and you might be able to find some answers that you need from this information. I am not knocking other diets that are out there; however, these diets didn't work for me, but may or may not work for you or they may even be dangerous for you. Try them, as they may well work for you but in the end you will find your own way and your own diet. All of these recipes are suitable for all the family, depending on your family's taste. Some Gluten Free flours are higher in carbohydrates so please remember this if you have to watch your carb count or a Diabetic. A recipe is not completely Fructose Free if it contains vegetables or fruit but it can be made Fructose friendly.

In the recipes, I have only mentioned what sort of flour, sweetener, etc. to use as I don't use any particular brand and if I did use one brand, you may not be able to buy it or find out what it is actually made of, so I'll leave it up to you to use what you feel is right or experiment with some suggestions in the first chapter. It will depend on what part of the world you live in as to the availability of the ingredients and how you buy, use and store them. I have mentioned two brands in the dairy line; however, they are my own personal choices.

Again, I will acknowledge and say thank you to everyone whose recipes that I have adapted to be part of my diet and in this book. I am really hoping that all our efforts will help other people who have been living with or who have just been diagnosed with some sort of "gut" issue or other issues that need a change of diet to help ease their symptoms, like Arthritis or Fibromyalgia.

This book contains basic everyday recipes from different parts of the world so you can take your taste buds to a different country every night. Some recipes you may like to try and other ones you may feel would not be suitable for you. That's okay; there are some foods that don't really interest me at all; however, I will be willing to give them a try.

Most people know how to cook and have their own favourite dishes; however, a few different recipes that have been adapted for this particular book have been included to show how easy it can be to cook for your needs if you have the right sort of information.

I have also placed a few homemade recipes in after the main recipes for each country; so that you can make your own if you want to, and have options for substituting them.

I am not a qualified professional so do listen to your own medical team, dietician and also your own body. You know what is right for you and if you would like to make one of my recipes and you can't have an ingredient; then change it to suit you. Make my recipe suggestions your recipes and enjoy them.

I cannot state enough; these recipes were adjusted to suit my needs and medical issues so please use them as basic recipes for yourself and adjust them to suit your own needs. Every recipe can be made using normal ingredients or adjusted again to make them Vegetarian or Vegan and the ingredients are everyday ones that you should already have at home.

I have placed the donated recipes under the Country's name so you know where they come from and I have purposely not put them in any particular order except for Southern Africa. This is because I didn't want similar recipe from the same part of the world together.

I wrote this book to give you new ideas for your meals, you now have it so make my ideas yours and have fun doing so. Don't worry about making mistakes because that is how we all learn and your mistake may become a roaring success to your family. If it is, your issue will be remembering your mistake to repeat it.

I have started this book with recipes from our own Indigenous people. As there are so many tribes here in Australia, these recipes will not cover every tribe although I wish I could cover more tribes. I have also included six recipes especially adapted for people who have Salicylate and Oxalate issues and each one may not fit exactly into the theme of this book, but it is still a medical issue. These recipes have been taken from other recipes from around the world that have been given to me.

The first thing to learn is how to get flavor in your food without the oxalate and low salicylates. Oils and extracts are typically much lower in oxalate than the whole herb or spice, and yet retain the flavor for baking and cooking purposes. Unless you know what you are doing or have used them before, I don't suggest that you use them. Using food grade cocoa butter, which has zero oxalate, in place of butter or oil, is another way to cook. Some countries have low salicylate and low oxalate spices and herbs in capsule form; however, I am still not certain if they are available here in Australia.

As there are many Vegetarians and Vegan in the world, I have included six recipes just for them and have adapted them to coincide with the theme of this book. Again I say, these are just basic recipes and have been adapted from the information that has been researched on the net. Please use ingredients to suit you and your taste.

Even though the recipes are made by people here in Australia, I have had to look up some adapted measurement and the measurements may not be as accurate because there are so many different measuring tables on the net. The Australian measurements are bigger than the US ones. American tablespoons are 15ml or 3 teaspoons and Australian tablespoons are larger, 20ml or 4 teaspoons. Different liquids also measure differently; 1 cup of water measures differently from 1 cup of cream cheese in grams and mls. The oven temperature could be a bit out as well, so watch your dishes as they may cook quicker; especially when cooking with dextrose powder also known as glucose powder.

The most important thing of all is to have fun with your baking and enjoy what you are doing because that's when the best recipes are usually cooked and enjoyed.

A BRIEF SUMMARY ON FRUCTOSE MALABSORPTION

This information was taken from:
http://www.marksdailyapple.com/fodmaps/#ixzz4Cqm7oyio

"You could be having a fairly routine conversation about health and nutrition where everything discussed is familiar. You hear things like "carbs" and "medium chain triglycerides" and "fructose" and "macros" and "gluten" and "PUFAs," thinking nothing of it. Like I said, routine. Then someone mentions FODMAPs. Huh? What the heck is that? Quite possibly one of the strangest, seemingly contrived acronyms in existence, FODMAPs represents a collection of foods to which a surprisingly large number of people are highly sensitive. To them, paying attention to the FODMAPs in their diets is very real and very serious if they hope to avoid debilitating, embarrassing, and painful digestive issues.

To begin, what exactly are FODMAPs?

As I said, it's an acronym:

F is for Fermentable – Fermentable carbohydrates are carbohydrates that are fermented by bacteria instead of broken down by our digestive enzymes. In most people, some fermentable carbohydrates are healthy sources of food for the (helpful) bacteria that ferment them; these can include the prebiotics I've championed in the past and can actually improve digestive and overall health. In people with FODMAPs intolerance, certain carbohydrates can become too fermentable, resulting in gas, bloating, pain, and poor digestion, as well as proliferation of unwanted pathogenic bacteria.

O is for Oligosaccharides – Oligosaccharides are short-chain carbohydrates, including fructans (fructooligosaccharides, or FOS, and inulin) and galactans (raffinose and stachyose). Fructans are chains of fructose with a glucose molecule at the end; galactans are chains of galactose with a fructose molecule.

D is for Disaccharides – These are pairs of sugar molecules, with the most problematic being the milk sugar lactose (a galactose molecule with a glucose molecule).

M is for Monosaccharides – This describes a single sugar molecule. Free fructose is the monosaccharide to watch out for with FODMAPs intolerance.

A is for And – Every list needs a good conjunction.

P is for Polyols – Polyols include sugar alcohols like xylitol, sorbitol, or maltitol. For an idea as to their effects, type one of them into Google and note the autofill choice (hint: it's usually "diarrhoea" or "constipation" or "gas"). Since large amounts of polyols rarely occur in nature, lots of people have trouble with them.

The reality, of course, is that digestive difficulties are widespread, particularly in the industrialized world. If it's not constipation, it is diarrhoea, or bloating, or gas, or hemorrhoids, or IBS, or all of the above. These complaints are sadly very common (even more common than the stats would suggest, since many people are too embarrassed to admit they have an issue).

For many of these people, FODMAPs may be exacerbating their symptoms.

Normal carbohydrate digestion takes place in the small intestine, where polysaccharides are broken up into glucose, fructose, and galactose and transporters like GLUT2 and GLUT5 absorb them for the body to use as nutrients. Sometimes those sugar molecules make it past the small intestine into the large intestine where colonic bacteria – the gut flora we (sorta) know and love – gobbles it up via fermentation, potentially causing gas and painful bloating. The presence of too many sugars in the colon can also cause an influx of fluid, which could lead to diarrhoea. Constipation is another common symptom, though it's not clear exactly how FODMAPs cause it. And some polysaccharides, like the oligosaccharides, make it through to the colonic bacteria as a rule because they resist digestion in everyone (in healthy people, these have a useful prebiotic effect).

You might be thinking, "Cool, so I can just avoid those weird sounding sugars and be fine, right?" Probably not. FODMAPs are very prevalent in the food supply. Even if you avoid free fructose, don't drink milk, and ditch processed food containing sugar alcohols, you'll still run into them in many fruits and vegetables.

FODMAP-containing vegetables include:
Asparagus (fructose, fructans), artichoke (fructose), beets (fructans), broccoli (fructans), Brussels sprouts (fructans), butternut squash (fructans), cabbage (fructans), celery (polyols), cauliflower (polyols), eggplant, fennel (fructans), garlic (fructans), leek (fructans), mushroom (polyols), okra (fructans), onion (fructans), shallots (fructans), sweet corn (fructose), radicchio (fructans), sweet potato (polyol)

FODMAP-containing fruits:
Apples (fructose, polyol), apricots (polyol), avocados (polyol), blackberries (polyol), cherries (fructose, polyol), plums (polyol), pluots (polyol), lychees (polyol), nectarines (polyol), peaches (polyol), pears (fructose, polyol), persimmons (polyol), grapes (fructose), mango (fructose), watermelon (polyol, fructose), dried fruit (fructose), juice (fructose)

Plus sweeteners like honey, agave nectar, maltitol, sorbitol, mannitol, and xylitol. And any dairy that contains significant amounts of lactose, like milk or soft cheeses. Depending on your sensitivity, cream or butter can even do the trick.

So it covers quite a few otherwise healthy Primal foods (and some non-Primal ones, like wheat and rye and the aforementioned refined sweeteners).

Let me reiterate before I go on, because I don't want to scare everyone away from berries and broccoli: not everyone has problems with FODMAPs. Most people probably don't. If you're eating all that stuff without issue, continue doing so and consider this post merely an academic curiosity.

Who might benefit from limiting FODMAPs?

Anyone with small intestinal bacterial overgrowth (SIBO)
Normally, the small intestine has relatively low numbers of gut flora residents. In SIBO, it's got tons that aren't supposed to be there. They interfere with nutrient absorption, digestion, and just generally muck everything up. SIBO has been shown to correlate quite strongly with lactase deficiency. Without enough lactase, you won't be able to digest lactose (one of the premier FODMAPs) and your colonic bacteria will have to do the job. Another, earlier study found that patients with SIBO also show malabsorption of fructose and sorbitol in addition to lactose; all three are FODMAPs.

Anyone with IBS
Low-FODMAP diets beat the pants off conventional dietary advice for people with IBS. One study found that while healthy subjects had increased flatulence on a high-FODMAP diet, subjects with IBS had increased flatulence in addition to lethargy and adverse GI symptoms. This could indicate that both groups were feeding FODMAPs to their gut bugs (which produce the flatulence through fermentation), but only the IBS patients had enough pathogenic gut flora to produce adverse symptoms.

Anyone suffering from chronic stress
Stress is a well-known disruptor of digestive function as anyone who's gotten queasy, lost their appetite, or had explosive diarrhoea before the big interview could tell you. There's evidence that stress might be causing FODMAP-intolerance, too. First, stress inhibits the action of GLUT2, a transporter responsible for the small intestinal absorption of glucose, fructose, and galactose in the gut. If you're unable to adequately absorb the sugar molecules in the small intestine, they end up making it to your large intestine for fermentation by colonic bacteria. Second, stress has an immediate impact on the composition and function of your gut flora, rendering your populations less diverse and allowing certain pathogenic species to overpopulate.

Anyone with otherwise unexplained digestive problems
Maybe you haven't had a diagnosis. Maybe you just don't feel right after eating almost anything. Maybe you're chronically constipated (or the opposite). Trying a low-FODMAP diet can help you narrow your focus and start to identify some culprits.

If you decide to embark on a low-FODMAP diet, consider keeping a diet journal to log your food and track your reactions to individual FODMAPs. Some people might really react poorly to fructose while having no issues with lactose. Point being: different FODMAPs affect different people differently. You can tolerate some and not others.

Dosage matters, too. A gram of inulin might be fine, while five grams could cause distress. Individual tolerance must be determined by, well, seeing what and how much you tolerate.

If you're interested in healing your gut, whether from SIBO or IBS or anything else that might be predisposing you to FODMAP intolerance, well-established protocol like GAPS (Gut and Psychology Syndrome) diet or SCD (specific carbohydrate diet) may help and are worth looking into.

If you have no digestive issues, I would caution against trying a low-FODMAP diet "just because". You'll be missing out on some very nutritious, important foods, probably unnecessarily, while adding a bunch of unnecessary stress to your eating. FODMAP-related digestive issues are very noticeable. You'll know it if you have it".

Some people can be born with Hereditary Fructose Malabsorption or get it when they are babies. The surgeon who did my Endoscopy thinks that's when I may have got it.

Another snippet about Fructose Malabsorption that we need to remember comes from http://www.strandsofmylife.com/8-symptoms-fodmap-intolerance-explained/

"All fruits and vegetables contain fructose and many contain fructans and polyols, which can cause us folk problems.

Some are lower in these substances than others and so can be tolerated in small helpings. Your digestive system rules your life.

Of course, this rules your life. I have always wondered what it would be like to not have to constantly think about this issue and how it would impact on each of my decisions in life. I know now because I have it under control – finally. I seldom worry about toilets any longer but must always be aware of what goes into my mouth. If I suffer or not is now up to me. Not to fate".

* * * * *

OXALATES AND SALICYLATES: http://www.pkdiet.com/pdf/oxalate%20lists.pdf

"Some folks are particularly bothered by oxalates and salicylates, which are plant chemicals and yet, if they were to ask their physicians about them, would find no answers concerning them.

Oxalates are chemicals in plants (and some animal foods) that bind with minerals in the body, such as magnesium, potassium, calcium, and sodium, creating oxalate salts. Most of these salts are soluble and pass quickly out of the body. However, oxalates that bind with Calcium are practically insoluble and these crystals solidify in the kidneys (kidney stones) or the urinary tract, causing pain and irritation. Oxalates, as far as I know, are not used in products but as flavourings for recipes. One spice is Cinnamon that is a very high oxalate spice with over 38 mg of oxalate for just one teaspoon. Choose instead cinnamon oil or cinnamon extract. Cinnamon oil is available from various outlets that sell culinary oils. You can get cinnamon extract in the supplement section of your grocery or health food store – generally, it is sold in capsules. When cooking with it, you simply open the capsules and put the powdered extract into your dish. Substitute about the equivalent amount of dry extract for ground cinnamon. (Not sure about here in Australia).

Salicylates are natural chemicals found in plants that protect the plant from being eaten by insects or attacked by disease. Although poisonous, salicylates are usually tolerated when ingested in small amounts, but when ingested too frequently, they can cause a wide range of symptoms. Salicylates are found to a higher degree in unripe food. This poses problems for Americans, as our food is often picked way too early. Salicylates are used to make prepared foods, hygiene (toothpaste, lotion, soap, etc.), cosmetic, and drug (Aspirin and others) products, which we are also using more and more of".

I know that there are a multitude of other well-known medical conditions and many more unknown medical conditions that require special diets; however, I am unable to cover all of them in these recipes. Again I state and please remember that I am not qualified in any field of medicine or nutrition and can only share my findings with you for many of the foods that I eat and in these freely given recipes for all of us to try. Please listen to your own professional advisors and your own body.

You could try blanching your green vegetables for 10 minutes to help lowered oxalic acid by 40-115% and may push many veggies back into the low oxalate/safe zone. Soaking rices and grains for 12 hours may help to lower the oxalates. Soaking beans and lentils overnight using warm water to start with and 2 teaspoons of bi-carb soda may help reduce the "gas" issue. Change this bi-carb water often and rinse well before cooking.

GLUTEN FREE FLOUR MIXES

There is a wide variety of Gluten Free flour mixes available at health food shops and grocery stores. Most "all purpose" blends are a mixture of rice flour, potato flour or potato starch, corn starch and tapioca flour. However, there are a wide variety of more exotic mixes available now, such as buckwheat mixes, quinoa flour and amaranth flour mixes.

Please note, that unlike the all-purpose mixes, these mixes might not be appropriate for every baking experience. For a more fail safe experience stick to the "all-purpose" mixes.

There are two kinds available; – plain (all-purpose) flour, and self-raising (or self-rising) flour. Self-raising flour is not commonly sold in America, but is widely used in Australia. It is all-purpose flour with added baking powder and salt that makes baked goods rise without the need to add anything.

The original writer of this article states "I have had success modifying conventional recipes using self-raising gluten free flour. But I really do prefer to mix my own gluten free flours for my specific requirements. But you can't beat these gluten free mixes for convenience. Just keep them fresh by storing these flours in sealed glass jars in the fridge. If you use stale self-raising flour, your baked goods may fall a little flat".

I have put a few different recipes for Gluten Free flour mixes for you to choose from.

ALL-PURPOSE FLOUR MIXES

The Gluten Free Lifesaver's own flour mix:
200 gm / 7 oz finely ground white rice flour
100 gm / 3.5 oz Buckwheat flour
100 gm / 3.5 oz Sorghum flour
300 gm / 10.6 oz Potato starch
300 gm / 10.6 oz Tapioca flour
50 gm / 1.76 oz non-fat dry milk powder (can be dropped for a dairy free option)
10 gm / 0.35 oz guar gum

Take care to mix the different flours together thoroughly, using an electric mixer if possible. More is more in this case.

When making your own flour mixes it is always better to use weight rather than volume measurements.

Great flour mixes from other recipe developers:

250g / 9oz of sorghum flour or brown rice flour 250g / 9oz tapioca flour 100g / 3½oz almond flour 1 teaspoon guar gum	6 cups white rice flour 3 cups tapioca flour 1½ cups potato starch 2 tablespoons xantan gum 1 tablespoon salt
2 cups white rice flour ⅔ cup potato starch ⅓ cup tapioca flour	6 parts rice flour 2 parts potato flour 1 part tapioca flour

2 parts soy flour 1 part rice flour 1 part potato flour	4 parts soy flour 4 parts potato flour 1 part rice flour 1 part glutinous rice flour
180g superfine white rice flour 145g cornstarch 85g tapioca starch/flour 80g superfine brown rice flour 60g non-fat dry milk 20g potato starch 10g guar gum	160g superfine brown rice flour 160g superfine white rice flour 80g tapioca starch/flour 80g potato starch 20g potato flour 18g guar gum 8g pure powdered pectin (no calcium)
200g oat flour (certified GF, for those who choose to include this in their diet) 100g millet flour 100g buckwheat flour 300g potato starch 300g tapioca flour	200g sorghum flour 200g millet flour 300g sweet rice flour 300g potato starch

SELF-RAISING:
Simply add 1½ teaspoon of Gluten Free baking powder per 250g / 9oz of your chosen all-purpose flour mix.

CAKE FLOURS:

3 cups fine ground brown rice flour 1 cup potato starch (not potato flour) ½ cup tapioca flour 1¼ teaspoon guar gum OR xantan gum	250g / 9oz brown rice flour 250g / 9oz sorghum flour 250g / 9oz tapioca flour
1¼ cup superfine white rice flour ¾ cup potato starch ½ cup sorghum or oat flour ¼ cup superfine brown rice flour 2 teaspoons baking soda 2 teaspoons gluten free baking powder 2 teaspoons guar gum	1 cup brown rice flour ½ cup ground arrowroot or cornstarch ½ cup sweet potato flour ⅔ cup potato starch ⅓ cup tapioca starch 1 tablespoon potato flour 1½ teaspoon guar gum
1¼ cup (300 ml) sorghum flour ⅔ cup (150 ml) amaranth flour ⅔ cup (150 ml) brown rice flour ¼ cup (50 ml) quinoa flour 2 tablespoons (25 ml) potato starch 2 tablespoons (25 ml) tapioca starch ¾ teaspoon (4 ml) guar gum ¾ teaspoon (4 ml) salt	

SUGARS AND SWEETENERS

This is the most important part of this book is for people who need to learn how to live with Fructose Malabsorption and still eat without the discomfort from the food. Many people can tolerate artificial sweeteners and Stevia; unfortunately, I am not one of them. If I have any sugar, it is usually raw sugar and the amount I have does not affect me or dextrose powder.

Since learning about Fructose, I have been changing the sugar content in my recipes. I have found that using either dextrose (Glucose Powder) or rice malt syrup doesn't really change the final cooked product; in fact, I personally think that the cakes are not as sweet as they used to be. Liquid Glucose is another product that I tend to use a lot of in my cooking. Liquid Glucose and Rice Malt Syrup are readily available in most supermarkets but I find it hard to get dextrose powder in the supermarket so I buy it in bulk from Simply Good in Alderley.

Again I say; you will find what works for you as far as sweeteners are concerned and I hope the following information will help you too.

Dextrose – which is simply the powdered form of glucose our body's favorite fuel. Dextrose is finer than sugar, similar in texture to caster sugar, and tastes similar to sugar, but isn't as sweet. And that last comment really applies to all of these sweeteners; not as sweet. Dextrose can be found in the brewing section of some supermarket – apparently it works better for beer making than sugar. **Make sure you don't buy 'brewing sugar', which is dextrose mixed with sugar. The packaging looks similar**.

Glucose Syrup – thick and sticky, clear and a bit sweet (any guesses about what it breaks down to?) I get this in the baking section of the supermarket.

Rice Malt Syrup – lovely and honey-like in colour and texture, and upon digestion, breaks down to good old glucose. I buy this in my local supermarkets and it can be in the sugar section, baking section or health food section. It should be easy to find in a health food shop too, but it's cheaper at the supermarket.

REFINED SUGAR SUBSTITUTES

Refined sugar has become something our society doesn't seem to be able to live without. It comes under many names – sugar, glucose-fructose, fructose, fruit sugar, corn syrup, glucose syrup (high-fructose corn syrup) and beet sugar. It's in everything from sweets to soups, sauces to bread – we can't seem to get away from it. Is this really a big issue? Does it really matter? For many people, Yes, it does matter considerably.

Crystallised refined sugars are pure sucrose and contain no nutrients beyond calories. Brown sugar, demerara, turbinado, and raw sugar have often been recommended as healthier alternatives to white sugar, but these sugars are virtually the same as white sugar. All these sugars are refined sugars of different sizes and various stages of processing. After processing, the crystals are reunited with some of the molasses in artificial proportions. Brown sugar is actually just refined white sugar with some molasses added to it.

The molasses contains vitamins and minerals, and is recommended for a healthy diet, but the crystals themselves are pretty much 'empty carbs'. These sugars have a glycemic index that is nearly as high as white sugar.

Some have switched to organic raw sugar in an effort to have a healthier sweetener, but it is not really any better than white sugar.

All 'raw' sugar is highly processed, whether organic or not – the only difference to regular raw sugar is that it's grown with organic agricultural methods, then refined as usual.

UNDERSTANDING THE TYPES OF SUGAR CATEGORY: FEATURED

Sugars are the simplest forms of carbohydrates, also known as saccharides. Sugars can be monosaccharides (meaning a single sugar molecule) and disaccharides (double), which are simply two monosaccharides bonded together. Our body actually breaks down almost everything we eat into these sugars, which are then combined to form more complex carbohydrates like starch.

This means that natural sugars are present in many foods, including those we wouldn't recognise as sweet. It also means different forms of sugar vary in their level and type of sweetness. For example the sweetness of honey and golden syrup is quite different to the sweetness of brown sugar, because they differ in chemical composition. This difference in composition also causes different sugars to act differently when cooked or baked, and will result in different levels of sweetness or a finished product that may brown easily or have a crumbly texture.

Glucose is a monosaccharide and is less sweet than other sugars. Fructose, on the other hand, is the sweetest known monosaccharide. Sucrose, or common sugar, has 1 part glucose and 1 part fructose. Sometimes knowing what parts certain sugars or syrups break down into can help when choosing a substitute.

Sugar There are many varieties of sugar and despite their similarities they aren't all interchangeable. Here's a quick guide to the most common types of sugar.

Common Sugar
White table sugar has a large variety of uses. Normal granulated sugar has a grain size of about 0.5mm across. You can also get larger grained sugars still considered 'common', such as hail sugar, which is popular for decorating cookies and other desserts.

Caster Sugar
Caster sugar is preferred in pastry and cake making as the granules are finer (around 0.35mm) and dissolve faster. With more sharp edges to cut through fat, batters become aerated more rapidly. Caster sugar also dissolves into beaten eggs for meringue with greater efficiency, and it's worthwhile to know that table sugar will typically produce a cake with a speckled crust.

A small note on etymology, the term caster or castor sugar is a British term given to sugar fine enough to fit through a sugar "caster" or sprinkler. In the United States this sugar is also sold as "superfine" sugar.

Icing Sugar (or confectioners' sugar)
This is crushed, powdered granulated sugar. It is used in icings, fillings and some pastries, such as friandes and sable. It's also one of the most important ingredients in cake decorating. This is because icing sugar is the basis of royal icing, which is used for decorating and writing, and it's also used to make "cake glue" and to dust surfaces before rolling out icings.

There are a few different sorts of icing sugar and they are not interchangeable. Pure **Icing Sugar** is pure unmixed sugar with no additives.

Pure icing sugar is quite lumpy and usually needs to be sifted. This is the sugar used for Royal icing.

Icing Sugar Mixture is sugar that has been blended with a small amount of cornflour (around 4%). It's not so good for cake decorating work as the small amounts of flour present can start to form mould if there is any moisture in the cake or decorated items (and there usually is).

Pure sugar will not grow mold. Icing sugar mixture, however, is fantastic for making simple glazes and icings, and fillings where a small amount of cornflour will not affect the result. It does not clump or lump and this is a definite advantage.

Snow Sugar is icing sugar with a mixture of cornflour and a touch of vegetable fat and dextrose. This mixture produces a sugar that doesn't melt when dusted onto cakes and tarts. This is its primary use, although some people bake with it very successfully.

Palm Sugar
Palm sugar is extracted from a sugar-giving tree, of which there are several varieties. The most generous is the Asian sugar palm. The sap is collected from the flowers or from a tap in the trunk, then boiled down to syrup (called palm honey) or crystallised to a mass. The dark sugar is often called jaggery and has a distinct almost winey aroma. It is mostly used in Indian, Indonesian and some African cuisines. A lighter palm sugar is also used extensively in Thai cuisine. This lighter palm sugar is the most common palm sugar used in our kitchens in Australia.

Brown Sugar
Brown sugars are softer and moister than granulated sugars. Their crystals are coated with a molasses like syrup. Darker sugars are more intensely flavoured, as the colour relates to the molasses retention. Glucose and fructose are present in the molasses syrup coating the crystals. These attract and retain more moisture in the sugar itself, making brown sugars great for baking, as the products will retain more moisture and stay fresher for longer periods.

Granulated sugars are 99% sucrose and brown sugars vary between 85-92%. If brown sugar is used instead of granulated sugar the result will be more flavourful and moist but the browning temperature will be lower.

Demerara sugar is also considered to be in this category, as it often comes from the first crystallisation of cane juice, producing yellow gold crystals that are frequently washed with alcohol to make them shiny and clear. Muscovado sugars are the crystallisation of the dark mother syrup forming very small, sticky, intensely flavoured sugars.

Invert Sugar
Invert sugar is made from a sucrose water solution (basic sugar syrup) that is heated with the addition of acid. Although invert sugar naturally occurs in honey, molasses and corn syrup, to name a few, it can also be purchased as a paste or syrup. It doesn't crystallise and it retains moisture. It is sweeter than sucrose (standard sugar), and when added to baked goods it will keep them moist longer. It also helps prevent ice formation in ice creams and sorbets.

Therefore, it is used extensively in ice cream, sorbet, glazes and sauces, fondant and candy making. Fudge and caramel sauce are two more examples where the non-grainy texture afforded by invert sugar is important.

Molasses (also known as treacle)
There are a number of grades of molasses. The darker the molasses, the more bitter it is. Blackstrap molasses is usually the last extracted and is very dark as its sugars have been caramelised over and over and an effort to extract as much sucrose as possible.

Most of the syrups available as molasses (or treacle) are a blend of molasses in various stages of caramelisation and sugar syrups. This is so the molasses can be sold in an almost uniform condition.

Molasses is generally added to a recipe for colour, flavour and moisture, rather than sweetness. This is why many recipes use molasses or treacle with sugar also added, such as gingerbread. Molasses is common in liquorice, baked beans, and barbecue sauce. Molasses are variably acidic, which makes them work well with bi-carbonate of soda as a leavening agent.

Golden Syrup
This is refinery syrup made from raw sugar filtered through charcoal to give it a clear appearance and delicate flavour.

Honey
Honey is great for longevity in baked goods. It is very high in fructose and glucose, and quite similar to invert sugar. It is approximately 1¼ times as sweet as granulated sugar. Heating honey makes it less liable to crystallise. The sweetness of the fructose in honey is registered almost immediately on the tongue, and fades very quickly. This quick action is said to enhance the flavours in some foods, especially fruitiness, tartness and spiciness without the sweetness lingering long enough to mask the flavour of the other ingredients. This is why honey and lemon work so well, and why honey is often used in a spicy marinade.

Maple Syrup and Maple Sugar
Maple syrup originates from the sap of the maple tree. The season for harvesting maple sap is very short (approximately six weeks). The water in the sap is separated from the sugars and boiled down, leaving heavily flavoured syrup. It takes about 40 parts sap to make 1 part syrup.

Maple syrup is graded by colour, flavour and sugar content. Grade A being the highest grade. The lower, darker grade syrups are used in baked goods and glazes. Cheap maple flavoured syrups are usually not maple at all; they're usually corn syrup with maple flavour added. Maple sugar is made by concentrating (boiling) the sap down for much longer than is needed to make the syrup until all that's left is a solid sugar.

Glucose (also known as dextrose)
Glucose is the building block of sugars, the chemical place from which sugar chains are started. It is found in fruits and honey, amongst other things. Glucose is less sweet than granulated sugar. It is less water soluble, producing a thinner solution. It melts and starts to caramelise at 150°C / 300°F, where granulated sugar will caramelise at around 170°C / 340°F. Used in toffees, candies and ice creams, it can keep the product soft and gooey while still caramelising and setting.

Corn Syrup
Corn is the second largest sugar producing crop. Corn syrup begins as a starchy liquid that is converted into sugars by the addition of acid. The thickness of corn syrup is due to the large number of carbohydrate molecules that are tangled up with each other. This results in a syrup that is much thicker than a standard sugar can produce.

Due to the tangled nature of its molecular composition, corn syrup has the valuable effect of preventing other sugars from crystallising and producing a grainy texture. This means that it helps minimise the size of ice crystals in ice cream encouraging a creamy consistency. Its viscosity helps impart a thick chewy texture to foods.

It is less sweet than sugar because it contains a lot of glucose, preventing moisture loss without being overbearingly sweet. Corn syrup is acidic, due to the way it is produced; therefore, it works well with baking soda.

Light corn syrup is a mixture of regular and high fructose corn syrup with the addition of vanilla. It contains around 75% fructose plus glucose making the sweetness similar to table sugar. The combination enhances the moisture and develops colour in baked goods. Dark Corn Syrup is a mixture of corn syrup and refiner's syrup, used for colour and flavour.

Date Syrup
This is made from date solids in a solution of sugar. Brands vary but can be a mix of approximately 37% solids with the remaining 63% being a mixture of glucose, fructose, and water.

Grape Syrup
A lovely syrup made from concentrated grape juice containing fructose and glucose, not unlike date syrup.

Our best option is, of course, to avoid sugar as much as possible, cutting down drastically on the amount of sweets we eat, reducing the ratios of sweeteners in recipes, and replacing refined sugar with more natural sweeteners. Most of the following suggestions are high in Fructose and/or Fructans and may contain Polyols, so please be aware if you have Fructose Malabsorption or a Diabetic as they may not be good for your glucose levels.

Only Maple Syrup and white sugar are reported to be "Negligible" on my Salicylates table and the rest of them have different amounts of Salicylates in them so please be careful in using them.

Raw Honey (GI 35-38) is very easy to digest, and has a lower glycemic index than refined sugar. It works well in cakes, drinks, custards, desserts and soft, chewy biscuits, and can be used in this ratio: 1 cup of sugar = ½ - ¾ cup of honey. Oven temperature needs to be lowered a little when cooking with honey, as it burns more easily than sugar. Some recipes may need a little less liquid (or more flour) when using honey, or the mixture can turn out too wet.

Dark Molasses (GI 54) can be used in place of brown sugar in baking, with a little stevia or ground up dates added for sweetness if needed. Again, the liquids/flours may need to be altered to make sure the mixture is not too wet.

Coconut Nectar (GI 35) – although that number is debated) is a mineral-rich liquid sweetener made from the coconut palm blossoms. It is minimally processed, and is an 'environmentally friendly' sugar. Coconut palms produce 50-75% more sugar than sugar cane per acre, and use less than 1/5th of the nutrients for that production.

Coconut Sugar (GI 35) – although that number is debated) is the evaporated, granular form of coconut nectar, and is very similar in taste and texture to Rapadura, except maybe a little milder. It's very much one of the more popular 'healthy sweeteners' these days. Use coconut sugar when you need the 'bulk' and 'texture' of sugar, as it's a healthy, low GI option.

Rapadura (GI 65) can be used just like sugar, but has a lot more goodness than refined sugars. It is a wholefood product, high in vitamins and minerals (compared to other sweeteners), and a form of it (Jaggery) is even used in Indian medicine for its healing properties.

It's minimally processed, won't alter the texture of baked goods when used instead of processed sugar, and has a richer, deeper flavour than sugar. Also known as Panela.

Ground Dates (GI 42) can be used in place of sugar (in equal amounts, cup for cup), especially brown sugar, as they have a caramel flavour. They work best in baking where the sugar does not need to be fine, as they don't dissolve like sugar does, unless they are cooked until soft first. They're also great for sweetening smoothies and raw treats. Process the dates on their own, or with nuts/seeds, before adding the remaining ingredients.

Stevia (GI 0) is an amazingly sweet substitute for sugar which is from the leaves of the stevia plant, which has a GI of zero, so is great for diabetics or those with fructose malabsorption. You only need about 1 teaspoon of stevia powder instead of a cup of sugar. It comes in a few different forms, liquid or powder, but use the natural, green stevia powder as it's just the dehydrated, ground leaves, and isn't refined like other forms of stevia. Stevia can have a slightly bitter aftertaste (especially the white, processed version), but tastes better if a little of another sweetener is added to the recipe with the stevia. Eg: instead of a cup of sugar, try ½ of a cup of Rapadura and a ¼ of a teaspoon of powdered stevia.

Pure Maple Syrup (GI 54) is boiled down from the sap of the maple tree, and can be used the same way as honey. It gives a lovely flavour, and is especially good in ice-creams, smoothies and pie fillings. Make sure you get the pure product, preferably organic, not the ones with added sugar.

Fruits are another option for healthy sweeteners as they contain plenty of fibre, which lowers the glycemic index, as well as living enzymes, vitamins and minerals. Many raw desserts use fruit as the only sweetener, and delicious fruit sorbets and 'ice-creams' can be made with frozen fruit and no other sweetener. Dried fruit can also be used to sweeten baking, but be aware the sugars in dried fruits are more concentrated.

So as you can see, there are many options other than refined white sugar, which you can use to sweeten your cooking. Don't be afraid to experiment – often the result is a lot better than it would have been with the white sugar anyway. And the improvement in your health will be worth it.

Please be careful with Aspartame (Methanol) (951) as it is a common yet dangerous artificial sweetener hidden in many common foods and beverages, especially baby food. Aspartame poisoning can be serious and even life threatening.

SPLENDA® NO CALORIE SWEETENER, GRANULATED
It measures cup for cup like sugar – so whatever amount of sugar your recipe requires just substitute the same amount of SPLENDA® Granulated Sweetener.

Sugar SPLENDA® Granulated Sweetener
1 cup 1 cup

Sugar SPLENDA® Packets
2 teaspoons = 1 packet
1 tablespoon = 1½ packets
1/8 cup = 3 packets
1/4 cup = 6 packets
1/3 cup = 8 packets
1/2 cup = 12 packets
2/3 cup = 16 packets

3/4 cup = 18 packets
1 cup = 24 packets

SPLENDA® Sugar Blend
It is part SPLENDA® Brand Sweetener and part sugar. That means you'll only need to use half as much to replace the sugar in your recipes.

Sugar SPLENDA® Sugar Blend
1 teaspoon = 1/2 teaspoon
1/4 cup = 1/8 cup or 6 teaspoons
1/3 cup = 8 teaspoons
1/2 cup = 1/4 cup
2/3 cup = 1/3 cup
3/4 cup = 6 tablespoons
1 cup = 1/2 cup

SPLENDA® Brown Sugar Blend
It's part SPLENDA® Brand Sweetener and part brown sugar. That means you'll only need to use half as much to replace the brown sugar in your recipes.

Sugar SPLENDA® Brown Sugar Blend
1 teaspoon = 1/2 teaspoon
1/4 cup = 1/8 cup or 6 teaspoons
1/3 cup = 8 teaspoons
1/2 cup = 1/4 cup
2/3 cup = 1/3 cup
3/4 cup = 6 tablespoon
1 cup = 1/2 cup

STEVIA
Stevia (SweetLeaf, Truvia, Pure Via) is 200 times sweeter than sugar and has 0 calories; it's made from the extract of the stevia plant. It's often blended with granulated sugar.

Manufacturer's guideline: Use 6 packets Truvia to replace 1/4 cup granulated sugar.

Substitutions:
Truvia: 1 teaspoon sugar = 1/2 packet or 1/2 teaspoon
Truvia Baking Blend: 1 cup sugar = 24 packets or 1/2 cup
Truvia Baking Blend - Pure Via: 1 teaspoon sugar = 1/2 packet or 1/4 teaspoon;
1 cup sugar = 24 packets or 12 teaspoons.
Stevia in the Raw: 1 teaspoon sugar = 1/2 packet or 1 teaspoon from Bakers Bag;
1 cup sugar = 24 packets or 1 cup from Bakers Bag.
Stevia LLC products, Sweetvia and Sweetvia.

1/33 of a teaspoon of stevia (liquid) (same as mini-spoon included in Sweetvia 1 oz. bottle) = 1 teaspoon sugar.
1/4 to 1/3 of a regular teaspoon of stevia (White Powder Extract Only) = 1 cup sugar.
The stevia powder referred to in this chart is the pure form, or the liquid made from the pure powder.

Stevia Conversion Chart

Sugar amount	Equivalent Stevia powdered extract	Equivalent Stevia liquid concentrate
1 cup	1 teaspoon	1 teaspoon
1 tablespoon	1/4 teaspoon	6 to 9 drops
1 teaspoon	A pinch to 1/16 teaspoon	2 to 4 drops

Substitutions: Sweet'N Low: 1 teaspoon sugar = 1/2 packet or 1/2 teaspoon bulk Sweet'N Low; 1 cup sugar = 24 packets or 8 teaspoons bulk Sweet'N Low.
Substitutions: Equal: 1 teaspoon sugar = 1/2 packet or 1 teaspoon Equal Spoonful/Granulated; 1 cup sugar = 24 packets or 1 cup Equal Spoonful/Granulated.
Substitutions: Sunett: No information available.
Sweet One: 1 teaspoon sugar = 1/2 packet; 1 cup sugar = 24 packets
Substitutions: Splenda: 1 teaspoon sugar = 1/2 packet or 1/2 teaspoon. Splenda Sugar Blend; 1 cup sugar = 24 packets or 1/2 cup Splenda Sugar Blend.
Substitutions: Nectresse: 1 teaspoon sugar = 1/2 packet or 1/4 teaspoon; 1 cup sugar = 24 packets.

SWEET'N LOW

In recipes for sweetened sauces and beverages, all the sugar can be replaced with Sweet'N Low. However, recipes for most baked goods require sugar for proper volume and texture. For best results, experiment by substituting half the amount of sugar in a recipe with the sweetening equivalence of Sweet'N Low.

Sweet'N Low Substitution Chart

Sweet'N Low	Packets Sweet'N Low	Bulk Sweet'N Low	Liquid
1/4 cup granulated sugar	6 packets	2 teaspoon	1 1/2 teaspoons
1/3 cup granulated sugar	8 packets	2 1/2 teaspoons	2 teaspoons
1/2 cup granulated sugar	12 packets	4 teaspoons	1 tablespoon
1 cup granulated sugar	24 packets	8 teaspoons	2 tablespoons

EQUAL®

Equal® sweetens like sugar, but its cooking properties are different. Equal® works very well in fruit pies; however, cakes, cookies and pastries depend on sugar for bulk, tenderness, and browning, properties that sugar alternatives don't have. When cooking with Equal®, use recipes designed for Equal® or add to recipes after removing from heat to maintain sweetness. Prolonged cooking at high heat levels may result in some loss of sweetness.

LEARN ABOUT THE FRUCTOSE RICH FOODS YOU SHOULD AVOID
FRUCTOSE IN COMMON FOODS

To put your average fructose consumption in perspective, consider the amounts in these common foods:

Figs, 1 cup – 23g
Raisins, 1/4 cup – 12g
Apple, 1 medium – 10g
Banana, 1 medium – 7g
Date (medjool, 1 medium) – 8g
Blueberries, 1 cup – 7g
Blackberries, 1 cup – 3.5g
Cranberries, 1 cup – 0.7g
Grapefruit, medium – 8.6g
Maple syrup, 1 tablespoon – 6g
Honey, 1 tablespoon – 12g

It's easy to see how using concentrated sources of sweetness – like dried fruits, maple syrup and honey – in "Paleo" dessert recipes can quickly drive fructose intake to unhealthy levels.

A Low Sugar Diet = A Longer, Healthier Life.

When reaching for fructose-containing foods – weigh the benefits. For example, a cup of dark berries is a better choice than a cup of melon, as it is rich in powerful antioxidants and lower in fructose. Similarly, raw honey – in small amounts – provides antioxidant benefits.

For natural sweetening power in your baking, consider creating a low sugar, low fructose blend of the following:
Non-GMO or Organic Erythritol – A zero calorie, zero glycemic sugar alcohol sweetener found in common foods like pears, watermelon and soy sauce. It has antioxidant properties and can be used in baking, cup for cup, just like sugar. Choose non-GMO and organic varieties. (Not sure about sugar alcohols?) (Polyols)

Stevia – A potent sweet herb that is best combined with erythritol to boost sweetness levels. Contains zero calories and zero sugar.

Luo Han Guo – Derived from a super-sweet melon, this potent sweetener has no calories or sugar and is best used with erythritol.

Coconut Sugar – Produced from the nectar of coconut flower buds, coconut sugar is 70-80% sucrose, of which half is fructose. Per tablespoon, coconut sugar contains 12 grams of sugar and 6 grams of fructose. Use sparingly – 1 tablespoon per 12 servings.

Coconut Nectar – Also produced from coconut flower buds, coconut nectar gives a rich caramel flavor to desserts. Per tablespoon, coconut nectar contains 13 grams of sugar and 6.5 grams of fructose. Use sparingly – 1 tablespoon per 12 servings.

Organic Molasses – Rich in minerals, a small amount of molasses can add a rich flavor to baked goods. Per tablespoon, molasses contains 14 grams of sugar and 7 grams of fructose. Use sparingly – 1 tablespoon per 12 servings.

For optimum health, enjoy the native foods our ancestors did – filling your plate with nutrient-dense grass-fed beef, pastured poultry, wild fish and colorful vegetables – while keeping total daily sugars and fructose low (25 grams and 15 grams, respectively).

Equal Substitution Chart

Sugar Equal®	Packets Equal®	For Recipes Equal®	Spoonful
2 teaspoons	1 packet	approx. 1/4 teaspoon	2 teaspoons
1 tablespoon	1 1/2 packets	1/2 teaspoon	1 tablespoon
1/4 cup	6 packets	1 3/4 teaspoons	1/4 cup
1/3 cup	8 packets	2 1/2 teaspoons	1/3 cup
1/2 cup	12 packets	3 1/2 teaspoons	1/2 cup
3/4 cup	18 packets	5 1/2 teaspoons	3/4 cup
1 cup	24 packets	7 1/4 teaspoons	1 cup
1 pound	57 packets	5 tablespoons plus 2 teaspoons	2 1/4 cups

DEXTROSE POWDER (GLUCOSE POWDER)

I buy my dextrose powder in bulk quantities; however you may not be able to do this. I have been trying to make this book as neutral as possible by not using brand names; however, I have purposely left this brand's name in so that it may be easier for you to find the product. I do know that you can by this brand in Rice Malt Syrup but I have not seen it in the powdered form. Please read the extra information on Dextrose following the Fructose Chart.

How to convert a sugar recipe to be sugar free and some tips that will make converting your traditional sugar recipes into Fructose Free easy

One cup of sugar means one cup of Dextrose powder. The Sugar Breakup Dextrose converts cup for cup with sugar. If the recipe says use 1 cup of sugar then use 1 cup of The Sugar Breakup Dextrose.

Weight matters 250g of Sugar = 180g of The Sugar Breakup Dextrose.

Scales: The Sugar Breakup Dextrose is lighter than sugar. A cup of sugar weighs approximately 250g; a cup of The Sugar Breakup Dextrose weighs approximately 180g. So if a recipe is done by weight not cups then multiple the sugar weight by 0.72.
For example: 125g of sugar = 90g of Dextrose.
60g of sugar = 43g of Dextrose.

Add more liquid.

Butter: Dextrose soaks up more fluid then sugar so you may need to add a little more of the liquid ingredients. Eg: if the recipe recommends 125gm of butter increase this to 140gm.

Eggs: Always use large eggs when cooking with Dextrose.

Temperature control on an oven: In cakes dextrose can cook faster than sugar so we recommend you turn the oven down 10°C / 50°F from the sugar recipe temperature. Eg: If the sugar recipe says 180°C / 350°F, then turn the oven down to 170°C / 330°F and keep an eye on your cake as you approach the anticipated cook time.

Double line with baking paper cake tin: For best results double line your cake and biscuit tins with non-stick paper.

Here's a quick reference list of some of the most common fruits that you can use to help you count your fructose grams (again different sites give different values and don't forget the Polyols):

Fruit	Serving Size	Grams of Fructose	Fruit	Serving Size	Grams of Fructose
Limes	1 medium	0	Boysenberries	1 cup	4.6
Lemons	1 medium	0.6	Tangerine/mandarin orange	1 medium	4.8
Cranberries	1 cup	0.7	Nectarine	1 medium	5.4
Passion fruit	1 medium	0.9	Peach	1 medium	5.9
Prune	1 medium	1.2	Orange (navel)	1 medium	6.1
Apricot	1 medium	1.3	Papaya	1/2 medium	6.3
Guava	2 medium	2.2	Honeydew	1/8 of med. melon	6.7
Date (Deglet Noor style)	1 medium	2.6	Banana	1 medium	7.1
Cantaloupe	1/8 of med. melon	2.8	Blueberries	1 cup	7.4
Raspberries	1 cup	3.0	Date (Medjool)	1 medium	7.7
Clementine	1 medium	3.4	Apple (composite)	1 medium	9.5
Kiwifruit	1 medium	3.4	Persimmon	1 medium	10.6
Blackberries	1 cup	3.5	Watermelon	1/16 med. melon	11.3
Star fruit	1 medium	3.6	Pear	1 medium	11.8
Cherries, sweet	10	3.8	Raisins	1/4 cup	12.3
Strawberries	1 cup	3.8	Grapes, seedless (green or red)	1 cup	12.4
Cherries, sour	1 cup	4.0	Mango	1/2 medium	16.2
Pineapple	1 slice (3.5" x .75")	4.0	Apricots, dried	1 cup	16.4
Grapefruit, pink or red	1/2 medium	4.3	Figs, dried	1 cup	23.0

Dextrose Contradictions are again at large. One site states that Dextrose powder comes from many sources including wheat but is safe for everyone to use. Another site states that it is not safe for people who are Gluten Free. The same goes with Diabetes; one site says yes and another says no. Being Diabetic myself, I say yes and use it in moderation like everything else I have to eat. You make up your own mind and follow what your medical advisers say and your own gut feeling. You know what is right for you.

HERBS AND SPICES

Most of the ingredients listed below are available in the supermarkets, health food and specialty stores. The spices comprise of valuable seeds, roots, barks, dried leaves and flowers. There are also a few recipes for you if you want to make your own mixtures.

Appetisers - a small portion of fruit, juice or any food served as the first course of a meal.

Aniseed - a small seed of an aromatic plant — used in sweet making and for flavouring puddings and pastries. Used in masalas as well.

Asafoetida - (Heeng) - a very strong smelling spice powder or crystals from Indian food stores. Use to replace onion as a seasoning. Heeng is used in minute quantities when cooking any legume family. Excellent for the digestive system. Also used by some religious groups to give an onion like flavour to food as they are prohibited to use onions in any form. My friend always used Heeng when cooking dhals and beans and some vegetables because it is famed as an antidote for flatulence, especially in Urad dhal and savoury snacks. May contain gluten.

Bayleaf - a herb used extensively in Western cooking around the world in its dried form. Dried bay leaf is excellent ground in spices. Fresh bay leaves have many uses in stocks, casseroles, soups, rice and masala chai etc.

Cumin - these tiny light greenish brown seeds are of the caraway family. These seeds are used more often in a large variety of Indian cooking. Cumin seeds are sprinkled on raitas (yoghurt salad) sambals, drinks, savoury snacks and others to give that special aromatic flavour. It is also mixed in masalas.

Coriander seeds - a small round, yellowish seed which is used in stocks, soups, pickling spice and sauces. Coriander seeds are usually ground and are used in innumerable dishes in Indian cooking.

Coriander powder: added to make special garam masala, sabzi masala and masala and used separately in curries, pulaos and biryanis. It is a very versatile spice.

Coriander leaves and stems are from the same plant as coriander seeds. It is the coriander leaves that give dishes the special characteristic pungent aroma usually associated with Indian fare. The fresh green leaves are used for garnishing a variety of dishes and also for making chutney.

Cinnamon - the inner tender bark of the cinnamon tree. This aromatic spice is powdered and used both in sweets (cakes and puddings) and savouries as well as in curry powder. In pulaos, cinnamon is mostly used whole. The piece is mostly removed from the dish just before serving if desired. Whole cinnamon stick is used in some special meat dishes as phoran.

Cloves - an aromatic spice used in so many ways. It is one of the most useful spices in garam masala and other ground masalas. Used as phoran occasionally in special meat dishes and rice. It is also used in soups, stocks, sauces, curries, gravies, puddings and masala chai. The spice is a dried flower with an unmistakable sweet and pungent appearance. It is also used in apple pies and other sweet dishes.

Cardamom - an aromatic spice, brownish and green pods containing fragrant seeds. The larger variety of green large pods is used entirely for curries, pulaos and biryanis either whole or powdered.

The smaller variety with brownish pods is generally used for Indian and Western sweets, cakes and puddings. It is also used along with other spices for curries, pulaos and biryanis. Very popular spice in masala chai and the seeds as an after dinner mint.

Chilies - Chilies are small capsicum family used to add heat to any dish. They range in colour from green, yellow, red, purple and orange. The shapes of round long, thin plump and bird's eye variety from tiny, medium to plump ones, yellow and green in colour.

If you like you can add green chillies in dishes for its special aroma and taste. Chillies are very versatile. (I am unable to digest chilies so I don't use them).

Chili wine is excellent in winter. Dried red chilies are excellent in meat and seafood dishes and sauces. Chili pickles, chili relish, chili jam and chili chutney are popular. Chili powder is used extensively in all cooking for convenience.

The following are different species of chilies:
Poblano - special flavour not so hot
Jalapeno - also mild in flavour
Ancho Chilli and Long Red - also mild and tasty, they dry well and will keep for years
Hot Chillies - Habanero- orange or yellow
Mexican - hot
Chinese - hot
African - frilly red and orange
Bird's Eye - green and yellow - excellent for drying
Mini bird's eye - a favourite in fresh chutneys and sambals Cayenne - hot
Thai bird's eye - hot
Salsa - medium
Dutch - medium

Chilli powder - Grind the dried red chillies in a coffee grinder to powder. Alternately grind with a mortar and pestle to powder.

Fenugreek - Methi - these brownish tiny bitter tasting bean like special spice, particularly good in fish, beans and certain dhal recipes to counteract inflatulence. In the Vedic Era, centuries ago fenugreek laddu was most prized sweet for special occasions. It is very rich and nutritious. The tender leaves are good to use in salads, chapatis and cooking.

Fennel Seeds - Greenish brown seeds - bit like caraway seeds. These are used whole and ground. Whole fennel seeds are used in phoran and many vegetable and dhal preparation. Serve lightly roasted fennel seeds as a mouth refreshers — chewed as an after dinner mint, It's often a focal point of conversation. Fennel seeds grow well in winter.
This is an excellent herb to use in salads sandwiches and cooking. Stems can be used in poaching, fish or chicken. Dry the seeds in the sun and keep in airtight containers. They are also Fructose Friendly.

Turmeric - Haldi - this is the spice that gives that distinctive yellow colour to every dish. It has medicinal properties. It is an essential ingredient in curry powder. The root (rhizome) of the turmeric plant is easily grown in the tropics. Saffron - the most used expensive spice in the world is bright orange in colour. Saffron is used to colour and flavour certain special dishes. A small pinch is a flavouring in sweets, pudding, chutney and drinks. It is most popular in pulaos, biryanis and special meat dishes. Buy in thread form. Saffron is obtained from a plant of the crocus species.

Pepper - a commonly used spice. There are four varieties - black, green, white and red. The black, green and white are from the same shrub. Green pepper is freshly plucked and black and white peppers are dried, white pepper is obtained by removing the outer husk of the seed.

Red or cayenne pepper is prepared from the seeds of certain types of red chilies or from red capsicum pods. Pepper is generally used in a powdered form in cooking but in some recipes it is also used whole such as pickles, sauces, stocks, masala chai. These dried whole berries are called peppercorns.

Mustard Seeds - there are two varieties, small black and brown. Small black seeds are mostly used in Indian cooking. It is used whole in phoran and many recipes at the beginning of cooking. It is especially good in omelettes, rice dishes and coconut chutney.

The brown variety is mostly used in pickles, powders and spices and spreads.

Mustard seeds one of the useful spices in Indian and other cuisines. So many varieties of mustard spreads are on the market.

Curry Powder - is readily available everywhere in the supermarkets and specialty stores. However, you can make your own mix without much effort to create that special magic into your kitchen.

Ginger - (Adrak) Fresh ginger, the aromatic rhizome is peeled, grated, minced, julienne and chopped and used in many recipes in all types of cook book. Ginger pickle and masala chai are just two types of uses for ginger.

Ginger is an important flavouring in Indian cooking. Ginger is regarded as a digestive aid, which is always added to beans, dhals and vegetables. Ginger powder is also used in tandoori marinade, chai masala, chutneys, relishes, sweets, cakes and other preparations. If fresh is unavailable, ginger powder (1 teaspoon ginger powder for 1 tablespoon fresh ginger), may be substituted.

Curry leaves - (Teg Patti) during summer, spread the leaves in your pantry for moths. They are the most important leaf in Indian cooking. This is the first ingredient fried with phoran (Indian Five Spice Blend) during any Indian recipe preparation to impart that special flavour to the oil. Fried curry leaves are excellent for garnishing.
Chopped curry leaves are used in savoury snacks and breads. Tender leaves make a delicious chutney.
Dried leaves are ground into masala and curry powder.

Curry leaves - fresh are available in supermarkets and vegetable outlets.

Mint Leaves - (Pudeena) Mint an aromatic herb used both in fresh and dry form. It is used for flavouring soups, some meat dishes, savoury dishes, garnishing, chutneys, pesto and raitas. There are so many varieties on the market. However, the old favourite, wild type is widely used. Dried mint leaves are also very useful in many recipes, crumbled over raitas or in recipes. Mint tea made from fresh mint leaves is very refreshing.

Parsley - a very popular herb grows easily around the globe. There are two varieties, the frilly and plain, also known as Italian parsley. This herb is used for flavouring and garnishing. It is one of the most useful herbs in the world. When coriander is out of season: use parsley in its place. Parsley is very nutritious. Make parsley pesto either plain or with other ingredients for excellent spreads or dips.

I use parsley in my scrambled egg and just about all my savoury dishes. Fried or raw parsley sprig is excellent as a garnish for fish or savoury dishes.

Tamarind - (Imli) A bean like fruit of the tamarind tree. Looks like a long brownish bean with feathery leaves. The pod clusters of the tamarind tree contain seeds and light brown sticky pulp. At maturity it turns darker. The pulp is very tasty to eat fresh from the tree with a touch of salt and chilli powder or sugar and chilli powder. This is used as a souring or acidifying in Indian cooking, often blended with palm sugar or brown sugar to produce that special sweet and sour effect. Dried pulp makes a very tasty chutney, sauces and drinks.

The juice, which is extracted by soaking a few pods in hot water for 15 - 20 minutes, squeezing the softened pods and then straining the juice. This juice, which is sour, is used in a number of curry and sauce dishes.

*   *   *   *   *

VEGETABLES HERBS AND SPICES

Here is a list of suggestions that you may like to use depending on your sensitivity.

You may use dried herbs in place of fresh herbs - simply add about half the amount of dried herbs as fresh (for example, 1 tablespoon fresh herbs equals 1-1½ teaspoons dried). The flavor of dried herbs is more concentrated so you don't need as much.

Blend 1 teaspoon dry mustard powder with 1 teaspoon white vinegar or water to use in place of 1 tablespoon prepared yellow mustard.

If you don't have fresh ginger, use ⅛ teaspoon ground ginger for each tablespoon fresh ginger called for in the recipe.

Two teaspoons dried Italian herb seasoning equals 1 teaspoon dried oregano leaves, ½ teaspoon dried basil leaves, and ½ teaspoon dried thyme leaves.

If a recipe calls for tarragon, it's fine to substitute the same amount of basil. They both have a similar, liquorice-like flavor.

Parsnips are a root vegetable that looks like a white carrot. Although parsnips are sweeter, it's fine to use an equal amount of carrots in place of parsnips in recipes.

There are two varieties of parsley: flat-leaf and curly. Flat-leaf is milder tasting than curly, but they may be used interchangeably.

Dried sage comes in two forms: rubbed, which is crumbled pieces of dried sage leaves, and ground, which is powdery. They may be used interchangeably, but crush the rubbed sage with your fingers to break up.

If a recipe calls for crystallized ginger, substitute an equal amount of minced fresh ginger root or half the amount of ground ginger. Galangal can also be used but has a peppery tone.

Shallots look like small, torpedo-shaped red onions. They have a mild onion flavor and can be eaten raw or cooked. If you don't have shallots, use finely minced red or yellow onion.

To make your own version of Cajun or Creole seasoning, combine equal parts paprika, ground black pepper, garlic powder, dried oregano leaves and dried thyme leaves. It's usually fairly spicy, so add cayenne to taste depending on how hot you want to make it.

Although the flavor of different dried herbs varies, most can be used interchangeably with each other. So don't worry if you don't have dried basil - swap it out with dried oregano, thyme or marjoram. The dish will still taste terrific.

It is fine to use ½ a sweet yellow onion in place of 1 bunch of green onions (scallions) in recipes. It's a good idea to sauté the onion in a little vegetable oil first to eliminate any strong taste.

Some stew and soup recipes call for adding a bay leaf to the liquid for flavor. But other hearty herbs work well too - try fresh rosemary or thyme sprigs. The flavor will be a little different but still good.

Lemongrass is a long, reed-like herb used extensively in Thai cooking. In place of 1 lemongrass stalk, use the minced zest of 1 lemon and ⅛ teaspoon minced fresh ginger.

For each teaspoon of poultry seasoning called for in a recipe, substitute ¼ teaspoon dried thyme leaves and ¾ teaspoon dried (rubbed) sage.

Generally, it's okay to use different hot fresh chili interchangeably in recipes. Depending on the variety, heat levels vary so you may need more or less than the recipe calls for. Jalapeños and serranos are the mildest (but still spicy); habaneros are the hottest.

*   *   *   *   *

SPICES

Spices are the magic ingredient of Indian cuisine and they determine the taste of each prepared dish.

Essential Points to Remember when Cooking Indian Food
Ghee - although it is traditional to use ghee in Indian cooking, if desired any fat such as butter or margarine and any oil can be used. (If on a diet, start with a teaspoon of oil and finish with water or cook in all stock).

Onions - In Indian cuisine onion plays a very important role in the preparation of the recipes as a thickening agent. Onions are never allowed to brown which would ruin the flavour and appearance of the dish. In some curries the finer the onions are chopped the better and in some cases spring onions or shallots are preferable.

Garlic and ginger is another major ingredient in Indian cooking. Garlic should never be allowed to brown, as it will spoil both the flavour and appearance of the curry. Garlic is only really pervasive when it is raw or only briefly cooked. Longer cooking brings out its sweet mild flavour and smooth consistency. Try cooking a few cloves in the microwave or oven less than a minute and enjoy the delicate special flavour.

Lemon Grass - tender fresh lemon grass stalk is excellent in meat gravies for poaching fish and chicken. Dried stalk is used in curry powder. The most popular being used as lemon grass tea, fresh or dried.

Curry Leaves - green leaves are used as Phoran: at the beginning of cooking. Dried leaves are used in curry powder and chutneys. Young shoots and leaves are also used to make chutney and savoury snacks.

Sour or Tang - tomatoes, lemon, lime, vinegar, tamarind pulp, and yoghurt are generally used.

The Masala - spices or curry powder ingredients, when added to the onion, garlic, ginger, curry leaves, chillies in oil with whole seeds before adding other ingredients should always be fried gently for 2-3 minutes on low heat to get rid of the raw flavour of the Masala or curry powder which is done by continually adding a splash of water to the pan and stirring all the while. This is known as 'chauch' and the whole seeds used are fenugreek, mustard, cumin, and fennel which is known as 'Phoran' and this is the most important step in the art of making an Indian curry. Knowing how to use spices with subtlety is the secret of authentic Indian cooking.

Instead of adding water to curry, add akni (stock) whenever gravy is required in a recipe. However, if you must use water, ensure that it is hot. By adding water you automatically dilute the flavour. By adding stock you automatically increase the flavour and nutritional value.

Coconut Milk - where recipes call for coconut milk, if time does not permit to extract milk and you are out of canned milk, use evaporated milk or carton milk instead. Try coconut milk next time. Otherwise use instant coconut milk powder. Follow directions on the packet. For best results, try to cook curry very slowly to extract all the richness and flavour of the curry spices. For seasoned curry eaters, make a good curry sauce base and keep in the fridge.

Yoghurt - is used frequently in the cooking as a base for curry or as a marinade and used in raitas (yoghurt salad) as well as made into a refreshing drink called Lassi by whisking and diluting with milk, a little sugar or honey, rose water and ice cubes, even soda water. Many of the recipes in this book give an alternative of red peppers or chillies as an ingredient. Use of red peppers will result in a mild curry; the chillies will give a hotter curry. The hotness of the curry will depend therefore, on the number of chillies used and their size. For a curry with medium heat, you might like to use a combination of both — a pepper and small chilli or half a chilli. For the beginners of Indian food, always make sure the seeds are removed from the chilli before using, as the seeds are very hot and most unpleasant to bite into if you are not used to it. Remove the seeds from peppers too (use plastic gloves).

Panch Phoron (Indian Five Spice Blend) Combine the following seeds in a small bowl and store in an airtight container: 1 tablespoon cumin seeds, 1 tablespoon brown mustard seeds, 1 tablespoon fennel seeds (Fructose Friendly), 1 tablespoon nigella seeds (also called black cumin or kalonji), 1½ teaspoons fenugreek seeds.

Here is a short list of herbs and spices with their Fructose values (based on levels per 200 calorie serving - I don't know what they mean by the serving size). Fructans, Polyols and Galactans are not mentioned so remember they come with and could be higher than Fructose.

Spice	Fructose	Spice	Fructose
Vinegar, balsamic	16773mg	basil, dried	598mg
Paprika	4645mg	Mustard, prepared, yellow	537mg
Vinegar, cider	2857mg	curry powder	486mg
chili powder	2732mg	parsley, dried	304mg
ginger, ground	1026mg	turmeric, ground	254mg
cinnamon, ground [Cassia]	899mg	Basil, fresh	174mg
oregano, dried	739mg	poppy seed	110mg
cloves, ground	662mg	mustard seed, yellow	9mg

FRUCTOSE FRIENDLY COOKING INGREDIENTS, HERBS AND SPICES

| Baking powder | Baking soda | Cacao powder | Cocoa powder | Cream, ½ cup |
| Gelatine | Ghee | Icing sugar | Lard | Salt |

Herbs: Basil, Cilantro, Coriander, Curry leaves, Fenugreek, Lemongrass, Mint, Oregano, Parsley, Rampa, Rosemary, Tarragon, Thyme.

Spices: All spice, Black pepper, Cardamon, Cinnamon, Cloves, Cumin, Curry powder, Fennel seeds, Five spice, Mustard seeds, Nutmeg, Paprika, Saffron, Star anise, Turmeric.

Oils: avocado oil, canola oil, coconut oil, olive oil, peanut oil, rice bran oil, sesame oil, sunflower oil, vegetable oil.

Asafoetida powder: - great onion and garlic substitute (may contain gluten) Use a tiny pinch for onion and/or garlic flavour. (Available from Indian spice markets and online)

HEALTHY BAKING: SURPRISING BUTTER SUBSTITUTES:

Baking calms the mind and feeds the soul, but all that buttery goodness can pack on the pounds. If looking to make healthier baked goods, omitting some or all of the butter from your favourite recipes greatly reduce the amount of calories, fat, and cholesterol in your sweet treats. There are countless ways to replace eggs in recipes, and here are healthier alternatives to using butter. These substitutes are great for vegan bakers too.

Apple sauce: Often used to replace oil in recipes, applesauce can also be used as butter alternative, and works best in cake-like recipes (like this Vegan Banana Apple Chunk Bread). Replace half the amount of butter in your recipe with applesauce; if the recipe calls for one cup of butter, use half a cup of butter and half a cup of applesauce. If you don't mind a denser, moister bread, replace all the butter with applesauce to cut even more calories and fat.

Avocado: Substitute half the amount of butter in a baking recipe with mashed avocado (it works well with cookies); use the same method as you would when using applesauce. Using avocado not only lowers the calorie content but also creates a softer, chewier baked good, and is perfect if you want to omit the dairy.

Keep reading for more healthy ways to replace butter in your baked goods but be mindful if you have Fructose Malabsorption and don't forget the Fructans and Polyols.

Nuttelex: Replace all of the butter with Nuttelex to reduce saturated fat and cholesterol. It is also good to use for all issues that I am trying to cater for in this book.

Canola/vegetable/olive oil: In certain recipes, replacing butter with oil works well, especially if the recipe calls for melted butter. Fiddle with your favourite recipes to figure out when the oil works instead of butter; when baking chocolate chip cookies, success has been made by substituting half a cup of canola oil for half a cup of unsalted butter.
Although slightly higher in calories, canola is much lower in saturated fat, cholesterol, and sodium.

Greek yoghurt: Replace half the amount of butter in your cookie recipes with half the amount of full-fat plain Greek yoghurt. For example, if the recipe calls for one cup of butter, use half a cup of butter and one quarter cup of yoghurt. You'll reduce the calories and the saturated fat. Play around with using more yoghurt and less butter to see if you still like the taste and consistency.

Prune purée: Often used to help little ones stay regular, prune purée also makes a low-calorie and low-fat alternative to butter.

Whatever amount of butter the recipe calls for, replace it completely with store-bought baby food prune puree (unless you have time to make your own; just purée prunes in the food processor). This option works well in recipes that involve chocolate and cinnamon.

Sucrose is also known as white table sugar, brown sugar, raw sugar and Rapadura sugar. It contains 50% fructose and 50% glucose.

Agave is a sugar substitute made from the same Mexican succulent that tequila is made from. It contains roughly 90% fructose – higher than sucrose. Look out for it in "health" bars and chocolate.

Coconut sugar/nectar/syrup: You'll often find one of these variations of coconut sugar in many health food products. Unfortunately it contains anywhere between 38% - 48.5% fructose, which is almost the same amount found in sucrose.

Honey: Whether it's raw or organic doesn't matter when it comes to fructose content. Honey contains 40% fructose, which is only 10% less than sucrose.

Maple syrup is often used as a healthier sugar alternative. Unlike other sugar substitutes it does have some health benefits but still contains up to 40% fructose.

Dates are often used to sweeten "sugar-free" recipes, but they contain roughly 30% fructose. Plus they often need to be used in large quantities to get the same sweetness.

Rice malt syrup is made from fermented cooked rice. It's a blend of complex carbohydrates, maltose and glucose. It's 100% fructose free. It is my preferred sweetener of choice.

Stevia is a plant-based sweetener. It's completely fructose free and 300 times sweeter than sugar. It's great in recipes where you want to add a little sweetness, but avoid using it in large quantities as it can have a bitter aftertaste.

Usage

Natural sweeteners can be used to replace sugar in any recipe. Here is a guide to substituting these products for sugar. The amount indicated is equivalent to 1 cup of sugar, and the third column details what it is best to use for. I've also found that sweet fruits and veggies are great for sweetening up recipes. Bananas are awesome in baked goods!

Sweetener	Amount = 1 cup Sugar	Use
honey	1/2-2/3 cup	all-purpose
maple syrup	1/2-3/4 cup	baking, desserts, sauces
maple sugar	1/2-1/3 cup	baking, candies
Sucanat	1 cup	baking, sauces
brown rice syrup	1-1 1/3 cups	baking, cakes, sauces
date sugar	2/3 cup	breads, baking, candies
coconut sugar	1 cup	all-purpose
blackstrap molasses	1 to 1 1/3 cups	all-purpose
stevia	See manufacturer's label for quantity and usage. Use the stevia conversion chart located above	

SOME LITTLE REMINDERS

At the end of the day, even natural sugars are still sugar and you should eat them in moderation.

If you are using "normal" flour you will not need to use xanthan gum, guar gum or chia seeds; however, you will need to remember that Gluten Free flours tend to need more liquids so you will need to tweak the recipe to slightly less liquid amounts or add a touch more of the dry ingredients.

Kosher salt is an edible salt with a much larger grain size to common table salt so use only half the amount of common salt if substituting.

This is just part of the tip of the "iceberg" that some of us have to conquer and many people don't understand what we have to go through. We also have Fructose, Polyols and Galactans in the following foods to contend with as well.

HIGH & LOW FRUCTAN FOODS (Fructose and Polyols not included)

	High Fructan Content	Alternative Lower Fructan Content
Fruits	Custard Apples, Persimmon, Rambutan, Watermelon	All fruits except those in High Fructan list
Vegetables	Artichokes, asparagus, beetroot, brussels sprouts, cabbage, chicory, dandelion leaves, fennel, garlic, leeks, okra, onions (brown, red, white, onion powder), peas, radicchio, spring onions (white part).	Alfalfa, avocado, bamboo shoots, bean shoots, bok choy, broccoli, capsicum, carrots, cauliflower, celery, chives, choy sum, cucumber, eggplant, endives, ginger, green beans, lettuce, marrow, mushrooms, olives, parsnips, potatoes, pumpkin, silver beet, snow peas, spinach, spring onions (green part only), squash, swedes, sweet potatoes, taro, tomatoes, turnips, yam, zucchini.
Grains, Cereals, etc	Wheat based products: bread, pasta, couscous, cracker and biscuits. Rye based Products: Bread, dry biscuits.	Amaranth, arrowroot, barley, buckwheat, corn (maize), millet, oats, potato, quinoa, rice, sorghum, tapioca.
Legumes	Chickpeas, lentils, all legume beans.	None

There are two small Fructose Charts on pages 24 &25. I acknowledge that the other medical issues that I am trying to address in these recipes are just as important as mine, so I hope that you all find something different for yourselves to enjoy.

When I stated earlier that the tip of the iceberg was Fructose, Fructans and Polyols, I was not kidding as there are still many more issues (Galactans) that each and every one of us have to deal with in our own ways.

A little bit of information on Galactans: "Galactooligosaccharides (GOS) are short chains of galactose molecules that can cause symptoms due to fermentation. It should be noted that the GOS are generally found in legumes and seaweed and many foods have not been characterized regarding their GOS content".

Yes, Fructose Malabsorption is a complicated medical condition and there will be more people out there, than what we know about, who will agree with me. It is not just Irritable Bowel Syndrome as some people think it is.

If you have read these last chapters well, you would notice that there are contradictions in there. On one site on the net, for instance, it stated that Honey is very high in excess Fructose where in the section above it states that Honey is 40% Fructose. What is not reported above is that another site states that honey also has some Fructans and Polyols.

This is why many times I will say that I will leave it up to you if you use certain ingredients or not. You should know what you can use and if you don't; then experiment with ingredients to find out.

This idea comes from http://sillyyaks.com.au/products/product-features/fructose-malabsorption-allergies/
"There is a simple way, however, to get the flavour of the onion into a dish without the fructose. The key is in understanding that the fructose in the onion is contained in the flesh of the onion and that this fructose is not liberated by soaking, boiling, etc., but remains in the flesh. It is therefore possible to make an "onion water" by taking a couple of large onions, quartering them and then tying them tightly into a mid-sized muslin bag. The bag can then be boiled in water, or as part of a more complex stock. So long as the flesh of the onion remains in the bag and is removed from the pot once it has cooled, the resulting stock or "onion water" will have all of the taste of the onion without the fructose". Onions are also high in Fructans and the Polyol mannitol.

LACTOSE FREE HARD CHEESES CHART

They are naturally Lactose Free and have strong flavors, pungency and character and a long shelf life.

Cheese Name	Flavor	Color	Texture	Description & Uses
Asiago	Sharp	Light yellow	Firm to very firm	Italian-style cheese with sharp, rich flavor. Used for eating and cooking. Harder, more aged versions used for grating in ways similar to Dry Jack or Parmesan.
Carmody	Medium sharp	Light yellow	Firm	A firm, flavorful, smooth-textured table cheese that also melts well. Typically aged four to six months.
Cheddar	Ranges from mild to extra sharp	Light yellow to orange; may also be white	Firm	Cheddar describes a family of cheeses — very popular and versatile cheeses available in a range of flavors from mild to very sharp. Good as is and in sandwiches. Melts well and is very good in cooked foods or shredded and sprinkled on top. Also available in an organic version.
Cheddar (raw milk)	Sharp, aged	White	Firm	Unpasteurized (raw) milk plus aging gives Cheddar a delicious sharpness. Eaten as is, with crackers, bread or fruit.
Colby/Jack	Mild to medium sharp	White and yellow/orange	Firm	A blend of Colby and Jack used for eating, especially sandwiches and snacks. Also called CoJack and Calico.
Cotija	Salty, pungent	White	Semi-firm to firm, crumbly	Hispanic-style cheese similar to Feta. Crumble and sprinkle over cooked dishes, soups, beans and salads. Also called Queso Anejo (aged cheese). Some types may be very dry and hard (see Very Hard Cheeses section).
Edam	Mild	Yellow with wax coating	Firm	Similar to Gouda, Edam is very tasty as is, with crackers or other snacks.
Enchilado	Aged, slightly spicy coating	Red spice coating, white interior	Firm, dry, crumbly	Slightly aged Hispanic-style cheese with mild red chili or paprika coating. When aged longer (Anejo-style) may be quite hard. Heated, it softens but does not melt. Crumble onto Mexican foods, soups and salads.
Fontina	Mild, nutty	Light yellow	Firm	Mild, pleasant cheese for snacking and sandwiches, similar to Gouda and Edam. (A variation, Fontinella, is firmer and drier.)
Frying Cheese	Mild, slightly salty	White	Firm	A Middle Eastern-style cheese typically cut into slices and fried. Holds shape when hot. Top with sauces or salsa. Used for saganaki.

Gouda	Mild, nutty	Yellow with wax coating	Firm	A popular mild cheese, eaten as is for snacks, also in cooked foods, salads and sandwiches. Similar to Edam.
Gouda (raw milk)	Sharp	Light yellow	Firm	A Dutch-style cheese also called Boere Kaas. Has a sharper, more complex flavor than most Goudas due to use of raw milk and aging. Used for eating and cooking.
Havarti	Mild, slightly tangy	Pale yellow	Semi-firm	Mild cheese similar to Edam and Gouda. Used both for snacks and in cooked foods and salads.
Longhorn	Mild to sharp	Light yellow to orange	Firm	A form of Cheddar. Used as is and in cooked foods.
Port Salut (also Port du Salut or St. Paulin)	Mild	Light yellow	Firm	A French-style cheese similar to Gouda or Edam in taste and appearance. Eaten as is, but also good for cooking.
St. George	Medium sharp	Light yellow	Firm	Portuguese-style table cheese with a rich, medium sharp flavor.

* * * * *

http://nutritiondata.self.com/foods-001011000000000000000.html?maxCount=15

Something for you to think about concerning Fructose in eggs (based on levels per 200-Calorie serving); Fresh raw egg white contains 292mg. Whole poached egg contains 155mg. Whole fresh raw egg contains 154mg. Whole fried egg contains 122mg. Whole cooked omelette contains 115mg. Egg yolk has 41 IU of Vitamin D.

* * * * *

LACTOSE FREE RICOTTA CHEESE

Ingredients for about 2 cups
8 cups or ½ gallon Lactose Free cow milk or goat milk
1 (6oz) container Lactose Free plain yogurt
¼ cup vinegar (L-MOX and VHS) of your choosing
1 teaspoon non-iodized salt

Directions
Whisk milk and yogurt together in a large cooking pot over medium heat. Stir often to avoid scorching. Bring the milk up to 175° (hot but not yet simmering; use a candy thermometer if you have one) and remove from heat. Add vinegar while stirring briefly. Tiny bits of curd will form. Set the mixture aside for 15 minutes.

Line a colander with several layers of cheesecloth. Pour curds and liquid (whey) into colander to strain. Let drain for at least an hour. Ideally, tie up the bundle with twine, thread the twine around a wooden spoon, and suspend the bundle over a pitcher to drain, in the refrigerator, for a couple of hours or more.

Transfer solids to a bowl and add salt, working in gently. (You can also add lemon zest, herbs, or anything you like for flavor). Refrigerate in a covered container; keeps for about a week.

HOMEMADE FARMER'S CHEESE

Ingredients
1 gallon or 4 litres whole Lactose Free milk (SEE NOTES)
1 pinch salt
1 large lemon, juiced (F, PO (sorbitol), VLOX and MS)

Directions
Pour the milk into a large pot, and stir in a pinch of salt. Bring to a boil over medium heat, stirring occasionally to prevent the milk from scorching on the bottom of the pot.

When the milk begins to boil (small bubbles will first appear at the edges), turn off the heat. Stir lemon juice into the milk and the milk will curdle. You may need to wait 5-10 minutes.

Line a sieve or colander with a cheesecloth and pour the milk through the cloth to catch the curds. What is left in the cheesecloth is the Farmer's Cheese. The liquid is the whey. Some people keep the whey and drink it, but you can throw it away if you don't want it.

Gather the cloth around the cheese, and squeeze out as much of the whey as you can. Wrap in plastic, or place in an airtight container. Store in the refrigerator.

Notes
Many sites state that Farmer's Cheese is very low in lactose so a little should be suitable for people who are Lactose intolerant. I will leave the decisions to you as to whether you use it or not.

* * * * *

LACTOSE FREE YOGURT CREAM CHEESE

Use Lactose Free yogurt to make "yogurt cheese," which is the consistency of cream cheese. All you have to do is line a colander with a dishtowel, pour in the yogurt, and let drain overnight in the fridge. Squeeze out any additional water, if necessary. You can mix in your choice of flavorings or leave it plain. Making a drained 'yogurt cheese' with Lactose Free yogurt would be similar in texture as if you used regular yogurt or milk, but the cheese would be tangier.

INDIGINENOUS
(Mainland Aborigines and Torres Strait Islanders)

I would like to acknowledge the Indigenous community here in Australia and thank them for donating the recipes to open my book with. These recipes do not represent all of the different tribes in Australia and the Torres Strait Islands. The meat or fish given in these recipes are not eaten by the tribes if it is their totem. Many of the recipes have been changed from the proper Bush ingredients over the years due to the different tribes moving to the cities and bigger towns and having to use ingredients available to them.

The first recipe, with written permission, was kindly donated to me by the Government of Western Australia, North Metropolitan Health Service to use their recipe "Kangaroo Soup" from their cookbook "More Deadly Tucker Cookbook". The other recipes were kindly donated by the Inala Community Elders here in Brisbane.

The vegetables and fruit in these recipes will only make them Fructose Friendly. I have tried to source out whether they have Fructose, Fructans, Polyols or Galactans in them and have indicated this beside the ingredient plus a few ingredients have alternatives beside them or in the notes at the end of each recipe. I am hoping that this will help you as much as it has helped me. Salicylates and Oxalates may also be issues for some people so I have added them as well. They will all be noted in the code form below or mentioned in the notes. Please read these.

Low – L, Medium – M, High – H, Very High – VH, Salicylates – S, Oxalates – OX
Fructose – F, Fructans – FOS, Polyols – PO, Galactans – GOS

I have placed some homemade recipes for substituting the ingredients after the main recipes. These recipes will be for Gluten Free, Fructose Friendly, Lactose Free or Friendly, Diabetic Friendly and IBS Friendly depending on your sensitivity so that you can make your own if you want to. Please remember that Fructans, Polyols and Galactans can also come with Fructose. Make these recipes your own and use your ingredients if you want to as you know what's best for you.

Kangaroo Soup	40
Namas	41
Bush Beef Stir Fry	42
Damper	43
Kangaroo And Tomato Stew With Dumplings	44
Pumpkin Damper	45
Sop Sop	46
Homemade Recipes For The Above Recipes	
Homemade Chili Powder	47
Garlic And Onion Free Chilli Powder	47
Chili Sauce Number 1	47
Chili Sauce Number 2	48
Homemade Chili Sauce Substitute	48
Homemade Ketchup / Tomato Sauce	48
Quick And Easy Homemade Fresh Tomato Soup	49
Homemade Curry Powder	49
How To Make Tomato Paste The Quick And Easy Way	50

KANGAROO SOUP

Ingredients to feed 12 people
1kg or 2.2lbs kangaroo meat
4 cups water
1 onion (HF, HFOS, PO (mannitol), LOX and LS) or 3 spring onions (green parts only) (white part has M-HF, FOS, PO (mannitol), MOX and LS) or a pinch of asafoetida powder (may contain Gluten) (see notes)
2 tomatoes (F, FOS, PO (mannitol), MOX and MS)
3 potatoes (see notes)
2 carrots (HF, FOS (raffinose), PO (sorbitol), GOS, VHOX and HS)
1 capsicum (green - HF, FOS, PO (sorbitol), MOX and VHS and red - HF, FOS, PO (sorbitol), LOX and VHS) (see Tucker Tips)
2 celery stalks (HF, FOS, PO (mannitol) and VHOX). Try using ½ cup of chopped leaves only)
2 teaspoons curry powder (VHS) (homemade recipe after main recipes)
2 sweet potatoes (HF, FOS, PO (mannitol), VHOX and HS)
½ cup sultanas or currants (see notes)
½ cup dried red lentils (FOS, GOS and boiled has MOX)
4 teaspoons canola oil (F, PO and LOX) or one to your liking

Directions (What to do)
Chop all vegetables and meat into cubes.

Add meat, curry powder and ½ the canola oil into a bowl and mix well. Heat frypan and add remaining oil and seal meat quickly and then transfer to a saucepan.

Add vegetables to same pan the meat was cooked in and cook for 3 - 4 minutes until slightly softened.

Add red lentils, water, potatoes and sweet potatoes to the saucepan with the meat. Bring to the boil.

Add all vegetables from the frypan to the saucepan. Cook until meat is tender.

Once meat is tender add sultanas.

TUCKER TIP
If you don't have red or green capsicums, you can use celery (HF, FOS, PO (mannitol) and VHOX), zucchini (HF, FOS, PO (sorbitol) VLOX and VHS) or frozen or canned vegetables.

Notes
Fructose in potatoes can range anything between 582 mg – 989 mg depending on the size, type and skin colour. They also have FOS, PO and GOS. They can also be VHOX and MS again depending on the type of potatoes, colour of skin and how they are cooked.

Asafoetida Powder is a strong spice that is used in place of onions and garlic so don't use more than the specified amount. It may contain Gluten as some suppliers cut it with wheat, corn or rice. It may also help to reduce gas from the lentils.

The Fructose count for Currants - 1 cup - 3.95g; Raisins, seedless - 1 cup, packed - 48.97g so exchange currants for the raisins. Both red and black currents have HF, PO (mannitol), HOX and VHS. Raisins have HF, PO (sorbitol), LOX and VHS.

NAMAS

Ingredients to feed 4
4 white fish fillets cut into thin strips (Trevally or Queen) or one to your liking
2 finely sliced onions (HF, HFOS, PO (mannitol), LOX and LS) or 6 spring onions (green parts only) (white part has M-HF, FOS, PO (mannitol), MOX and LS)
2 sliced tomatoes (F, FOS, PO (mannitol), MOX and MS)
1 chopped green capsicum (HF, FOS, PO (sorbitol), MOX and VHS) (see Tucker Tips)
1 chopped red capsicum (HF, FOS, PO (sorbitol), LOX and VHS) (see Tucker Tips)
1 tablespoon salt reduced soy sauce (FOS)
3 cups brown vinegar (L-MOX and VHS) to cover the fish
1 small fresh chilli (F, PO (mannitol) HOX and HS) (omit if you can't tolerate)
1 finely sliced lemon (F, PO (sorbitol), VLOX and MS)

Directions (What to do)
Place the sliced fish fillets into a container that has an airtight lid (don't seal it yet).

Add onion, tomato, red capsicum, green capsicum and soy sauce.

Add vinegar so the fish is covered.

If you like a hot chilli taste, chop the chilli and mix in thoroughly. If not, just add whole chilli and you can remove it before serving.

Cover with lemon slices or squeeze the juice on top of the mixture.

Put lid on the container.

Let the mixture marinate overnight in the fridge before serving.

Namas can be eaten with rice and salad.

TUCKER TIP
If you don't have red or green capsicums, you can use celery (HF, FOS, PO (mannitol) and VHOX), zucchini (HF, FOS, PO (sorbitol) VLOX and VHS) or frozen or canned vegetables.

Add diced apples (M-HF, FOS (raffinose), PO (sorbitol), LOX and M-HS (depending on the type of apple) or oranges (F, PO (sorbitol), HOX and VHS) to the mixture before marinating to add extra texture and a sweet flavour.

Make sure you leave enough time to cook this recipe – remember that it has to marinate overnight.

BUSH BEEF STIR FRY

Ingredients to feed 6
Canola oil (F, PO, and LOX) or olive oil (LOX and HS) spray
1 onion, diced (HF, HFOS, PO (mannitol), LOX and LS) or 3 spring onions (green parts only) (white part has M-HF, FOS, PO (mannitol), MOX and LS) or a good pinch of asafoetida powder (may contain Gluten) (see notes)
1 crushed garlic clove (F, FOS, GOS, LOX and LS) (omit if you can't tolerate) (see notes)
1 tablespoon crushed ginger (F, FOS, LOX and MS)
750g or 1.7 lbs lean beef cut into strips
1 sliced green capsicum (HF, FOS, PO (sorbitol), MOX and VHS) (see notes)
1 sliced red capsicum (HF, FOS, PO (sorbitol), LOX and VHS) (see notes)
1 bunch broccoli (HF, FOS, PO (sorbitol), GOS, MOX and HS)
2 large peeled and sliced carrots (HF, FOS (raffinose), PO (sorbitol), GOS, VHOX and HS)
1 cup sliced mushrooms (HF, FOS (raffinose), PO (mannitol and xylitol), GOS, VLOX and MS) (see notes)
1 cup snow peas (HFOS, PO (mannitol), GOS, MOX and MS)
1 sliced zucchini (HF, FOS, PO (sorbitol), VLOX and VHS)
2 tablespoons water
1 tablespoon cornflour (MOX and HS)
1 teaspoon honey (HF, FOS, VLOX and VHS) or rice malt syrup (Fructose Free)
3 tablespoons salt reduced soy sauce (FOS)
1 tablespoon sweet chilli sauce (can't find any info for anything. Homemade Chili Sauce recipes after main recipes)

Directions (What to do)
Lightly spray pan or wok with oil and cook onion, garlic and ginger on medium heat for 2 minutes.

Add beef strips and cook until slightly brown all over.

Add red capsicum, green capsicum, broccoli, carrot, mushroom, snow peas, and zucchini and cook for 3 minutes.

In a bowl mix water, cornflour, honey, soy sauce and sweet chilli sauce. Pour this over the meat and vegetables. Stir and simmer for 5 minutes.

Serve with rice or noodles.

TUCKER TIP
If fresh vegetables are not available try frozen or tinned vegetables.

Other types of meat such as chicken (with the skin removed) or kangaroo can be used in the place of beef if desired.

Notes
Try substituting normal mushrooms (HF, FOS (raffinose), PO (mannitol and xylitol), GOS, VLOX and MS) for the gourmet style. It has been stated that Shiitake, Enoki, Oyster have low to no Polyols and information for Fructose, Fructans, Oxalates and Salicylates could not be found at all. Usually only "Mushrooms" in general comes up when researching so this ingredient will be your call as what you want to use. I don't have any issues when eating the Gourmet Style mushrooms.

If you don't have red or green capsicums, you can use celery (HF, FOS, PO (mannitol) and VHOX), zucchini (HF, FOS, PO (sorbitol) VLOX and VHS) or frozen or canned vegetables.

Asafoetida Powder is a strong spice that is used in place of onions and garlic. It may contain Gluten as some suppliers cut it with wheat, corn or rice. Use only the specified amount if you are not using onion and garlic.

*　　　*　　　*　　　*　　　*

DAMPER

Ingredients to feed 6
2⅓ cups Gluten Free wholemeal self-raising flour or one to your liking (see notes)
1 cup Gluten Free white self-raising flour or one to your liking (see notes)
1⅓ cups Lactose Free low fat milk or one to your liking or extra water if needed
Canola oil (F, PO, and LOX) or olive oil (LOX and HS) to grease baking tray

Directions (What to do)
Preheat oven to 200°C / 400°F.

In a large bowl, mix wholemeal and white flour together.

Add milk and mix until combined and dough starts to form.

Knead the dough on a lightly floured surface until dough is nice and soft (about 5 - 8 minutes).

Make dough into a round shape and then place on a lightly greased oven tray.

Cook for 30 - 40 minutes. You can tell when the damper is ready as it will be golden brown and have a hollow sound when tapped.

Cut into slices and serve warm.

TUCKER TIP
Damper can also be cooked on a hot open fire. Wrap the damper in aluminium foil or a banana leaf and place on or under the hot ashes.

If using a camp oven, place hot ashes on the top of the lid and cook for 10 - 15 minutes.

You will be able to tell when the damper is ready as it will have a hollow sound when tapped.

Notes
You can also add some frozen or fresh mixed berries to the damper for a fruity type of snack but make sure that the berries are well drained or some cheese and a herb of your choice.

You will need to adjust the amount of liquid if you use Gluten Free flour as it needs more liquid. Gluten Free flour is also higher in carbs so be mindful if you have to watch your carb count or you are diabetic. Optional mixes on pages 13 & 14.

KANGAROO AND TOMATO STEW WITH DUMPLINGS

Ingredients to feed 6

Canola oil (F, PO and LOX) or olive oil (LOX and HS) spray or one to your liking
500g or 1lb kangaroo meat, cubed (trim off the fat)
1 chopped onion (HF, HFOS, PO (mannitol), LOX and LS) or 3 spring onions (green parts only) (white part has M-HF, FOS, PO (mannitol), MOX and LS) or ⅛ teaspoon asafoetida powder (may contain Gluten and is a strong spice so only use the specified amount)
1 x 420g or 15oz tin tomato soup (reduced salt) (HF, PO (aspartame), M-HOX and MS) (homemade recipe after main recipes)
2 cups water
2 peeled and cubed potatoes (see notes)
1 peeled and cubed sweet potato (HF, FOS, PO (mannitol), VHOX and HS)
2 peeled and diced carrots (HF, FOS (raffinose), PO (sorbitol), GOS, VHOX and HS)
1 cup frozen mixed vegetables of your choice
1 teaspoon dried mixed herbs of your choice
2 tablespoons Gluten Free plain flour or one of your choosing
Water
Extra Gluten Free flour or any flour of your choosing and water may be needed for the gravy

Directions (What to do)

Lightly spray a large saucepan with oil and cook the kangaroo on medium heat until browned all over.

Add onion, tomato soup and water and cook covered until the meat is tender.

Add potato, sweet potato, carrot, mixed vegetables and mixed herbs.

In a bowl mix flour and water to make a thick smooth paste and add to stew.

Cook on low heat until sauce has thickened and stew is heated through.

TUCKER TIP

If the tomato paste is in a jar, store the jar upside down in the fridge and make sure that only clean utensils are used to scoop paste out (HF, FOS, PO (mannitol) HOX and VHS). (Not used in recipe).

DUMPLINGS

Ingredients to make 10

2¾ cups Gluten Free self-raising flour or one to your liking (options on pages 13 &14)
1 teaspoon Nuttelex Original or canola margarine or one of your choosing
1 tablespoon fresh or dried parsley (F, PO (mannitol) LOX and LS) or mixed herbs of your choice
1 cup water (extra water may be needed)

Directions (What to do)

In a large bowl, rub flour and margarine together with fingers.

Add parsley or herbs and water and mix until a soft dough is formed (add a little extra water if mixture seems too dry or add a little extra flour if mixture seems too wet). Roll and cut dough into bite size balls.

Carefully drop dumplings into the finished stew and cook on low heat for 20 minutes or until dumplings are firm.

TUCKER TIP
Damper can also be cooked on a hot open fire. Wrap the damper in aluminium foil or a banana leaf and place on or under the hot ashes. If using a camp oven, place hot ashes on the top of the lid and cook for 10 - 15 minutes. You will be able to tell when the damper is ready as it will have a hollow sound when tapped.

Notes
Fructose in potatoes can range anything between 582 mg – 989 mg depending on the size, type and skin colour. They also have FOS, PO and GOS. They can also be VHOX and MS again depending on the type of potatoes, colour of skin and how they are cooked.

*   *   *   *   *

PUMPKIN DAMPER

Ingredients to feed 6 - 8
2½ cups Gluten Free self-raising flour or one to your liking (see notes)
2½ cups Gluten Free wholemeal self-raising flour or one to your liking (see notes)
1 teaspoon cinnamon (F, HOX and VHS)
¼ cup dextrose powder (may contain Gluten) or sugar
1 tablespoon Nuttelex Original or margarine or one to your liking
2 cups cooked mashed pumpkin (M-HF, FOS, PO (mannitol) and MS)
1 lightly beaten egg
½ cup Lactose Free reduced fat milk or one to your liking
Extra Lactose Free or low fat milk to brush over the dough
Canola oil (F, PO and LOX) or olive oil (LOX and HS) to grease baking tray

Directions (What to do)
Preheat oven to 200°C / 400°F.

In a large bowl mix together self-raising flour, wholemeal self-raising flour, cinnamon and sugar. Rub the margarine into this dry mixture with your fingers.

Add pumpkin, egg and milk and mix ingredients until dough starts to form.

Knead on a lightly floured surface until smooth (about 5 - 8 minutes). Shape dough into a round circle.

Place dough on a lightly greased oven tray and use a sharp knife to cut across the top of the dough.

Brush the top of the dough with extra milk and bake for 30 - 35 minutes or until golden brown.

TUCKER TIP
Damper can also be cooked on a hot open fire. Wrap the damper in aluminium foil or a banana leaf and place on or under the hot ashes. If using a camp oven, place hot ashes on the top of the lid and cook for 10 - 15 minutes. You will be able to tell when the damper is ready as it will have a hollow sound when tapped.

Notes
You will need to adjust the amount of liquid if you use Gluten Free flour as it needs more liquid. Gluten Free flour is also higher in carbs so be mindful if you have to watch your carb count or you are diabetic. (Optional mixes on pages 13 & 14).

SOP SOP

Ingredients to feed 8
2 peeled and sliced sweet potatoes (HF, FOS, PO (mannitol), VHOX and HS)
2 peeled and sliced potatoes (see notes)
1 cup sliced yam or white sweet potato (see notes) (FOS, PO (mannitol), HOX and HS)
2 peeled and sliced carrots (HF, FOS (raffinose), PO (sorbitol), GOS, VHOX and HS)
200g or 7oz peeled and sliced pumpkin (M-HF, FOS, PO (mannitol) and MS)
2 medium peeled and diced taros (FOS but has not been tested for Salicylates and Oxalates)
2 peeled and sliced bananas (F, FOS (inulin) PO (sorbitol), GOS and MOX)
1 x 270g tin or 8oz light coconut milk (HF, FOS, PO (sorbitol) GOS, and S) or low fat Lactose Free evaporated milk or one of your choice

Directions (What to do)
In a large saucepan add potato, sweet potato, yam, carrots, pumpkin, taro and place sliced banana on top.

Add the evaporated milk. The liquid should not cover the vegetables.

Cook on a low heat with the lid on for 30 minutes, until vegetables are cooked but still firm. Stir occasionally so vegetables don't stick to the bottom of the pan.

Serve with meat or chicken dish.

TUCKER TIP
If you can't buy coconut milk, you can use a tin of low fat evaporated milk plus 3 tablespoons low fat coconut milk powder.

Add a different flavour by putting fish pieces in with the vegetables.

Notes
Fructose in potatoes can range anything between 582 mg – 989 mg depending on the size, type and skin colour. They also have FOS, PO and GOS. They can also be VHOX and MS again depending on the type of potatoes, colour of skin and how they are cooked.

Bush Yam (Anaty) http://www.mbantua.com.au/bush-tucker/
The Desert Yam is another staple food of the Aboriginal people of Central Australia. The yam can be hard to locate as it can be growing up to 80 or 90cms underground. The yam is cooked by placing coals over it for about 20 minutes and then peeled before being eaten.

Long yam: https://www.darwinfreespiritresort.com.au/your-complete-guide-to-bush-tucker-in-the-northern-territory/
Wild yams are the potatoes and carrots of Australian bush tucker, although caution must be taken with preparation as they can be poisonous. A twining vine, the long yam is a staple food in many parts of Australia, particularly along rainforest edges. Yams are at their best when the leaves turn yellow, and are best eaten boiled or roasted. Be prepared to dig deep for these guys!

HOMEMADE RECIPES FOR THE ABOVE RECIPES

HOMEMADE CHILI POWDER

Ingredients
1 tablespoon ground cumin (VHS)
2 teaspoons garlic powder (optional) (F, FOS, GOS and LS)
1 teaspoon cayenne pepper (LOX and VHS)
1 teaspoon paprika (F and VHS)
1 teaspoon ground oregano (F, HOX and VHS)

Directions
Mix the ingredients together until well blended and you're ready to go. This will make a little less than 3 tablespoons of chili powder. Double it if you need more. Store in an airtight container.

*   *   *   *   *

GARLIC AND ONION FREE CHILLI POWDER

Ingredients to make 2 tablespoons (double quantities if you want more to keep on hand)
1 tablespoon cayenne pepper (or less if you don't want it too hot) (LOX and VHS)
½ teaspoon paprika (F and VHS)
½ teaspoon dried oregano (F, HOX and VHS)
1½ teaspoons ground cumin (VHS)
1 teaspoon salt
1 teaspoon ground black pepper (HOX and VHS)

Directions
Using a small clean and dry storage jar measure out all the ingredients into the jar - put the lid on and give this a good shake to mix it up. Store in a dry and cool place.

*   *   *   *   *

CHILI SAUCE NUMBER 1

Ingredients
1 cup tomato sauce (HF, PO (aspartame), HOX and VHS) / ketchup (HF, FOS, PO, VLOX and VHS) (homemade recipe in this section for Fructose Friendly)
1 tablespoon dextrose powder (for Fructose Free and may contain Gluten) or sweetener of your choice
2 tablespoons rice vinegar or one to your liking
¼ teaspoon dried chives (F, FOS (raffinose) PO (mannitol), VLOX and LS)
¼ teaspoon ground cumin (VHS)
¼ teaspoon ground allspice (VHS)
⅛ teaspoon ground clove (F and HS)
1 teaspoon hot sauce (or ¼ teaspoon red pepper flakes (chili flakes - F and HS) or ¼ teaspoon paprika (F and VHS) or homemade substitute recipe in this section

Directions
In a heavy sauce pan, mix all ingredients together until well combined and bring to the boil over medium heat. Reduce heat and simmer for 3 - 5 minutes, stirring occasionally. Remove from heat and use. Store any unused portion in a covered container in the refrigerator.

CHILI SAUCE NUMBER 2

Ingredients
800g / 4 cups / 29oz diced tomatoes (F, FOS, PO (mannitol), MOX and MS)
1 cup dextrose powder (for Fructose Free and may contain Gluten) or sweetener of your choice
⅔ cup white wine vinegar (L-MOX and VHS) or rice wine vinegar
A pinch of asafoetida powder (may contain Gluten. This is a strong spice so don't use more than the specified amount)
3 teaspoons ground cinnamon (F, HOX and VHS)
1 teaspoon ground ginger (F, FOS, LOX and LS)
½ teaspoon salt
2 teaspoons cayenne pepper or to suit your own taste (LOX and VHS)

Directions
Mix all dry ingredients in a large saucepan. Add the vinegar, tomatoes, and asafoetida, mix well. Bring to a boil over medium heat and continue to cook, uncovered until it is reduced by half. Cool and cover tightly and store in the refrigerator.

* * * * *

HOMEMADE CHILI SAUCE SUBSTITUTE

Ingredients for about 1 cup
Mix together:
1 cup tomato sauce (HF, PO (aspartame), HOX and VHS) / ketchup (HF, FOS, PO, VLOX and VHS) (homemade recipe in this section)
¼ cup brown sugar or rice malt syrup or dextrose powder (may contain Gluten) (all three are Fructose Friendly or Free)
2 tablespoons vinegar (L-MOX and VHS)
¼ teaspoon cinnamon (F, HOX and VHS)
1 dash ground cloves (F and HS)
1 dash allspice (VHS)

* * * * *

HOMEMADE KETCHUP/TOMATO SAUCE

Ingredients
One 6oz can of tomato paste (HF, FOS, PO (mannitol), HOX and VHS) or homemade recipe in this section
½ cup white vinegar (L-MOX and VHS)
½ cup + 2 tablespoons dextrose powder (may contain Gluten)
1 teaspoon salt
⅛ teaspoon ground celery (HF, FOS, PO (mannitol) and VHOX)
Pinch of ground cloves (F and HS)

Directions
Put all ingredients into a saucepan and whisk together until smooth. Heat on medium heat until just boiling; immediately reduce heat and simmer for 20 more minutes, stirring frequently.

Remove from heat and let cool on the counter or stove. Store in a covered container in the fridge.

QUICK AND EASY HOMEMADE FRESH TOMATO SOUP

Ingredients to Serves 4

2 onions, peeled and chopped (HF, HFOS, PO (mannitol), LOX and LS) or 6 spring onions (green parts only) (white part has M-HF, FOS, PO (mannitol), MOX and LS) or a pinch of asafoetida powder (may contain Gluten. This is a strong spice so don't use more than the specified amount)
1 carrot, peeled and diced finely (HF, FOS (raffinose), PO (sorbitol), GOS, VHOX and HS)
1 stick of celery finely chopped (HF, FOS, PO (mannitol) and VHOX) or ¼ cup chopped celery leaves
2 tablespoons olive oil (LOX and HS) or one to your liking
450g / 1lb fresh ripe tomatoes, halved (F, FOS, PO (mannitol), MOX and MS)
1 litre / 1¾ pints vegetable stock (minus garlic and onion) (see notes)
1 teaspoon dextrose powder (may contain Gluten) or sugar (see notes)
Salt and freshly ground black pepper (HOX and VHS)
Handful fresh basil, shredded (optional) (F, MOX and VHS)

Directions

Heat the oil in a large saucepan and add the onions, carrot and celery/leaves. Cover and cook gently for 10 minutes until soft.

Add the dextrose powder or sugar, salt, pepper and tomatoes. Stir and cook for another 5 minutes.

Add the stock, bring to the boil and simmer for 10 minutes. Liquidise until smooth. If using the basil, stir in at the end.

Notes

Using the dextrose powder may help reduce a little of the Fructose in the tomatoes.

In Australia, Massel make a liquid Vegetable stock without the onion and garlic.

*   *   *   *   *

HOMEMADE CURRY POWDER

Ingredients

2 tablespoons whole cumin seeds, toasted (VHS)
2 tablespoons whole cardamom seeds, toasted (LOX)
2 tablespoons whole coriander seeds, toasted (VLOX)
¼ cup ground turmeric (VHOX, VHS)
1 tablespoon dry mustard (F, GOS, VLOX and VHS)

Directions

Grind the cumin seeds, cardamon seeds and coriander seeds to a powder. Add the turmeric and dry mustard and mix well. Store in an airtight container.

HOW TO MAKE TOMATO PASTE THE QUICK AND EASY WAY

This recipe makes about 5 heaped tablespoons.

Soak 2 kilos (4½ lbs) of tomatoes (F, FOS, PO (mannitol), MOX and MS) in boiling water for five minutes or until the skins can be easily peeled off. Drain and carefully remove the tomato skin. The tomatoes may be hot to handle.

Carefully cut tomatoes in half or quarters longways and de-seed completely. Place tomato pieces in to processor and process to a very liquidy paste.

If you have a slow cooker, then place this liquid paste in it and leave it to reduce and thicken up. Stir occasionally. I left mine on all day and got a beautiful thick tomato paste to use in my recipes.

If you don't have a slow cooker you can cook the paste in a 350°F / 180°C preheated oven on shallow trays until it is reduced to a paste. Check the tomatoes every half hour, stirring the paste and switching the position of the trays so that they reduce evenly. Over time, the paste will start to reduce to the point where you can make one tray.

The paste is done when shiny and brick-colored, and it has reduced by more than half. There shouldn't be any remaining water or moisture separating from the paste at this point. This will take 3 - 4 hours, though exact baking/cooking times will depend on the juiciness of your tomatoes and your oven.

After the paste was cold; I put it in a container and kept it in the refrigerator or freezer.

Making small batches when you need it can be useful; however, if you use a lot of tomato paste then just double or triple the amount of tomatoes used. I made a very small batch using the same prep method but I cooked them down in my non-stick frypan over low heat and I continually stirred the mixture. I did not add anything to the paste because I can do that when I use it in a recipe.

SALICYLATES AND OXALATE

The following recipes are taken from recipes that have been kindly donated to me by the International communities here in Brisbane. I have selected them just for people who have Salicylate and Oxalate intolerances and I hope that I have done this correctly so I have not worried too much about Fructose, Fructans, Polyols and GOS content of the fruit and vegetables. They are also under their country's name. I have also placed any homemade recipes after the main recipes; however, they might not be suitable to make and use due to the Oxalates and Salicylates.

The vegetables and fruit in these recipes will only make them Fructose Friendly. I have tried to source out whether they have Fructose, Fructans, Polyols or Galactans in them and have indicated this beside the ingredient plus a few ingredients have alternatives beside them or in the notes at the end of each recipe. I am hoping that this will help you as much as it has helped me. Salicylates and Oxalates may also be issues for some people so I have added them as well. They will all be noted in the code form below or mentioned in the notes. Please read these.

Low – L, Medium – M, High – H, Very High – VH, Salicylates – S, Oxalates – OX
Fructose – F, Fructans – FOS, Polyols – PO, Galactans – GOS

Substituting ingredients will alter the original taste; however, it is a way to try different recipes from other countries and you can adjust the taste to your liking. Make these recipes your own and use your ingredients if you want to as you know what's best for you. Some spices or herbs may have a Medium Oxalates or Salicylates; however you may only use a small amount but if you can't have it, then substitute it or omit it.

Australian tablespoons and cups measurements are used and they are: 1 teaspoon equals 5ml; 1 tablespoon equals 20ml; 1 cup equals 250ml. Oven temperatures are for conventional; if using fan-forced (convection), reduce the temperature by 20°C.

Tompoes (Tom Thumbs) (Holland)	52
Boiled Beef And Vegetables (Philippines)	53
Walnut Kuchen (Chile) (Special Recipe For This Section Only)	54
Cheese And Herb Flan (Vegetarian)	55
Onion Jam (France) (Special Recipe For This Section Only)	56
Sigara Böreği - Stuffed Pastries (Turkey)	57
Homemade Recipes For The Above Recipes	
Gluten & Dairy Free Pie Crust - Sweet Or Savory	58
Gluten Free Filo Pastry Number 1	58
Filo Dough Number 2	59
Chili Sauce Number 1	59
Chili Sauce Number 2	60
Homemade Chili Sauce Substitute	60
Homemade Dijon Mustard	60
Homemade Ketchup	61
How To Make Tomato Paste The Quick And Easy Way	61
Homemade Alternative Ideas For Food Colourings	62

TOMPOES (TOM THUMBS) (Holland)

The tompoes is a traditional Dutch pastry that is often served with afternoon coffee or at celebratory events like birthdays. It's similar to what's known as a Napoleon in the United States, Napoleonbakelse in Sweden and Finland, and Napoleon-cake in Norway and Denmark. In Holland and Belgium it is called a tompoes, or tompouce.

What sets the Dutch variety apart is the sweet pink (or orange for Queen's Day) icing on top, often topped with a complimentary white stripe of whipped cream. It's a pastry that is much favored by all and, as the national sense of humor dictates, is the traditional choice for being served when one is visiting with one's family in-laws for the first time or when one has to make a good impression of oneself and is now challenged with having to eat a pastry that is going to fall to pieces the moment one bites into one end.

Both the tompoes and the Bossche Bol are the two top pastries that are a devil to eat, either by hand or with cutlery, without making an absolute mess. But in case you were in a situation where manners do not matter, the easiest way to consume this lovely baked good is to grab the bottom layer firmly between thumb and index and attack it, one bite at a time, short side first.

Ingredients
250ml (8.5 fl oz) of Lactose Free milk or one to your liking
1 vanilla bean (or 1 tablespoon of vanilla flavoring) (F, VLOX and VHS)
2 egg yolks
4 tablespoons of dextrose powder (Fructose Free may contain Gluten) or sugar
4 tablespoons of Gluten Free flour or one to your liking (options on pages 13 & 14)
Pinch of salt
1 sheet of puff pastry (homemade Gluten Free recipe after main recipes)
1 egg, beaten
3 tablespoons of dextrose powder (Fructose Free may contain Gluten) or powdered or icing sugar
2 teaspoons Lactose Free milk or one to your liking
1 drop red food coloring or red berry juice (homemade substitute ideas after main recipes)

Directions
Warm the milk, add the vanilla bean and steep for 15 minutes.

Mix the egg yolks with the sugar and the salt, and one tablespoon of flour. Stir until creamy.

Take the vanilla bean out of the milk, open it up and scrape out the seeds (or add the vanilla essence to the milk) and stir.

Take two tablespoons of warm milk and stir it into the egg yolk mix, then stir in the rest of the flour.

Carefully stir all this back into the warm milk into the pan, put it back on a low heat and stir until it becomes a thick mass.

Take off the stove and cover with a piece of plastic, to avoid forming a skin when it cools down.

Heat the oven to 200°C / 400°F). Spray a baking sheet or pan with cooking spray.

Cut the puff pastry sheet in 4 equal rectangular sections and place them on the baking sheet. Brush the top with the beaten egg, prick holes into the pastry with the tines of a fork and bake for fifteen minutes, or until the dough is golden.

Remove from the oven, and taking care not to burn your fingers, quickly and carefully pull the top from the bottom sheet. Set all eight pieces aside on a rack to cool.

Stir powdered sugar with the milk and the red food coloring into a thick icing.

Take the bottom part of one of the baked puff pastries and spread the cooled down vanilla cream on it. Top it with its corresponding top half of the pastry.

When all four are done, carefully spread the pink icing on top: let it dry and eat.

*   *   *   *   *

BOILED BEEF AND VEGETABLES (Philippines)

Ingredients (use the amount not mentioned to suit your family)
500g or 1.1lb beef cuts with bones
Potatoes - cut in cubes (see notes)
Peppercorns (HOX and VHS) (omit if you want to)
½ a cabbage - slice half then quarter (HF, HFOS, PO (sorbitol), GOS, LOX and LS)
Chinese vegetables - one bunch (see notes)
Salt and white pepper (VLOX and VHS) to taste
Onions (HF HFOS, PO (mannitol), LOX and LS) or use the green parts only of spring onions. (Use 3 spring onions for 1 medium - small onion (white part has M-HF, FOS, PO (mannitol), MOX and LS)
One teaspoon oil of your liking

Directions
Sauté onions in a teaspoon of oil then add beef.

When the beef is brownish and soft add one and a half cups of water and then add potatoes.

When the potatoes are cooked, add the cabbage and then add the salt and pepper to taste.

Add peppercorns (if using).

Serve with steamed rice with a sauce (Basmati (FOS, LOX and MS) and Doongara (FOS and LOX) rice is low GI. Soaking rice and grains for 12 hours lowers oxalates).

Notes
Fructose in potatoes can range anything between 582 mg – 989 mg depending on the size, type and skin colour. They also have FOS, PO and GOS. They can also be VHOX and MS again depending on the type of potatoes, colour of skin and how they are cooked.

Chinese Vegetables
Bok Choy - PO (sorbitol) GOS and VLOX.
Choy sum - FOS, PO, GOS and VHS
Chinese broccoli (gai-lan or kai-lan) - unsure of any F, FOS, PO or GOS but has HS.
Daikon - HF, PO, VLOX and VHS
Bamboo Shoots - FOS and LOX
Bean sprouts - F, FOS, LOX and LS

WALNUT KUCHEN (Chile)

I think that I have found a nut that would be very suitable for this recipe; however, they might be a little expensive. See notes to see what I have found and they are only in this recipe and not in the original recipe.

Ingredients for 10-12 people
For the dough
115g or ⅔ cup of Nuttelex Original or butter
150g or ⅔ cup of dextrose powder (for Fructose Free and may contain Gluten) or granulated sugar
1 egg
200g or 1½ cups of all-purpose Gluten Free flour (high in carbs) or normal flour or one to your liking
½ teaspoon baking powder (VLOX)
Pinch of salt

Directions
Preheat oven to 180°C / 350°F. Butter a round cake pan of 22cm in diameter (9") or 20 × 20cm square (9" x 9").

In a medium bowl beat butter with a fork until creamy, add the sugar and beat until creamy, add the egg and beat well until incorporated fully into the mix.

Add the flour, salt and baking powder. Mix to form a soft dough.

Scoop the batter into the pan and spread with a spoon or your wet fingers. Form an even layer and bake for 12 - 15 minutes until lightly browned.

For the filling
300g of chopped walnuts (VHOX and HS) (see notes for substitute)
1 can (375g or 13oz) Lactose Free condensed milk (3 homemade recipes after main recipes)
1 egg (see notes)
115g or ⅔ cup Nuttelex Original or butter, melted or oil to your liking
Pinch of salt

Directions
In a bowl mix the chopped nuts with the condensed milk and egg, pinch of salt, stir to mix. Add the melted butter and stir well.

Pour over baked dough (hot) and cover the pan with foil. Bake for 30 minutes and then remove the foil gently and carefully.

Bake for another 10 - 13 minutes until golden and then let cool completely on a wire rack.

Refrigerate before cutting and serving.

Notes
A substitute for walnuts
There are four species of chestnuts; Japanese, Chinese, American and European. The European chestnut is considered the sweetest. Chestnuts should not be confused with Horse Chestnuts or Chinese water chestnuts.

Chestnuts (LOX) Salicylates: (No information available on anything else)

Cooking Tips: Chestnuts can be boiled in the shell for 30 minutes before cutting in half to scoop out the flesh. Roast them in the oven or over hot coals. (Shells must be pierced first to prevent them from exploding when they cook). Once cooked use them in place of the walnuts and adjust the sweetness to your liking.

*   *   *   *   *

CHEESE AND HERB FLAN (Vegetarian)

Ingredients
1½ sheets frozen Gluten Free shortcrust pastry or one of your choosing (homemade alternative for Gluten and Dairy Free after main recipes)
4 eggs, whisked (see notes)
120g / 4oz goat's cheese chopped (may contain Lactose) (options on page 36)
100g / about 4oz fresh ricotta cheese (homemade Lactose Free recipe on page 37)
½ cup Lactose Free thickened cream or one to your liking
1 bunch chives snipped (F, FOS (raffinose), PO (mannitol) VLOX and LS) (substitute tarragon (VLOX and VHS to taste) (see notes)
¼ cup grated parmesan cheese (Lactose Friendly)
2 teaspoons Dijon mustard (F, LOX and HS) (homemade recipe after main recipes)
2 tomatoes thinly sliced (HF, FOS, PO (mannitol), MOX and MS)
Baby salad leaves to serve of your choice

Directions
Preheat oven to hot; 200°C / 400°F and lightly grease a 22cm (9") quiche pan.

Join pastry sheets and ease pastry into the pan, trimming it to fit. Bake blind for 10 minutes using bake paper with pastry weights, dry pasta or dry rice.

Remove from oven and remove paper and weights before returning to the oven to bake for a further 5 - 6 minutes.

Reduce oven temperature to 180°C / 350°F.

In a large bowl, using an electric mixer; beat the eggs, goat's cheese, ricotta, cream, chives/tarragon, parmesan and mustard together.

Pour into pastry case and arrange the tomatoes on top and bake for 30 - 35 minutes until just set in the centre.

Cool for 10 minutes and top with leaves and then serve in wedges.

Notes
I have never used an egg replacer so I don't know if it would be suitable for this recipe. If you use it, then you would know.

ONION JAM (France)

This recipe is very hard to adapt so I'm leaving it pretty much as such. Remember that Onions and Garlic are high in any of The Fructose, Fructans, Polyols and Galactan (GOS) groups and are low in Salicylates and Oxalates.

Ingredients to serve 8
3 or 4 halved, thinly sliced onions (HF, HFOS, PO (mannitol) LOX and LS)
2 or 3 crushed garlic (F, FOS, GOS, LOX and LS)
Salt, pepper (black - HOX and VHS, white - VLOX and VHS) to taste
50g of dextrose powder (Fructose Free and may contain Gluten) or sugar
20ml blackberry syrup (Fructose in Blackberries - 1 cup - 3.46g also HPO (sorbitol), VHOX and VHS) (**see variation**)
⅓ - ½ bottle of red wine (varies in Ox and S) (see notes for substitutes)

Directions
Heat the oil in a saucepan. Sauté the onions briefly, tossing with a wooden spatula. When the onions are well greased, but not brown, reduce the heat and cook the onions slowly, stirring from time to time, for about 15 minutes.

Add the sugar and cook, stirring, until the sugar is dissolved. Add the red wine and bring to the boil. Reduce the heat to low and simmer until the mixture thickens (around 20 minutes). Remove from heat, put in a nice ramequin to serve.

Can be eaten cold or warm and can be kept in an airtight container in fridge for a few days.

Notes
Red wine substitute
Non-alcoholic wine with a tablespoon of vinegar (L-MOX and VHS) added to cut the sweetness, grape juice (Purple has HF, FOS, PO (sorbitol) and S. Red has HF, FOS, PO (sorbitol), MOX and S. White has MF, FOS, PO (sorbitol), LOX and S), cranberry juice (LF, PO, VLOX and VHS), tomato juice (HF, PO (aspartame), MOX and MS), or water. Use equal amounts of liquid as called for in the recipe.

Variation for people who can't eat berries

FRUCTOSE FRIENDLY PEAR AND FENNEL SYRUP

Ingredients to make about 3 cups of syrup
Juice from 3 lbs peeled pears (VHF, PO (sorbitol) and LOX). (Use the amount to suit your needs. Pears 1 pound (4 medium) = 2 cups sliced)
½ cup dextrose powder (may contain Gluten)
1 tablespoon lemon juice (F, PO (sorbitol), LOX and L-HS) or lime juice (F, PO and LOX)
¼ teaspoon fennel seed (FOS, LOX and M-HS) or dried fennel (FOS, MOX and LS) tied in a spice bag or mesh tea infuser (see notes)
Pinch sea salt

Directions
Juice the pears by halving or quartering stemmed pears (with cores), covering with water in a large stockpot and adding ¼ cup of dextrose powder and simmering for about 1 hour until mushy.

Take off and mash with a potato masher or push through a food mill. Put into cheesecloth and strain over a large pot overnight.

Add pear and lemon/lime juice, ¼ cup dextrose powder, fennel seeds or dried fennel and salt to a large, wide-bottomed saucepan. Bring to a boil over medium-high heat; stir until dextrose is completely dissolved. Continue to boil, stirring occasionally, until juice is reduced by at least half and is thick and syrupy (about 20 minutes). Watch carefully to assure it does not boil over.

Allow to cool and put into a container of your choice and store in the refrigerator.

Notes
Fennel seeds are Fructose Friendly; however, the bulb has F, HFOS, and PO (mannitol) and LS.

*   *   *   *   *

SIGARA BÖREĞI - STUFFED PASTRIES (Turkey)

Börek is one of THE great indulgences of Turkish cuisine. It is a small cylindrical roll of filo pastry (shaped like cigarettes), stuffed with white cheese and parsley, and served hot and crispy as a mouth-watering meze (appetizer).

Ingredients to serve 4 people
2 sheets of filo pastry (known as yufka in Turkish) (2 Gluten Free homemade recipes after main recipes)
250ml oil Olive (LOX and HS) or Sunflower (LOX) for frying (or you can bake them, in which case you will need 50g of Nuttelex Original or butter)

Filling
200g of crumbled white cheese (Turkish white cheese, or feta cheese (VLOX)
1 egg yolk
¼ bunch parsley (F, PO (mannitol), LOX and LS) or coriander (MOX and HS) finely chopped
¼ bunch dill (F, L-MOX and VHS) or tarragon (VLOX and VHS) or chives (F, FOS (raffinose), VLOX and LS) finely chopped
Pinch of salt

Directions
Divide the filo pastry sheets into two semi circles, and then into four curved triangles. Cover any filo pastry you are not using with a towel to stop it drying out.

Mix the filling ingredients together and then place a spoonful the filling at the wide end, fold up the long sides to hold in the filling and then roll it up like a small cigar. Wet the pointed end with a wet (use water/milk/egg) pastry brush and stick it down.

Fry in hot oil until golden, making sure you turn the cigars frequently, and serve piping hot.

Alternatively, you can brush them with melted butter and bake in a preheated oven 200°C / 400°F on a greased baking sheet until they are golden and crisp. This should take approx 15 minutes.

Other fillings suggestions for your Sigara Böreği
Savoury lamb / beef (even chicken) mince filling (preferably cooked with some onions (HF, HFOS, PO (mannitol), LOX and LS or substitute 3 spring onions (green parts only) diced (white part has M-HF, FOS, PO (mannitol) MOX and LS) for each onion, tomato puree (HF, FOS, PO (mannitol), HOX and VHS) and herbs of your choice).

HOMEMADE RECIPES FOR THE ABOVE RECIPES

GLUTEN & DAIRY FREE PIE CRUST - SWEET OR SAVORY
(Taken from my first book)

This recipe makes 2 Bottom Pie Crusts or 1 Set (top & bottom) Pie Crusts.

Ingredients
2 cups of all-purpose Gluten Free flour of your liking (options on pages 13 & 14)
½ cup palm shortening (LOX), coconut oil (HS), or real butter or Nutellex Original
1 egg
⅔ cup water (approx. depending on consistency)
½ teaspoon salt (or season to taste)
2 teaspoons dextrose (for Fructose Friendly and may contain Gluten) or alternative sweetener for desserts if desired (or sweeten to taste)

Directions
Mix together Gluten Free Flour along with optional salt and dextrose and then add in shortening (or butter), and mix until crumbly. Add in egg and mix until well incorporated - mixture will still be crumbly.

Add water by stirring in 1 tablespoon at a time until dough holds together for rolling - better a little moist, then too dry. Cut mixture in half and roll into 2 balls (one for each crust or topping).

Shape dough balls into disc with floured hands and place onto a sheet of well-floured parchment or wax paper. Cover with an additional sheet of parchment or wax paper. Roll crust out to slightly larger than your pie tin.

Remove top parchment/wax paper and Slip hand gently under the bottom paper to flip into pie tin, carefully peeling back the paper as you press it into the pan. Don't worry if it breaks apart a little, you can always press it together and it will look great.

Crimp edges of crust to make a decorative edge or top with an additional crust layer after adding your pie filling. Pierce bottom slightly with fork (and slit top layer with knife to vent).

Fill with your favorite recipe and bake following the pie recipe you are using for bake time and temperature.

*   *   *   *   *

GLUTEN FREE FILO PASTRY NUMBER 1

Ingredients
¼ cup water
2 cups Gluten Free flour (probably use amaranth flour (HOX))
4 teaspoons olive oil (LOX and HS) or one to your liking
¼ teaspoon salt

Directions
Sift flour and salt and make a well, then add the water and oil in it. Work the dough, and on a dusted board, knead it for about 5 minutes. It gets smooth. Roll it out in a huge rectangle, put a damp towel over it, and let it stay for about 15 minutes. Work it out again so it's about 3 x 3 feet (92 x 92cm). Cut it with a knife to sheet size, and then use for your recipe.

FILO DOUGH NUMBER 2

Ingredients
1¾ cups fine white rice flour
¼ cup sweet rice flour
4 teaspoons of guar gum or xanthan gum or chia seed powder (OX and HS)
1 teaspoon gelatin (LOX)
1 egg
¼ - ½ cup Lactose Free milk or one of choice
1 stick butter or ½ cup or 4oz or 113g Nuttelex Original, melted or margarine or oil to your liking
1 teaspoon rice malt syrup

Directions
Mix together rice flour, sweet rice flour, xanthan gum/guar gum/chia seed powder and gelatin. Make a well in dry ingredients large enough to hold the liquids.

Lightly beat egg with ¼ cup milk, butter and rice malt syrup. Pour this into well in dry ingredients. Mix everything together until you have a soft dough. (Depending on brand of rice flour, you may want to stir in more milk).

Wrap dough in plastic wrap until ready to use for your favorite holiday pastry. Store in refrigerator if not using immediately.

*   *   *   *   *

CHILI SAUCE NUMBER 1

Ingredients
1 cup tomato sauce (HF, PO (aspartame), HOX and VHS) / ketchup (HF, FOS, PO, VLOX and VHS) (homemade recipe in this section for Fructose Friendly)
1 tablespoon dextrose powder (for Fructose Free and may contain Gluten) or sweetener of your choice
2 tablespoons rice vinegar (no information available)
¼ teaspoon dried chives (F, FOS (raffinose), PO (mannitol), VLOX and LS)
¼ teaspoon ground cumin (VHS)
¼ teaspoon ground allspice (VHS)
⅛ teaspoon ground clove (F, VHOX and HS)
1 teaspoon hot sauce (VHS) or ¼ teaspoon red pepper flakes / chili flakes (VHS) or
¼ teaspoon paprika (VHS) or homemade substitute recipe in this section

Directions
In a heavy sauce pan, mix all ingredients together until well combined and bring to the boil over medium heat. Reduce heat and simmer for 3 - 5 minutes, stirring occasionally.

Remove from heat and use. Store any unused portion in a covered container in the refrigerator.

CHILI SAUCE NUMBER 2

Ingredients
800 grams / 4 cups / 29oz diced tomatoes (HF, FOS, PO (mannitol), MOX and MS)
1 cup dextrose powder (for Fructose Free and may contain Gluten) or sweetener of your choice
⅔ cup white wine vinegar (L-MOX and VHS) or rice wine vinegar (no info available)
⅛ teaspoon asafoetida powder (may contain Gluten. This is a strong spice so don't use more than the specified amount)
3 teaspoons ground cinnamon (F, HOX and VHS)
1 teaspoon ground ginger (F, FOS, LOX and LS)
½ teaspoon salt
2 teaspoons cayenne pepper (LOX and VHS) or to suit your own taste

Directions
Mix all dry ingredients in a large saucepan. Add the vinegar; tomatoes, and asafoetida; mix well. Bring to a boil over medium heat and continue to cook, uncovered until it is reduced by half. Cool and cover tightly and store in the refrigerator.

* * * * *

HOMEMADE CHILI SAUCE SUBSTITUTE

Ingredients for about 1 cup
Mix together:
1 cup tomato sauce (HF, PO (aspartame), HOX and VHS) / ketchup (HF, FOS, PO, VLOX and VHS) (homemade recipe in this section)
¼ cup brown sugar or rice malt syrup or dextrose powder (may contain Gluten) (all three are Fructose Friendly or Free)
2 tablespoons vinegar (L-MOX and VHS) or rice wine vinegar (no info available)
¼ teaspoon cinnamon (F, HOX and VHS)
1 dash ground cloves (F, VHOX and HS)
1 dash allspice (VHS)

* * * * *

DIJON MUSTARD

1 cup of onion (HF, HFOS, PO (mannitol) LOX and LS) (chopped) don't use if using asafoetida powder (may contain Gluten)
2 cloves of garlic (F, FOS, GOS, LOX and LS) (minced) or ⅛ teaspoon asafoetida powder (may contain Gluten. This is a strong spice so don't use more than the specified amount)
2 tablespoons of honey (HF, FOS, VLOX and VHS) or rice malt syrup (Fructose Free)
4oz (8 tablespoons) of dry mustard (seeds ground) (F, GOS, VLOX and VHS)
1 tablespoon of vegetable oil or one to your liking
2 teaspoons of salt
4 drops of Tabasco sauce (no info available) (check label for unwanted ingredients) (homemade Hot sauce substitute in this section)
2 cups of dry white wine (varies in OX and S) (can use non-alcoholic wine)

HOMEMADE KETCHUP

Ingredients

One 6oz can of tomato paste (HF, FOS, PO (mannitol), HOX and VHS) or homemade recipe in this section
½ cup white vinegar (L-MOX and VHS) or rice wine vinegar (no info available)
½ cup + 2 tablespoons dextrose powder (may contain Gluten)
1 teaspoon salt
⅛ teaspoon ground celery (HF, FOS, PO (mannitol) and VHS)
Pinch of ground cloves (F, VHOX and HS)

Directions

Put all ingredients into a saucepan and whisk together until smooth.

Heat on medium heat until just boiling; immediately reduce heat and simmer for 20 more minutes, stirring frequently.

Remove from heat and let cool on the counter or stove. Store in a covered container in the fridge.

*   *   *   *   *

HOW TO MAKE TOMATO PASTE THE QUICK AND EASY WAY

This recipe makes about 5 heaped tablespoons.

Soak 2 kilos (4½ lbs) of tomatoes (HF, FOS, PO (mannitol), MOX and MS) in boiling water for five minutes or until the skins can be easily peeled off. Drain and carefully remove the tomato skin. The tomatoes may be hot to handle.

Carefully cut tomatoes in half or quarters longways and de-seed completely. Place tomato pieces in to processor and process to a very liquidy paste.

If you have a slow cooker, then place this liquid paste in it and leave it to reduce and thicken up. Stir occasionally. I left mine on all day and got a beautiful thick tomato paste to use in my recipes.

If you don't have a slow cooker you can cook the paste in a 350°F / 180°C preheated oven on shallow trays until it is reduced to a paste. Check the tomatoes every half hour, stirring the paste and switching the position of the trays so that they reduce evenly. Over time, the paste will start to reduce to the point where you can make one tray.

The paste is done when shiny and brick-colored, and it has reduced by more than half. There shouldn't be any remaining water or moisture separating from the paste at this point. This will take 3 - 4 hours, though exact baking/cooking times will depend on the juiciness of your tomatoes and your oven.

After the paste was cold; I put it in a container and kept it in the refrigerator or freezer.

Making small batches when you need it can be useful; however, if you use a lot of tomato paste then just double or triple the amount of tomatoes used. I made a very small batch using the same prep method but I cooked them down in my non-stick frypan over low heat and I continually stirred the mixture. I did not add anything to the paste because I can do that when I use it in a recipe.

HOMEMADE ALTERNATIVE IDEAS FOR FOOD COLOURINGS

And as an alternative, you can use natural food dye in a savory recipe. Remember, food dye isn't reserved just for sweets and treats. Remember that working with natural coloring will be different than the artificially amplified colors you're probably used to. In general you can expect a paler, more pastel-type of result. It is best if you experiment, play around with quantities and combinations, add a little at a time, and always taste as you go. Most importantly, let your creative juices flow, and have fun with it.

Pink and Red

You can use any number of options, but for a ton of color with almost no flavor, beets are your best bet. Use the juice from the canned kind, or make your own by either boiling or juicing the raw vegetable. Alternately, you can also use any red fruit, like raspberries or pomegranate. Just know that these may change the flavor – which can be a great thing. To procure your dye, pulverize the berries in a food processor or blender, then strain out the colored liquid using a mesh sieve or cheesecloth.

Pink/Red/Magenta: Juiced berries, Juiced cranberries, Juiced beetroot Juiced red capsicum, Juiced tomato, choose dark red tomatoes, rhubarb juiced or boiled, pomegranate juice, chili powder or paprika powder.

VEGETARIAN

The following recipes were kindly donated to me by the minister of my church.

I would like to thank the people who originally wrote or adapted the recipes that she has passed on to me as they will help me and many other people with new and exciting meal ideas.

The vegetables in these recipes will only make them Fructose Friendly. I have tried to source out whether they have Fructose, Fructans, Polyols or Galactans in them and have indicated this beside the ingredient plus a few ingredients have alternatives beside them. I am hoping that this will help you as much as it has helped me. Salicylates and Oxalates may also be issues for some people so I have added them as well. They will all be noted in the code form below or mentioned in the notes. Please read these.

Low – L, Medium – M, High – H, Very High – VH, Salicylates – S, Oxalates – OX
Fructose – F, Fructans – FOS, Polyols – PO, Galactans – GOS

I have placed some homemade recipes for substituting the ingredients after the main recipes. These recipes will be for Gluten Free, Fructose Friendly, Lactose Free or Friendly, Diabetic Friendly and IBS Friendly depending on your sensitivity so that you can make your own if you want to. Please remember that Fructans, Polyols and Galactans can also come with Fructose.

Substituting ingredients will alter the original taste; however, it is a way to try different recipes from other countries and you can adjust the taste to your liking. Make these recipes your own and use your ingredients if you want to as you know what's best for you.

Australian tablespoons and cups measurements are used and they are: 1 teaspoon equals 5ml; 1 tablespoon equals 20ml; 1 cup equals 250ml. Oven temperatures are for conventional; if using fan-forced (convection), reduce the temperature by 20°C.

Thai Sweet Potato and Carrot Soup	64
Vegie and Lentil Soup	65
Cheese and Herb Flan	66
Goat's Cheese and Sun-Dried Tomato Tarts	67
Quinoa and Black Bean Burgers with Guacamole	68
Curried Chickpeas	69
Homemade Recipes For The Above Recipes	
Gluten & Dairy Free Pie Crust - Sweet or Savory	70
Homemade Thai Red Curry Paste	71
Homemade Simple Curry Powder	72
Homemade Curry Powder	72
Homemade Curry Paste	72
Vegan Fish Sauce	73
Homemade Dijon Mustard	73
Lactose Free Ricotta Cheese	74
Shrimp Paste Homemade	74
Onion And Garlic Free Mild Thai Sweet Chili Sauce	75
Homemade Tin/Can Tomatoes Substitute	75
Lactose Free Evaporated Milk	75

THAI SWEET POTATO AND CARROT SOUP

Ingredients

1 onion, finely chopped (HF, HFOS, PO (mannitol), LOX and LS) or 3 spring onions (green parts only) (white part has M-HF, FOS, PO (mannitol), MOX and LS) or a pinch of asafoetida powder (may contain Gluten. This is a strong spice so don't use more than the specified amount)

¼ cup Thai red curry paste (homemade recipe after main recipes) or your own

1kg or 36oz sweet potato peeled, cut into small pieces (F, FOS, PO (mannitol), HOX and HS)

2 large carrots, peeled and cut into small pieces (F, FOS (raffinose), PO (sorbitol), GOS, (MOX and L-MS)

1 litre (4 cups) vegetable stock (minus onion and garlic)

270ml can or 8oz coconut milk (F, FOS, PO (sorbitol) and S) or Lactose Free milk or one to your liking

Roti bread to serve (optional) (homemade recipe below)

Directions

Heat an oiled stockpot over a medium to high heat and add the onion and cook until soft. Add curry paste and stir for 1 minute and then add the vegetables and stock and bring to the boil.

Simmer covered for about 15 minutes or until tender and then remover from the heat and cool slightly.

Blend soup in 2 batches until smooth and then return to the same pot and add the milk and stir over a low heat until hot.

Season with salt and pepper and serve hot with Roti bread.

Homemade Roti (Indian Bread)
Ingredients to make approx 12 Roti's

2 cups Gluten Free whole wheat flour (Chapati Flour) (see notes)
½ teaspoon salt (optional)
4 teaspoons oil of your choice
¾ cup warm water or more if needed
Gluten Free all-purpose flour, for rolling and dusting (see notes)

Method

In a large mixing bowl, mix the flour and salt well and then add the oil and mix until all the lumps are gone.

Add warm water a little at a time to form a medium soft dough ball but do not overwork the dough.

Add few drops of oil and coat the dough ball. Cover and let it rest for 15 minutes.

Heat Tawa or skillet or frypan on medium heat.

Knead the dough once and divide into golf ball size balls.

Dip one ball into the all-purpose flour to coat and roll it out into a thin disc. Keep dipping the roti into the dry flour to prevent it from sticking to the rolling surface.

Shake or rub off excess flour from the roti and place it onto the hot tawa or skillet.

Flip to the other side once you see bubbles appear on the surface. Allow it to cook for 10 - 15 seconds.

Increase the stove heat to High, gently pick the roti up with tongs, remove the tawa/skillet/frypan off of the flame, flip the roti over and place onto an open flame.

The roti should balloon up. Flip it over and cook on the other side.

Place the cooked roti into an insulated container and smear it with Ghee or clarified butter and repeat the process for the remaining dough.

Notes: Gluten Free flours are higher in carbohydrates. Adjust liquid if using normal flour.

*   *   *   *   *

VEGIE AND LENTIL SOUP

Ingredients
2 tablespoons olive oil (LOX and HS) or one to your liking
1 onion, finely chopped (HF, HFOS, PO (mannitol), LOX and LS) or 3 spring onions (green parts only) (white part has M-HF, FOS, PO (mannitol), MOX and LS) or a pinch of asafoetida powder (may contain Gluten) (see notes)
3 teaspoons curry powder (F and VHS) (homemade recipe after main recipes)
1 cup dried red lentils, rinsed and drained (FOS, GOS and boiled has MOX)
400g or 14oz can of chopped tomatoes (HF, PO (aspartame), H-VHOX and LS?) (homemade recipe after main recipes)
2 carrots, chopped into 1cm pieces (F, FOS (raffinose), PO (sorbitol), GOS, MOX and L-MS)
2 potatoes, chopped into 1cm pieces (see notes)
1 cup frozen peas and corn (corn has HF, FOS, PO (xylitol), LOX and MS; Peas have HF, HFOS, GOS, and boiled have VLOX and LS)
Salt and pepper, (black - HOX and VHS, white - VLOX and VHS) to taste
Crusty bread and natural yoghurt (bought has VLOX) to serve or Lactose Free yoghurt

Directions
Heat oil in a large saucepan and add the onion and cook, stirring occasionally until soft.

Add curry powder and cook, stirring for about 30 seconds or until fragrant. Add stock, lentils, tomatoes, carrots and potatoes and bring to the boil.

Simmer covered for about 20 minutes or until vegetables are tender and lentils are cooked.

Stir in peas and corn and simmer uncovered for 5 minutes or until peas and corn are tender.

Season with salt and pepper and serve with rusty bread and natural yoghurt.

Notes
Asafoetida powder may help reduce some of the "gas" from the lentils. This is a strong spice so don't use more than the specified amount.

The lentils may make this soup not ISB Friendly depending on your Fructose and Galactan tolerance level. Galactans are gas makers.

Fructose in potatoes can range anything between 582 mg – 989 mg depending on the size, type and skin colour. They also have FOS, PO and GOS. They can also be VHOX and MS again depending on the type of potatoes, colour of skin and how they are cooked.

CHEESE AND HERB FLAN

Ingredients
1½ sheets frozen Gluten Free shortcrust pastry or one of your choosing (homemade alternative for Gluten and Dairy Free after main recipes)
4 eggs, whisked (see notes)
120g / 4oz goat's cheese chopped (may contain Lactose) (see notes)
100g / about 4oz fresh ricotta cheese (see notes)
½ cup Lactose Free thickened cream or one to your liking
1 bunch chives snipped (F, FOS (raffinose), PO (mannitol) VLOX and LS) (substitute tarragon (VLOX and VHS to taste) (see notes)
¼ cup grated parmesan cheese (Lactose Friendly)
2 teaspoons Dijon mustard (F, LOX and HS) (homemade recipe after main recipes)
2 tomatoes thinly sliced (HF, FOS, PO (mannitol), MOX and MS)
Baby salad leaves to serve of your choice

Directions
Preheat oven to hot; 200°C / 400°F and lightly grease a 22cm (9") quiche pan.

Join pastry sheets and ease pastry into the pan, trimming it to fit.

Bake blind for 10 minutes using bake paper with pastry weights, dry pasta or dry rice.

Remove from oven and remove paper and weights before returning to the oven to bake for a further 5 - 6 minutes.

Reduce oven temperature to 180°C / 350°F.

In a large bowl, using an electric mixer; beat the eggs, goat's cheese, ricotta, cream, chives/tarragon, parmesan and mustard together.

Pour into pastry case and arrange the tomatoes on top.

Bake for 30 - 35 minutes until just set in the centre.

Cool for 10 minutes and top with leaves and then serve in wedges.

Notes
There is a Lactose Friendly Cheese Chart on page 36 for other options.

Ricotta cheese has a low fat, (20g) content with Lactose being around 0.4 (homemade Lactose Free recipe on page 37)

Chives are high in Polyols (and have raffinose) where tarragon is not and Chives have very low oxalates and low salicylates where tarragon has very low oxalates and very high salicylates.

I have never used an egg replacer so I don't know if it would be suitable for this recipe. If you use it, then you would know.

GOAT'S CHEESE AND SUNDRIED TOMATO TARTS

Ingredients

3 sheets Gluten Free frozen shortcrust pastry, thawed or one of your choosing (homemade alternative for Gluten and Dairy Free after the main recipes)
½ cup semi sun-dried tomatoes chopped (F, FOS, PO and HS)
100g / 4 oz / ½ cup crumbled goat's cheese (may contain Lactose) (see notes)
2 tablespoons chives snipped or 2 teaspoons dried (F, FOS (raffinose), PO (mannitol) VLOX and LS) (substitute tarragon (VLOX and VHS)
300ml carton / 1¼ cups Lactose Free cream or one to your choosing
3 eggs
1 teaspoon Dijon mustard (F, LOX and HS) (homemade recipe after main recipes)

Directions

Preheat the oven to 180°C / 350°F and lightly grease a 12 hole (⅓ cup) muffin pan.

Cut twelve 10cm (4") circles from the pastry sheets and ease the pastry rounds into the muffin holes.

Divide the sun-dried tomatoes, cheese and chives evenly between tart shells.

In a jug, whisk the cream, eggs and mustard together and then season to taste.

Fill the tarts with the egg mixture.

Bake for 25 - 30 minutes until set and golden. Cool in the pan for 5 minutes and then transfer to a wire rack to cool completely.

Store in an airtight container in the fridge.

Variations

Wilted spinach (F, FOS, PO (sorbitol), VHOX and VHS) and Feta (VLOX); chopped cooked vegetables and Brie.

Caramelised onion (HF, HFOS, PO (mannitol), LOX and LS) or green parts only of the spring onion (white part has M-HF, FOS, PO (mannitol), MOX and LS) and blue cheese.

Notes

You will have to use your own judgement and consider how the ingredients could affect your issue.

If you are unable to eat Goat's cheese, Blue cheese or Brie, then there is a Lactose Friendly Cheese Chart on page 36 for more options.

I have never used an egg replacer so I don't know if it would be suitable for this recipe. If you use it, then you would know.

QUINOA AND BLACK BEAN BURGERS WITH GAUCAMOLE

Ingredients
1 cup vegetable stock (minus onion and garlic)
½ cup white quinoa, rinsed (Gluten Free and has a high carb count, FOS and HS)
400g or 14oz tin black beans, drained or 400g dried (FOS, GOS and HOX) (see notes)
4 spring onions, thinly sliced (green parts only) (white part has M-HF, FOS, PO (mannitol), MOX and LS)
½ cup fresh coriander leaves (VLOX)
1 teaspoon ground cumin (VHS)
½ teaspoon ground chili powder (HF and HS) or paprika (HF and VHS)
½ cup dried Gluten Free breadcrumbs or one to your liking
1 egg, lightly beaten
Salt and pepper (black - HOX and VHS, white - VLOX and VHS) to taste
2 tablespoons vegetable oil or one to your choosing
4 Gluten Free multigrain bread rolls, halved or ones to your liking
Tomato Chutney of your choosing, lettuce (HF, FOS, PO (sorbitol), and VLOX), sliced tomatoes (HF, FOS, PO (mannitol), MOX and MS) and sliced red onion (HF, HFOS, PO (mannitol), MOX and MS) (optional) to serve
Coriander sprigs to garnish (MOX and HS)

Guacamole
1 large avocado, peeled and de-seeded (F, FOS, PO (sorbitol), VLOX and HS)
2 tablespoons fresh coriander, finely chopped (MOX and HS)
2 teaspoons lime juice (F, PO and LS)

Directions
In a medium pot bring stock to the boil and then add the quinoa. Cover and simmer for 12 - 15 minutes until tender and the liquid is absorbed.

Remove from the heat and stand covered for another 5 minutes before fluffing with a fork and letting it cool.

Place the beans, onions, coriander, cumin and chili/paprika in a processor and process until smooth.

Transfer to a large bowl and stir in the breadcrumbs, egg, quinoa, salt and pepper and then divide and shape into 4 patties 2cm (½") thick. Cover and refrigerate until firm.

To make the Guacamole
Mash the avocado in a bowl with salt and pepper and stir in the coriander and lime juice.

Heat the oil in a large non-stick frypan/skillet over a medium to high heat. Add the patties and cook for 5 - 6 minutes on each side or until golden brown.

Top the roll bases with the chutney, lettuce, patties, tomato, onion and guacamole.

Garnish with coriander and then replace the tops.

Notes
I have never used an egg replacer so I don't know if it would be suitable for this recipe. If you use it, then you would know.

Soaking the beans for at least 12 hours in warm water with 2 teaspoons bi barb soda should soften them a little and may help with "gas" issues. Drain and rinse beans and re-soak at least twice before using.

*   *   *   *   *

CURRIED CHICKPES

Ingredients
1 tablespoon olive oil (LOX and HS) or one to your choosing
1 onion, finely chopped (HF, HFOS, PO (mannitol), LOX and LS) or 3 spring onions, thinly sliced (green parts only) (white part has M-HF, FOS, PO (mannitol), MOX and LS) or a pinch of asafoetida powder (may contain Gluten) (see notes)
2 tablespoons mild Gluten Free curry paste (homemade recipe after main recipes)
375g or 13oz can Light and Creamy Coconut flavoured evaporated milk (F, FOS, PO and S) (homemade Lactose Free or normal evaporated milk recipes after main recipes)
2 x 400g or 13oz cans chickpeas, drained (FOS, GOS and MS) or 800g dried chickpeas (see notes)
1½ cups brown rice (Basmati (FOS, LOX and MS) and Doongara (FOS and LOX) rices are both low GI. Soaking rice and grains for 12 hours lowers oxalates)
3 Gluten Free vegetarian chicken-style stock cubes or ones to your liking (minus onion and garlic for Fructose Free)
½ cup chopped coriander (MOX and HS)
1 cup frozen peas (HF, HFOS, GOS, VLOX and N-LS)
2½ cups boiling water
Extra coriander to garnish

Directions
Hear the oil in a saucepan over medium heat and add the onion and cook until soft. Add the paste and cook, stirring for 2 minutes.

Add the milk, chickpeas, ½ cup of rice, crumbled cubes and 2½ cups of boiling water and mix well and bring to the boil.

Simmer stirring occasionally for 35 - 40 minutes or until thick.

Stir in the coriander and peas and cook for another 2 minutes.

Cook the remaining rice in boiling water until tender and then drain well.

Serve the curry with the rice.

Notes
Soaking the chickpeas for at least 12 hours in warm water with 2 teaspoons bi barb soda should soften them a little and may help with "gas" issues. Drain and rinse peas and re-soak at least twice before using.

Cooking with the asafoetida powder may help with the "gas" issue. This is a strong spice so don't use more than the specified amount.

HOMEMADE RECIPES FOR THE ABOVE RECIPES

GLUTEN & DAIRY FREE PIE CRUST - SWEET OR SAVORY
(Taken from my first book)

This recipe makes 2 Bottom Pie Crusts or 1 Set (top & bottom) Pie Crusts.

Ingredients
2 cups of all-purpose Gluten Free flour of your liking (options page 13 & 14)
½ cup palm shortening (LOX), coconut oil (HS), or real butter or Nutellex Original (see notes)
1 egg (see notes)
⅔ cup water (approx. depending on consistency)
½ teaspoon salt (or season to taste)
2 teaspoons dextrose powder (may contain Gluten) or alternative sweetener for desserts if desired (or sweeten to taste)

Directions
Mix together flour along with salt and dextrose.

Add in shortening (or butter), and mix until crumbly.

Add in egg and mix until well incorporated - mixture will still be crumbly.

Add water by stirring in 1 tablespoon at a time until dough holds together for rolling - better a little moist, then too dry.

Cut mixture in half and roll into 2 balls (one for each crust or topping).

Shape dough balls into disc with floured hands and place onto a sheet of well-floured parchment or wax paper.

Cover with an additional sheet of parchment or wax paper. Roll crust out to slightly larger than your pie tin.

Remove top parchment/wax paper and Slip hand gently under the bottom paper to flip into pie tin, carefully peeling back the paper as you press it into the pan. Don't worry if it breaks apart a little, you can always press it together and it will look great.

Crimp edges of crust to make a decorative edge or top with an additional crust layer after adding your pie filling. Pierce bottom slightly with fork (and slit top layer with knife to vent).

Fill with your favorite recipe and bake following the pie recipe you are using for bake time and temperature.

Notes
Coconut oil is reported to be Fructose Friendly but still may affect some people.

I have never used an egg replacer so I don't know if it would be suitable for this recipe. If you use it, then you would know.

HOMEMADE THAI RED CURRY PASTE

Ingredients

1 or 2 shallots, green part only (white part has M-HF, FOS, PO (mannitol), MOX and LS) OR ¼ cup purple onion, chopped (HF, HFOS, PO (mannitol) LOX and LS) (see notes)
1 stalk fresh lemongrass, minced, OR 3 tablespoons frozen prepared lemongrass (available at Asian stores) (only info found is that it may contain Polyols)
1 - 2 red chilies (F, PO (mannitol), HOX and HS) or peppers (HF, PO (sorbitol), VLOX and VHS), OR ½ - 1 teaspoon cayenne pepper, (VHS) OR 1 teaspoon paprika (HF and VHS) OR 2 - 3 teaspoons Thai chili sauce (homemade mild, onion and garlic free sauce recipe in this section)
4 cloves garlic (F, FOS, GOS, LOX and LS) or ⅛ teaspoon asafoetida powder (may contain Gluten) (see notes)
1 thumb-size piece galangal OR ginger, sliced (HF, FOS, LOX and MS) (see notes)
2 tablespoons tomato ketchup (HF, FOS, PO, VLOX and VHS) OR good-tasting tomato puree (F, FOS, PO (mannitol), HOX and VHS)
1 teaspoon ground cumin (VHS)
¾ teaspoon ground coriander (MOX and HS)
¼ teaspoon ground white pepper (VLOX and VHS)
2 tablespoons fish sauce, OR for vegetarians: 2 tablespoons soy sauce, plus salt to taste or Vegan Fish Sauce (homemade recipe in this section)
1 teaspoon shrimp paste (homemade recipe in this section), OR for vegetarians: 1 tablespoon Thai golden mountain sauce, both available at Asian stores
1 teaspoon sugar or dextrose powder (Fructose Free and may contain Gluten)
1½ - 2 tablespoons chili powder (F and VHS), depending on how spicy you want it or paprika (F and VHS)
3 tablespoons thick coconut milk (HF, FOS, PO (sorbitol) and S), or just enough to keep the blades turning or milk to your liking
2 tablespoons fresh squeezed lime juice (F, PO, MOX and LS)
Optional: ¼ teaspoon cinnamon powder (HF, HOX and VHS) (see notes)

Directions

Place all ingredients in a food processor or blender and process well to create a fragrant Thai red curry paste.

If too thick, add a little more coconut milk to help blend ingredients. Note that it will taste very strong at this point, but will mellow when you add your curry ingredients plus remaining coconut milk. Also, it will turn 'redder' once it is cooked, bringing out the red chili color.

Notes

You do not need to use both onion and garlic if you are using asafoetida powder and don't use any more than ⅛ teaspoon as it is a strong spice.

If you want to keep the heat down, completely de-seed and de-vein your chili/peppers.

Galangal has more of a peppery tone where ginger has a more sweet and spicy tone.

HOMEMADE CURRY POWDERS

HOMEMADE SIMPLE CURRY POWDER

Combine in a screw top jar and shake to mix well. Use in your favourite recipes.
¼ cup coriander powder (MOX and HS)
1¼ tablespoons turmeric (VHOX, VHS)
2 teaspoon cumin powder (VHS)
1 teaspoon mustard powder (F, GOS, VLOX and VHS
1 teaspoon black pepper (HOX and VHS)
1 teaspoon chilli powder (F and HS) or cayenne pepper (LOX and VHS)
1 tablespoon roasted paprika (VHS)

* * * * *

HOMEMADE CURRY POWDER

Ingredients
2 tablespoons whole cumin seeds, toasted (VHS)
2 tablespoons whole cardamom seeds, toasted (LOX)
2 tablespoons whole coriander seeds, toasted (MOX and HS)
¼ cup ground turmeric (VHOX, VHS)
1 tablespoon dry mustard (F, GOS, VLOX and VHS)

Directions
Grind the cumin seeds, cardamon seeds and coriander seeds to a powder. Add the turmeric and dry mustard and mix well.

Store in an airtight container.

* * * * *

HOMEMADE CURRY PASTE

Ingredients
2 tablespoons coriander (ground or fresh or dry leaves) (MOX and HS)
1 tablespoon ground cumin (VHS)
1½ tablespoons ground cardamon (LOX and HS)
1 teaspoon turmeric (F, VHOX and VHS)
1 teaspoon ground fennel seed (FOS, LOX and M-HS) (Fennel seeds are Fructose Friendly and safe to use but the rest of the plant isn't due to its Fructose value)
2 teaspoons crushed or ground ginger (F, FOS, LOX and MS)
2½ tablespoons lemon juice (F, PO (sorbitol) LOX and L-HS)

Directions
Combine coriander, cumin, turmeric, ginger, cardamon, fennel seed and lemon to form a paste.

VEGAN FISH SAUCE

Ingredients for about ½ cup or 125 ml
¼ cup warm filtered or spring water
2 tablespoons raw turbinado sugar (Fructose Friendly)
¼ cup fresh or canned 100% pineapple juice (HF, PO (mannitol), VLOX and MS)
2 tablespoons light soy sauce (FOS) or tamari

Directions
Stir the water and sugar together in a bowl until sugar dissolves. Add the pineapple juice and light soy sauce and mix well.

Refrigerate in a glass container or jar with a lid for an hour or so. This can last up to 3 - 4 days.

Notes
This version is intended to make it saltier like 'light soy sauce': Alternatively instead of 2 tablespoons light soy sauce, use 1 tablespoon Gluten Free tamari and 1 tablespoon Gluten Free chicken free broth. You want it to be slightly saltier and lighter.

*   *   *   *   *

HOMEMADE DIJON MUSTARD

Ingredients
1 cup of onion (chopped) (HF, HFOS, PO (mannitol), LOX and LS) or a pinch of asafoetida powder (may contain gluten) (see notes)
2 cloves of garlic (F, FOS, GOS, LOX and LS) (minced) or ⅛ teaspoon asafoetida powder (may contain gluten) (see notes)
2 tablespoons of honey (HF, FOS, VLOX and VHS) or rice malt syrup (Fructose Free)
4 oz (8 tablespoons) of dry mustard (seeds ground) (F, GOS, VLOX and VHS)
1 tablespoon of vegetable oil or one to your liking
2 teaspoons of salt
4 drops of Tabasco sauce (check label for unwanted ingredients)
2 cups of dry white wine (varies in OX and S) or white wine vinegar (L-MOX and VHS) to your liking

Directions
Take the dry ingredients and grind in a spice grinder until relatively fine. This way you won't have to do any soaking.

Add the liquid ingredients to a glass bowl and then add the dry to the liquid and mix well with a fork.

Microwave on high for 1 minute and then mix well with a stick blender until creamy. Let the mixture rest. It will thicken as it cools.

Notes
Try using 3 spring onions (green parts only) (white part has M-HF, FOS, PO (mannitol), MOX and LS) instead of the onion but it will change the colour, taste and texture.

Don't use the onion and garlic if using the asafoetida powder and as this is a strong spice only use the amount specified.

LACTOSE FREE RICOTTA CHEESE

Ingredients for about 2 cups
8 cups Lactose Free cow milk or goat milk (VLOX)
1 (6oz) container or ¾ cup Lactose Free plain yogurt (LOX)
¼ cup vinegar (F and LOX) of your choosing
1 teaspoon non-iodized salt

Directions
Whisk milk and yogurt together in a large cooking pot over medium heat. Stir often to avoid scorching. Bring the milk up to 175° (hot but not yet simmering; use a candy thermometer if you have one) and remove from heat. Add vinegar while stirring briefly. Tiny bits of curd will form. Set the mixture aside for 15 minutes.

Line a colander with several layers of cheesecloth. Pour curds and liquid (whey) into colander to strain. Let drain for at least an hour. Ideally, tie up the bundle with twine, thread the twine around a wooden spoon, and suspend the bundle over a pitcher to drain, in the refrigerator, for a couple of hours or more.

Transfer solids to a bowl and add salt, working in gently. (You can also add lemon zest, herbs, or anything you like for flavor). Refrigerate in a covered container; keeps for about a week.

*   *   *   *   *

SHRIMP PASTE

Ingredients for about 2 cups
1 cup or 16 tablespoons Nuttelex Original or unsalted butter or one to your liking
1lb or 450g medium shrimp, shelled and de-veined
½ teaspoon salt to taste
½ teaspoon ground black pepper (HOX and VHS)
¼ cup red wine vinegar (L-MOX and VHS) + ½ tablespoon dextrose powder (may contain Gluten) or sugar - mixed
2 tablespoons fresh lemon juice (F, PO (sorbitol), LOX and L-HS)
¼ teaspoon cayenne pepper (LOX and VHS)

Directions
In a large frypan, melt 6 tablespoons of the butter until it foams and then add the shrimp, the salt and pepper. Cook over high heat, stirring, until the shrimp are pink and cooked through, about 5 minutes. Using a slotted spoon, transfer the shrimp to a food processor.

Return the frypan to high heat. Add the red wine vinegar mix, lemon juice and cayenne and cook until reduced to 3 tablespoons, 2 - 3 minutes. Pour the liquid over the shrimp and process until very smooth. With the machine on, add the remaining butter, 1 tablespoon at a time, and process until smooth and silky.

Transfer the shrimp paste to a serving bowl and let cool. Press a piece of plastic wrap directly onto the surface and refrigerated for at least 1 day.

Bring to room temperature before serving.

Notes
The shrimp paste can be refrigerated for up to 1 week.

ONION AND GARLIC FREE MILD THAI SWEET CHILI SAUCE

Ingredients for 2 cups
5 red chili/peppers (completely and utterly de-veined and de-seeded)
⅛ teaspoon asafoetida powder (may contain Gluten. This is a strong spice so don't use more than the specified amount)
1 cup dextrose powder (may contain Gluten) or sugar or sweetener to your liking
1 cup rice wine vinegar (no info available) or one to your liking
¾ cup water
½ teaspoon salt
2 tablespoons cornstarch (MOX) for thickening (optional)
2 tablespoons hot water for thickening (optional)

Directions
Slice peppers in half and completely remove all the seeds and veins.

In the bowl of a food processor or blender combine chili/peppers, asafoetida powder, dextrose powder, vinegar, water and salt. Blend until only very small flecks of the peppers remain.

Transfer to a saucepan and simmer over medium heat until sugar is completely dissolved, 4 - 5 minutes. (Make sure you stir the sauce frequently as it cooks - it's prone to bubble over). Keep simmering the sauce down until it reduces by about half which takes 15 - 20 minutes and will be a watery style sauce.

If you would like a thicker style of sauce, just whisk together the hot water and cornstarch and add it to the sauce. Simmer for a couple minutes longer, until the sauce is thickened to your liking.

*   *   *   *   *

HOMEMADE TIN/CAN TOMATOES SUBSTITUTE

Place the weight amount of tomatoes needed in a bowl of boiling water for 5 minutes. Carefully remove and peel tomatoes; they will be hot. Place them in a saucepan and bring them to a boil. Cook until soft but not soggy. Follow the recipe as to their use. For crushed tomatoes, process by pulsing for a few seconds in your processor or chop finely.

*   *   *   *   *

HOMEMADE LACTOSE FREE EVAPORATED MILK

Well, in my search for the best way to make homemade evaporated milk; it seems like there are basically three ways: either with whole or low fat milk, cooked down to ½ it's volume, or reconstituted whole milk dry powder or low fat dry powder milk cooked down to ½ it's volume OR mixing up a batch of whole powdered milk, using twice as much powdered milk than called for. All of these ways work. It seems that boiling the whole milk down is the best tasting.

CHILE

The following recipes were kindly donated by Alejandra Stanko.

The vegetables and fruit in these recipes will only make them Fructose Friendly. I have tried to source out whether they have Fructose, Fructans, Polyols or Galactans in them and have indicated this beside the ingredient plus a few ingredients have alternatives beside them or in the notes at the end of each recipe. I am hoping that this will help you as much as it has helped me. Salicylates and Oxalates may also be issues for some people so I have added them as well. They will all be noted in the code form below or mentioned in the notes. Please read these.

Low – L, Medium – M, High – H, Very High – VH, Salicylates – S, Oxalates – OX
Fructose – F, Fructans – FOS, Polyols – PO, Galactans – GOS

I have placed some homemade recipes for substituting the ingredients after the main recipes. These recipes will be for Gluten Free, Fructose Friendly, Lactose Free or Friendly, Diabetic Friendly and IBS Friendly depending on your sensitivity so that you can make your own if you want to. Please remember that Fructans, Polyols and Galactans (GOS) can also come with Fructose and that Gluten Free flour is high in carbs so they may not be Diabetic friendly.

Substituting ingredients will alter the original taste; however, it is a way to try different recipes from other countries and you can adjust the taste to your liking. Make these recipes your own and use your ingredients if you want to as you know what's best for you.

The ingredients can also be changed slightly to make them Vegan, Vegetarian or just a plain simple basic recipe for you to try. If you are using normal flour, then please be mindful that you may have to use less liquid in the recipe. As to what liquid you decrease; this I will leave to you.

Australian tablespoons and cups measurements are used and they are: 1 teaspoon equals 5ml; 1 tablespoon equals 20ml; 1 cup equals 250ml. Oven temperatures are for conventional; if using fan-forced (convection), reduce the temperature by 20°C.

Carbonada, Chilean Soup	77
Stuffed Potatoes, Chilean Recipe	78
Walnut Kuchen	79
Corn and Beef Pie, Pastel De Choclo	80
Chilean Zucchini Casserole	81
Pear Empanadas	82
Homemade Recipes For The Above Recipes	
Homemade Lactose Free and Fructose Friendly Sweetened Condensed Milk	84
Dairy Free Sweetened Condensed Milk	84
Instant Dairy Free Sweetened Condensed Milk Alternatives	85
Homemade Pumpkin Puree	85
Homemade Panko (Japanese Bread Crumbs)	86

CARBONADA, CHILEAN SOUP

Ingredients for 6 people
½ kilo or 1 pound of meat of your choice
1 onion (HF, HFOS, PO (mannitol), LOX and LS) or 3 spring onions (green parts only) (white part has M-HF, FOS, PO (mannitol), MOX and LS) or a pinch of asafoetida powder (may contain Gluten and is a strong spice so only use the specified amount)
3 carrots (boiled HF, FOS (raffinose), PO (sorbitol), GOS, MOX and HS)
2 stalks celery or ½ cup chopped celery leaves (celery is HF, FOS PO (mannitol) and VHOX)
½ bell pepper (red - F, HPO (sorbitol), VLOX and HS or green - F, HPO (sorbitol), MOX and VHS, to taste)
3 medium red potatoes (see notes)
6 handfuls of rice (Basmati and Doongara rice is low GI) (see notes)
Spinach or Swiss chard (see notes)
Peas (F, FOS, VLOX and LS)
Salt, pepper (black - HOX and VHS, white - VLOX and VHS), parsley (F, PO (mannitol), LOX and LS)
1 tablespoon oil to your liking

Directions
Cut meat into cubes, onion into small cubes, same with carrots, pepper and celery.

In a large pot place 1 tablespoon of oil and brown the meat for 2 minutes per side over medium-high heat. Add the onion and season with salt and pepper and let it sauté for about 5 minutes and then add carrots and celery and sauté for 3 minutes more, stirring occasionally.

Add 6 to 9 cups water until it is all covered. Add potatoes and rice and stir well and add more salt and pepper if necessary. Cook covered for 20 minutes over medium heat.

Test, adjust the seasoning. Add the chopped chard or spinach and peas, cook 5 minutes more. Serve hot.

Notes
Substitute for bell peppers; add more spinach or Swiss chard for the colour or make a spice mix for 'strong spicy' (cumin (VHS), ginger (HF, FOS, LOX and MS) and mustard powder (F, GOS,VLOX and, VHS).

Fresh Spinach has HF, FOS, PO (sorbitol), VHOX and HS
Frozen Spinach has HF, FOS, PO (sorbitol), VHOX and MS
Swiss Chard/Chard has F, FOS, PO and VHOX

Fructose in potatoes can range anything between 582 mg – 989 mg depending on the size, type and skin colour. They also have FOS, PO and GOS. They can also be VHOX and MS again depending on the type of potatoes, colour of skin and how they are cooked.

Basmati rice has FOS, LOX and MS. Doongara rice has FOS and LOX. Soaking rice and grains for 12 hours lowers oxalates.

STUFFED POTATOES, CHILEAN RECIPE

Ingredients
10 - 12 medium potatoes (see notes)

For the meat
1 pound or ½ kilo of ground beef
½ cup beef broth (minus onion and garlic)
2 medium onions, chopped into small cubes (HF, HFOS, PO (mannitol) LOX and LS) or green parts only 6 spring onions (white part has M-HF, FOS, PO (mannitol) MOX and LS) or ⅛ teaspoon of asafoetida powder (may contain Gluten and is a strong spice so don't use more than the specified amount)
1 tablespoon Gluten Free flour or one to your liking
1 tablespoon paprika or to taste (F and VHS)
¼ teaspoon cumin (VHS)
Salt and pepper (black - HOX and VHS, white - VLOX and VHS)
2 tablespoons oil of your choosing

Directions
Heat the oil in a large pot or pan, fry the meat until lightly browned, about 8 minutes, and then add the paprika, salt, pepper and cumin, sauté a few more minutes. Add the onions or asafoetida powder, incorporate well, sauté for 5 minutes add the broth and cook 30 minutes over low heat.

Turn off the heat, add the flour and stir well, adjust the seasoning if necessary.

For the potatoes
2 pounds or 1 kilo of potatoes (Yukon gold or red) (see notes)
2 eggs
4 tablespoons all-purpose Gluten Free flour or one to your liking
1 cup Panko or Gluten Free breadcrumbs (homemade Panko breadcrumb recipe after the main recipes)
Salt, pepper (black - HOX and VHS, white - VLOX and VHS)
Oil to your liking for frying

Directions
Peel the potatoes and cut into slices about ¼" or 6½ mm.

Place in a pot with cold water and salt. Cook covered over high heat until it boils, and then lower the heat a bit, but should continue boiling. Cook for 18 - 20 minutes, until you can easily pierce the potatoes with a fork. Drain and let cool slightly before mashing the potatoes very well, should be smooth, no lumps left.

Working with floured hands, make a ball with about ½ cup of mashed potatoes, form a disc in your hand, fill with 1 generous tablespoon of meat mixture and close, forming a stuffed potato. Roll in flour. Repeat with remaining puree and meat.

Beat eggs with salt for 30 seconds and pass the potatoes through the egg, then through the Panko or breadcrumbs.

Preheat the broil/grill and place potatoes in a greased oven tray. Bake for 3 - 4 minutes until golden and then turn and repeat until browned all around, about 20 minutes.

They can also be fried in hot oil, with care because they are fragile.

Notes
Fructose in potatoes can range anything between 582 mg – 989 mg depending on the size, type and skin colour. They also have FOS, PO and GOS. They can also be VHOX and MS again depending on the type of potatoes, colour of skin and how they are cooked.

*   *   *   *   *

WALNUT KUCHEN

Ingredients for 10-12 people
For the dough
115g or ⅔ cup of Nuttelex Original or butter
150g or ⅔ cup of dextrose powder (for Fructose Free and may contain Gluten) or granulated sugar
1 egg (see notes)
200g or 1½ cups of all-purpose Gluten Free flour (high in carbs) or normal flour or one to your liking
½ teaspoon baking powder (VLOX)
Pinch of salt

Directions

Preheat oven to 180°C / 350°F. Butter a round cake pan of 22cm in diameter (9") or 20 × 20cm square (9" x 9").

In a medium bowl beat butter with a fork until creamy, add the sugar and beat until creamy, add the egg and beat well until incorporated fully into the mix. Add the flour, salt and baking powder. Mix to form a soft dough.

Scoop the batter into the pan and spread with a spoon or your wet fingers. Form an even layer and bake for 12 - 15 minutes until lightly browned.

For the filling
300g of chopped walnuts (VHOX and HS)
1 can (375g or 13oz) Lactose Free condensed milk (3 homemade recipes after main recipes)
1 egg
115g or ⅔ cup Nuttelex Original or butter, melted or oil to your liking
Pinch of salt

Directions

In a bowl mix the chopped nuts with the condensed milk and egg, pinch of salt, stir to mix. Add the melted butter and stir well.

Pour over baked dough (hot) and cover the pan with foil. Bake for 30 minutes and then remove the foil gently and carefully.

Bake for another 10 - 13 minutes until golden and then let cool completely on a wire rack.

Refrigerate before cutting and serving.

CORN AND BEEF PIE, PASTEL DE CHOCLO

Ingredients for 4-6 persons
For the corn mixture
2 tablespoons Nuttelex Original or butter or one to your liking
4 bags of frozen corn kernels or 10 cups or equivalent from corn off the cob (HF, FOS, PO (xylitol), LOX and MS)
½ cup whole Lactose Free milk or one to your liking
1 tablespoon cornstarch (MOX) dissolved in ¼ cup cold Lactose Free milk or water
1 bunch basil, about 10 leaves; sweet basil if fine (F, MOX and VHS)
Salt, pepper (black - HOX and VHS, white - VLOX and VHS) and Merkén (see notes) or paprika (HF and VHS)

For the meat
2 tablespoon of vegetable oil or one to your liking
1 kilo or 2 pounds ground beef
1 cup water or beef broth (minus onion and garlic)
3 onions, diced small (HF, HFOS, PO (mannitol) LOX and LS) or 9 spring onions (green parts only) (white part has M-HF, FOS, PO (mannitol) MOX and LS)
Merkén (see notes) or 1 tablespoon chili powder (HF and HS) or paprika (HF and VHS) use less if you don't want it "hot"
½ teaspoon ground cumin (VHS)
Salt to taste
Pepper (black - HOX and VHS, white - VLOX and VHS)
2 tablespoons Gluten Free flour or plain flour or one to your liking
Grilled chicken, and raisins or currants if you like them to go on top of the meat (see notes)

Directions
Heat the oil in a large pot, sauté the meat until lightly browned, about 8 minutes, stirring occasionally, add the paprika, salt, pepper and cumin, sauté 2 minutes more. Add the broth and simmer 30 minutes over low heat.

Add the onion and mixed well and cook over medium heat until the onion is tender, about 30 minutes, stirring occasionally. Turn off heat and add the flour and stir well, adjust seasoning if necessary. Cool and refrigerate.

For the corn mixture
In a large pot with a thick bottom, I use my cast iron, melt the butter over medium-high heat, add the frozen corn and stir occasionally, about 8 minutes.

Add milk, basil, salt, pepper and paprika and continue to cook stirring occasionally for about 10 minutes longer. (You may need to longer if using corn off the cob).

With a hand blender, blend the corn trying to not to go uniform, leave some chunky parts, when happy with the consistency, add the dissolved cornstarch and continue cooking over medium heat 5 minutes, taste and adjust seasoning, it will thicken slightly.

To assemble the pie
In a clay or baking dish, put one layer of cooked meat, add grilled chicken and raisins or currants. Cover with the corn mixture, sprinkle with dextrose powder or granulated sugar and bake at 400°F / 200°C on a preheat oven for 45 - 60 minutes until bubbling and golden on top.

Let stand 10 minutes before serving.

Notes

Merkén or merquén (from the Mapuche mezkeñ) is a smoked chili pepper (or, in Spanish, "ají") used as a condiment that is often combined with other ingredients when in ground form. Merkén is a traditional condiment in Mapuche cuisine in Chile.

1 cup Currants = 3.95g Fructose and 1 cup Raisins = 48.97g Fructose. Both red and black currents have HF, PO (mannitol), HOX and VHS. Raisins have HF, PO (sorbitol), LOX and VHS.

*   *   *   *   *

CHILEAN ZUCCHINI CASSEROLE

Ingredients for 6 servings
3 zucchinis thinly sliced (HF, FOS, PO (sorbitol), VLOX and VHS)
1 large onion, diced (HF, HFOS, PO (mannitol), LOX and LS) or 3 spring onions (green parts only) (white part has M-HF, FOS, PO (mannitol) MOX and LS)
2 cloves garlic, (F, FOS, GOS, LOX and LS) optional (see notes for onion and garlic substitutes)
1 tablespoon oil to your liking
3 slices of Gluten Free bread soaked in Lactose Free milk or ones to your liking
2 eggs
3 slices of Lactose Free cheese (Lactose Friendly Cheese Chart on page 36) or ones to your liking

Directions

In a skillet/frypan heat the oil over medium-high heat and fry the onion until it is translucent, about 5 minutes, add garlic finely chopped or passed through a garlic press, cook for 1 more minute.

Add the zucchini and cook until it is tender and just cooked through, about 8 - 10 minutes, season and taste. Add the soaked and squeezed bread (discard the leftover milk) to the zucchini. Turn off heat and let stand 5 minutes to cool slightly. Add the egg yolks to the zucchini mixture, and mix well.

Preheat oven to 180°C / 350°F.

In the meantime separate the eggs and beat the egg whites to soft peaks. Add the egg whites, fold carefully.

Cover with slices of cheese and bake for 35 - 40 minutes or until golden and cheese is melted. Serve warm.

Notes

Onion and garlic are both high in FODMAPs. An alternative to onion is the green part of a spring onion or fresh chives (F, FOS (raffinose), PO (mannitol), VLOX and LS). Substitute 3 spring onions (green part only) (white part has M-HF, FOS, PO (mannitol) and LS) for 1 small onion.

There is no substitute for garlic, but a couple of flavorful and aromatic alternatives are cumin seeds (VHS) and fresh ginger (HF, FOS, LOX and MS) or something else of your choosing.

PEAR EMPANADAS

Ingredients for up to 24 small Empanadas
For the filling
250g or 2 cups or 9oz of dried pears or about 2 fresh pears (VHF, PO (sorbitol), Peeled LOX and Unpeeled MOX and HS)
100g or ½ cup of dextrose powder (may contain Gluten) or sugar
½ teaspoon cinnamon (F, HOX and VHS)
Pinch of nutmeg (VLOX and VHS)
2 tablespoons of dextrose powder for fresh pears only
2 tablespoons of glucose syrup for fresh pears only

For the dough
3 cups Gluten Free flour or one to your liking (options on pages 13 & 14)
2 teaspoons baking powder (VLOX)
½ teaspoon salt
½ cup or 125g of cold Nuttelex Original or butter or one to your liking
2 eggs
¼ cup pumpkin puree (MHF, FOS, PO (mannitol) and MS) (homemade recipe after main recipes)
¼ cup Lactose Free milk or one to your liking
2 tablespoons dextrose powder (may contain Gluten) or sugar
1 egg for brushing or milk of your liking
Dextrose powder (may contain Gluten) or sugar for sprinkling

Directions
Preheat oven to 350°F / 180°C.

For Dried Pears
In a small saucepan, place the pears and mostly submerge with boiling water. Let stand 15 minutes.

Place over medium heat and add sugar, stirring until sugar dissolves. Using a hand blender: grind the pears to a puree, add the cinnamon and nutmeg. Cook until it boils softly and when you stir you can see the bottom of the pot.

Allow to cool completely.

For Fructose Friendly Fresh Pears
Peel and slice the pear and place in a saucepan with the dextrose powder and enough water to cover the pears and dissolve the dextrose powder.

Bring to the boil and simmer for about 10 minutes, moving the pears around gently to stop them sticking.

Add the glucose syrup and raise the heat so the pears boil in the made syrup. Add more water if necessary. Boil for about 10 minutes more then turn off the heat and cool.

Strain and puree the pears when cool enough to do so.

For the dough
Combine flour, baking powder and salt in a bowl, add the chopped butter in small pieces, and work with two knives or the paddle attachment of the mixer until it look like a coarse sand. Add eggs, sugar, milk and pumpkin and mix everything into a smooth dough.

Beat the egg with 1 tablespoon water until blended, 20 seconds.

Divide dough into 2 halves, place one half in the refrigerator. Roll the dough on a floured counter until a thickness of about 2 - 3mm. Cut circles of 12cm in diameter.

Place a tablespoon of filling into the center. Wet the border with the egg wash, close, and make small indentations with a fork to seal.

Repeat with other half of dough and place Empanadas on a parchment paper covered or greased baking sheet.

Brush with beaten egg and sprinkle with dextrose or sugar. Use a fork to pierce each Empanada.

Bake for 25 minutes or until golden browned on both sides.

Let cool 5 minutes on the baking sheet and then move to a wire rack to cool completely and serve cold.

HOMEMADE RECIPES FOR THE ABOVE RECIPES

HOMEMADE LACTOSE FREE AND FRUCTOSE FRIENDLY SWEETENED CONDENSED MILK

Ingredients for ⅔ - 1 cup (adjust the ingredient amounts depending on how much your recipe calls for)

1½ cups whole Lactose-Free milk of your choosing
⅔ cup dextrose powder (may contain Gluten)
3 tablespoons Nuttelex Original or butter or one to your choosing
1 teaspoon vanilla (F, VLOX and VHS)
Pinch of salt

Directions

In a heavy-bottomed saucepan, stir the milk and dextrose together. Bring the mixture to a low simmer, stirring often. When you can see steam coming up from the milk mixture, lower the heat a little further, and once the sugar is dissolved, keep the milk at a very low heat.

You want to reduce the milk and sugar to about half. Reducing the mixture will take anywhere from 1 - 2 hours, depending on how low you have your burner and how thick you want your condensed milk.

Once the mixture is reduced and thickened; stir in the Nuttelex and vanilla until combined.

You can use it warm (depending on the recipe) or you may need to let it cool before adding to the rest of your ingredients.

*   *   *   *   *

DAIRY FREE SWEETENED CONDENSED MILK

Ingredients

1 can of unsweetened coconut milk (HF, FOS PO (sorbitol), GOS and S)
⅓ - ½ cup granulated sugar, honey (F, FOS, VLOX and VHS) or rice malt syrup (Fructose Free) or dextrose powder (may contain Gluten and Fructose Free)
1 tablespoon brown sugar (optional but adds good flavour and is Fructose Friendly)

Directions

Place the coconut milk, sweetener of choice, and brown sugar (if using) into a saucepan and whisk gently over medium heat for 2 - 3 minutes. This will help the solid bits of coconut milk melt and incorporate with the sugar.

When the mixture is just beginning to bubble around the edges, reduce the heat to the lowest flame/setting. Set a timer for one hour (you may need to go a bit longer depending on your stove) and simmer uncovered, whisking every 5 - 10 minutes to release steam and aid in evaporation.

The mixture will reduce by about half and should be quite thick. You will also notice that it is a darker color.

Remove from heat, stir thoroughly and pour into a glass jar or container.

Cool in the refrigerator. It will continue to thicken as it cools.

INSTANT DAIRY FREE SWEETENED CONDENSED MILK ALTERNATIVES

I would like to say a special thank you to the person who has supplied the following information and recipe.

Special Diet Notes & Options: Dairy-Free Sweetened Condensed Milk
By ingredients, this recipe is dairy-free / non-dairy, egg-free, Gluten Free, nut-free, peanut-free, soy-free, vegan / plant-based, vegetarian, and generally food allergy-friendly.

Ingredients
1 cup + 2 tablespoons Dairy Free vanilla milk powder (Vanilla Rice Milk Drink)
¾ cup sugar (use dextrose powder (may contain Gluten) for Fructose Friendly)
½ cup hot water
2 tablespoons non-GMO canola, rice bran, grapeseed, or melted coconut oil (coconut oil is reported to be Fructose Friendly but still may affect some people and has HS)
Generous pinch salt

Directions
Place the rice milk powder and sugar in your blender. Whiz the ingredients for about 30 seconds, or until powdered.

Add the water, oil, and salt to your blender and blend for 2 minutes, or until thick and creamy.

Use as a substitute for sweetened condensed milk in recipes.

*   *   *   *   *

HOMEMADE PUMPKIN PUREE

Ingredients
2 cups cooked Kent or Jap pumpkin (MHF, FOS, PO (sorbitol) and MS)
1¼ cup skim milk or Lactose Free milk or one to your liking
½ teaspoon salt + more to taste
⅛ teaspoon black pepper (HOX and VHS)
1 cup shredded mozzarella or Lactose Free Cheese (see notes) or omit if you don't want to have the cheese taste with the pears

Directions
Place pumpkin, 1 cup of milk, salt, and pepper in a bowl. Using an immersion blender, (stick blender); blend the pumpkin mixture until smooth. If you don't have an immersion blender you can use a food processor or blender and puree in batches.

Add additional ¼ cup of milk as necessary, you want a thick sauce but you don't want it too chunky. Stir in 1 cup mozzarella and additional salt and pepper to taste (if using).

Notes
Mozzarella cheese claims to be a Lactose Friendly cheese. There is a Lactose Free or Friendly Cheese Chart on page 36 for more options.

You may wish to add a bit of spice like nutmeg (VLOX and VHS) or cinnamon (F, HOX and VHS) in place of the pepper.

It is completely up to you to use other ingredients to suit your taste.

HOMEMADE PANKO (JAPANESE BREAD CRUMBS)

Carefully trim only the brown crust from 2 slices of fresh Gluten Free white bread and lay them out on the counter (or somewhere safe) for 1 - 2 hours. Some people have had to leave their bread out to dry for much longer, even up to 12 hours, depending on the type of bread used. (You can use any type of bread if you desire).

When it is dried out, crumble gently using your fingers. Use as desired.

POLAND

The following recipes were kindly donated by Biblioteka Polonii, Basia, Malgosia i Ewa.

The vegetables and fruit in these recipes will only make them Fructose Friendly. I have tried to source out whether they have Fructose, Fructans, Polyols or Galactans in them and have indicated this beside the ingredient plus a few ingredients have alternatives beside them or in the notes at the end of each recipe. I am hoping that this will help you as much as it has helped me. Salicylates and Oxalates may also be issues for some people so I have added them as well. They will all be noted in the code form below or mentioned in the notes. Please read these.

Low – L, Medium – M, High – H, Very High – VH, Salicylates – S, Oxalates – OX
Fructose – F, Fructans – FOS, Polyols – PO, Galactans – GOS

I have placed some homemade recipes for substituting the ingredients after the main recipes. These recipes will be for Gluten Free, Fructose Friendly, Lactose Free or Friendly, Diabetic Friendly and IBS Friendly depending on your sensitivity so that you can make your own if you want to.

Substituting ingredients will alter the original taste; however, it is a way to try different recipes from other countries and you can adjust the taste to your liking. Make these recipes your own and use your ingredients if you want to as you know what's best for you.

The ingredients can also be changed slightly to make them Vegan, Vegetarian or just a plain simple basic recipe for you to try. If you are using normal flour, then please be mindful that you may have to use less liquid in the recipe. As to what liquid you decrease; this I will leave to you. Please remember that Fructans, Polyols and Galactans (GOS) can also come with Fructose and that Gluten Free flour is high in carbs so they may not be Diabetic friendly.

Australian tablespoons and cups measurements are used and they are: 1 teaspoon equals 5ml; 1 tablespoon equals 20ml; 1 cup equals 250ml. Oven temperatures are for conventional; if using fan-forced (convection), reduce the temperature by 20°C.

Zupa Pomidorowa Z Ryżem (Tomato Soup with Rice)	88
Piernik (Hania's Spiced Gingerbread)	89
Ruskie Pierogi Z Ziemniakami I Serem (Dumplings with Potato and Quark) and with (Pierogi Z Kapusta I Grzybami) Sauerkraut and Mushrooms	90
Zupa Ogorkowa (Cucumber Soup)	91
Gołąbki (Cabbage Roll)	92
Bigos (Hunter's Stew)	94
Barszcz (Borshsch) (Beetroot Soup)	95
Cheesecake - Polish Version Sernik	96
Homemade Recipes For The Above Recipes	
Homemade Farmer's Cheese	97
Homemade Sauerkraut	97
How To Make Tomato Paste The Quick And Easy Way	98

ZUPA POMIDOROWA Z RYŻEM (TOMATO SOUP WITH RICE)

Ingredients to serve 4

1kg or 500g tomatoes (HF, FOS, PO (mannitol) MOX and MS)

1 medium-sized onion (HF, HFOS, PO (mannitol) LOX and LS), or 3 spring onions (green parts only) (white part has M-HF, FOS, PO (mannitol) MOX and LS) or a pinch of asafoetida powder if you can't tolerate onion. (This is a strong spice so use only specified amount)

2 tablespoons fresh flat leaf parsley (FOS, PO (mannitol), LOX and LS) or coriander (MOX and HS) (see notes)

3 carrots (F, FOS (raffinose), PO (mannitol), GOS, M-VHOX and HSL)

½ swede (F, FOS and VLOX)

1 parsnip (F, FOS and HS)

1 small stalk of celery (FOS, PO (mannitol) and VHOX) or try using ¼ cup of celery leaves for the flavour

3 tablespoons tomato paste (**see notes**) (homemade recipe after main recipes)

1 litre (4 cups) chicken stock (bouillon) (minus garlic and onion)

400g (2 cups) long grain rice (Basmati - FOS, LOX and MS and Doongara - FOS and LOX and both rices are low GI. Soaking rice and grains for 12 hours lowers oxalates)

200ml or ¾ cup + 4 teaspoons fresh Lactose Free cream or normal cream or one to your liking

Directions

Dice onion, carrot, celery, parsley, parsnip and swede and gently fry in oil in a heavy bottomed pot.

Blanch tomatoes in hot water for 5 minutes, rinse in cold water and peel off the skin.

Add tomatoes to the pot, pour in the stock and oil for 20 - 30 minutes until the vegetables are soft.

Add 2 tablespoons tomato paste, remove from heat and blend with a hand blender.

Stir in the cream and simmer for a couple more minutes. Do not boil.

Cook rice separately according to instruction on the packet. Drain rice but don't rinse with cold water, so it stays sticky.

Fill a cup with rice and invert into soup bowl. Fill bowl with hot tomato soup.

Notes

Dried parsley has 304mg Fructose. (Substitution is 1 teaspoons of dried parsley for every tablespoon of fresh parsley).

Tomato paste may naturally contain a high load of Fructose, i.e. over 3g per serving, or of Fructans, i.e. over 0.5g/serving. It also has PO (mannitol), HOX and VHS.

A cup of a raw tomato has 2.5 grams of Fructose, FOS, PO (mannitol), MOX and MS.

PIERNIK (HANIA'S SPICED GINGERBREAD)

I have named this gingerbread after my Aunt who has given me this recipe many years ago and I still use it. In Poland, the gingerbread is usually baked at Christmas.

Ingredients

250g (just over ⅔ cup) of honey (HF, FOS, VLOX and VHS) or rice malt syrup (Fructose Free)
125g or ½ cup Nuttelex Original or butter or one to your liking
1 cup of dextrose powder (may contain Gluten) or sugar (brown, caster, white) (see notes)
1 cup of Lactose Free milk or one of your choosing
1 teaspoon of cinnamon (cinnamon, ground [Cassia] Fructose: 899mg per 100g, HOX and VHS)
1 tablespoon of cocoa powder (FOS, GOS, VHOX and MS)
1 teaspoon mix of ground spices (cloves (HS), nutmeg (VLOX, VHS), allspice (VHS), ginger (F, FOS, LOX, MS), cardamom (S), pepper (black - HOX, VHS, white - VLOX, VHS) star of anise (VHS), coriander (MOX, HS) or ones of your choosing
2 cups of Gluten Free plain flour or normal plain flour or one to your liking (see notes)
3 eggs separated
1 teaspoon of baking soda
Delicacies/dried fruit and nut of your choice (raisins, currants and almonds (F, PO (xylitol), VHOX and VHS) or other nuts) (see notes)

Directions

Preheat the oven to 160°C / 320°F. Grease and flour a 28cm or 11" loaf tin.

Place honey/rice malt syrup, Nuttelex Original/butter, dextrose powder/sugar, and milk in the saucepan, simmer on medium heat, until all melted.

Add cinnamon, cocoa and the mix of ground spices. Stir well and set aside to cool.

When the mixture has cooled, add egg yolks, and mix it well.

Add the flour and baking soda and blend well.

Add the beaten egg white and delicacies/nuts and dried fruit, and gently stir.

Pour the gingerbread mixture in the tin and bake for about 60 minutes until slightly firm on the outside but still soft and moist inside.

Allow to cool in the baking tin.

Notes

Gluten Free flour is high in carbs and if using Gluten Free flour, you made need to add a little more liquid.

Be mindful when cooking with dextrose powder that it may cook slightly quicker. I use dextrose in my cooking and find that my baking comes out fine when using the temperature suggested. I will leave this up to you to judge when it is done.

The Fructose count for Currants - 1 cup - 3.95g; Raisins, seedless - 1 cup, packed - 48.97g so exchange currants for the raisins. Both red and black currents have HF, PO (mannitol), HOX and VHS. Raisins have HF, PO (sorbitol), LOX and VHS.

RUSKIE PIEROGI Z ZIEMNIAKAMI I SEREM (DUMPLINGS WITH POTATO AND QUARK) AND WITH (PIEROGI Z KAPUSTA I GRZYBAMI SAUERKRAUT AND MUSHROOMS)

Ingredients
For the dough
400g Gluten Free plain flour or normal flour or one to your liking (see notes)
1 egg
225ml or 1 cup of cold or tap water
Pinch of salt
60g of Nuttelex Original or unsalted butter, melted or oil to your liking

For the filling (A)
800g potatoes, boiled, choose the best for making mashed potatoes (see notes)
400g of drained quark/farmers cheese (homemade Farmer's Cheese recipe after main recipes)
2 onions chopped finely or 6 spring onions, green parts only (white part has M-HF, FOS, PO (mannitol) MOX and LS) (see notes)
Cooking oil of your choice
Salt and pepper (black - HOX and VHS, white - VLOX and VHS)

For the filling (B)
800g of sauerkraut (from European delis, markets, some supermarkets, fresh, canned or in jar) (homemade recipe after main recipes) (see notes)
300g of Swiss/brown/forest mushrooms, chopped finely or Shiitake, Oyster and Enoki mushrooms (see notes)
1 onion sliced finely or 3 spring onions (green parts only) sliced finely (white part has M-HF, FOS, PO (mannitol) and LS) (see notes)
Salt and pepper (black - HOX and VHS, white - VLOX and VHS)
Cooking oil of your choosing

Directions
Make a dough from the flour, salt, egg, adding water gradually to ensure the dough is not too soft and runny. The dough should not stick to your fingers.

Roll out, with rolling pin, on floured kneading board until about 3mm thick. Using a biscuit cutter or drinking glass, cut out circles of 5cm or 2½" in diameter.

Put a teaspoon of the filling of your choice in the centre of each cut circle and holding it gently in your hand, seal the outer edges to make a half-circle, half-moon shaped Pierogi.

Drop the Pierogi into salted boiling water (use big pan) and boil for 3 minutes until they bob to the surface. Remove with a slotted spoon and serve hot and fresh with melted butter, cream, or lightly fried chopped bacon.

To make Filling A
Finely mince the potatoes, combine with quark/Farmer's Cheese and sautéed onion. Season to taste.

To make Filling B
Combine sauerkraut with sautéed onion, mushrooms. Season to taste.

Pierogi taste nice lightly fried the following day, served with caramelized onion or cream or melted butter.

Notes
This is information is from my files back in 2014: Sauerkraut, canned, solids and liquids Fructose: 421mg, FOS, GOS, PO and MOX.

Onions, sweet, raw Fructose: 12622mg, HFOS and PO (mannitol). They also are LOX and LS.

Fructose in potatoes can range anything between 582 mg – 989 mg depending on the size, type and skin colour. They also have FOS, PO and GOS. They can also be VHOX and MS again depending on the type of potatoes, colour of skin and how they are cooked.

Gluten Free flour is high in carbs so if using Gluten Free flour, you made need to add a little more liquid.

Swiss/brown/forest mushrooms are high in Polyols (mannitol and xylitol) and contain moderate amounts of both raffinose and fructans and are therefore a potential source of bad gas. They are VLOX and MS. Many sites class all mushrooms under one heading so very little other information is available. Shiitake, Oyster and Enoki mushrooms have less or no Polyols.

*   *   *   *   *

ZUPA OGORKOWA (CUCUMBER SOUP)

Ingredients
4 Polish dill cucumbers in brine cut in fine slices, (available at European delis) (see notes)
2 litres or 8 cups of good quality vegetable or chicken broth stock (minus onion or garlic)
200ml or 1 cup of Lactose Free cooking or Lactose Free sour cream or one to your liking, mixed with 1 tablespoon Gluten Free plain flour or normal flour or one to your liking
Salt and pepper (black - HOX and VHS, white - VLOX and VHS) to taste
Reserve some brine from which cucumbers have been preserved

Directions
Add sliced dill cucumbers to the stock and boil/cook for about 20 minutes.

Add cream mixture and bring to the boil to dissolve any flour remains.

Check the seasoning, add salt and pepper if needed, if the soup is not tart/sour enough for your liking, add some reserved brine.

Serve hot with finely chopped fresh dill (F, L-MOX and VHS) and crusty European bread roll.

Notes
I could not find out if these Polish Dill cucumbers contain Fructose, Fructans or Polyols. The pre-packaged ones stated on the label that there was a low amount of sugar in them. The only main information is on cucumbers and it is reported that they contain HF, FOS, PO (sorbitol), VLOX and HS

I did find this in my files though: Pickles, cucumber, dill, low sodium Fructose: 7110mg.

This is another one of your call ingredients as to whether you eat them or not because you know what your tolerance level is and the consequences of eating them are.

These may or similar ones may be available now in some supermarkets.

GOŁĄBKI (CABBAGE ROLL)

This recipe is definitely not Fructose, Fructan, Polyol, Galactan and IBS friendly.

Gołąbki (cabbage roll) is a typical traditional Polish food made of minced pork with some rice, onion, mushrooms, wrapped in white cabbage leaves. There are also other variations of fillings such as poultry, mutton or without meat. Before serving cabbage are simmered / fried in fat.

Traditional Polish Gołąbki Recipe combining ground beef, ground pork and rice and topped with a sweet and tangy tomato sauce.

Ingredients
1 large head green cabbage or 2 small green cabbages (Fructose: 10087mg, FOS, PO (sorbitol), GOS, LOX and LS)

For The Sauce
2 tablespoons extra virgin olive oil (LOX and HS) or one to your liking
3 garlic cloves, chopped (F, FOS, GOS, LOX and LS) (see notes for substitutes)
2 x 28oz cans diced tomatoes (HF, PO (aspartame), H-VHOX and LS?)
2 tablespoons white wine vinegar (L-MOX and VHS) or one to your liking
1 tablespoon sugar or dextrose powder (Fructose Free and may contain Gluten)
½ teaspoon kosher salt (an edible salt with a much larger grain size to common table salt so use only half the amount of common salt if substituting)
¼ teaspoon black pepper (HOX and HVS)

For The Cabbage Rolls
2 tablespoons extra virgin olive oil (LOX and HS) or one to your liking
1 medium onion, chopped (HF, HFOS, PO (mannitol) LOX and LS) or 3 spring onions (green parts only) (white part has M-HF, FOS, PO (mannitol) MOX and LS) (see notes for other substitutes)
2 garlic cloves, minced (F, FOS, GOS, LOX and LS) (see notes for substitutes)
2 tablespoons tomato paste (HF, PO (mannitol), HOX and VHS) (homemade recipe after main recipes)
2 tablespoons red wine (varies in OX and S) or red wine vinegar (L-MOX and VHS) or water
1lb or 450g ground beef (see notes for Vegetarian)
1lb or 450g ground pork (see notes for Vegetarian)
1 large egg, lightly beaten
1½ cups cooked white rice (Basmati - FOS, LOX and MS and Doongara - FOS and LOX and both rices are low GI. Soaking rice and grains for 12 hours lowers oxalates)
½ teaspoon kosher salt (an edible salt with a much larger grain size to common table salt so use only half the amount of common salt if substituting)
¼ teaspoon black pepper (HOX and VHS)

Directions
Bring a large pot of water to a boil.

Remove the large, damaged outer leaves of the cabbage and discard and then carefully peel off the large cabbage leaves from the head of the cabbage, setting aside the leaves that are whole and big enough to stuff. Blanch the cabbage leaves in the pot of water, boiling for 4 - 5 minutes.

Drain the cabbage in a colander and run the leaves under cold water. Lay the leaves out on a cutting board and pat dry with a paper towel.

Make the sauce

Coat a large saucepan with oil and place over medium heat. Add the garlic or substitute and sauté for 1 minute. Add the 2 cans of diced tomatoes with their juices to the saucepan and stir and cook for 3 minutes.

Add the vinegar and sugar/dextrose powder; simmer until the sauce thickens, about 5 minutes. Season with the salt and pepper and remove from the heat.

Make the Onion and Garlic Mixture

Place a skillet over medium heat and add the olive oil. Sauté the onion and the garlic or substitutes for about 5 minutes. Stir in the tomato paste, red wine and ¾ cup of the prepared tomato sauce, mix and remove from the heat.

Prepare the filling

Preheat the oven to 350° F / 180°C.

In a large mixing bowl, combine the ground beef and the ground pork. Add the egg, the cooked rice, the sautéed onion and garlic mixture and the salt and pepper. Stir or toss the filling together using your hands to combine. Set aside.

To Assemble

Pour ½ cup of the tomato sauce onto the bottom of a 13 x 9" (33 x 23cm) baking dish and spread the sauce with a spoon so it covers the entire bottom of the dish.

Take each cabbage leaf and place ¼ - ⅓ cup of the filling in the center. Fold the base of the leaf up and over the filling until it's completely covered. Fold the sides in and roll up the cabbage to enclose the filling.

Place the cabbage rolls side by side in rows, seam side down in the baking dish and then pour the remaining tomato sauce over the cabbage rolls. Cover with aluminium foil and bake for 1½ hours or until done to your satisfaction.

Notes
Garlic Substitutes

You might want to try using cumin (VHS) as a garlic substitute. Its rich, savory character will go a long way to disguise the lack of garlic in whatever you're cooking. OR Asafoetida powder is a strong spice that replaces onion and garlic. Don't use more than a pinch in the sauce and a pinch in the cabbage. Asafoetida is said to prevent flatulence.

Substitutes for onions

Fennel pairs well with some surprising foods. The seeds may be fine but the Fennel bulb is HF, FOS and LS. OR Celery seed powder is said to be fine to use but raw celery stalks have HF, FOS, PO and VHOX. Cumin (VHS) can mimic the rich depth of onions.

To make this dish Vegetarian you can substitute the meat for mushrooms. Portabella, White, Swiss/brown/forest mushrooms are high in Polyols (mannitol and xylitol) and contain moderate amounts of both raffinose and fructans and are therefore a potential source of bad gas. They are VLOX and MS. Many sites class all mushrooms under one heading so very little other information is available. Shiitake, Oyster and Enoki mushrooms have less or no Polyols. Not too sure about the King Brown even though one site states that they are in the same category as the other Gourmet mushrooms. I am fine using "Gourmet Style" mushrooms.

BIGOS (HUNTER'S STEW)

Ingredients

600g or 4 cups sauerkraut (FOS, PO (mannitol) GOS and MOX) (from European delis, markets, some supermarkets, fresh, canned or in jar) (homemade recipe after main recipes)
400g or 4 cups fresh cabbage (has 10087mg of Fructose per 100g, FOS, PO (mannitol), GOS, LOX and LS)
300g or 10.5oz neck of pork
250g or 8oz of stewing steak
200g or 7oz of good quality Polish sausage (Continental delis, Polish markets/delis/butchers)
150g or 5oz bacon
70g or 2.5oz unsmoked belly pork
60g or ⅜ cup onions (HF, HFOS, PO (mannitol) LOX and LS) or same weight in the green parts only of a spring onion (white part has M-HF, FOS, PO (mannitol) MOX and LS)
5 dried porcini mushrooms (Continental delis, Polish shops, markets, Gourmet food shops) (Stated to be safe and in the same category as Gourmet mushrooms with little or no PO, VLOX and MS)
Couple of prunes (optional) (F, HPO (sorbitol) and VHS)
50g or just under ¼ cup of tomato paste (F, PO (mannitol), HOX and VHS) (homemade recipe after main recipes)
25g or just under ¼ cup Gluten Free or normal plain flour or one to your choosing
Salt, pepper (black - HOX and VHS, white - VLOX and VHS), bay leaves (VHS), all-spice berries (VHS), juniper berries (L-MOX and VHS) - few (optional)
Splash of good quality red wine (varies in OX and S) - optional

Directions

Chop the sauerkraut finely and add crumbled dried porcini.

Cover with boiling water and cook until almost tender. Add the fresh cabbage and boil for 10 minutes. Lower the heat and continue to simmer.

In a separate saucepan brown the whole neck of pork and the stewing steak. Add the bacon and braise until tender.

Cut the cooked meat into 2cm cubes and add to cabbage mixture.

Chop the belly of pork into small pieces and cook until golden brown before adding to the cabbage mixture.

In the same frypan cook the chopped onion until translucent. Add the flour to make a roux (fat and flour mixture) and cook until golden before adding to cabbage mixture.

Remove the skin from Polish sausage, slice it into 3 - 4mm slices and add to cabbage.

Add prunes, tomato paste, red wine, seasoning. Stir. Continue to simmer for at least 2 hours or until mixture has reduced to golden stew.

Bigos (Hunter's Stew) taste can be enhanced by adding a variety of good quality and cut meats such as poultry, game or a variety of different sausages. It is well recognised and agreed upon that the flavour of the Bigos improves with reheating, while kept in cold conditions between reheating (fridge, cold larder etc)

It can be served with a slice of good quality continental dense rye or sourdough bread or bread rolls.

BARSZCZ (BORSHSCH) (BEETROOT SOUP)

Ingredients to serve 4-6
900g or 2lb of uncooked, fresh beetroot/s, peeled (HF, FOS, PO (mannitol), GOS, VHOX and MS)
2 carrots peeled **(see notes)**
2 celery sticks **(see notes)**
3 tablespoon of Nuttelex Original or unsalted butter or one to your liking
2 brown onions, sliced thinly (HF, HFOS, PO (mannitol) LOX and LS) or 6 spring onions (green parts only) (white part has M-HF, FOS, PO (mannitol) MOX and LS) or ⅛ teaspoon asafoetida powder only (may contain Gluten) (use instead of onion and garlic)
2 garlic cloves, crushed (F, FOS, GOS, LOX and LS) (see notes above in onions)
4 ripe tomatoes, peeled, seeded, and chopped roughly (F, FOS, PO (mannitol), MOX and MS)
1 bay leaf (VHS)
2 sprigs of fresh continental parsley (F, PO (mannitol), LOX and LS)
2 cloves (F and HS)
4 whole black peppercorns (HOX)
5 cups of good quality beef or chicken stock (minus onion and garlic)
150ml or 5 fl oz of beetroot juice or the liquid from the pickled/canned beetroots (HF, FOS, PO (mannitol), GOS, VHOX and MS)
Seasoning - salt, freshly ground black pepper (HOX and VHS), pinch of sugar, squeeze of lemon juice (F, PO, LOX and L-HS)
To serve and garnish - sour cream with snipped fresh chives (F, FOS (raffinose), PO (mannitol), VLOX and LS) and dill (F, L-MOX and VHS)

Directions
Cut the beetroot, carrots, celery into fairly thick stripes.

Melt the butter in a large pan and cook the onions over a low heat for 5 min, stirring occasionally, until translucent. Add the beetroot, carrots, celery and cook for further 5 minutes, stirring occasionally. Add the garlic, chopped tomatoes to the pan and cook, stirring, for 2 more minutes.

Place the bay leaf, parsley, cloves and peppercorns in a piece of muslin and tie with a string. You can use ready to use bouquet garni seasoning/blend for the supermarket, deli or gourmet food store. Add the muslin bag to the pan with the stock and all vegetables. Bring to the boil, reduce the heat, cover and simmer for 75 minutes or until the vegies, including beetroot are very tender.

Discard the bag, add beetroot juice or liquid, stir and season to taste - salt, pepper, sugar, squeeze of lemon juice. Bring to the boil. Ladle into the bowls or deep soup plates and serve with a dollop of sour cream, garnished with fresh chives and dill.

Notes
A little information: Raw baby carrots have 5741mg of Fructose per 100g and normal carrots have 2683mg of Fructose per 100g and all carrots have FOS (raffinose), PO (mannitol) and raw carrots are VHOX and HS.

A little information: Celery, cooked, boiled, drained, with or without salt has 7332mg of Fructose: 7332mg whereas raw celery has 6376mg of Fructose which shows that the Fructose increases when you cook it. Celery also has FOS, PO (mannitol) and VHS.

CHEESECAKE - POLISH VERSION SERNIK

This recipe would be easier made by weight as conversions differ greatly.

Ingredients
Biscuit pastry
150g of Gluten Free plain flour or one to your liking
120g of Nuttelex Original or unsalted butter or one to your liking
50g dextrose powder (Fructose free and may contain Gluten) or icing sugar
1 egg yolk

Cheese filling
1kg or 2 cups Quark/Farmers Cheese, moisture well squeezed out, available in European delis, Gourmet Food stores, some supermarkets, Polish shops and markets (homemade recipe after main recipes)
12 egg yolks
8 egg whites
50g candied orange peel / orange peel mix (F, PO (sorbitol) and HOX)
50g sultanas or currants (see notes)
Vanilla essence or good quality vanilla extract (VLOX and VHS)
400g of dextrose powder (Fructose free and may contain Gluten) or icing sugar
300g of Nuttelex Original or unsalted butter cut into small cubes
50g of semolina (high in carbs)
Juice of small lemon (F, PO (sorbitol), LOX and L-HS)

Directions
Preheat the oven at 200°C / 400°F and grease a round spring form cake tin.

To make the biscuit pastry
Add the dextrose powder or icing sugar to the flour and rub in the butter until the mixture looks like coarse crumbs. Add egg yolk and make soft dough, assembling all ingredients together.

Pour the pastry mixture to a circle/round bottom of the base of the cake tin, and bake in a for up to 15 minutes. Remove from the oven.

To make a cheese mixture
Cream the butter and sugar until fluffy and soft. Combine with well drained quark and add egg yolks, one at the time. Add semolina, and mix well and then add the orange peel, sultanas, vanilla essence and lemon juice. Whip the egg whites to a stiff peaks/foam and gently fold into the cheese mixture.

Spread over the partly baked biscuit base and continue baking in a preheated oven at 180° C / 350°F for 30 - 40 minutes or until the top has turned into a light golden colour.

Turn off the oven and let it rest in the oven for next 10 min, and then rest on a cake rake. Dust with dextrose powder or icing sugar and Enjoy with dollop of whipped cream, ice cream or fresh berries. Even better next day.

Notes
1 cup Currants = 3.95g Fructose and 1 cup Raisins = 48.97g Fructose. Both red and black currents have F, PO (mannitol), HOX and VHS. Raisins have HF, PO (sorbitol), LOX and VHS.

HOMEMADE RECIPES FOR THE ABOVE RECIPES

HOMEMADE FARMER'S CHEESE

Ingredients
1 gallon or 4 litres whole Lactose Free milk or one to your choosing (SEE NOTES)
1 pinch salt
1 large lemon, juiced (F, PO (sorbitol), LOX and L-HS)

Directions
Pour the milk into a large pot, and stir in a pinch of salt. Bring to a boil over medium heat, stirring occasionally to prevent the milk from scorching on the bottom of the pot.

When the milk begins to boil (small bubbles will first appear at the edges), turn off the heat. Stir lemon juice into the milk and the milk will curdle. You may need to wait 5 - 10 minutes.

Line a sieve or colander with a cheesecloth and pour the milk through the cloth to catch the curds. What is left in the cheesecloth is the Farmer's Cheese. The liquid is the whey. Some people keep the whey and drink it, but you can throw it away if you don't want it.

Gather the cloth around the cheese, and squeeze out as much of the whey as you can. Wrap in plastic, or place in an airtight container. Store in the refrigerator.

Notes
Many sites state that Farmer's Cheese is very low in lactose so a little should be suitable for people who are Lactose intolerant. I will leave the decisions to you as to whether you use it or not.

*   *   *   *   *

HOMEMADE SAUERKRAUT

Ingredients
1 medium head of cabbage (has 10087mg of Fructose per 100g, FOS, PO (sorbitol), GOS, LOX and LS)
1 - 3 tablespoons sea salt

Directions
Chop or shred cabbage. Sprinkle with salt.

Knead the cabbage with clean hands, or pound with a potato masher or cabbage crusher for about 10 minutes, until there is enough liquid to cover the cabbage.

Stuff the cabbage into a quart jar, pressing the cabbage underneath the liquid. If necessary, add a bit of water to completely cover cabbage.

Cover the jar with a tight lid, airlock lid, or coffee filter secured with a rubber band.

Culture at room temperature (60 - 70°F is preferred) for at least 2 weeks until desired flavor and texture are achieved. If using a tight lid, burp daily to release excess pressure.

Once the sauerkraut is finished, put a tight lid on the jar and move to cold storage. The sauerkraut's flavor will continue to develop as it ages.

HOW TO MAKE TOMATO PASTE THE QUICK AND EASY WAY

This recipe makes about 5 heaped tablespoons.

Soak 2 kilos (4½ lbs) of tomatoes (HF, FOS, PO (mannitol), MOX and MS) in boiling water for five minutes or until the skins can be easily peeled off. Drain and carefully remove the tomato skin. The tomatoes may be hot to handle.

Carefully cut tomatoes in half or quarters longways and de-seed completely. Place tomato pieces in to processor and process to a very liquidy paste.

If you have a slow cooker, then place this liquid paste in it and leave it to reduce and thicken up. Stir occasionally. I left mine on all day and got a beautiful thick tomato paste to use in my recipes.

If you don't have a slow cooker you can cook the paste in a 350°F / 180°C preheated oven on shallow trays until it is reduced to a paste. Check the tomatoes every half hour, stirring the paste and switching the position of the trays so that they reduce evenly. Over time, the paste will start to reduce to the point where you can make one tray.

The paste is done when shiny and brick-colored, and it has reduced by more than half. There shouldn't be any remaining water or moisture separating from the paste at this point. This will take 3 - 4 hours, though exact baking/cooking times will depend on the juiciness of your tomatoes and your oven.

After the paste was cold, I put it in a container and kept it in the refrigerator or freezer.

Making small batches when you need it can be useful; however, if you use a lot of tomato paste then just double or triple the amount of tomatoes used. I made a very small batch using the same prep method but I cooked them down in my non-stick frypan over low heat and I continually stirred the mixture. I did not add anything to the paste because I can do that when I use it in a recipe.

FRANCE

The following recipes were kindly donated to me by Catherine.

The vegetables and fruit in these recipes will only make them Fructose Friendly. I have tried to source out whether they have Fructose, Fructans, Polyols or Galactans in them and have indicated this beside the ingredient plus a few ingredients have alternatives beside them or in the notes at the end of each recipe. I am hoping that this will help you as much as it has helped me. Salicylates and Oxalates may also be issues for some people so I have added them as well. They will all be noted in the code form below or mentioned in the notes. Please read these.

Low – L, Medium – M, High – H, Very High – VH, Salicylates – S, Oxalates – OX
Fructose – F, Fructans – FOS, Polyols – PO, Galactans – GOS

These recipes will be for Gluten Free, Fructose Friendly, Lactose Free or Friendly, Diabetic Friendly and IBS Friendly depending on your sensitivity so that you can make your own if you want to. Please remember that Fructans, Polyols and Galactans (GOS) can also come with Fructose.

Substituting ingredients will alter the original taste; however, it is a way to try different recipes from other countries and you can adjust the taste to your liking. Make these recipes your own and use your ingredients if you want to as you know what's best for you.

Australian tablespoons and cups measurements are used and they are: 1 teaspoon equals 5ml; 1 tablespoon equals 20ml; 1 cup equals 250ml. Oven temperatures are for conventional; if using fan-forced (convection), reduce the temperature by 20°C.

Classics Bistro Terrine	100
Potatoes and Parsnip Galettes	101
Onion Jam	102
Poires au Vin From Burgundy	103
Friands (Gluten-Free cakes)	104
Crème Anglaise	104

CLASSICS BISTRO TERRINE

Preparation: 20 minutes
Cooking: 35 minutes

Ingredients to serve 8
300g or 1⅓ cups each of veal and pork mince (you could use turkey, chicken or any other meat)
3 or 4 onions thinly sliced (HF, HFOS, PO (mannitol) LOX and LS) or 9 or 12 spring onions (green parts only) (white part has M-HF, FOS, PO (mannitol) MOX and LS) or ⅛ teaspoon asafoetida powder (see notes)
3 or 4 gloves of crushed garlic (F, FOS, GOS, LOX and LS) (see notes for substitutes)
200g or 1 cup of thawed spinach (frozen is good in this recipe (LF, FOS, PO (sorbitol), VHOX and MS), squeezed dry (1 cup of raw spinach has 0.04 Fructose and has FOS, PO (sorbitol), VHOX and HS)
50ml port (VHS) (see notes for substitutes)
Very thin slices of either prosciutto or pancetta to cover the terrine dish
Salt, pepper (black - HOX and VHS, white - VLOX and VHS) to taste
Peppercorn (HOX and VHS)

Directions
Preheat the oven to moderate 200°C / 400°F.

Heat the oil in a saucepan and sauté the onions briefly, tossing with a wooden spatula. When the onions are well greased, reduce the heat and cook the onions slowly, stirring from time to time, for about 40 minutes or until they are completely softened. (Add the asafoetida now if using and cook for a minute).

Meanwhile, mix all the other ingredients in a bowl. Add onions when they are ready.

Put into a terrine dish lined with prosciutto or pancetta. Put in a baking dish with hot water (bain-marie).

Cover the terrine with foil and cook in the oven for 30 - 35 minutes.

When done, turn off the oven and leave it in the oven to cool down.

Serve cold with cornichons (see notes), onion jam and toasted sliced bread.

Notes
Garlic Substitutes
Try Ginger (F, FOS, LOX and MS) and Chili Powder (F and HS) - it won't taste like garlic at all, but its spicy-sweet taste combined with the chili's heat will provide depth and aroma for whatever dish you're preparing.
OR
You might want to try using cumin (VHS) as a garlic substitute. Its rich, savory character will go a long way to disguise the lack of garlic in whatever you're cooking.
OR
Asafoetida
Asafoetida is a strong spice that is used to substitute onion and garlic or both. Don't use more than the amount specified. Asafoetida is said to prevent flatulence.

Substitute for Port
Concord grape juice (Purple has HF, FOS, PO (sorbitol) and S. Red has HF, FOS, PO (sorbitol), MOX and S.
White has MF, FOS, PO (sorbitol), LOX and S) mixed with lime zest (F, PO and HOX); or cranberry juice (LF, PO, VLOX and VHS) mixed with lemon juice (LF, PO (sorbitol), LOX and L-HS) or grape juice concentrate (see above). Substitute orange juice (HF, PO (sorbitol), VLOX and MS) or apple juice (F, PO (sorbitol), VLOX and MS) for lighter ports. Cranberry juice is reported to be very low in Fructose and so is lemon juice so should be the best choice for substituting. All the other fruits are high in Fructose.

Cornichons are little gherkins. Cornichon substitutes: dill pickle slices (PO, VLOX and VHS).

*   *   *   *   *

POTATOES AND PARSNIP GALETTES

Preparation: 20 minutes
Cooking: 25 minutes

Ingredients to serve 8
5 peeled, grated and squeezed dry potatoes (see notes)
3 peeled, grated and squeezed dry parsnips (LF, LFOS, PO and HS)
50ml or 2½ tablespoons oil to your liking
Salt, pepper (black - HOX and VHS, white - VLOX and VHS)
2 cloves of crushed garlic (F, HF, GOS, LOX and LS) (omit if you can't tolerate)

Directions
Heat 20ml / 1 tablespoon of oil in your biggest frypan and add the garlic, potatoes and parsnips.

When starting to colour, reduce heat and cook stirring regularly to separate the pieces of vegetable. Add more oil when necessary.

It is ready to serve when it is golden. Season then.

(You could also "mould" the grated vegetable in ramequins and glide the formed galette in the frypan. Cook without stirring but flatten with the back of a spatula. Turn after 10 minutes. Cook for a further 10 minutes. These are the usual galettes).

Notes
Fructose in potatoes can range anything between 582 mg – 989 mg depending on the size, type and skin colour. They also have FOS, PO and GOS. They also have VHOX and MS again depending on the size, type and skin colour.

ONION JAM

This recipe is very hard to adapt so I'm leaving it pretty much as such. Remember that Onions and Garlic are high in any of The Fructose, Fructans, Polyols and Galactan (GOS) groups and are low in Salicylates and Oxalates.

Preparation: 10 minutes
Cooking: 40 mins

Ingredients to serve 8
3 or 4 halved, thinly sliced onions (HF, HFOS, PO (mannitol) LOX and LS)
2 or 3 crushed garlic (F, FOS, GOS, LOX and LS)
Salt, pepper (black - HOX and VHS, white - VLOX and VHS) to taste
50g of dextrose powder (Fructose Free and may contain Gluten) or sugar
20ml blackberry syrup (Fructose Blackberries - 1 cup - 3.46g also PO (sorbitol), VHOX and VHS) (see variation)
⅓ - ½ bottle of red wine (varies in OX and S) (see notes for substitutes)

Directions
Heat the oil in a saucepan. Sauté the onions briefly, tossing with a wooden spatula. When the onions are well greased, but not brown, reduce the heat and cook the onions slowly, stirring from time to time, for about 15 minutes.

Add the sugar and cook, stirring, until the sugar is dissolved. Add the red wine and bring to the boil. Reduce the heat to low and simmer until the mixture thickens (around 20 minutes). Remove from heat, put in a nice ramequin to serve.

Can be eaten cold or warm and can be kept in an airtight container in fridge for a few days.

Notes
Red wine substitute
Non-alcoholic wine with a tablespoon of vinegar (L-MOX and VHS) added to cut the sweetness, grape juice (Purple has HF, FOS, PO (sorbitol) and S. Red has HF, FOS, PO (sorbitol), MOX and S. White has MF, FOS, PO (sorbitol), LOX and S), cranberry juice (LF, PO, VLOX and VHS), tomato juice (HF, PO (aspartame), MOX and MS), or water. Use equal amounts of liquid as called for in the recipe.

VARIATION FOR PEOPLE WHO CAN'T EAT BERRIES

FRUCTOSE FRIENDLY PEAR AND FENNEL SYRUP

Ingredients to make about 3 cups of syrup
Juice from 3 lbs peeled pears (VHF, PO (sorbitol) and LOX) (Pears 1 pound (4 medium) = 2 cups sliced)
½ cup dextrose powder (may contain Gluten)
1 tablespoon lemon juice (F, PO (sorbitol), LOX and L-HS) or lime juice (F, PO and LOX)
¼ teaspoon fennel seed (FOS, LOX and M-HS), tied in a spice bag or mesh tea infuser (see notes)
Pinch sea salt

Directions
Juice the pears by halving or quartering stemmed pears (with cores), covering with water in a large stockpot and adding ¼ cup of dextrose powder and simmering for about 1 hour until mushy.

Take off and mash with a potato masher or push through a food mill. Put into cheesecloth and strain over a large pot overnight.

Add pear and lemon/lime juice, ¼ cup dextrose powder, fennel seeds and salt to a large, wide-bottomed saucepan. Bring to a boil over medium-high heat; stir until dextrose is completely dissolved. Continue to boil, stirring occasionally, until juice is reduced by at least half and is thick and syrupy (about 20 minutes). Watch carefully to assure it does not boil over.

Allow to cool and put into a container of your choice and store in the refrigerator.

Notes
Fennel seeds are Fructose Friendly; however, the bulb has F, HFOS, and PO (mannitol) and LS.

*   *   *   *   *

POIRES AU VIN FROM BURGUNDY

Pears were cooked this way when they were not looking good or were not all good. The "vignerons" will peel and cut them in pieces and cooked them in wine with whatever spices was available. This is one of the recipes that my great uncle would have done.

Preparation: 5 minutes Cooking: 35 minutes

Ingredients to serve 6
6 small pears (Beure Bosc) (HF, HPO (sorbitol) and peeled pears are LOX)
150g of dextrose powder (Fructose Free and my contain Gluten) or sugar
50ml of red wine (varies in OX and S) (see notes for substitute)
Vanilla (F, VLOX and VHS), nutmeg (VLOX and VHS), orange zest (PO (sorbitol) and HOX), 2 cloves (cloves, ground Fructose: 662mg. It has VHOX and HS)

Directions
Peel and core the pears.

Put the wine, dextrose powder/sugar and spices to boil in a saucepan big enough to put in all the pears.

Lower the heat. Add the pears (they should be covered by the liquid. If not, add some water) and poach them for 20 - 30 minutes until they are soft (time depends on the size and type of pears). Strain and put them in a plastic or ceramic container.

The cooking liquid is then put back onto the heat and thickened, before being poured on top of the pears.

Serve the pears cold with the syrup and crème anglaise if desired.

Notes
Red wine substitute
Non-alcoholic wine with a tablespoon of vinegar (L-MOX and VHS) added to cut the sweetness, grape juice (Purple has HF, FOS, PO (sorbitol) and S. Red has HF, FOS, PO (sorbitol), MOX and S. White has MF, FOS, PO (sorbitol), LOX and S), cranberry juice (LF, PO, VLOX and VHS), tomato juice (HF, PO (aspartame), MOX and MS), or water. Use equal amounts of liquid as called for in the recipe.

FRIANDS (GLUTEN-FREE CAKES)

Ingredients
60ml or ½ cup of macadamia oil or one of your choosing
Whites of 2 eggs, lightly beaten
80g or ½ cup of almond meal (FOS, PO (xylitol), VHOX and VHS)
75g or ⅓ cup dextrose powder (Fructose Free and main contain Gluten) or sugar
Slivered almonds (FOS, PO (xylitol), VHOX and VHS)
A drop of almond essence (stated to be safe in everything to use)

Directions
Preheat oven to moderately hot 190°C / 375°F. Grease 12 (⅓ cup / 80ml) rectangular or small patty cakes moulds. Stand on oven tray.

Combine oil, almond meal, sugar, egg whites and flour in medium bowl: Stir until just combined.

Divide mixture among prepared pans. Scatter with slivered almonds. Bake in moderately hot oven about 25 minutes: stand in pans 5 minutes, turn onto wire rack to cool. Serve dusted with dextrose powder or icing sugar.

*   *   *   *   *

CRÈME ANGLAISE

Ingredients
5 yolks
150g or ¾ cup of dextrose powder (Fructose Free and may contain Gluten) or sugar
500ml of Lactose Free milk or one to your liking (see notes)
Vanilla essence to your taste (F, VLOX and VHS)

Directions
Heat the milk.

Mix yolks and sugar until whitish. Pour the milk into mixture while whisking continuously.

Put back on low heat still whisking using a wooden spoon until set. The custard should adhere to the spoon when it is ready. Don't overheat.

Add vanilla essence. Leave to cool before placing in fridge.

Notes
You can also replace half of the milk with Lactose Free, normal or any cream of your choice.

PHILIPPINES

The following recipes were kindly donated to me by Genoveva F Phillips (Jenny).

All these recipes do not have quantities beside them so you can make them as small or as large as you need.

The vegetables and fruit in these recipes will only make them Fructose Friendly. I have tried to source out whether they have Fructose, Fructans, Polyols or Galactans in them and have indicated this beside the ingredient plus a few ingredients have alternatives beside them or in the notes at the end of each recipe. I am hoping that this will help you as much as it has helped me. Salicylates and Oxalates may also be issues for some people so I have added them as well. They will all be noted in the code form below or mentioned in the notes. Please read these.

Low – L, Medium – M, High – H, Very High – VH, Salicylates – S, Oxalates – OX
Fructose – F, Fructans – FOS, Polyols – PO, Galactans – GOS

I have placed some homemade recipes for substituting the ingredients after the main recipes. These recipes will be for Gluten Free, Fructose Friendly, Lactose Free or Friendly, Diabetic Friendly and IBS Friendly depending on your sensitivity so that you can make your own if you want to. Please remember that Fructans, Polyols and Galactans can also come with Fructose.

Substituting ingredients will alter the original taste; however, it is a way to try different recipes from other countries and you can adjust the taste to your liking. Make these recipes your own and use your ingredients if you want to as you know what's best for you.

Australian tablespoons and cups measurements are used and they are: 1 teaspoon equals 5ml; 1 tablespoon equals 20ml; 1 cup equals 250ml. Oven temperatures are for conventional; if using fan-forced (convection), reduce the temperature by 20°C.

Boiled Beef and Vegetables	106
Boiled Chicken with Vegetables	107
Crab in Coconut Milk	107
Chokos Shoots and Corn Soup	108
Egg Plant Omelette	108
Dessert Sweet Potato Spider	108
Homemade Recipes For Above Recipes	
Homemade Soy Sauce Substitute	109
Homemade Seafood Sauce	110
Vegan Fish Sauce	110
Homemade Hoisin Sauce	111
Homemade Chinese Five-Spice Powder	111
Homemade Five-Spice Powder	112
Homemade Simple Curry Powder	112
Homemade Curry Powder	112
Homemade Yellow Mustard Recipe	113
Homemade Chili Powder	113
Onion And Garlic Free Mild Thai Sweet Chili Sauce	114
Homemade Almond Butter	114
Sweet And Spicy Thai Dipping Sauce	115

BOILED BEEF AND VEGETABLES

Ingredients (use the amount to suit your family)
500g beef cuts with bones
Potatoes - cut in cubes (see notes)
Peppercorns (HOX)
½ cabbage - slice half then quarter (HF, HFOS, PO (sorbitol), GOS, LOX and LS)
Chinese vegetables - one bunch (see notes)
Salt and pepper (black - HOX and VHS, white - VLOX and VHS) to taste
Onions (HF HFOS, PO (mannitol) LOX and LS) or use the green parts only of spring onions. (Use 3 spring onions for 1 medium - small onion) (White part has M-HF, FOS, PO (mannitol) MOX and LS)
One teaspoon oil of your liking

Directions
Sauté onions in a teaspoon of oil then add beef.

When the beef is brownish and soft add one and a half cups of water and then add potatoes.

When the potatoes are cooked, add the cabbage and then add the salt and pepper to taste.

Add peppercorns.

Serve with steamed rice with a sauce (see notes) (tablespoon of soya sauce with a drop of lemon). (Homemade soy sauce substitute recipe and a homemade Hoisin Recipe follow the main recipes).

Notes
Fructose in potatoes can range anything between 582 mg – 989 mg depending on the size, type and skin colour. They also have FOS, PO and GOS. They also have VHOX and MS again depending on the type of potatoes, colour of skin and how they are cooked

Chinese Vegetables
Bok Choy - PO (sorbitol) GOS and VLOX.
Choy sum - FOS, PO, GOS and VHS
Chinese broccoli (gai-lan or kai-lan) - unsure of any F, FOS, PO or GOS but has HS.
Daikon - HF, PO, VLOX and VHS

Doongara rice has FOS and LOX. Basmati rice has FOS, LOX and MS. Both are low GI. Soaking rice and grains for 12 hours lowers oxalates.

BOILED CHICKEN WITH VEGETABLES

Ingredients (Use the amount of ingredients to suit your family)
One teaspoon oil of your liking
Chicken pieces (thighs, drumstick or wings)
Green pawpaw (FOS, PO (xylitol), MOX and LS) or Chokos cut in squares (LF, FOS, PO (mannitol), GOS and LS)
Chilli leaves (Unknown for F, FOS, PO or GOS) although Chili powder has HF and HS)
Ginger (HF, LOX and MS) try substituting with Galangal (no info available but has a peppery taste)
Salt and pepper (black - HOX and VHS, white - VLOX and VHS) to taste

Directions
Sauté the chicken in oil and then add one and a half cups of water.

When cooked, add green pawpaw or Chokos and when that is cooked add the chilli leaves and ginger and then salt and pepper to taste.

Serve with steam rice. (Doongara rice has FOS and LOX. Basmati rice has FOS, LOX and MS. Both are low GI. Soaking rice and grains for 12 hours lowers oxalates).

*   *   *   *   *

CRAB IN COCONUT MILK

Ingredients (Use the amount of ingredients to suit your family).
Fresh crabs cut in half with no shell
One tin of coconut milk (F, FOS, PO (sorbitol) and HS) or equivalent amount of milk to your liking
Pumpkin - cut in cubes (F, FOS, PO (mannitol) and MS)
Salt and pepper (black - HOX and VHS, white - VLOX and VHS)
Optional - add green Chinese vegetables to your liking

Directions
Boil the whole crabs, when cooked take the shell off then cut in half.

Cook the coconut milk and let it boil for a few moments and then add the pumpkin.

When the pumpkin is cooked add the crab, simmer let sauce thickens.

When cooked served with steam Doongara rice (see notes), the vegetables and have a spicy sauce on the side. (2 homemade spicy type sauces after main recipes).

Notes
Doongara rice has FOS and LOX and is low GI. (Soaking rice and grains for 12 hours lowers oxalates).

CHOKOS SHOOTS AND CORN SOUP

Ingredients (Use the amount of ingredients to suit your family)
Young Choko shoots from Asian grocers or markets (choko has LF, FOS, PO (mannitol), GOS and LS)
Fresh corn - sliced from off the corn cob (HF, FOS, PO (xylitol), LOX and MS)
Garlic crushed (F, FOS, GOS, LOX and LS)
Onions sliced (HF HFOS, PO (mannitol) LOX and LS) or use the green parts only of spring onions. (Use 3 spring onions for 1 medium - small onion) (White part has M-HF, FOS, PO (mannitol) MOX and LS)

Directions
In a teaspoon of oil sauté the garlic and onions then add the corn add one cup of water. When corn is cooked add the choko shoots. If you want a thick soup (mix a teaspoon of corn flour (MOX and HS) or cornstarch (MOX) in 5 tablespoon of water mix thoroughly then add to the soup.

*   *   *   *   *

EGG PLANT OMELETTE

Ingredients (Use the amount of ingredients to suit your family)
Skinny eggplant (F, FOS, PO (xylitol), MOX and HS)
Eggs
Salt and pepper (black - HOX and VHS, white - VLOX and VHS)

Directions
Grill the eggplant take the skin off, then flattened it on a chopping board. Pat the eggplant with paper towel to take excess water.

Beat the eggs add pepper and salt and dip the eggplant in it or leave it in the egg mixture for few minutes.

Fry the eggplant turning from one side to the other until brown.

Serve with steam rice as a meal. (Doongara rice has FOS and LOX. Basmati rice has FOS, LOX and MS. Both are low GI. Soaking rice and grains for 12 hours lowers oxalates).

*   *   *   *   *

DESSERT SWEET POTATO SPIDER

Ingredients (Use the amount of ingredients to suit your family)
Sweet potato sliced like French fries (F, FOS, PO (mannitol), VHOX and HS)
One cup of Gluten Free plain flour or one to your liking
Oil of your liking

Directions
Mix the flour with water to a thick consistency and then mix in the cut up sweet potato. Fry the battered sweet potato, turning to each side until brown and soft.

Served sprinkle with brown sugar or dextrose powder (may contain Gluten).

Notes
You can have it as a meal by mixing your favourite mincemeat into the mixture before frying.

HOMEMADE RECIPES FOR ABOVE RECIPES
HOMEMADE SOY SAUCE SUBSTITUTE

Ingredients for about ⅔ cup
1 cup beef broth (Gluten Free and minus the garlic and onion)
2 tablespoons balsamic vinegar (F, VLOX and HS) (homemade substitute recipe in this section)
2 teaspoons white wine vinegar (L-MOX and HS) or rice wine vinegar (no info available)
3 teaspoons rice malt syrup (Fructose Free)
⅛ teaspoon ground black pepper (HOX and VHS)
A pinch of asafoetida powder (may contain Gluten. This is a strong spice so don't use more than the specified amount)
⅛ teaspoon ground ginger (F, FOS, LOX and MS)
¼ teaspoon salt or to taste
½ teaspoon fish sauce (optional) (homemade substitute next or Vegan substitute below)

Directions
Place the following in a small saucepan: broth, both vinegars, rice malt syrups, black pepper, asafoetida and ground ginger. Bring to a brief boil over medium-high heat, then reduce heat to a gentle simmer - small bubbles should just break on the surface.

Cook until reduced to about ⅔ cup - this takes about 7 - 10 minutes. (NOTE: If you accidentally cook it longer, the flavors of the vinegar and syrup will be concentrated, and it becomes quite sweet. Keep an eye on the clock and don't miss that 10 minute max).

Remove the pan from the heat and add the salt and fish sauce; stir to combine and taste to make sure it's salty enough for you.

Pour into a glass container and allow to cool. Store in the refrigerator for up to 10 days. This sauce can be used in any recipe that calls for soy sauce.

Notes
⅛ teaspoon coarse (granulated) garlic powder (F, FOS, GOS, LOX and LS) can replace the asafoetida powder.

2 teaspoons cider vinegar (F, L-MOX and VHS) can replace white wine vinegar or rice wine vinegar.

Molasses (F and MS) will replace rice malt syrup for a stronger flavour.

HOMEMADE SEAFOOD SAUCE

Ingredients
2 egg yolks
1 teaspoon mustard (F, LOX and HS) (homemade recipes in this section)
150ml (about ⅔ cup) vegetable oil or one to your liking
1 teaspoon white vinegar (L-MOX and VHS)
½ teaspoon sea salt
1 tablespoon ketchup (HF, FOS, PO, VLOX and VHS)
1 tablespoon Worcestershire sauce (HS) (read ingredients for added anchovy)
1 teaspoon lemon juice (F, PO (sorbitol) and LOX)
½ teaspoon curry powder (F and VHS) (homemade recipes in this section)
½ teaspoon Lactose Free cream or one to your liking
½ tablespoon finely chopped anchovies (optional)

Directions
Combine the egg yolks and mustard in a clean bowl. Whisk vigorously for 30 seconds. Slowly add the oil a few drops at a time, while continuing to whisk vigorously. The mixture will thicken and become creamy like store-bought mayo.

When you've added about 80mls (about ⅓ cup) of the oil to the yolks, add the vinegar to the mixture and continue to whisk. This will lighten the color of the mayo. Season with ½ teaspoon of salt and add remaining oil slowly while continuing to whisk.

Add your other ingredients to make your sauce.

*   *   *   *   *

VEGAN FISH SAUCE

Ingredients for about ½ cup or 125 ml
¼ cup warm filtered or spring water
2 tablespoons raw turbinado sugar (Fructose Friendly)
¼ cup fresh or canned 100% pineapple juice (F, PO (mannitol), VLOX and MS)
2 tablespoons light soy sauce (FOS) or tamari

Directions
Stir the water and sugar together in a bowl until sugar dissolves. Add the pineapple juice and light soy sauce and mix well.

Refrigerate in a glass container or jar with a lid for an hour or so. This can last up to 3 - 4 days.

Notes
This version is intended to make it saltier like 'light soy sauce': Alternatively instead of 2 tablespoons light soy sauce, use 1 tablespoon Gluten Free tamari and 1 tablespoon Gluten Free chicken free broth. You want it to be slightly saltier and lighter.

HOMEMADE HOISIN SAUCE

Ingredients for about 1 cup
Juice of 1 orange (remove any pits) (HF, PO (sorbitol), VLOX and MS)
2 tablespoon almond butter (homemade recipe in this section) or sunflower butter or one to your liking
⅛ teaspoon asafoetida powder (may contain Gluten. This is a strong spice so don't use more than the specified amount)
1 tablespoon grated ginger (thumb size knob of fresh ginger) or 1 teaspoon powdered ginger (F, FOS, LOX and MS)
1 teaspoon rice wine vinegar or white vinegar (L-MOX and VHS)
1 teaspoon rice malt syrup (Fructose Free)
5 tablespoons Gluten Free soy sauce (FOS) such as Tamari or coconut aminos or homemade substitute in this section
½ teaspoon Chinese Five Spice powder (2 homemade recipes in this section)
1 teaspoon sesame oil (VHOX and MS) or one to your liking
½ teaspoon chilli flakes or powder (omit if you can't tolerate) (F and VHS) (homemade Chili powder in this section) or substitute ½ teaspoon paprika (HF and VHS)
1 teaspoon tomato paste (HF, FOS, PO (mannitol), HOX and VHS)

Directions
Add all ingredients to a small saucepan and heat over medium heat to boil. Turn the heat down to very low, whisk and simmer gently for 3 - 5 minutes, stirring frequently to prevent sticking. The mixture will thicken and darken.

Remove to a ramekin and set aside.

Store the leftovers in an air-tight container in the refrigerator for up to two weeks.

Notes: For those who want to avoid soy all together, use coconut aminos or the substitute instead and it will still taste hoisin delicious.

1 teaspoon of grated garlic (about 1 large clove) (F, FOS, GOS, LOX and LS) will replace the asafoetida powder.

*   *   *   *   *

HOMEMADE CHINESE FIVE-SPICE POWDER

Ingredients
Mix together and store in an airtight jar:
1 teaspoon ground cinnamon (F, HOX and VHS)
1 teaspoon ground cloves (HS)
1 teaspoon fennel seed, toasted and ground (FOS, LOX and M-HS)
1 teaspoon ground star anise (VHS)
1 teaspoon Szechuan peppercorns, toasted and ground (No information on the Szechuan peppercorns)

HOMEMADE FIVE-SPICE POWDER

Ingredients for about ¼ cup of spice powder
3 tablespoons cinnamon (F, HOX and VHS)
6 star anise or 2 teaspoons anise seeds (VHS)
1½ teaspoons fennel seeds (see Notes)
1½ teaspoons Szechuan peppercorns or 1½ teaspoons whole black peppercorns (HOX and VHS) (No information on the Szechuan peppercorns)
¾ teaspoon ground cloves (HS)

Directions
Combine all ingredients in blender or coffee grinder and blend until finely ground.
Stored in airtight container, it will keep up to 2 months.

Note
You could "roast" the whole spices a bit for a more intense flavor in a dry frying pan. Watch closely to prevent spices from burning.

Fennel seeds are Fructose Friendly but the fennel bulb isn't. (One site states seeds are M-HS but fennel bulb is LS)

*   *   *   *   *

HOMEMADE CURRY POWDERS

HOMEMADE SIMPLE CURRY POWDER

In a screw top jar combine and shake to mix well
¼ cup coriander powder (MOX and HS)
1¼ tablespoons turmeric (VHOX and VHS)
2 teaspoon cumin powder (VHS)
1 teaspoon mustard powder (F, GOS, VLOX and VHS)
1 teaspoon black pepper (HOX and VHS)
1 teaspoon chilli powder (F and HS) (homemade recipe in this section) or cayenne pepper (LOX and VHS)
1 tablespoon roasted paprika (VHS). Use in your favourite recipes.

*   *   *   *   *

HOMEMADE CURRY POWDER

Ingredients
2 tablespoons whole cumin seeds, toasted (VHS)
2 tablespoons whole cardamom seeds, toasted (LOX)
2 tablespoons whole coriander seeds, toasted (MOX and HS)
¼ cup ground turmeric (VHOX, VHS)
1 tablespoon dry mustard (F, GOS, VLOX and VHS)

Directions
Grind the cumin seeds, cardamon seeds and coriander seeds to a powder. Add the turmeric and dry mustard and mix well.

Store in an airtight container.

HOMEMADE YELLOW MUSTARD

Ingredients for about 1 cup
1 cup cold water
¾ cup yellow dry mustard (VLOX and VHS)
¾ teaspoon coarse sea salt or kosher salt (an edible salt with a much larger grain size to common table salt so use only half the amount of common salt if substituting)
½ teaspoon ground turmeric (F, VHOX and VHS)
A pinch of asafoetida powder (may contain Gluten. This is a strong spice so don't use more than the specified amount) or 1 teaspoon garlic purée, (F, FOS, GOS, LOX and LS)
⅛ teaspoon paprika (F and VHS)
½ cup white distilled vinegar (L-MOX and VHS)

Directions
Place the water, dry mustard, salt, turmeric, garlic, and paprika in a small non-reactive saucepan and whisk until smooth. Cook the mixture over medium-low to low heat, stirring often, until it bubbles down to a thick paste, 30 - 45 minutes (Note: You're definitely going to want to do this in a well-ventilated kitchen).

Whisk the vinegar into the mustard mixture and continue to cook until it's thickened to the desired consistency - you know, the usual prepared mustard consistency, which ought to take anywhere from 7 - 15 minutes.

Let the mustard cool to room temperature. Transfer the mustard to an airtight container, cover, and refrigerate for up to 3 months. The mustard will be quite pungent the first few days or even weeks, but will mellow with time.

*   *   *   *   *

HOMEMADE CHILI POWDER

Ingredients
2 tablespoons paprika (F and VHS)
2 teaspoons oregano (F, HOX and VHS)
1½ teaspoons cumin (VHS)
1½ teaspoons garlic powder (F, FOS, GOS, LOX and LS)
¾ teaspoon onion powder (HF, HFOS, PO (mannitol), LOX and LS)
½ teaspoon cayenne pepper (LOX and VHS) (omit or increase to taste)

Directions
Place all ingredients in a bowl.

Blend thoroughly.

Store in an airtight container in the refrigerator.

Notes
Paprika is a pepper and should be refrigerated for maximum shelf life and potency.

ONION AND GARLIC FREE MILD THAI SWEET CHILI SAUCE

Ingredients for 2 cups
5 red chili/peppers (completely and utterly de-veined and de-seeded) (F, PO (mannitol), HOX and HS) (see notes)
A pinch of asafoetida powder (may contain Gluten and is a strong spice so only use specified amount)
1 cup dextrose powder (may contain Gluten) or sugar or sweetener to your liking
1 cup rice wine vinegar
¾ cup water
½ teaspoon salt
2 tablespoons cornstarch (MOX) for thickening (optional)
2 tablespoons hot water for thickening (optional)

Directions
Slice peppers in half and completely remove all the seeds and veins.

In the bowl of a food processor or blender combine chili/peppers, asafoetida powder, dextrose powder, vinegar, water and salt. Blend until only very small flecks of the peppers remain.

Transfer to a saucepan and simmer over medium heat until sugar is completely dissolved, 4 - 5 minutes. (Make sure you stir the sauce frequently as it cooks - it's prone to bubble over).

Keep simmering the sauce down until it reduces by about half which takes 15 - 20 minutes and will be a watery style sauce.

If you would like a thicker style of sauce, just whisk together the hot water and cornstarch and add it to the sauce. Simmer for a couple minutes longer, until the sauce is thickened to your liking.

Notes
If you would like to keep some heat in this sauce, leave the veins and some seeds in the chili/peppers.

*　　*　　*　　*　　*

HOMEMADE ALMOND BUTTER

Ingredients for about 1.5 cups
3 cups almonds (preferably dry-roasted, unsalted) (FOS, PO (xylitol), VHOX and VHS)

Directions
Pour almonds into food processor. Pulse/process until the nuts go from coarsely chopped, to crumbly, to finely ground. Stop and scrape down the sides as needed.

Process again until the almonds resemble a thick and relatively smooth almond butter.

Notes
Add 1 - 2 tablespoons of a neutral tasting oil during the blending process to make the almond butter extra creamy.

You could stop processing when it reaches the finely ground Almond meal stage and use the meal for baking.

SWEET AND SPICY THAI DIPPING SAUCE

Ingredients makes about 1 cup

¼ cup or ¼ onion finely minced (HF HFOS, PO (mannitol) LOX and LS) or use the green parts only of spring onions. (White part has M-HF, FOS, PO (mannitol) MOX and LS)
⅛ cup finely chopped fresh red pepper (HF, PO (sorbitol), VLOX and VHS)
1¼ cup white vinegar (L-MOX and VHS)
1¼ cup pineapple juice (F, PO (mannitol), VLOX and MS)
¼ cup water
¾ cups dextrose powder (may contain Gluten) or white sugar or sweetener to your liking
2 teaspoons red pepper flakes (to taste) (HF, PO (sorbitol), VLOX and VHS)

Directions

Combine all of the ingredients, (except the red pepper flakes) in a small saucepan over medium-high heat. Bring the mixture to a boil and then reduce to a simmer.

Allow the sauce to simmer until reduced by half, 20 minutes.

Pour the sauce into a bowl through a small sieve to remove the onion and pepper. (If you want the sauce to have some spice, return the strained sauce to the pan over medium heat and add red pepper flakes to taste and heat for 1 minute more).

Chill the sauce in a glass jar the refrigerator until ready to use.

OR

You can mince/chop the onion and red pepper by hand, or you can also pulse the onion and red pepper in a blender or food processor until they are nearly a paste.

Simply combine the onion/red pepper paste with the other ingredients and cook them down and there will be no need to strain the sauce at the end. Store in a glass jar the refrigerator for several weeks.

JEWISH

The following recipes were kindly donated to me by the "Anonymous" Jewish ladies.

Sources: Tari's Batmitzvah Cookbook 2016 – recipes from Brisbane relatives/family & others, "Curry not Gefilte Fish" Melbourne's Bene Israel and Baghdadi Jewish Cookbook 2014 Published by NCJWA Victoria, Cook in Israel 2013 Orly Ziv.

The vegetables and fruit in these recipes will only make them Fructose Friendly. I have tried to source out whether they have Fructose, Fructans, Polyols or Galactans in them and have indicated this beside the ingredient plus a few ingredients have alternatives beside them or in the notes at the end of each recipe. I am hoping that this will help you as much as it has helped me. Salicylates and Oxalates may also be issues for some people so I have added them as well. They will all be noted in the code form below or mentioned in the notes. Please read these.

Low – L, Medium – M, High – H, Very High – VH, Salicylates – S, Oxalates – OX
Fructose – F, Fructans – FOS, Polyols – PO, Galactans – GOS

I have placed some homemade recipes for substituting the ingredients after the main recipes. These recipes will be for Gluten Free, Fructose Friendly, Lactose Free or Friendly, Diabetic Friendly and IBS Friendly depending on your sensitivity so that you can make your own if you want to. Please remember that Fructans, Polyols and Galactans can also come with Fructose.

Substituting ingredients will alter the original taste; however, it is a way to try different recipes from other countries and you can adjust the taste to your liking. Make these recipes your own and use your ingredients if you want to as you know what's best for you.

Fish in Tomato Sauce Jewish-Turkish Style	117
Green Shakshuka	118
Israeli Salad with Pomegranate and Avocado	119
Hummus	120
Potato Kugel	121
Firm Kneidlach	121
Baked Brisket With Vegetables	122
Kneidlach Recipe 1	122
Kneidlach Recipe 2	123
Chermoula	124
Chicken Soup	125
Challah	126
Honey Cake	127
Chocolate Cake	128
Homemade Recipes For The Above Recipes	
How To Make Tomato Paste The Quick And Easy Way	129
Homemade Ketchup	130
Quick And Easy Tahini/Sesame Paste	130
Homemade Preserved Lemons or Limes	131
Grain-Free Matzo Crackers	132
Homemade Normal Matzoh Recipe 1	133
Homemade Normal Matzah Recipe 2	134
Grain-Free Matzo	135

FISH IN TOMATO SAUCE JEWISH-TURKISH STYLE

This dish reminds me of my childhood flavors as my mother included tomato sauce in many dishes. It tastes so good. Be sure to have plenty of bread on hand to sop up any leftover sauce.

Ingredients
Olive oil (LOX and HS) or one to your liking (see notes)
1 onion chopped (F, FOS, PO (mannitol) LOX and LS) or 3 green parts only of spring onions chopped (white part has M-HF, FOS, PO (mannitol) MOX and LS) (see notes)
1 - 2 tablespoons tomato paste (HF, FOS, PO (mannitol), HOX and VHS) (homemade recipe after main recipes)
1 - 2 cloves garlic, sliced (F, FOS, GOS LOX and LS) (see notes)
3 - 4 tomatoes, diced (HF, FOS, PO (mannitol), MOX and MS)
Chopped cilantro (VLOX) or parsley (F, PO (mannitol), LOX and LS)
1 hot pepper, sliced (optional) (F, PO (mannitol), HOX and HS)
1 teaspoon dextrose powder (may contain Gluten) or sugar (optional)
Salt and pepper (black - HOX and VHS, white - VLOX and VHS)
5 fish fillets (grouper, mullet, or tilapia all work well)

Directions
Preheat oven 190°C / 375°F.

Fry the chopped onion in olive oil until soft.

Add the tomato paste, garlic, tomatoes, cilantro or parsley, hot pepper, sugar (if using), salt and pepper and a bit of water. Cook until tomatoes soften. Keep warm.

Place the fish in a large baking pan and pour the sauce over.

Bake for about 10 minutes, until the fish is cooked through and the sauce dense.

Garnish with additional fresh cilantro or parsley before serving.

Variation
Fry the fish in a non-stick pan for 2 minutes each side, until cooked through. Transfer the fish to plates and spoon the sauce over.

Notes
Olive oil is LOX and VHS where Canola Oil (F, PO and LOX), Safflower Oil, Soy Oil (VLOX), Sunflower Oil are reported to be negligible in Salicylates.

A good pinch of asafoetida powder can replace the onion and garlic but only use a pinch because this is a strong spice.

GREEN SHAKSHUKA

This version of Shakshuka can only be found in Israeli cafes and restaurants for those who want a change of pace from regular Shakshuka. The color is great, as it is the taste – especially with fresh bread on the side.

Ingredients
3 - 4 tablespoons of olive oil (LOX and HS) or one to your liking (see notes)
1 onion diced (HF, HFOS, PO (mannitol) LOX and LS) or 3 spring onions (green parts only) (white part has M-HF, FOS, PO (mannitol) MOX and LS) OR ⅛ teaspoon of asafoetida powder for both onion and garlic. This is a strong spice so don't use more)
3 - 4 cloves garlic, minced (F, FOS, GOS, LOX and LS) (see above and notes)
1 - 2 spring onions sliced green parts only (optional) (white part has M-HF, FOS, PO (mannitol) MOX and LS)
1 bunch Swiss chard roughly chopped (leaves and stalks separated) (see notes)
1 bunch spinach leaves roughly chopped (see notes)
2 tablespoons of white wine (varies in OX and S) (substitute white wine vinegar (L-MOX and VHS), rice wine vinegar or chicken stock (minus garlic and onions)
½ cup Lactose Free heavy cream or one to your liking
Salt and pepper (black - HOX and VHS, white - VLOX and VHS) to taste
Nutmeg to taste (VLOX and VHS)
4 - 6 eggs
Feta cheese crumbled - optional (Low Lactose and VLOX)

Directions
Heat oil in a large skillet/frypan and sauté the onion, garlic, spring onions and Swiss chard stalks until the onions are golden brown.

Add the spinach and Swiss chard leaves. Cook for a few minutes, stirring, until the leaves lose half their volume.

Stir in the wine and cream and season with salt and pepper and a pinch of nutmeg.

Bring to a boil and lower the heat. Cook for 20 minutes on low heat.

Break an egg into a small dish and gently slide into the pan. Repeat with remaining eggs, evenly spacing them within the pan.

Cover and cook until the egg whites are set but the yolks are still soft (or to your preference).

Remove the lid, sprinkle with cheese, if using and serve with plenty of fresh bread.

Notes
A few substitute suggestions for garlic; Fennel (dried Fennel has F, FOS, PO (mannitol) and LS), Bell peppers (HF, FOS, PO (sorbitol), GOS, Red are VLOX and HS, Green are MOX and VHS), Celeriac (LF, PO and HOX).

Peppercorns: white, pink (HOX and VHS), or Szechuan pepper (no info available) can add different flavors to your cooking.

Cumin's (VHS) distinctive taste may work well in some recipes, especially where garlic is used raw.

Canola Oil (F, PO and LOX), Safflower Oil, Soy Oil (VLOX), Sunflower Oil are reported to be negligible in Salicylates.

Swiss chard is also known as Spinach and silverbeet. Fresh spinach has F, FOS, PO (sorbitol), VHOX and HS and frozen spinach has F, FOS, PO (sorbitol), VHOX and MS. Swiss chard has F, FOS, PO (sorbitol) and VHOX (no info for Salicylates available), Silverbeet has F, FOS, GOS, HOX and HS.

*   *   *   *   *

ISRAELI SALAD WITH POMEGRANATE AND AVOCADO

The basic Israeli salad, which is simply chopped tomatoes and cucumbers, is served with every meal at every time of the day in Israel. This is my dressed up version with radish, avocado, mint and pomegranate seeds. One past student wrote to tell me, "I have served your salad with the pomegranate seeds with rave reviews. It is a flavor and texture most are not familiar with and was liked by all".

Ingredients
1 - 2 tomatoes cut into cubes (HF, FOS, PO (mannitol), MOX and MS)
1 - 2 cucumbers cut in cubes (see notes)
1 - 2 radishes cut into strips (HF, FOS, PO and VHS)
1 avocado cut in cubes (F, FOS, PO (sorbitol), VLOX and HS)
½ cup roughly chopped mint (Unknown for F, FOS and PO but VHS)
Pomegranate seeds - optional (see notes)
Chopped preserved lemon - optional (homemade recipes after main recipes)
Lemon juice (F, PO (sorbitol), LOX and L-HS)
Olive oil (LOX and HS) or one to your liking
Salt
Sumac (no information of any type is available) (Substitute lemon zest and salt to your taste)

Directions
Put the tomatoes, cucumbers, radishes, avocado, mint, pomegranate seeds and preserved lemon in a bowl and toss to combine.

Whisk together lemon juice, olive oil, salt and sumac to taste and toss with the salad. Garnish with additional pomegranate seeds and serve.

Notes
It is stated that Lebanese cucumber are HF where green/continental cucumber has F, FOS, PO (sorbitol), VLOX and HS.

It is stated that Pomegranates contain Fructans and the skin also contains Polyols; however it is not stated whether it is the seeds or skins that contain the Fructans. Pomegranates also are moderate in Salicylates.

HUMMUS

This recipe is the superstar of any culinary tour in Israel. Although you can use canned chickpeas, if you want to make authentic hummus you must start with dry chickpeas. It takes a little bit of forethought but not that much more work and it's worth it.

Ingredients
2 cups dried chickpeas (FOS, GOS and MOX)
1 medium onion, peeled and cut in quarters (F, FOS, PO (mannitol) LOX and LS) or 3 spring onions (green parts only) diced (white part has M-HF, FOS, PO (mannitol) MOX and LS) (see notes)
5 cloves garlic (F, FOS, GOS, LOX and LS) (see notes)
1 bunch of fresh parsley (optional) (F, PO (mannitol) LOX and LS)
1 teaspoon cumin (optional) (VHS)
4 - 5 tablespoon tahini (VHOX and HS)
Juice of 1 lemon (F, PO (sorbitol), LOX and L-HS)
Salt
Olive oil (LOX and HS) or one to your liking (see notes)
Paprika (F and VHS)
Coarsely chopped parsley leaves (F, PO (mannitol) LOX and LS)

Directions
Put the chickpeas in a large bowl, cover with water and soak overnight. Change the soaking water at least once. (Try putting 1 tablespoon of bicarb soda in the soaking water and change often as this may lessen the wind/gas issue and soak for a longer period. It also helps lower oxalates).

Drain and rinse the chickpeas, put in a large pot and cover with plenty of cold water. Add the onion and garlic and bring to the boil.

Simmer till the chickpeas are tender, 2 - 3 hours. (Alternatively, cook in a pressure cooker for at least 1½ hours after it starts to boil). Add the parsley and cumin to the cooking water if you like.

Drain the chickpeas and remove the herbs, reserving some of the cooking liquid.

Set aside ¼ cup of the chickpeas. Grind the remaining chickpeas along with the cooked onion and garlic in a food processor or hand blender.

Gradually add tahini, lemon juice and salt until you have a smooth, uniform paste. Slowly pour in reserved chickpea liquid until the desired consistency is reached.

Taste and adjust seasoning.

Pour into a bowl and serve topped with a drizzle of olive oil, the reserved chickpeas, paprika and coarsely chopped parsley leaves.

Variation
Make green hummus by adding ½ bunch fresh parsley (F, PO (mannitol) LOX and LS) and a ½ bunch fresh cilantro (VLOX).

Notes
Olive oil is (LOX and HS) where Canola Oil (F, PO and LOX), Safflower Oil, Soy Oil (VLOX), Sunflower Oil are reported to be negligible in Salicylates.

About ⅛ teaspoon of asafoetida powder can be used instead of the garlic and onion. This is a strong spice so don't use more than the specified amount.

*   *   *   *   *

POTATO KUGEL (Chana Giberstein)

Ingredients
5 large potatoes, grated and squeezed of excess moisture (see notes)
1 onion grated (HF, HFOS, PO (mannitol) LOX and LS) or 3 finely sliced spring onion - green parts only (white part has M-HF, FOS, PO (mannitol) MOX and LS)
3 eggs
⅓ cup matzo meal or breadcrumbs of your liking (4 homemade recipes after main recipes)
½ cup melted fat or oil of your choice
1 teaspoon salt
¼ teaspoon pepper (black - HOX and VHS, white - VLOX and VHS)

Directions
Combine all ingredients and mix well.

Place into a well-greased pie or pudding dish and bake at 200°C / 390°F for about 1 hour or until crusty.

Notes
To make a lighter textured Kugel, substitute one large cooked mashed potato for a raw one.

Fructose in potatoes can range anything between 582 mg – 989 mg depending on the size, type and skin colour. They also have FOS, PO and GOS. They also have VHOX and MS again depending on the type of potatoes, colour of skin and how they are cooked.

*   *   *   *   *

FIRM KNEIDLACH (Yafa Goldschmidt)

Ingredients to make 6 large or 12 small balls
2 eggs
½ cup Gluten Free matzo meal or matzo meal or saltine crackers - salted or unsalted or Gluten Free crackers (4 homemade recipes after main recipes)
½ teaspoon salt
1 - 2 tablespoons chicken fat or oil to your liking

Directions
Beat eggs slightly and add matzo meal, salt and oil, stirring constantly until a soft dough is formed. Allow mixture to stand for 15 minutes.

Rub the palms of hands with oil, form mixture into balls and drop into rapidly boiling water.

Cook covered for 20 - 30 minutes.

Drain and place in soup.

BAKED BRISKET WITH VEGETABLES (Yafa Goldschmidt)

Ingredients
1½ - 2kg brisket
1 large onion, sliced (F, FOS, PO (mannitol), LOX and LS) or 3 spring onions (green parts only) cut in half (white part has M-HF, FOS, PO (mannitol) MOX and LS)
1 large carrot, sliced (HF, FOS (raffinose), PO (sorbitol), GOS, VHOX and HS)
250g mushrooms, quartered (F, FOS (raffinose), PO (mannitol and xylitol), GOS, VLOX and MS) (**see notes**)
1½ cups sweet red wine (varies in OX and S) or beef stock (minus onion and garlic)
2 tablespoons tomato sauce (HF, PO (aspartame), HOX and VHS) (homemade recipe after main recipes)
1 - 2 cups boiling water

Directions
Place brisket in a large covered pan. Arrange onion, carrot, and mushrooms around meat.

Pour wine, tomato sauce and enough water to cover the vegetables (about 1 cup).

Cover tightly and place in a preheated 175°C / 390°F oven for 3 - 4 hours or until meat is tender.

Cut into thin slices across the grain to serve.

Notes
Shiitake and King Brown mushroom could be used in the beginning as they will take the long cooking time. You could add Enoki and Oyster mushrooms towards the end of the cooking as these take to short cooking times. All these mushrooms have little to no Fructans and Polyol to cause any issues and there isn't any listing for Oxalates and Salicylates.

* * * * *

KNEIDLACH RECIPE 1

Ingredients
4 eggs
Salt
Pepper (black - HOX and VHS, white - VLOX and VHS) to taste
¾ cup water
¼ cup oil to your liking
1 tablespoon soda water (no info available for anything)
1 cup Gluten Free or normal matza meal (4 homemade recipes after main recipes)

Directions
Mix and leave in the fridge for ½ hour.

Fill pot to ¾ with water and bring to the boil.

Roll kneidlach into balls and drop them into the water.

Boil them for about 8 minutes until they are all floating at the top of the pot.

KNEIDLACH RECIPE 2 (Michelle Kronberg)

WHAT YOU NEED
Bowl, Little cup, Hand beater, Little frypan, Wooden spoon, Cutting board, Sharp knife
Slotted spoon, Large pot

Ingredients:
12 eggs
2 cups Gluten Free or normal fine matzah meal (4 homemade recipes after main recipes)
2 cups Gluten Free or normal coarse matzah meal (4 homemade recipes after main recipes)
4 tablespoons margarine (melted) or one to your liking or your choice of oil can be used as the margarine is melted
2 teaspoons salt
2 cups warm - hot water
2 onions + a little oil to fry it in (HF, HFOS, PO (mannitol) LOX and LS) or 6 shallots (green parts only) cut very small (white part has M-HF, FOS, PO (mannitol) MOX and LS)

Directions
Peel the onion. Chop it in half and then finely chop as small as you can. Fry this in the frypan with a little oil until brown. Let it cool on a plate.

Now crack each egg into the little cup and if ok add it to the bowl. Add the salt, margarine and water in with the eggs and beat them together. Add the Matzah meal and mix thoroughly. Mix in the fried onions also. Put the bowl in the fridge for about 30min - 1 hour for the mixture to get firm.

Boil some diluted stock on the stove. When boiling take the bowl of mixture out of the fridge and roll balls of the mixture in the palms of your hands (it is easier if you wet your hands a bit) and drop them into the pot of boiling diluted stock. If you are doing it in a large pot you should be able to cook 15 - 20 at a time.

Cook for about 15 minutes and then use the slotted spoon to take each out and place on a plate or in a container. You will need to do about 3 rounds to cook them all.

Keep them in the fridge if you will eat them in the next few days or else they freeze very well.

CHERMOULA (Peta Briner)

My best recipes are ones that I have pinched from others. I channel my non-existent Sephardi/Mizrachi heritage via Myriam and love cooking that style of food. So here's a recipe for Chermoula which works equally well as a marinade for chicken or salmon and even as a dressing for a couscous and roast vegetable salad. It's especially good I think because the chicken or salmon can be cooked in advance and don't dry out in the oven when warming them for Shabbat or Yom Tov. And can you believe it, everyone to my slightly fussy family eats it – hooray!

Ingredients
This is enough for 1kg of salmon or chicken.
In a small bowl mix:
1½ teaspoons ground cumin (VHS)
½ teaspoon ground coriander (MOX and HS)
1 tablespoon of sweet paprika (F and VHS)
2 teaspoons of kosher salt (an edible salt with a much larger grain size to common table salt so use only half the amount of common salt if substituting)
¼ teaspoon cayenne pepper (LOX and VHS)
Dash white pepper (VLOX and VHS)

Directions
Place in a processor:
4 cloves minced garlic (F, FOS, GOS, LOX and LS) (try substituting with ⅛ teaspoon asafoetida powder (may contain Gluten) (see notes) (This is a strong spice so don't use more than the specified amount)
½ cup packed continental flat leaf parsley (LOX and LS) (unknown for F, FOS, PO, and GOS)
½ cup packed fresh coriander (MOX and HS)
Zest of 1 lemon (F, PO (sorbitol) and HOX)
Zest of 1 lime (F, PO and HOX)
Juice of 1 lemon (F, PO (sorbitol), LOX and L-HS)
Juice of 1 lime (F, PO and LOX)
½ cup olive oil (LOX and HS) or one to your liking

Directions
Add spices to the food processor with the chopping blade.

While the motor is running, slowly add the oil.

Marinate with the mixture for at least 2 hours in the fridge. You could keep a small amount of the marinade covered in the fridge and use it as a garnish. We haven't, but could be good.

Chicken and salmon are best barbequed, but can also be baked in the oven. Make sure the salmon is only just cooked - about 20 minutes in a moderate oven. (It will continue to cook in the pan and when re-heated).

CHICKEN SOUP (Jennifer Paneth)

This is my Nanna's famous chicken soup recipe that she learnt from her mother. There is nothing like the smell of chicken soup cooking on the stove! This chicken soup has the "magic power" to make you feel better when you are feeling unwell and to bring the family together on a Friday night to celebrate Shabbat together.

Ingredients and Directions
Combine in a large pot (12L)
1 large piece top rib cut into two pieces.

Cut the tops (ie the leaves) of half a large celery and add to the pot (should be friendly in all F, FOS, PO, GOS and unknown if leaves have VHOX like the stalk does) (see notes).

Cut the top half of a leek - the leaf bits (don't use the bottom half in the soup. Should be friendly in all F, FOS, PO, GOS and unknown if leaves have MOX and LS like the stalk does) (see notes).

Chop one onion into four cubes and add to the pot (HF, HFOS, PO (mannitol) LOX and LS) or 3 spring onions (green parts only) diced (white part has M-HF, FOS, PO (mannitol) MOX and LS) (see notes).

Peel one turnip, cut it in half and add it to the pot (MF, LFOS, PO (sorbitol), MOX and LS).

Add half a celeriac (do not chop it) (F, PO and HOX). Peel and cut 3 parsnips lengthways into 3 parts and add to the pot (F, LFOS, PO and HS).

Fill the pot ¾ with water and cover with the lid. Cook for one hour.

After one hour add:
6 washed chicken frames. (Nanna washes them really well and cuts off all the excess fat from them)
9 wings
4 peeled whole carrots (HF, FOS (raffinose), PO (sorbitol), GOS, VHOX and HS)
½ peeled sweet potato (HF, FOS, PO (mannitol), VHOX and HS)
2 tablespoons salt (use less if you think this amount is too high for you)
½ bunch parsley (F, PO (mannitol), LOX and LS) or coriander (HOX and HS)
½ bunch dill (F, L-MOX and VHS) can substitute tarragon (VLOX and VHS)
3 whole cloves garlic (F, FOS, GOS, LOX and LS) (see notes)
1 tablespoon sugar or dextrose powder (may contain Gluten)
Chicken stock to taste at end (minus onion and garlic)

Cook for another half an hour – an hour.

Remove chicken and vegetables and drain soup into another pot.

Notes
A pinch or ⅛ teaspoon asafoetida powder (may contain Gluten) can be used instead of the garlic and onions if you can't tolerate them. This is a strong spice so don't use more than the specified amount.
Celery-Raw HF, FOS, PO (mannitol), VHOX and Neg S (it is stated that the leaves should be safe to use for their flavour).
Leek F, FOS, PO (mannitol), GOS, MOX and LS (it is stated that the leaves should be safe to use for their flavour).

CHALLAH (Nana Goldman via Gary Goldman)

This recipe belongs to your great grandmother Broncha Goldman (Tarl's Papa's mother) – it is a family treasure.
During the school holidays the grandchildren got to come to Nana's house to bake Challah. We learnt to plait six strands and got to eat the Challah hot out of the oven!

Ingredients

2lb (about 300g) Gluten Free bakers flour (plain will suffice) or one to your liking (options on pages 13 & 14) (wheat flour has FOS and VHOX) (you may need to adjust the amount of liquid)
5 large tablespoons dextrose powder (may contain Gluten) or sugar
1 desert spoon salt (lessen this if you feel that it is too much for your liking)
1¾ cups water
3 sachets (21g) dried yeast (bakers - MOX and LS, non-bakers - MOX and VHS)
2 eggs beaten
2 tablespoons oil of your choosing
Additional egg to glaze challot before baking
Poppy (L-Neg S) sesame (FOS, VHOX and HS) or other seed to decorate

Directions

Place the flour into a bowl and make a well in the centre of the bowl.

Place the balance of the dry ingredients into the well followed by wet ingredients.

Combine ingredients in well and then mix in flour until dough begins to form. Turn out onto a floured bench.

Knead vigorously for 5 - 10 minutes until there is a smooth elastic dough. It may be necessary to add some additional flour.

Place the dough back into the bowl and cover with cling wrap. Leave dough to rise for 40 - 60 minutes in a warm place until the dough doubles in size.

Remove the dough from the bowl and knead briefly to knock the dough back to original size. The dough will make 2 large or 3 medium sized challot. Divide the dough into pieces as required and make each into a ball.

Divide each ball into pieces which should be rolled into strands on a floured bench. The surface of the stands should be dry or the strands will lose their form and their plaited effect during the further rise.

The strands should be joined as the top and plaited into a loaf. The width of the challah should be one third to one quarter of the length. The more strands used for the plait, the higher the loaf and the better shape of the challah.

Using your hands as a knife cut off one portion at one end to perform the mitzvah of separating challah and say the appropriate blessing. This should set aside and cooked with challah, but not eaten.

Place the loaves on a flat tray lined with baking paper and leave to rise again for another 40 - 50 minutes.

Cover with egg wash and sprinkle with seeds.

Cook in a preheated oven at 180°C / 350°F for 35 - 40 minutes until the loaves are golden brown. When cooked, the loaves should have a hollow sound if knocked gently.

Leave the loaves to cool on a cooling rack.

*   *   *   *   *

HONEY CAKE (Aunty Carolyn (Goldsmith)

This honey cake is one of my favourite cakes and a favourite with my friends. It is a recipe that won a Honey Cake competition is an Israel newspaper. I am not sure the original chef was but I claim it now.

Ingredients
4 eggs
1 cup bland oil of your choice
1 cup brown sugar (Fructose Friendly) or dextrose powder (Fructose Free and may contain Gluten)
1 cup honey (F, FOS, VLOX and VHS) or rice malt syrup (Fructose Free)
1 cup double strength black coffee (beans have F, FOS, PO (mannitol), GOS, VLOX and varies in S. Instant has F, FOS, PO (mannitol), GOS, VLOX and varies in S)
2½ cups Gluten Free self-raising flour or one to your liking (options on pages 13 & 14) (may need to adjust liquid)
1 teaspoon all spice (VHS)
1 teaspoon cinnamon (F, HOX and VHS)

Directions
Beat eggs, oil and sugar until the sugar has dissolved. Add honey/rice malt syrup and coffee.

Then gently mix into the flour until mixture is smooth.

Bake in a large round fluted tin at 170°C / 340°F for 1 hour.

Leave to cool in pan before turning out. Sprinkle with icing sugar or drizzle with icing.

CHOCOLATE CAKE (Grandma Sharryn Goldman)

This is a great Chocolate Cake recipe because it rarely falls and if you use an unlined chiffon tin and turn it upside down after coming out of the oven it is a very high cake. However I normally bake it in a large springform tin that I line with baking paper to make sure it does not stick to the sides. It is also parave so it suits many situations.

Ingredients
6 eggs separated
¾ cup hot water from the tap (may need to adjust if using Gluten Free flour)
2 cups Gluten Free flour or one to your choosing (see notes)
½ cup cocoa, sifted (FOS, GOS, VHOX and MS)
2 cups of dextrose powder (may contain Gluten) or caster sugar
¾ cup canola oil (F, PO and LOX)
2 teaspoonsful vanilla essence (VLOX and VHS)

Directions
Beat egg whites until very stiff and put aside in a bowl.

Mix yolks and sugar til creamy and sugar dissolves. Add sifted cocoa, hot water, oil, sifted flour, and vanilla essence in that order and beat till all mixed.

Remove from mixer and fold in egg whites using a wooden spoon until they are incorporated and the mixture is not streaky. Pour into a lined baking tin. Bake at 170°C / 340°F for 60 - 75 minutes.

Test with a skewer at 60 minutes as that is usually enough.

HOMEMADE RECIPES FOR THE ABOVE RECIPES
HOW TO MAKE TOMATO PASTE THE QUICK AND EASY WAY

This recipe makes about 5 heaped tablespoons.

Soak 2 kilos (4½ lbs) of tomatoes (HF, FOS, PO (mannitol), MOX and MS) in boiling water for five minutes or until the skins can be easily peeled off. Drain and carefully remove the tomato skin. The tomatoes may be hot to handle.

Carefully cut tomatoes in half or quarters longways and de-seed completely. Place tomato pieces in to processor and process to a very liquidy paste.

If you have a slow cooker, then place this liquid paste in it and leave it to reduce and thicken up. Stir occasionally. I left mine on all day and got a beautiful thick tomato paste to use in my recipes.

If you don't have a slow cooker you can cook the paste in a 350°F / 180°C preheated oven on shallow trays until it is reduced to a paste. Check the tomatoes every half hour, stirring the paste and switching the position of the trays so that they reduce evenly. Over time, the paste will start to reduce to the point where you can make one tray.

The paste is done when shiny and brick-colored, and it has reduced by more than half. There shouldn't be any remaining water or moisture separating from the paste at this point. This will take 3 - 4 hours, though exact baking/cooking times will depend on the juiciness of your tomatoes and your oven.

After the paste was cold; I put it in a container and kept it in the refrigerator or freezer.

Making small batches when you need it can be useful; however, if you use a lot of tomato paste then just double or triple the amount of tomatoes used. I made a very small batch using the same prep method but I cooked them down in my non-stick frypan over low heat and I continually stirred the mixture. I did not add anything to the paste because I can do that when I use it in a recipe.

HOMEMADE KETCHUP

Ingredients
One 6oz can of tomato paste (HF, FOS, PO (mannitol), HOX and VHS) or homemade recipe in this section
½ cup white vinegar (L-MOX and VHS)
½ cup + 2 tablespoons dextrose powder (may contain Gluten) or sugar
1 teaspoon salt
⅛ teaspoon ground celery (celery has FOS, PO (mannitol) and VHOX. No info at all for celery seeds or powder) (see notes)
Pinch of ground cloves (F, VHOX and HS)

Directions
Put all ingredients into a saucepan and whisk together until smooth.

Heat on medium heat until just boiling; immediately reduce heat and simmer for 20 more minutes, stirring frequently.

Remove from heat and let cool on the counter or stove. Store in a covered container in the fridge.

Notes
Celery oil and celery seeds have been noted by several sources as unsafe during pregnancy.

*   *   *   *   *

QUICK AND EASY TAHINI/SESAME PASTE

Making tahini at home is easy and much less expensive than buying from the store especially if you look for sesame seeds in bulk bins or at International, Asian and Middle Eastern markets for the best deals.

While tahini can be made from unhulled, sprouted and hulled sesame seeds, preference is to use hulled (or natural) sesame seeds for tahini. Tahini can be kept in the refrigerator for a month.

Ingredients for about ½ cup of Tahini
1 cup (5oz or 140g) sesame seeds, your preference to hulled or unhulled (FOS, VHOX and HS)
3 - 4 tablespoons neutral flavored oil such as grape seed, rice bran, canola (F and LOX) or a light olive oil (LOX and HS)
Pinch of salt, optional

Directions
Toast Sesame Seeds (optional): Add sesame seeds to a wide, dry saucepan over medium-low heat and toast, stirring constantly until the seeds become fragrant and very lightly colored (not brown), 3 - 5 minutes. (Careful here, sesame seeds can burn quickly).

Transfer toasted seeds to a baking sheet or large plate and cool completely.

Make Tahini Paste: Add sesame seeds to the bowl of a food processor then process until a crumbly paste forms, about 1 minute. Add 3 tablespoons of the oil then process for 2 - 3 minutes more, stopping to scrape the bottom and sides of the food processor a couple times.

Check the tahini's consistency. It should be smooth, not gritty and should be pourable. You may need to process for another minute or add the additional tablespoon of oil. Taste the tahini for seasoning then add salt to taste. Process for 5 - 10 seconds to mix it in.

How to Store Tahini: Store tahini covered in the refrigerator for one month. You may notice it separates over time, like a natural peanut butter would. If this happens, give the tahini a good stir before using.

* * * * *

HOMEMADE PRESERVED LEMONS OR LIMES

Ingredients
1 kg (2lb 4 oz) lemons or limes - if using limes, you may need a few extra if they aren't particularly juicy (see notes)
100 - 150g (3½ - 5½oz) salt

For each jar of preserved lemons (optional) (Moderate in Salicylates)
1 bay leaf (PO and HVS) or 1 cinnamon stick (F, HOX and HVS) and 2 cloves (F and HS)
1 all spice berry (VHS)
5 black peppercorns (HOX)

For each jar or preserved limes (optional) (Negligible for Salicylates)
1 red chilli (F, PO, HOX and HS)
½ teaspoon coriander seeds (MOX and HS)
5 black peppercorns (HOX)

Directions
First sterilise your jars, then leave to cool completely.

Cut the lemons or limes into quarters, or halves if very small. Place a tablespoon of salt into the bottom of each jar. Put a few layers of lemon or lime quarters into the jar, pressing down as you go to release the fruit's juices.

Slide your chosen spices down the side of each jar. Sprinkle over another layer of salt, then add another layer of lemon or lime quarters and repeat these layers until the jar is full. Remember to keep pushing down as you go. The fruit needs to be completely covered in salty juice - if your fruit hasn't released enough of its own juices, squeeze a few extra and pour in this juice to cover.

Leave 1 cm (½") of space between the top of the fruit and the lid of the jar - you don't want the salty fruit touching the lid or it will corrode the metal. Seal the jars and let them sit in a cool, dark place for 6 weeks.

You know your lemons or limes are preserved when the salt has completely dissolved into a gel-like liquid. Preserved lemons and limes will keep for years, but opened jars are best stored in the fridge (if the top layer of fruit looks discoloured, just discard it and the rest should be fine to use).

Notes
Zest of 1 lemon (F, PO (sorbitol) and HOX); Juice of 1 lemon (F, PO (sorbitol), LOX and L-HS)
Zest of 1 lime (F, PO and HOX); Juice of 1 lime (F, PO and LOX)

Before I was diagnosed with Fructose Malabsorption, I used to cook a lot of Jewish recipes as they were easy to adapt and were very tasty and filling. I have gathered a large stock pile of recipes. I have put in 4 different recipes for you to make homemade Matzah; however, these recipes may not be Kosher to eat during Passover. The following snippets have come from my files that I have had for almost six years. If you recognise them, please do not be offended that I have not acknowledged you for them.

"The downside to making matzo at home is that it's difficult to keep it kosher. Jewish law gives us only 18 minutes from the time the flour is first mixed with water to get the breads cooked. If you're speedy and work in small batches, you can just accomplish this at home. It also helps to have a few helpers to keep the process going smoothly!"

"Dough is considered to begin the leavening process 18 minutes from the time it gets wet; sooner if eggs, fruit juice, or milk is added to the dough. The entire process of making matzo takes only a few minutes in efficient modern matzo bakeries.

After baking, matzo may be ground into fine crumbs, known as matzo meal. Matzo meal can be used like flour during the week of Passover when flour can otherwise be used only to make matzo".

GLUTEN-FREE MATZO CRACKERS

Ingredients to serve 4
1 cup Kosher Gluten Free all-purpose flour or one to your liking (options pages 13 & 14)
½ cup almond flour (almonds have FOS, PO (xylitol), VHOX and VHS)
4 tablespoons extra virgin olive oil (LOX and HS) or one to your liking
3 tablespoons water (adjust liquid if using normal flour)
½ teaspoon sea salt or kosher salt (an edible salt with a much larger grain size to common table salt so use only half the amount of common salt if substituting)

Directions
Preheat oven to 450°F / 230°C.

Whisk together flour and almond flour then add in the liquid slowly while stirring with a fork or pastry cutter. If the dough is too dry, add additional water by the ½ teaspoonful in order to get dough wet enough to form a ball but not be sticky.

Form a ball with the dough and pat out onto a clean surface or pastry mat dusted with flour.

Pat with your fingers to flatten the dough and roll to the thickness of matzo, then prick with a fork. Sprinkle with additional coarse kosher salt, if desired.

Bake for 10 minutes on a parchment-lined baking sheet, or just until slightly browned.

HOMEMADE NORMAL MATZOH RECIPE 1

Ingredients

4½ cups sifted all-purpose flour, plus more for rolling or one to your liking
1 teaspoon kosher salt, plus more for sprinkling (an edible salt with a much larger grain size to common table salt so use only half the amount of common salt if substituting)
2 tablespoons mild olive oil (LOX and HS) or, if you're not keeping kosher for Passover, you can substitute canola oil (F, PO and LOX)
¾ cup plus up to ¼ cup more warm water

Directions

Preheat the oven to 500°F / 260°C. Ideally you would place a pizza stone on the bottom oven rack, but realistically a 10 x 15" (26 x 38cm) baking sheet will work just dandy.

In a large bowl, mix together all the ingredients, using ¾ cup water, until everything comes together to form a dough. If the dough seems dry, add a little more water, a few drops at a time.

If you do not need the matzoh to be kosher for Passover, let the dough rest for 10 - 15 minutes. If you do need the matzoh to be kosher for Passover, proceed immediately to the next step so that you can finish everything in 18 minutes.

Divide the dough into 8 pieces and then you can either, flatten a piece slightly and pass it repeatedly through a pasta maker, reducing the thickness each time until you reach the minimum setting or you can simply roll the dough as thinly as possible with a rolling pin on a lightly floured surface. Repeat with the remaining dough pieces.

Trim the rolled-out dough pieces into rectangles. (How many pieces of matzoh you get depends on how thinly you rolled the dough).

Use a fork to prick holes in the surface of the dough. If salted matzoh are desired, brush or spray the dough surface lightly with water and sprinkle with salt to taste.

Carefully place some of the rectangles onto the pizza stone or baking sheet. They should fit snugly but should not touch. Bake until the surface of the matzoh is golden brown and bubbly, 30 - 90 seconds.

Using tongs; carefully flip the matzoh pieces and continue to bake until the other side is golden browned and lightly blistered, 15 - 30 seconds. Keep careful and constant watch to keep the matzoh from burning; the exact baking time will vary from oven to oven and will get longer with subsequent batches.

You want to let the matzoh get a few dots of light brown but do not let the matzoh turn completely brown or it will taste burnt. Let it cool before serving.

HOMEMADE NORMAL MATZAH RECIPE 2

Ingredients for 8 servings
1 teaspoon all-purpose flour for dusting
1 cup all-purpose flour
⅓ cup water or more if needed
½ teaspoon kosher salt, or as needed (optional) (an edible salt with a much larger grain size to common table salt so use only half the amount of common salt if substituting)
1 teaspoon olive oil (LOX and HS), or as needed or oil to your liking if not for kosher (optional)

Directions
Move an oven rack near the top of oven and preheat oven to 475°F / 245°C. Preheat a heavy baking sheet in the oven.

Dust a clean work surface and a rolling pin with 1 teaspoon flour, or as needed.

Place 1 cup of flour into a mixing bowl; set a timer for about 16 minutes (18 minutes maximum). Start the timer; pour the water, about 1 tablespoon at a time, into the flour.

Stir the water and flour together with a fork until the dough forms a rough ball, remove the dough to the prepared work surface, knead rapidly and firmly until smooth, about 30 seconds to 1 minute.

Divide the dough into four equal pieces; cut each piece in half again to get 8 pieces total.

Swiftly roll each piece into a ball. Roll each piece of dough out into a 5" pancake, dusting the top and rolling pin with flour as needed. Gradually roll the pancakes out to a size of about 8 inches, increasing the size of each by about 1" and then letting the dough rest for a few seconds before rolling again to the finished size. Roll from the center out. The bread rounds should be very thin.

Using a fork, quickly pierce each bread about 25 times, all over, to prevent rising. The holes should go completely through the bread. Flip the bread over, and pierce each piece another 25 times with the fork.

With at least 5 minutes left on the timer, remove the hot baking sheet from the preheated oven, and place the rounds onto the baking sheet. Place the baking sheet onto the rack near the top of the oven, and bake for 2 minutes; turn the breads over and bake an additional 2 minutes, until the matzot are lightly browned and crisp.

Transfer to a wire rack to cool. Lightly anoint each matzah with olive oil, using a brush, and sprinkle generously with salt.

GRAIN-FREE MATZO

Ingredients to serve 2
1 cup blanched almond flour (not almond meal) (almonds have FOS, PO (xylitol), VHOX and VHS) **(see notes)**
¼ cup coconut flour (FOS and PO (sorbitol)
½ teaspoon Celtic sea salt or one to your liking
1 large egg
2 tablespoons olive oil (LOX and HS) or one to your liking
1 tablespoon water

Directions
In a food processor combine almond flour, coconut flour, and salt and then pulse in the egg, oil, and water.

Divide dough into 2 pieces and roll out the dough between 2 pieces of parchment paper to 1/16" or 1½ mm thick.

Remove top piece of parchment paper and transfer matzo to a baking sheet. Prick holes in matzo using a fork.

Bake at 350°F / 180°C for 10 - 13 minutes, watching very closely. Cool for 2 hours then serve.

Notes
Almond meal is a coarser grind made from almonds that might still have their skins. Almond flour is ground more finely and usually made from blanched almonds (no skins).

CREOLE

The following recipes were kindly donated to me by Leena.

The vegetables and fruit in these recipes will only make them Fructose Friendly. I have tried to source out whether they have Fructose, Fructans, Polyols or Galactans in them and have indicated this beside the ingredient plus a few ingredients have alternatives beside them or in the notes at the end of each recipe. I am hoping that this will help you as much as it has helped me. Salicylates and Oxalates may also be issues for some people so I have added them as well. They will all be noted in the code form below or mentioned in the notes. Please read these.

Low – L, Medium – M, High – H, Very High – VH, Salicylates – S, Oxalates – OX
Fructose – F, Fructans – FOS, Polyols – PO, Galactans – GOS

I have placed some homemade recipes for substituting the ingredients after the main recipes. These recipes will be for Gluten Free, Fructose Friendly, Lactose Free or Friendly, Diabetic Friendly and IBS Friendly depending on your sensitivity so that you can make your own if you want to. Please remember that Fructans, Polyols and Galactans can also come with Fructose.

Substituting ingredients will alter the original taste; however, it is a way to try different recipes from other countries and you can adjust the taste to your liking. Make these recipes your own and use your ingredients if you want to as you know what's best for you.

Australian tablespoons and cups measurements are used and they are: 1 teaspoon equals 5ml; 1 tablespoon equals 20ml; 1 cup equals 250ml. Oven temperatures are for conventional; if using fan-forced (convection), reduce the temperature by 20°C.

Corn Pudding	137
Creole Baked Chicken	137
Meatballs With Creole Red Sauce	138
New Orleans Fried Eggplant Sticks	139
Blueberry Cobbler	140
Homemade Recipes For The Above Recipes	
Homemade Worcestershire Sauce	141
Homemade Ketchup	141
Homemade Balsamic Vinegar Substitute	141
How To Make Tomato Paste The Quick And Easy Way	142
Homemade Cocktail Sauce With Homemade Ingredients	142
Homemade Soy Sauce Substitute	143
Homemade Chili Powder	143
Vegan Fish Sauce	144
Homemade Mushroom "Soy" Sauce	144
Homemade Tin/Can Tomatoes Substitute	144

CORN PUDDING

Ingredients
6 ears of corn (HF, FOS, PO (xylitol) LOX and MS)
2 tablespoons Nuttelex Original or butter or one to your liking
1 tablespoon fresh lime juice (F, PO and LOX)
Cayenne pepper to taste (LOX and VHS)
Salt to taste
Vegetable oil for cooking or one to your liking

Directions
Coarsely grate corn into a bowl.

Heat a heavy skillet or bake pan and coat with oil.

Spread corn and juices into skillet/pan and bake in the oven till browning around edges.

Scrape corn into bowl add butter, lime, cayenne pepper and salt.

This is a great accompaniment to Creole Baked Chicken.

*   *   *   *   *

CREOLE BAKED CHICKEN

Ingredients
1 chicken of your choice

Creole seasoning
2 tablespoons paprika (F and VHS)
1 tablespoon salt
1 tablespoon garlic powder (F, FOS, GOS, LOX and LS) (see notes)
¼ tablespoon black pepper (HOX and VHS)
¼ tablespoon white pepper (VLOX and VHS)
½ tablespoon onion powder (onions have HF, HFOS, PO (mannitol), LOX and LS but no info on onion powder) (see notes)
½ tablespoon dried oregano (F, HOX and VHS)
¼ tablespoon dried basil (F, MOX and VHS)
¼ teaspoon dried thyme (LOX and VHS)
Pinch cayenne pepper (LOX and VHS)

Directions
Mix all the dry ingredients together until well combined and rub the chicken with the Creole seasoning and oven roast.

Notes
I don't know how it will go but you could try substituting a good pinch of asafoetida powder (may contain Gluten) for the onion and garlic. I know that it would change the taste. This is a strong spice so don't use more than the specified amount.

MEATBALLS WITH CREOLE RED SAUCE

Ingredients
Meatballs
500g or 1.1lb pork mince
500g or 1.1lb beef mince
3 tablespoons onion powder (onions have HF, HFOS, PO (mannitol), LOX and LS but no info on onion powder) or a pinch of asafoetida powder (see notes)
2 teaspoons crushed black pepper (HOX and VHS)
1 tablespoon Worcestershire sauce (HS) (read label for added anchovies) (homemade recipe after main recipes)
1 tablespoon ketchup (F, FOS, PO, VLOX and VHS) (homemade recipe after main recipes)
6 sprigs fresh oregano (F, HOX and VHS)
1 teaspoon chili flakes (F and VHS)
1 teaspoon salt
2 tablespoons mushroom soy sauce (**see notes**) (homemade recipe after main recipes)
4 pieces crust less Gluten Free white bread soaked in milk or one to your liking

Directions
Preheat oven to 180°C / 350°F.

Mix together and roll into 40g balls placing them together in rows on a baking tray.

Cook 20 min.

Notes
A pinch of asafoetida powder (may contain Gluten) should be enough to substitute for the garlic and onion. This is a strong spice so don't use more than the specified amount.

Normal mushrooms are high in Polyols (mannitol and xylitol) and contain moderate amounts of both raffinose and Fructans and are therefore a potential source of bad gas. They are VLOX and MS. It has been stated that Shiitake, Enoki, Oyster have low to no Polyols and information for Fructose, Fructans, Oxalates and Salicylates could not be found at all. Usually only "Mushrooms" in general comes up when researching so this ingredient will be your call as what you want to use. I don't have any issues when eating the Gourmet Style mushrooms. Not too sure about the King Brown even though one site states that they are in the same category as the other Gourmet mushrooms.

CREOLE RED SAUCE
Ingredients
½ cup of olive oil (LOX and HS) or one to your liking
8 sticks of celery (HF, FOS, PO (mannitol) and VHOX) or 1 packed cup of chopped celery leaves
4 onions (HF, HFOS, PO (mannitol), LOX and LS) or 12 spring onions (green parts only) diced (white part has M-HF, FOS, PO (mannitol) MOX and LS) (see notes)
6 cloves of garlic (F, FOS, GOS, LOX and LS) (see notes)
3 carrots (F, FOS (raffinose), PO (sorbitol), GOS, VHOX and HS)
3 green capsicums (HF, FOS, PO (mannitol) and VHOX)
1 teaspoon cayenne pepper (LOX and VHS)
2 tablespoons of salt
2 teaspoons black pepper (HOX and VHS)
1 tablespoon dried thyme (LOX and VHS)

2 teaspoons white pepper (VLOX and VHS)
2 tablespoons Worcestershire sauce (HS) (read label for anchovies) (homemade sauce after main recipes)
4 tablespoons chopped parsley (F, PO (mannitol), LOX and LS)
6 finely sliced green onion/shallots (green ends only) (white part has M-HF, FOS, PO (mannitol), MOX and LS)
5 bay leaves (VHS)
4 kilo crushed tomatoes (HF, FOS, PO (mannitol) MOX and MS) (homemade recipes after main recipes)
4 cups stock (minus onion and garlic) of your choice

Directions
Blitz the first 6 ingredients together and then cook for 10 minutes constantly stirring until vegetables are tender.

Stir in the remaining ingredients before adding the crushed tomatoes and stock. Simmer for at least an hour until flavours have blended.

Notes
⅛ teaspoon of asafoetida powder (may contain Gluten) should be enough to substitute for the garlic and onion. This is a strong spice so don't use more than the specified amount.

If you don't have green capsicums, you can use celery (HF, FOS, PO (mannitol) and VHOX), zucchini (HF, FOS, PO (sorbitol) VLOX and VHS) or frozen or canned capsicums.

*   *   *   *   *

NEW ORLEANS FRIED EGGPLANT STICKS

Ingredients
6 cups vegetable oil or one to your liking
1 large eggplant (F, FOS, PO (xylitol), MOX and HS)
1 cup Gluten Free flour or one to your liking (options on pages 13 & 14)
2 tablespoons Creole Seasoning (see previous recipe)
2 large eggs
½ cup buttermilk (homemade recipe after main recipes)
1 cup dextrose powder (may contain Gluten) or icing sugar or sweetener to your liking

Directions
Heat oil to 180°C / 350°F in heavy pan or alternatively use a deep fryer.

Peel and cut eggplant in 1cm thick batons.

Mix flour and seasoning.

Whisk egg and buttermilk together.

Toss eggplant in flour mix then in egg mix then back in flour mix to coat.

Fry in batches turning frequently until golden (about 2 mins).

Drain on paper towel then dust heavily with icing sugar.

We serve ours with American cocktail sauce for dipping but you can also eat as is (homemade cocktail sauce after main recipes).

BLUEBERRY COBBLER

Some Gluten Free flours are higher on the carbohydrate scale and may not be Diabetic Friendly.

In making the fillings for Apple, Apricot and other fruit pies, tarts and slices, stew the fruit with dextrose monohydrate (commonly called glucose). During the cooking process the excess fructose in the fruit bonds with the dextrose, creating a sugar molecule (sucrose) which still tastes sweet but which should not provoke an allergic reaction in a person who suffers from a Fructose Malabsorption Allergy.

Ingredients
Filling
6 cups frozen blueberries (F, PO (xylitol) and VHS) (**see above**)
1 cup dextrose powder (may contain Gluten) or sugar
2 teaspoons lemon zest (F, PO (sorbitol) and HOX)
3 tablespoons Gluten Free plain flour or one to your liking (options pages 13 & 14)

Directions
Pre-heat oven 180°C / 350°F.

Mix together and put in a lightly buttered pie dish.

Topping
1 cup Gluten Free plain flour or one to your liking (options pages 13 & 14)
6 tablespoons dextrose powder (may contain Gluten) or sugar
1½ teaspoon baking powder (VLOX)
¼ teaspoon salt
6 tablespoons Nuttelex Original or butter - cut into 1cm dice or one to your liking
1 egg slightly beaten
¼ teaspoon fresh grated nutmeg (VLOX and VHS)

Directions
Whisk together flour, baking powder, sugar, salt and nutmeg until well combined.

Work butter into flour mix until it resembles a course pea like crumble.

Crumble on top of blueberries and bake until golden about 30 - 40 mins.

HOMEMADE RECIPES FOR THE ABOVE RECIPES

HOMEMADE WORCESTERSHIRE SAUCE

Ingredients
½ cup white wine vinegar (L-MOX and VHS) or rice wine vinegar
2 tablespoons water
2 tablespoons coconut aminos, Tamarin or Soy Sauce (FOS) substitute in this section
¼ teaspoon ground ginger (F, FOS, LOX and MS)
¼ teaspoon mustard powder (F, GOS, VLOX and VHS)
A good pinch of asafoetida powder (may contain gluten)
⅛ teaspoon cinnamon (F, HOX and VHS)
⅛ teaspoon freshly ground black pepper (HOX and VHS)

Directions
Combine all the ingredients in a saucepan and slowly bring to a boil while stirring frequently.
Let simmer for about a minute for the flavors to develop.
Cool and store in the refrigerator.

Notes
¼ teaspoon onion powder (onions have HF, HFOS, PO (mannitol), LOX and LS but no info on onion powder) and ¼ teaspoon garlic powder (F, FOS, GOS and LS) will replace the asafoetida which is a strong spice so only use the specified amount.

* * * * *

HOMEMADE KETCHUP

Ingredients
One 6oz can of tomato paste (HF, FOS, PO (mannitol), HOX and VHS) or homemade recipe in this section
½ cup white vinegar (L-MOX and VHS)
½ cup + 2 tablespoons dextrose powder (may contain Gluten)
1 teaspoon salt
⅛ teaspoon ground celery (celery has HF, FOS, PO (mannitol) and VHOX)
Pinch of ground cloves (F and HS)

Directions
Put all ingredients into a saucepan and whisk together until smooth.

Heat on medium heat until just boiling; immediately reduce heat and simmer for 20 more minutes, stirring frequently.

Remove from heat and let cool on the counter or stove. Store in a covered container in the fridge.

* * * * *

HOMEMADE BALSAMIC VINEGAR SUBSTITUTE

For about 1 tablespoon of balsamic vinegar (F, VLOX and HS), combine 1 tablespoon red wine vinegar (L-MOX and VHS) and ½ teaspoon sugar

For Fructose friendly, substitute the sugar for dextrose.

HOW TO MAKE TOMATO PASTE THE QUICK AND EASY WAY

This recipe makes about 5 heaped tablespoons.

Soak 2 kilos (4½ lbs) of tomatoes (HF, FOS, PO (mannitol), MOX and MS) in boiling water for five minutes or until the skins can be easily peeled off. Drain and carefully remove the tomato skin. The tomatoes may be hot to handle.

Carefully cut tomatoes in half or quarters longways and de-seed completely. Place tomato pieces in to processor and process to a very liquidy paste.

If you have a slow cooker, then place this liquid paste in it and leave it to reduce and thicken up. Stir occasionally. I left mine on all day and got a beautiful thick tomato paste to use in my recipes.

If you don't have a slow cooker you can cook the paste in a 350°F / 180°C preheated oven on shallow trays until it is reduced to a paste. Check the tomatoes every half hour, stirring the paste and switching the position of the trays so that they reduce evenly. Over time, the paste will start to reduce to the point where you can make one tray.

The paste is done when shiny and brick-colored, and it has reduced by more than half. There shouldn't be any remaining water or moisture separating from the paste at this point. This will take 3 - 4 hours, though exact baking/cooking times will depend on the juiciness of your tomatoes and your oven.

After the paste was cold; I put it in a container and kept it in the refrigerator or freezer.

Making small batches when you need it can be useful; however, if you use a lot of tomato paste then just double or triple the amount of tomatoes used. I made a very small batch using the same prep method but I cooked them down in my non-stick frypan over low heat and I continually stirred the mixture. I did not add anything to the paste because I can do that when I use it in a recipe.

*   *   *   *   *

HOMEMADE COCKTAIL SAUCE WITH HOMEMADE INGREDIENTS

Ingredients
1½ cups ketchup (HF, FOS, PO, VLOX and VHS) (homemade in this section)
1 tablespoon chili powder (F and VHS) (homemade recipe below)
1 tablespoon lemon juice (F, PO (sorbitol), LOX and L-HS)
2 teaspoons dextrose powder (may contain Gluten) or sugar
½ teaspoon salt
¼ teaspoon black pepper (HOX and VHS)

Directions
Mix everything together and chill for at least one hour before serving if desired.

If you like lots of lemon juice you can add another teaspoon for more zip.

HOMEMADE SOY SAUCE SUBSTITUTE

Ingredients for about ⅔ cup
1 cup beef broth (Gluten Free and minus the garlic and onion)
2 tablespoons balsamic vinegar (F, L-MOX and VHS) (substitute recipe in this section)
2 teaspoons white wine vinegar (L-MOX and VHS) or rice wine vinegar
3 teaspoons rice malt syrup (Fructose Free)
⅛ teaspoon ground black pepper (HOX and VHS)
A pinch of asafoetida powder (may contain Gluten and is a strong spice)
⅛ teaspoon ground ginger (F, FOS, LOX and MS)
¼ teaspoon salt or to taste
½ teaspoon fish sauce (optional) (homemade Vegan Fish sauce substitute in this section)

Directions
Place the following in a small saucepan: broth, both vinegars, rice malt syrups, black pepper, asafoetida and ground ginger. Bring to a brief boil over medium-high heat and then reduce heat to a gentle simmer - small bubbles should just break on the surface. Cook until reduced to about ⅔ cup - this takes about 7 - 10 minutes. (NOTE: If you accidentally cook it longer, the flavors of the vinegar and syrup will be concentrated, and it becomes quite sweet. Keep an eye on the clock and don't miss that 10 minute max).

Remove the pan from the heat. Add the salt and fish sauce; stir to combine and taste to make sure it's salty enough for you.

Pour into a glass container and allow to cool before storing in the refrigerator for up to 10 days. This sauce can be used in any recipe that calls for soy sauce.

Notes
⅛ teaspoon coarse (granulated) garlic powder can replace the asafoetida.
2 teaspoons cider vinegar (F, L-MOX and HS) can replace white wine vinegar or rice wine vinegar.
Molasses (F and MS) will replace rice malt syrup for a stronger flavour.

*   *   *   *   *

HOMEMADE CHILI POWDER

Ingredients
2 tablespoons paprika (F and VHS)
2 teaspoons oregano (F, HOX and VHS)
1½ teaspoons cumin (VHS)
1½ teaspoons garlic powder (F, FOS, GOS, LOX and LS)
¾ teaspoon onion powder (Onions white & yellow HF, HFOS, PO (mannitol), LOX and LS)
½ teaspoon cayenne pepper (LOX and VHS) (omit or increase to taste)

Directions
Place all ingredients in a bowl.
Blend thoroughly.
Store in an airtight container in the refrigerator.

Notes
Paprika is a pepper and should be refrigerated for maximum shelf life and potency.

VEGAN FISH SAUCE

Ingredients for about ½ cup or 125 ml
¼ cup warm filtered or spring water
2 tablespoons raw turbinado sugar (for Fructose Friendly use dextrose powder (may contain Gluten) instead
¼ cup fresh or canned 100% pineapple juice (F, PO (mannitol), VLOX and MS)
2 tablespoons light soy sauce (FOS) (homemade substitute in this section) or tamari

Directions
Stir the water and sugar together in a bowl until sugar dissolves. Add the pineapple juice and light soy sauce and mix well.

Refrigerate in a glass container or jar with a lid for an hour or so. This may last up to 3 - 4 days.

Notes
This version is intended to make it saltier like 'light soy sauce': Alternatively instead of 2 tablespoons light soy sauce, use 1 tablespoon Gluten Free tamari and 1 tablespoon Gluten Free chicken free broth. You want it to be slightly saltier and lighter.

* * * * *

HOMEMADE MUSHROOM "SOY" SAUCE

Ingredients to make 3½ cups
2 lb or 1kilo sliced white button mushrooms or shiitake mushrooms (see notes)
1 tablespoon fine sea salt
Cheesecloth

Directions
Toss mushrooms with sea salt; let sit 1 hour. Transfer to a cheesecloth-lined colander set over a bowl. Gather edges of cheesecloth; squeeze mushrooms dry and save for another use. Chill sauce up to 2 weeks.

Notes
Portabella, White, Swiss/brown/forest mushrooms are high in Polyols (mannitol and xylitol) and contain moderate amounts of both raffinose and Fructans and are therefore a potential source of bad gas. They are VLOX and MS. It has been stated that Shiitake, Enoki, Oyster have low to no Polyols and information for Fructose, Fructans, Oxalates and Salicylates could not be found at all. Usually only "Mushrooms" in general comes up when researching so this ingredient will be your call as what you want to use. I don't have any issues when eating the Gourmet Style mushrooms. Not too sure about the King Brown even though one site states that they are in the same category as the other Gourmet mushrooms.

* * * * *

HOMEMADE TIN/CAN TOMATOES SUBSTITUTE

Place the weight amount of tomatoes needed in a bowl of boiling water for 5 minutes. Carefully remove and peel tomatoes; they will be hot. Place them in a saucepan and bring them to a boil. Cook until soft but not soggy. Follow the recipe as to their use. For crushed tomatoes, process by pulsing for a few seconds in your processor or chop finely.

HOLLAND

The following Dutch recipes were kindly donated to me by Brisa

The vegetables and fruit in these recipes will only make them Fructose Friendly. I have tried to source out whether they have Fructose, Fructans, Polyols or Galactans in them and have indicated this beside the ingredient plus a few ingredients have alternatives beside them or in the notes at the end of each recipe. I am hoping that this will help you as much as it has helped me. Salicylates and Oxalates may also be issues for some people so I have added them as well. They will all be noted in the code form below or mentioned in the notes. Please read these.

Low – L, Medium – M, High – H, Very High – VH, Salicylates – S, Oxalates – OX
Fructose – F, Fructans – FOS, Polyols – PO, Galactans – GOS

I have placed some homemade recipes for substituting the ingredients after the main recipes. These recipes will be for Gluten Free, Fructose Friendly, Lactose Free or Friendly, Diabetic Friendly and IBS Friendly depending on your sensitivity so that you can make your own if you want to. Please remember that Fructans, Polyols and Galactans can also come with Fructose.

Substituting ingredients will alter the original taste; however, it is a way to try different recipes from other countries and you can adjust the taste to your liking. Make these recipes your own and use your ingredients if you want to as you know what's best for you.

Australian tablespoons and cups measurements are used and they are: 1 teaspoon equals 5ml; 1 tablespoon equals 20ml; 1 cup equals 250ml. Oven temperatures are for conventional; if using fan-forced (convection), reduce the temperature by 20°C.

Hutspot Met Klapstuk (Stew With Beef)	146
Split Pea Soup (Erwtensoep)	147
Dutch Asparagus	148
Vegetable Soup With Meatballs (Groentesoep Met Balletjes)	149
Appelflappen (Apple Turnover)	150
Tompoes (Tom Thumbs)	152
Dough Balls (Oliebollen)	153
Homemade Recipes For The Above Recipes	
Gluten Free Rough Puff Pastry	154
Homemade Alternative Ideas For Food Colourings	155

HUTSPOT MET KLAPSTUK (STEW WITH BEEF)

Hutspot is traditionally served with klapstuk, a piece of braised beef, but sometimes will also be eaten with a typical Dutch meatball. The best carrots to use for this dish are a larger and thicker variety of the orange carrot. The sugars in the carrot add a hint of sweetness to this dish that will appeal to almost any eater, young or old.

Ingredients
500g (1.1lb) beef chuck rib roast
400ml (13.5 fl oz) water
½ beef bouillon or stock cube (minus onion and garlic)
1 bay leaf (VHS)
8 black pepper corns, whole (HOX)
1 tablespoon Gluten Free flour, or one to your liking, dissolved in ½ cup water
6 large potatoes peeled and quartered (see notes)
8 large carrots, peeled and diced (HF, FOS (raffinose), PO (sorbitol), GOS, VHOX and HS)
4 large onions, peeled and sliced (HF, HFOS, PO (mannitol), LOX and LS) or 12 shallots (green parts only) (white part has M-HF, FOS, PO (mannitol) MOX and LS) (see notes)
Salt and pepper (black - HOX and VHS, white - VLOX and VHS)

Directions
Add the water to a Dutch oven or a braising pan, add the bouillon/stock cube and stir until dissolved. Add the beef, the bay leaf and the pepper corns and braise on low heat for approximately 90 minutes or until beef is tender.

Remove the meat to a serving dish, discard the bay leaf and peppercorns and stir the dissolved flour into the pan juices. Stir scraping the bottom of the pan, loosening any meat particles that may be stuck. Bring the heat slowly up until the gravy starts to thicken. Pour the gravy over the meat and set aside, keeping it warm.

In the meantime, place the potatoes on the bottom of a pan, and add water so that the potatoes are just covered. Put the carrots on top, and finish with the onions. Add salt. Cover and bring to a boil, then lower the heat and boil for about 20 minutes or until the potatoes are cooked.

Pour off the cooking water, but save it. Mash the potatoes, carrots and onions until you achieve a mashed potato consistency. If you need more liquid to make it smoother, add a tablespoon of cooking liquid at a time. Taste, adjust with salt and pepper.

Serve the hutspot family style on a large platter, slice the beef and serve with the gravy.

Notes
Fructose in potatoes can range anything between 582 mg – 989 mg depending on the size, type and skin colour. They also have FOS, PO and GOS. They can also be VHOX and MS again depending on the type of potatoes, colour of skin and how they are cooked.

You can replace the onion with ⅛ teaspoon asafoetida powder and as this is a strong spice, don't use any more than the specified amount.

SPLIT PEA SOUP (ERWTENSOEP)

The Dutch love soup in all flavors, shapes and sizes. Most Sunday dinners will have soup as a starter, whether it's a broth-based or a cream soup. Often throughout the week, they will have a thicker, filling soup as a meal, together with a slice of bread or a small roll.

Served traditionally with a slice of dark rye bread, this typical Dutch soup will give you enough energy to keep going.

Ingredients
500g (1.1lb) green split peas (FOS, GOS and MOX) (**see notes**)
1 litre (34 fl oz) water
1 carrot, peeled (HF, FOS (raffinose), PO (sorbitol), GOS, VHOX and HS)
1 small potato, peeled (see notes)
2 ribs celery (HF, FOS, PO (mannitol) and VHOX) try using ½ cup of chopped celery leaves instead
1 small onion (HF, HFOS, PO (mannitol), LOX and LS) or 3 shallots (green parts only) (white part has M-HF, FOS, PO (mannitol) MOX and LS)
1 bay leaf (VHS)
1 small smoked ham hock, ham bone or sausage to your liking
Salt and pepper (black - HOX and VHS, white - VLOX and VHS)

Directions
Rinse and wash the split peas, and add them with the water to a pot. Chop the vegetables and add them to the water and add the bay leaf. Add the smoked meat.

Bring to a boil and simmer for about 40 minutes. When the peas are soft, remove the bay leaf and either puree or just stir the soup several times, the peas will dissolve and give it a creamy consistence. Cut the meat off the bone, or slice the sausage and stir it back in the soup. Adjust the flavor with salt and pepper if needed.

Serve with a slice of buttered dark rye bread. This soup is best served the next day, when the flavors all have a chance to blend. Do reheat carefully, as the soup thickens overnight and can scorch easily. Thin with a little bit of warm water if needed.

Notes
Soaking the peas for at least 12 hours or overnight in water with 2 teaspoons of bicarb soda may help to reduce the "gas". Change the water often and rinse the peas between water changes.

Fructose in potatoes can range anything between 582 mg – 989 mg depending on the size, type and skin colour. They also have FOS, PO and GOS. They can also be VHOX and MS again depending on the type of potatoes, colour of skin and how they are cooked.

DUTCH ASPARAGUS

Asparagus has rightfully earned itself nicknames like 'white gold' and 'queen among vegetables'. It is indeed a very flavourful vegetable, which is traditionally harvested and enjoyed from the second Thursday in April.

Ingredients to serve 4
1kg (2.2lb) white asparagus (HF, FOS, PO (mannitol), LOX and MS)
1kg (2.2lb) potatoes (see notes)
4 eggs
100g (5.3oz) Nuttelex Original or butter or one to your liking
8 slices cooked ham
1 pinch freshly grated nutmeg (VLOX and VHS)
Fresh parsley (chopped), garnish (F, PO (mannitol), LOX and LS) or coriander (MOX and HS)
Other requirements – asparagus or potato peeler

Directions
Wash asparagus and cut about 2cm from bottom. Remove skin with peeler.

Place washed and peeled asparagus in pan and cover with water. Season with salt, bring to a boil and reduce fire, leave to simmer for 10 minutes.

Boil potatoes in water for about 20 minutes until cooked.

Remove pan with asparagus from heat and leave for another 15 - 20 minutes. Test with fork to see if asparagus are done: prick bottom section, must be tender but not soggy.

Boil eggs 10 minutes in boiling water. Drain and rinse eggs briefly in cold water to remove shells more easily. Shell and halve lengthwise.

Melt butter on low heat, and season with salt and pepper to taste.

Use skimmer to take asparagus from pan and leave to drip dry on tea towel. Pour molten butter into gravy boat. Drain potatoes.

Divide asparagus amongst 4 plates and garnish with 4 rolled slices of ham, 2 half eggs and potatoes. Sprinkle asparagus with nutmeg and parsley for garnish.

Notes
Fructose in potatoes can range anything between 582 mg – 989 mg depending on the size, type and skin colour. They also have FOS, PO and GOS. They can also be VHOX and MS again depending on the type of potatoes, colour of skin and how they are cooked.

VEGETABLE SOUP WITH MEATBALLS (GROENTESOEP MET BALLETJES)

Holland's cuisine knows many soups, from the sturdy thick split pea soup to a brothy, light, appetite-arousing Groentesoep, or vegetable soup. A standard item in Groentesoep are, besides the vegetables, these so-called soup balls, or soepballetjes. Not the big softball-size meatballs, or gehaktballen, that the Dutch serve for dinner, but bitesize balletjes the size of marbles.

The meat used for these fleshy globes is "half-om-half", half pork and half beef. The fattiness of the pork makes sure that the meatballs stay juicy and tender, and the beef adds body and flavor.

Omas, or grandmas, usually had a "pannetje soep" on the back of the stove, simmering, and many of us associate soup with Sunday afternoon visits to grandma's house. Soup is still a favorite starter for an evening meal or a Sunday lunch, and an easy and affordable dish to feed a family with.

Ingredients
Select a variety of chopped vegetables (typical Dutch soup vegetables are leeks, cauliflower, carrots and celery) or, if you're in a pinch, even a bag of frozen stir-fry vegetables will do.
200g (7oz) soup vegetables (see notes for what is in the vegetables) or ones to your liking
150g (5.3oz) ground pork
150g (5.3oz) ground beef
1 tablespoon Gluten Free breadcrumbs or ones to your liking
¼ teaspoon nutmeg (VLOX and VHS)
½ teaspoon salt
½ teaspoon ground black pepper (HOX and VHS)
1 litre (34 fl oz) bouillon or stock cube (minus onion and garlic)

Directions
Mix the meats with the breadcrumbs, the salt, pepper and nutmeg until well blended. Roll small meatballs the size of a marble.

In the meantime, heat the bouillon to a slow boil. Add the fresh vegetables and simmer for a good twenty minutes.

Put several soepballetjes (soup balls) at a time in the bouillon, wait ten seconds, then add some more, until they're all in the soup. The meatballs are done when they start to float, within a minute or two.

Notes
Leeks (F, FOS, PO (mannitol), GOS and MOX) try using the green parts only
Cauliflower (F, FOS, PO (mannitol), GOS, LOX and MS)
Carrots (HF, FOS (raffinose), PO (sorbitol), GOS, VHOX and HS)
Celery (HF, FOS, PO (mannitol) and VHOX) try using chopped celery leaves instead

APPELFLAPPEN (APPLE TURNOVER)

The apple is one of the most versatile and used fruits in the Dutch kitchen. Welcome in savory dishes such as Hemel-en-aarde, a mashed potato dish with smoked bacon, potatoes and tart apples; the apple is equally as appreciated in sweet baked goods such as our famous apple pie.

If you have the time, sample some of the varied apple-based dishes around the country. Most good bakeries in town will have an apple dessert for you to try, and feel free to ask for recommendations: the bakery staff most often have their own favorites! But in case you're in a rush, or just want to carry on exploring the city, don't miss out on an equally delectable treat that you can eat on the go: the triangular Appelflap. Made with tender, buttery flaked pastry and filled with fresh apples, sweet currants and raisins, this apple turnover is a wonderful start to exploring the rich and varied history of Dutch baked goods.

Ingredients
20g (0.7oz) currants (see notes for Fructose Friendly tip)
20g (0.7oz) raisins (see notes for Fructose Friendly tip)
3 dried apricots (Fresh apricots have F, PO (sorbitol), VLOX and VHS) (see notes for Fructose Friendly tip)
100ml (3.3 fl oz) apple juice (F, PO (sorbitol), VLOX and MS)
2 Jonagold apples (or similar crisp red apples) (F, FOS (raffinose), PO (sorbitol), LOX and M or HS, depending on the type of apple used) (see notes for Fructose Friendly tip)
2 tablespoons dextrose powder (Fructose Free may contain Gluten) or sugar
Pinch of cinnamon (F, HOX and VHS)
1 package puff pastry (usually ten squares) (homemade Gluten Free recipe after the main recipes)
Dextrose powder (Fructose Free and may contain Gluten) or coarse sugar

Directions
Add the currants, raisins and apricots to the apple juice and allow to soak, preferably overnight, but at least for a good hour.

Allow the puff pastry to thaw, while you peel and core the apples. Chop the apples into small pieces.

Drain the soaked fruit, but keep the water. Finely chop the apricots and add them together with the currants and raisins to the apples and stir.

Then add the sugar and the cinnamon and stir until everything is well mixed. Set aside.

Peel the separate squares of puff pastry apart. Place them before you with one corner pointing downwards.

Place approximately 1 - 1½ tablespoons of filling on the bottom half of the square, wet the edges of the dough with some of the soaking water that you saved before and fold the top part over, forming a triangle. Carefully press the dough around the filling and on the edges, making sure they are sealed.

Place the triangles on parchment paper on a baking sheet and place in the fridge while you pre-heat the oven to 200°C / 400°F.

Remove the baking sheet from the fridge, and moisten the top of each triangle with a little bit of water, before sprinkling the coarse sugar on top. Place the baking sheet on the middle shelf in the oven, and bake the turnovers for 20 minutes or until golden.

These can be eaten warm or cold.

Notes
Currants (the Fructose count for Currants - 1 cup - 3.95g; Raisins, seedless - 1 cup, packed - 48.97g so exchange currants for the raisins) Currants also have PO (mannitol), HOX and VHS and Raisins also have PO (sorbitol), LOX and VHS.

Fructose Friendly Fruits
In making the fillings for Apple Tarts and Apricot Tarts or just about any fruit filling; stew the fruit with dextrose monohydrate (commonly called glucose) for at least 10 minutes. During the cooking process the excess fructose in the fruit bonds with the dextrose, creating a sugar molecule (sucrose) which still tastes sweet but which should not provoke an allergic reaction in a person who suffers from Fructose Malabsorption Allergy.

TOMPOES (TOM THUMBS)

Ingredients
250ml (8.5 fl oz) of Lactose Free milk or one to your liking
1 vanilla bean (or 1 tablespoon of vanilla flavoring) (F, VLOX and VHS)
2 egg yolks
4 tablespoons of dextrose powder (Fructose Free may contain Gluten) or sugar
4 tablespoons of Gluten Free flour or one to your liking (options pages 13 & 14)
Pinch of salt
1 sheet of puff pastry (homemade Gluten Free recipe after main recipes)
1 egg, beaten
3 tablespoons of dextrose powder (Fructose Free may contain Gluten) or powdered or icing sugar
2 teaspoons Lactose Free milk or one to your liking
1 drop red food coloring or red berry juice (homemade substitute ideas after main recipes)

Directions
Warm the milk, add the vanilla bean and steep for 15 minutes.

Mix the egg yolks with the sugar and the salt, and one tablespoon of flour. Stir until creamy.

Take the vanilla bean out of the milk, open it up and scrape out the seeds (or add the vanilla essence to the milk) and stir.

Take two tablespoons of warm milk and stir it into the egg yolk mix, then stir in the rest of the flour.

Carefully stir all this back into the warm milk into the pan, put it back on a low heat and stir until it becomes a thick mass.

Take off the stove and cover with a piece of plastic, to avoid forming a skin when it cools down.

Heat the oven to 200°C / 400°F. Spray a baking sheet or pan with cooking spray.

Cut the puff pastry sheet in 4 equal rectangular sections and place them on the baking sheet. Brush the top with the beaten egg, prick holes into the pastry with the tines of a fork and bake for fifteen minutes, or until the dough is golden.

Remove from the oven, and taking care not to burn your fingers, quickly and carefully pull the top from the bottom sheet. Set all eight pieces aside on a rack to cool.

Stir powdered sugar with the milk and the red food coloring into a thick icing.

Take the bottom part of one of the baked puff pastries and spread the cooled down vanilla cream on it. Top it with its corresponding iced top half of the pastry.

When all four are done, carefully spread the pink icing on top: let it dry and eat.

DOUGH BALLS (OLIEBOLLEN)

Ingredients
125g (4.4oz) Gluten Free flour or one to your liking (options pages 13 & 14)
75ml Lactose Free milk, warm or one to your liking (may need to adjust for Gluten Free flour)
7g (0.25oz) active dry yeast (non-bakers MOX and VHS and bakers MOX and LS)
20g (0.7oz) Nuttelex Original or butter, softened or one to your liking
15g (0.5oz) dextrose powder (Fructose Free may contain Gluten) or sugar
1 teaspoon lemon zest (F, PO (sorbitol) and HOX)
Pinch of salt
1 egg
20g (0.7oz) raisins and currants or other dried fruits (see notes)
1 heaping tablespoon of dextrose powder (Fructose Free may contain Gluten) or powdered sugar

Directions
Soak the raisins in some rum or warm water several hours before, preferably the night prior to the frying.

Dissolve the yeast in the warm milk.

Mix the flour, sugar and the lemon zest, and stir the milk and yeast mix carefully.

Add the egg and the salt and stir the batter for several minutes until everything is nicely blended. Stir in the drained raisins.

Cover and let rise until it doubled its volume, stir down and let rise again.

In the meantime, heat the oil in the fryer up to 190°C / 375°F. Place a plate with several paper towels to soak up the excess fat of the fried goods.

Stir the batter down. Now use a large spoon or an ice cream scoop to scoop out a portion, drop it into the hot oil and fry for about four minutes on each side or until brown. It's important to gauge the temperature of your oil: too hot and the oil will scorch the outside but leave the inside of the balls uncooked.

Drain the balls on paper towels, then transfer onto a new plate and sprinkle with powdered sugar.

Notes
Currants (the Fructose count for Currants - 1 cup - 3.95g; Raisins, seedless - 1 cup, packed - 48.97g so exchange currants for the raisins). Currants also have PO (mannitol), HOX and VHS and Raisins also have PO (sorbitol), LOX and VHS.

Fructose Friendly Fruits
In making the fillings for Apple Tarts and Apricot Tarts or just about any fruit filling; stew the fruit with dextrose monohydrate (commonly called glucose) for at least 10 minutes. During the cooking process the excess fructose in the fruit bonds with the dextrose, creating a sugar molecule (sucrose) which still tastes sweet but which should not provoke an allergic reaction in a person who suffers from Fructose Malabsorption Allergy.

HOMEMADE RECIPES FOR THE ABOVE RECIPES
GLUTEN FREE ROUGH PUFF PASTRY

I have had this recipe for nearly a year now, so I forget where it came from, so thank you to the person who quoted from the adaptor "Bake by weight and you'll be able to play. Play and let it be imperfect. Don't expect to be good at this the first time. I promise you this is a project you will master eventually. Allow yourself time in front of the kitchen counter, more than just once". (I still use cup measures because it's easier for me).

Ingredients
345g (¾ lb or 1½ cups or 3 sticks) unsalted butter Or Nuttelex Original
137g (4⅞ oz or ¾ cup) potato starch (or tapioca flour) (FOS)
137g (4½ oz or 1 cup) cornstarch (MOX) (or arrowroot powder (FOS)
52g (1⅞ oz or ⅓ cup) superfine brown rice flour (MOX) (or sorghum (FOS)
52g (1⅞ oz or ⅓ cup) superfine sweet rice flour (or millet flour VHOX)
2 teaspoons xanthan gum (omit if you are not sure of this gum)
½ teaspoon guar gum (plus the amount of xanthan gum if you choose to omit it)
OR 2½ teaspoons chia seeds ground to a powder (FOS, LOX and HS)
1 teaspoon fine sea salt
180ml (¾ cup) ice water

Directions
Prepping the butter
Cut the butter into ½" cubes and arrange them on a plate, making sure they are separated. Put the plate in the freezer until the butter is frozen, at least 1 hour.

Combining the flours
Mix the potato starch, cornstarch, brown rice flour, and superfine sweet rice flour together. Whisk the flours together to aerate them. (Whirl the flours in the food processor for a few moments, to fully combine them). Add the xanthan gum, guar gum or chia seed powder and salt. Stir to combine.

Making the rough dough
Put the combined flours in the bowl of a stand mixer. (This batch is too big for a standard size food processor, or you could have done it there. You can also do this by hand, with the help of a pastry scraper).

Add the frozen butter. When you turn on the mixer, on the lowest speed, the butter will fly and your stand mixer will sound like it is suffering. Keep going. Turn it off and on a few times until the edges of the butter pieces have started to soften.

Turn off the mixer. Pour in the ice water and turn on the mixer again. Let it run until the flours have absorbed the water. This dough is going to look crazy ragged and unfinished.

Rolling out and turning (see notes below about a Silpat)
Pour the dough onto a Silpat or piece of parchment paper about the same size as a Silpat. Knead it together with your hands for a moment or two, just enough to bring it together. Put a piece of parchment paper on top and roll this out to a rough rectangle, with a rolling pin. (Aim for roughly the size of a piece of notebook paper, with just a bit more length.) You might like to pat it down with your hands.

Roll from the center outward, going both ways. Take care not to roll over the edges. Go gently.

Gently, using the edges of the Silpat or parchment paper, fold the bottom third of the dough toward the middle, then fold the top third on top of it. Eventually, this will look like a book. Right now, it might be hard to distinguish the folds from each other.

Rotate the dough one-quarter turn to your right (clockwise). You have now completed one turn.

Again, roll out the dough to roughly the same size as a piece of notebook paper, with just a bit more length. Go gently. In these early turns, you're going to think this is impossible but keep going. With each turn, the dough will become smoother and more cohesive. Once you are done rolling, fold the bottom third up, and overlap the top third over it. Try as best you can to align the edges.

Rotate the dough one-quarter turn to your right (clockwise). You have now completed two turns.

Follow the same process, rolling carefully, then turning, until you have completed four turns. Wrap the folded dough in plastic wrap and let it chill in the refrigerator for 2 hours.

Finishing the dough
Pull the puff pastry dough out of the refrigerator and let it sit on the counter for about 20 minutes before working with it again, since it will be hard from the cold. Don't let it sit out too long; however, you want the dough to be cold but pliable.

Complete the fifth and sixth turns, following the same procedure as above. Wrap the dough in plastic again and refrigerate for at least another 2 hours.

And there you have it; rough puff pastry, gluten-free. This batch makes enough for 2 large tarts or whatever recipes that you have made it for. This dough does well in the refrigerator for 3 days or in the freezer for 1 month.

Notes
Silpat baking sheets replace parchment paper, and are heat-resistant up to 480°F / 250°C. The Silpat makes any baking sheet non-stick so no greasing is necessary.

*   *   *   *   *

HOMEMADE ALTERNATIVE IDEAS FOR FOOD COLOURINGS

Pink and Red
You can use any number of options, but for a ton of color with almost no flavor, beets are your best bet. Use the juice from the canned kind, or make your own by either boiling or juicing the raw vegetable. Alternately, you can also use any red fruit, like raspberries or pomegranate. Just know that these may change the flavor – which can be a great thing. To procure your dye, pulverize the berries in a food processor or blender, then strain out the colored liquid using a mesh sieve or cheesecloth.

Pink/Red/Magenta: Juiced berries, Juiced cranberries, Juiced beetroot Juiced red capsicum, Juiced tomato, choose dark red tomatoes, rhubarb juiced or boiled, pomegranate juice, chili powder or paprika powder.

EASTERN EUROPE

The following recipes were kindly donated to me by Anastasiya Sukhinina.

The vegetables and fruit in these recipes will only make them Fructose Friendly. I have tried to source out whether they have Fructose, Fructans, Polyols or Galactans in them and have indicated this beside the ingredient plus a few ingredients have alternatives beside them or in the notes at the end of each recipe. I am hoping that this will help you as much as it has helped me. Salicylates and Oxalates may also be issues for some people so I have added them as well. They will all be noted in the code form below or mentioned in the notes. Please read these.

Low – L, Medium – M, High – H, Very High – VH, Salicylates – S, Oxalates – OX
Fructose – F, Fructans – FOS, Polyols – PO, Galactans – GOS

I have placed some homemade recipes for substituting the ingredients after the main recipes. These recipes will be for Gluten Free, Fructose Friendly, Lactose Free or Friendly, Diabetic Friendly and IBS Friendly depending on your sensitivity so that you can make your own if you want to. Please remember that Fructans, Polyols and Galactans can also come with Fructose.

Substituting ingredients will alter the original taste; however, it is a way to try different recipes from other countries and you can adjust the taste to your liking. Make these recipes your own and use your ingredients if you want to as you know what's best for you.

Australian tablespoons and cups measurements are used and they are: 1 teaspoon equals 5ml; 1 tablespoon equals 20ml; 1 cup equals 250ml. Oven temperatures are for conventional; if using fan-forced (convection), reduce the temperature by 20°C.

Bulgarian cabbage rolls "Sarmi"	157
Ukrainian Traditional " Borsh" Soup	158
Russian Crepes "Blini"	159
Hungarian Beef Goulash	160
Homemade Recipes For The Above Recipes	
Homemade Sauerkraut	161
How To Make Tomato Paste The Quick And Easy Way	161

BULGARIAN CABBAGE ROLLS "SARMI"

Ingredients
500g or 1.1lbs ground pork
150g or ¾ cup rice (Basmati is low in carbs and has FOS, LOX and MS. Doongara is low in carbs and has FOS and LOX. Soaking rice and grains for 12 hours lowers oxalates)
The leaves of sauerkraut (Bulgaria cabbage is salted entirely)
1 onion (HF, HFOS, PO (mannitol), LOX and LS) or 3 shallots (green part only) (white part has M-HF, FOS, PO (mannitol) MOX and LS)
1 carrot (F, FOS (raffinose), PO (sorbitol), GOS, VHOX and HS)
100ml or 2¾ fl oz of vegetable oil or one to your liking
Salt
Red pepper (use cayenne pepper if you don't have red (LOX and VHS) to taste
1 cup (0.200 ml) of cabbage pickle
100ml canned tomatoes (HF, PO (aspartame), H-VHOX and LS?)
200ml or 7 fl oz of sour Lactose Free milk or one to your liking (homemade mix the milk required with 1 tablespoon of lemon juice (F, PO (sorbitol), LOX and L-HS) or vinegar (L-MOX and VHS). Stir and leave for 5 minutes until soured and then use)
1 egg

Directions
First prepare the cabbage leaves (about 10 - 12 pieces). Cut out the middle of the thick leaves, which can be used for salad.

Finely cut the onions and carrots and mixed with minced meat.

Put it in a pan and add the rice, 100ml of vegetable oil and 200ml of water. Sprinkle with spices and fry, stirring for about 10 - 15 minutes. Cool.

In a saucepan (preferably - in a ceramic gyuvech) pour canned tomatoes, cabbage juice and 1 tablespoon of vegetable oil.

On each cabbage leaf spread about 1 tablespoon of stuffing and roll forming cabbage leaf rolls. Densely stacked rolls in the pan, pour 400ml or 1¾ cups of water and close the lid tightly and bake at 200°C / 400°F for about 60 minutes.

Then open the lid and cool for half an hour.

In a bowl, mix lightly beaten egg and sour milk, add a little liquid in which the cooked Sarmi and constantly whisk with a whisk or fork.

Carefully return the mixture back into the pan. When serving pour Sarmi a thick sauce.

UKRAINIAN TRADITIONAL "BORSH" SOUP

Ingredients

500g or 1.1lbs meat of your choice
1 tablespoon of tomato paste (F, FOS, PO, HOX and VHS) (homemade recipe after main recipes) or 2 - 3 pieces of salt or fresh tomatoes (HF, FOS, PO (mannitol), MOX and MS)
½ lb or 500g thick slab bacon or Spec or pancetta (diced)
50g Fat or 100ml of vegetable oil or one to your liking
1 cup sauerkraut (F, FOS, PO and HOX) (homemade recipe after main recipes)
6 - 7 medium size pieces Potatoes (see notes)
1 piece (whole) beet (beetroot) (HF, FOS, PO, VHOX and MS) coarsely shredded
2 pieces (whole) carrots (F, FOS (raffinose), PO (sorbitol), GOS, VHOX and HS) chop one and coarsely grate the other
2 onions (heads) (HF, HFOS, PO (mannitol), LOX and LS) or 6 shallots (green part only) (white part has M-HF, FOS, PO (mannitol) MOX and LS) both diced but 1 finer than the other
2 - 3 pieces bay leaf (PO and VHS)
3 - 5 pieces peppercorn (HOX)
3 - 4 cloves garlic (F, FOS, GOS, LOX and LS) crushed
Greenery; any green vegetables of your liking
0.5 teaspoon or ½ teaspoon salt

Directions

In a saucepan, pour the volume of six litres of cold water, a little more than half. (Water is required to be filtered or settle, free of chlorine. Some countries add chlorine to their tap water).

The meat is rinsed with cold water and place in the prepared pan. For the broth to have richness, it is better to take the meat from the bone and cook whole with the bone and then divided into portions pieces. (De-bone meat but leave whole until cooked and then cut to required portions).

Put the saucepan with the meat over high heat.

Clean the potatoes, carrots and onions. Meanwhile, boil the broth, (skim any scum from the top of the broth): the broth will be more transparent. If you do not have time - do not worry, the hot broth can drain through a sieve.

Cut half of brushed potatoes into wedges and place in a broth. If you cook pork soup, the potatoes should be put in immediately after boiling broth, and if you use beef, then after 30 minutes. This is done in order to seethe good potatoes and the broth is more intense.

After half an hour add to the saucepan the second half of potatoes, diced, the chopped carrot and the larger diced onion, peppercorn and bay leaves.

When all the vegetables are already in the pot, add salt, (do not forget that adding sauerkraut is adding salted cabbage).

After boiling, cook for about 15 minutes and add the sauerkraut. In the finished soup, pickled cabbage can remain resilient - it is normal, or seethe, which is also very tasty, it all depends on the characteristics of its ambassador.

(This process is known as making zazharku). While in another pan cooked bacon until the fat drips out and then remove the bacon. Add the shredded beets and fry a little. Add grated carrots and continue to cook.

After 5 - 7 minutes add the smaller diced onions to the beets mix and continue to fry for 10 minutes on medium heat and then add the tomatoes, tomato paste and continue to simmer all together for another 5 minutes.

Add the zazharku to the other pot and stir until well combined. Add crushed garlic, let the soup boil again and immediately remove from heat. The Borsch is almost ready, try it for taste, and add salt, if the salt is not enough.

Give the borscht little stir to catch and remove the bay leaves.

Serve with sour cream and herbs.

Notes
Fructose in potatoes can range anything between 582 mg – 989 mg depending on the size, type and skin colour. They also have FOS, PO and GOS. They can also be VHOX and MS again depending on the type of potatoes, colour of skin and how they are cooked.

*   *   *   *   *

RUSSIAN CREPES "BLINI"

Ingredients
3 (pieces) chicken eggs
1 tablespoon sugar or dextrose powder (Fructose Free and may contain Gluten)
1 teaspoon salt
500ml or 2 cups Lactose Free Milk or one to your liking
280g or 2 cups Gluten Free Flour or one to your liking (options pages 13 & 14)
3 tablespoons Vegetable oil or one to your liking

Directions
In a bowl, lightly whisk the eggs with the sugar and salt. Add half the milk and stir.

Gradually add the flour, stirring until smooth consistency of thick cream. Add the rest of the milk and mix thoroughly.

Add butter, stir and leave for 10 - 15 minutes.

Heat a cast-iron pan, brush with oil and fry the pancakes on both sides.

HUNGARIAN BEEF GOULASH

Ingredients
600 - 700g about 1½ lbs beef blade cut into slices (**see notes**)
700 - 900g around 2 lbs potatoes, (not the very crumbly variety) diced medium (1.5cm cubes) (see notes)
2 - 3 onions (HF, HFOS, PO (mannitol), LOX and LS) or 6 - 9 shallots or spring onions (green part only) (white part has M-HF, FOS, PO (mannitol) MOX and LS)
2 - 3 cloves of garlic (F, FOS, GOS, LOX and LS)
A pinch pepper (white - VLOX and VHS, black - HOX and VHS)
1 pod of hot pepper cut into strips (**see notes**)
A pinch of cumin (VHS)
3 tablespoons dry sweet paprika (F and VHS)
Vegetable oil or lard to your liking
Salt

Optional extras
Several pods of hot pepper (if you want it really hot) (**see notes**)
Green onions (shallots or spring onions) or parsley (F, PO (mannitol), LOX and LS)

Directions
For roasting meat we can take a vegetable oil or lard (classic) (which had previously been melted in a pan, rendered and skimmed and is ready to start to cooking with).

Place the cut slices of meat in a pan and fry in oil or lard until golden on high heat. Add chopped onion cubes and fry a little more over medium heat and then add cumin and garlic. Add the peppers or capsicum, potatoes, paprika and salt to taste.

Pour boiling water or hot vegetable broth over the meat and vegetables and cover. Reduce the heat to low and simmer until ready, about 30 - 40 min. Remove from heat and let stew for 15 - 20 minutes more for a more authentic taste.

Optionally, you can sprinkle with green onion or parsley on the top of the served dish. (Well, if the day is cool and moist, place the extra hot pepper (not chilli) in the goulash pot and eat. I promise you your body and soul will experience bliss and satisfaction of the extra warming heat).

Notes
It is important to take a good fresh piece meat. If it is blade or the sacrum, the meat is cooked quickly enough and will be very tender. Meat must be cleaned of veins.

Fructose in potatoes can range anything between 582 mg – 989 mg depending on the size, type and skin colour. They also have FOS, PO and GOS. They can also be VHOX and MS again depending on the type of potatoes, colour of skin and how they are cooked.

Peppers, Capsicums and Chilis Substitutes
Avoid green bell peppers or capsicums as they have a completely different flavor profile.
Chili Peppers has F, PO (mannitol) HOX and HS
Red Capsicums has HF, FOS, PO (sorbitol), LOX and VHS
Green Capsicums has HF, FOS, PO (sorbitol), MOX and VHS
Yellow Capsicums has HF, FOS, PO (sorbitol), MOX and VHS
Red Bell Peppers has HF, PO (sorbitol), VLOX and HS
Green Bell Peppers has HF, PO (sorbitol), MOX and VHS
Yellow Bell Peppers has HF, PO (sorbitol), MOX and VHS

HOMEMADE RECIPES FOR THE ABOVE RECIPES

HOMEMADE SAUERKRAUT

Ingredients

1 medium head of cabbage (has 10087mg of Fructose per 100g, FOS, PO (sorbitol), GOS, LOX and LS)
1 - 3 tablespoons sea salt

Directions

Chop or shred cabbage. Sprinkle with salt. Knead the cabbage with clean hands, or pound with a potato masher or cabbage crusher for about 10 minutes, until there is enough liquid to cover the cabbage.

Stuff the cabbage into a quart jar, pressing the cabbage underneath the liquid. If necessary, add a bit of water to completely cover cabbage. Cover the jar with a tight lid, airlock lid, or coffee filter secured with a rubber band.

Culture at room temperature (60 - 70°F is preferred) for at least 2 weeks until desired flavor and texture are achieved. If using a tight lid, burp daily to release excess pressure. Once the sauerkraut is finished, put a tight lid on the jar and move to cold storage. The sauerkraut's flavor will continue to develop as it ages.

* * * * *

HOW TO MAKE TOMATO PASTE THE QUICK AND EASY WAY

This recipe makes about 5 heaped tablespoons.

Soak 2 kilos (4½ lbs) of tomatoes (HF, FOS, PO (mannitol), MOX and MS) in boiling water for five minutes or until the skins can be easily peeled off. Drain and carefully remove the tomato skin. The tomatoes may be hot to handle. Carefully cut tomatoes in half or quarters longways and de-seed completely. Place tomato pieces in to processor and process to a very liquidy paste.

If you have a slow cooker, then place this liquid paste in it and leave it to reduce and thicken up. Stir occasionally. I left mine on all day and got a beautiful thick tomato paste to use in my recipes.

If you don't have a slow cooker you can cook the paste in a 350°F / 180°C preheated oven on shallow trays until it is reduced to a paste. Check the tomatoes every half hour, stirring the paste and switching the position of the trays so that they reduce evenly. Over time, the paste will start to reduce to the point where you can make one tray.

The paste is done when shiny and brick-colored, and it has reduced by more than half. There shouldn't be any remaining water or moisture separating from the paste at this point. This will take 3 - 4 hours, though exact baking/cooking times will depend on the juiciness of your tomatoes and your oven. After the paste was cold; I put it in a container and kept it in the refrigerator or freezer

Making small batches when you need it can be useful; however, if you use a lot of tomato paste then just double or triple the amount of tomatoes used. I made a very small batch using the same prep method but I cooked them down in my non-stick frypan over low heat and I continually stirred the mixture. I didn't add anything to the paste.

TONGA

The following recipes were kindly donated to me by Leafa.

The vegetables and fruit in these recipes will only make them Fructose Friendly. I have tried to source out whether they have Fructose, Fructans, Polyols or Galactans in them and have indicated this beside the ingredient plus a few ingredients have alternatives beside them or in the notes at the end of each recipe. I am hoping that this will help you as much as it has helped me. Salicylates and Oxalates may also be issues for some people so I have added them as well. They will all be noted in the code form below or mentioned in the notes. Please read these.

Low – L, Medium – M, High – H, Very High – VH, Salicylates – S, Oxalates – OX
Fructose – F, Fructans – FOS, Polyols – PO, Galactans – GOS

I have placed some homemade recipes for substituting the ingredients after the main recipes. These recipes will be for Gluten Free, Fructose Friendly, Lactose Free or Friendly, Diabetic Friendly and IBS Friendly depending on your sensitivity so that you can make your own if you want to. Please remember that Fructans, Polyols and Galactans can also come with Fructose.

Substituting ingredients will alter the original taste; however, it is a way to try different recipes from other countries and you can adjust the taste to your liking. Make these recipes your own and use your ingredients if you want to as you know what's best for you.

Australian tablespoons and cups measurements are used and they are: 1 teaspoon equals 5ml; 1 tablespoon equals 20ml; 1 cup equals 250ml. Oven temperatures are for conventional; if using fan-forced (convection), reduce the temperature by 20°C.

Raw Fish	163
Curry Tin Fish Soup	163
Hangi	164
Stuffing	164
Homemade Recipes For The Above Recipes	
Homemade Curry Paste	165
Homemade Curry Powder	165

RAW FISH

This is a recipe for you to cook to suit the size of your family

Basic Ingredients
Fish to your liking
Juice of half a lemon (F, PO (sorbitol), LOX and L-HS)
Shallots (green parts only) (white part has M-HF, FOS, PO (mannitol) MOX and LS)
Tomatoes (HF, FOS, PO (mannitol), MOX and MS)
Coconut cream (HF, FOS, PO (sorbitol) and HS) or Lactose Free cream or one to your liking
Salt and pepper (black - HOX and VHS, white - VLOX and VHS)

Directions
Dice the fish and soak in the lemon juice, salt and pepper.

Chop shallots, dice the tomatoes and add to the fish and mix together.

Add the cream and mix to combine thoroughly.

*   *   *   *   *

CURRY TIN FISH SOUP

This is a recipe for you to cook to suit the size of your family

Basic Ingredients
Tin fish (**not sardines**)
Garlic (F, FOS, GOS, LOX and LS) (see notes)
Onion (HF, HFOS, PO (mannitol), LOX and LS) or 3 shallots per onion (green part only) (white part has M-HF, FOS, PO (mannitol) MOX and LS) (see notes)
Rice (Basmati is low in carbs and has FOS, LOX and MS. Doongara is low in carbs and has FOS and LOX. Soaking rice and grains for 12 hours lowers oxalates)
Curry powder or paste (F and VHS) (homemade recipes after main recipes)
Gluten Free flour or one to your liking (options pages 13 & 14)
Nuttelex Original or butter or oil for frying to your liking
Water
Salt and pepper (black - HOX and VHS, white - VLOX and VHS)

Directions
Dice garlic and onion and fry in butter until transparent and then add the tin fish.

In a different pot, cook the rice.

Mix the flour and water together to make a paste and add to the fish mix.

Add the curry, salt and pepper and stir until thick or to your desired texture.

Serve with the rice.

Notes
If you can't tolerate onions and garlic; try using a pinch - ⅛ teaspoon of asafoetida powder (may contain Gluten) instead of using both depending on the amount you are making. Asafoetida powder is a strong spice so only use the amount specified.

HANGI

Hangi's are a traditional way for not only Tongans but other Islanders to come together to eat as a family or as a celebration. Most of the Islanders have large families and this is a good way to feed them all without having to spend hours in the kitchen cooking. This recipe can also be cooked using slow cookers or a low oven setting but that will depend on the size of the family that you are cooking for. If you are cooking for just a few people, you may wish to decrease the amount of ingredients mentioned to suit.

Ingredients
1kg or 2.2lbs of pork
1kg or 2.2lbs of lamb
1kg or 2.2lbs of chicken
½ kg or 1lb of potatoes (see notes)
½ kg or 1lb of pumpkin (M-HF, FOS, PO (mannitol) and MS)
½ kg or 1lb of cabbage (HF, HFOS, PO (sorbitol), GOS, LOX and LS)

Directions
Dig a hole in the ground and build a fire and place coals in the fire. Allow the fire to die done leaving the red hot coals.

Wrap the meats, potatoes, pumpkin and cabbage separately in foil and place on the coals and cover with a layer of soil. Let cook for at least 4 hours or until you feel the meat will be cooked through or to your liking. Remove the dirt on top carefully and remove the food. Unwrap and place on serving plates.

For slow cookers place the vegetables in the bottom and place the meat on top. Cover and cook slowly until the meat is cooked to your liking.

For cooking in the over, you can cover the vegetables and meat with foil and cook in roast pans in a low over until the meat is done to your liking.

Notes
If you would like you can cook other vegetables as well or instead of those mentioned. Just remember that some vegetables might go very soft if cooked for too long.

Fructose in potatoes can range anything between 582 mg – 989mg depending on the size, type and skin colour. They also have FOS, PO and GOS. They can also be VHOX and MS again depending on the type of potatoes, colour of skin and how they are cooked.

*   *   *   *   *

STUFFING
This is a recipe for you to cook to suit the size of your family

Basic Ingredients
Gluten Free bread or one to your liking (options on pages 13 & 14)
Nuttelex Original or butter to your liking
Mixed herbs of your choice

Directions
Crumb the bread, mix in the butter and then add the mixed herbs.
Mix until dough like and wrap in foil. Cook in the ground, slow cooker or oven with the rest of the Hangi or when you need some stuffing to go with your meal.

HOMEMADE RECIPES FOR THE ABOVE RECIPES

HOMEMADE CURRY PASTE

Ingredients
2 tablespoons coriander (ground or fresh or dry leaves) (MOX and HS)
1 tablespoon ground cumin (VHS)
1½ tablespoons ground cardamon (LOX and HS)
1 teaspoon turmeric (F, VHOX and VHS)
1 teaspoon ground fennel seed (LS) (see notes)
2 teaspoons crushed ginger or ground (F, FOS, LOX and MS)
2½ tablespoons lemon juice (F, PO (sorbitol), LOX and L-HS)

Directions
Combine coriander, cumin, turmeric, ginger, cardamon, fennel seed and lemon to form a paste.

Notes
Fennel seeds are Fructose Friendly and safe to use but the rest of the plant isn't due to its fructose value.

* * * * *

HOMEMADE CURRY POWDER

Ingredients
2 tablespoons whole cumin seeds, toasted (HOX)
2 tablespoons whole cardamom seeds, toasted (LOX and HS)
2 tablespoons whole coriander seeds, toasted (MOX and HS)
¼ cup ground turmeric (F, VHOX and VHS)
1 tablespoon dry mustard powder (VLOX and VHS)

Directions
Grind the cumin seeds, cardamon seeds and coriander seeds to a powder. Add the turmeric and dry mustard and mix well. Store in an airtight container.

HUNGARY

The following recipes were kindly donated to me by Tommy Gaál and other people from the Hungarian Community.

The vegetables and fruit in these recipes will only make them Fructose Friendly. I have tried to source out whether they have Fructose, Fructans, Polyols or Galactans in them and have indicated this beside the ingredient plus a few ingredients have alternatives beside them or in the notes at the end of each recipe. I am hoping that this will help you as much as it has helped me. Salicylates and Oxalates may also be issues for some people so I have added them as well. They will all be noted in the code form below or mentioned in the notes. Please read these.

Low – L, Medium – M, High – H, Very High – VH, Salicylates – S, Oxalates – OX
Fructose – F, Fructans – FOS, Polyols – PO, Galactans – GOS

I have placed some homemade recipes for substituting the ingredients after the main recipes. These recipes will be for Gluten Free, Fructose Friendly, Lactose Free or Friendly, Diabetic Friendly and IBS Friendly depending on your sensitivity so that you can make your own if you want to. Please remember that Fructans, Polyols and Galactans can also come with Fructose.

Substituting ingredients will alter the original taste; however, it is a way to try different recipes from other countries and you can adjust the taste to your liking. Make these recipes your own and use your ingredients if you want to as you know what's best for you.

All measurements are Australian tablespoons and cups: 1 teaspoon equals 5ml; 1 tablespoon equals 20ml; 1 cup equals 250ml. Oven temperatures are for conventional; if using fan-forced (convection), reduce the temperature by 20°C.

Paprika's Csirke	167
Salte Things	167
Rakott Krumpli	168
Nudels	168
Paloc Soup	169
Hungarian Gulyas	170
Hungarian Baked Bluefish	171
Hungarian Walnut Pastries or Kiffles	172
Homemade Recipes For The Above Recipes	
Homemade Pinched Noodles	173

PAPRIKA'S CSIRKE

Ingredients
Chicken pieces to suit your family
2 capsicum cut into 4 - 5 pieces (HF, FOS, PO (sorbitol), (Green) MOX and VHS, (Red) LOX and VHS)
1 small tomato (HF, FOS, PO (mannitol), MOX and MS)
3 onions cut up small (HF, HFOS, PO, (mannitol), LOX and LS) or 9 spring onions (green parts only) (white parts have M-HF, FOS, PO (mannitol) MOX and LS)
½ glass water and oil (to your choosing) mixed
2 - 3 teaspoons paprika (F and VHS)
Small Lactose Free sour cream bottle or carton or one to your liking
Salt and pepper (black - HOX and VHS, white - VLOX and VHS) to taste

Directions
Place the capsicum, tomato, onion and water and oil mixture in a pot and simmer for half an hour. Add more water if needed.

Add salt, pepper and paprika and cook for a further 5 minutes.

Add the chicken pieces and simmer in the covered pot over a medium heat until chicken is cooked.

When the chicken is cooked, take it out and add the small sour cream and stir while simmering until the cream has dissolved. Sift sauce if you want to.

*   *   *   *   *

SALTE THINGS

Ingredients
Small packet/bag (7g) yeast (bakers - MOX and LS, non- bakers - MOX and VHS)
1 cup warm, **not hot,** water
½ teaspoon salt (see notes)
1 cup Gluten Free plain flour or one to your liking (see notes) (options on pages 13 & 14)
2 teaspoons lard/shortening/unsalted butter to your liking (**see notes**)

Directions
Place yeast, water and salt in a bowl and let sit for 5 minutes until it bubbles. Add flour and lard and mix together by hand. Let it sit until it rises.

Put it on a board and flatten and then cut into 4 - 5" square. Slice it in the middle and let it sit to rise further.

Deep fry the pieces until brown and drain on absorbent paper towel.

Notes
Do not use sugar as the salt will activate the yeast.

You can't substitute butter for lard one to one because butter is about 80% fat, 20% liquid. The correct ratio is one cup + 3 tablespoons of butter per one cup of lard If you want to use all vegetable shortening, you can substitute one to one because both are 100% fat.

Gluten Free flour is high in carbs and needs more liquid so you may need to adjust the water.

RAKOTT KRUMPLI

Ingredients (use the amount to suit your size family)
Potatoes, boiled until tender, then peeled and sliced (see notes)
Eggs, hard boiled
Hungarian csabai (sausage), thickly sliced (If you can't find csabai, you can use Spanish chorizo sausage which is similar) or one to your liking
Red onion, diced (HF, HFOS, PO (mannitol), MOX and MS) (see notes)
Lactose Free Sour cream or one to your liking
Gluten Free Fresh breadcrumbs or one to your liking
Mild Hungarian paprika (F and VHS)

Directions
Preheat oven to 180°C / 350°F.

Lightly brush ceramic baking dish with oil.

Sauté onion until soft and add sour cream, stirring.

Layer the potato then egg then csabai, seasoning in between.

Pour over sour cream mixture.

Repeat layers, finishing with a layer of potato.

Sprinkle over breadcrumbs and paprika and bake for 35 - 40 minutes until golden.

Notes
Fructose in potatoes can range anything between 582 mg – 989 mg depending on the size, type and skin colour. They also have FOS, PO and GOS. They can also be VHOX and MS again depending on the type of potatoes, colour of skin and how they are cooked.

Instead of using red onion, you could try using the green parts only of 3 spring onions (for each onion) (white parts have M-HF, FOS, PO (mannitol) MOX and LS). This will also change the flavour.

*   *   *   *   *

NUDELS

Ingredients
2 eggs
½ teaspoon salt
3 cups Gluten Free plain flour or one to your choosing (see notes) (options on pages 13 & 14)

Directions
Mix the ingredients together until you get a paste or glue like mixture.

Drop spoonfuls of mixture into boiling salt water and cook for 5 - 10 minutes or until they come to the top.

Rinse in fresh water.

Notes
You may need to thin with a little milk if using Gluten Free flour and mixture is too thick.

PALOC SOUP

Ingredients
3 lb (about 1.4kg) neck of mutton (or 1¾ lb (900g) without bones)
1 clove of garlic (F, FOS, GOS, LOX and LS) (see notes)
1 bay leaf (VHS)
1 lb or 500g potatoes (see notes)
A few caraway seeds (HS)
1 lb or 500g French/green beans (HF, FOS, PO (sorbitol), VLOX and MS)
Salt
½ lb (250g) onions (HF, HFOS, PO, (mannitol), LOX and LS) or ¼ lb (125g) spring onions (green parts only) (white parts have M-HF, FOS, PO (mannitol) MOX and LS) (see notes)
2 heaped teaspoons Gluten Free flour or one to your liking
2 oz lard/ shortening/unsalted butter to your liking (see notes)
4 tablespoons Lactose Free sour cream or one to your liking
1 teaspoon red paprika (F and VHS)

Directions
Cut the mutton into small cubes, and prepare the vegetables.

Fry the chopped onions in the smoking hot lard until golden brown, sprinkle with paprika, and quickly add the mutton, garlic, bay leaf, caraway seeds and salt, and cook for 15 minutes.

Meanwhile, cut the potatoes into cubes, and cook them and the beans.

When both are soft, pour them with their liquid over the meat.

Add the flour, blended with a little cold water, re-boil, and lastly add the cream.

Do not re-boil after adding the cream.

Notes
Fructose in potatoes can range anything between 582 mg – 989 mg depending on the size, type and skin colour. They also have FOS, PO and GOS. They can also be VHOX and MS again depending on the type of potatoes, colour of skin and how they are cooked.

You can't substitute butter for lard one to one because butter is about 80% fat, 20% liquid. The correct ratio is one cup + 3 tablespoons of butter per one cup of lard If you want to use all vegetable shortening, you can substitute one to one because both are 100% fat.

If you can't tolerate onions and garlic, try using a pinch of asafoetida powder instead (may contain Gluten and is a strong spice, so only use specified amount).

HUNGARIAN GULYAS

Ingredients to serve 4 to 6 people
4 slices smoked bacon
2 medium-sized onions, sliced (HF, HFOS, PO, (mannitol), LOX and LS) or 6 spring onions (green parts only) (white parts have M-HF, FOS, PO (mannitol) MOX and LS) (see notes)
1 - 1½ tablespoons Hungarian paprika (F and VHS)
2 lbs (900g) chuck blade or boneless pot roast, cut into small cubes
1 tablespoon salt
1 teaspoon caraway seeds (HS)
3 green peppers (HF, FOS, PO (sorbitol), MOX and VHS) or capsicums (HF, FOS PO (sorbitol), MOX and VHS), sliced (see notes for substitute ideas)
3 tomatoes, sliced (HF, FOS, PO (mannitol), MOX and MS)
2 cloves garlic through garlic press (F, FOS, GOS, LOX and LS) (see notes)
4 small potatoes, pared and quartered (you can use new unpeeled potatoes) (see notes)
Pinched noodles (homemade recipe after main recipes)
Green pepper rings (HF, FOS, PO (sorbitol), MOX and VHS) or green capsicum rings (HF, FOS PO (sorbitol), MOX and VHS) for garnish (optional)

Directions
Brown the bacon in a Dutch oven or heavy, 3 quart pot.

Remove bacon and brown onions in the bacon drippings until transparent.

Remove pot from heat and stir in paprika (paprika is high in sugar and burns easily).

Add the beef, salt, caraway seeds, cooked bacon and half of the green pepper and tomato.

Return to heat and cover tightly. Simmer over low heat, stirring occasionally and adding small amounts of warm water if needed.

Cook 1½ - 2 hours or until meat is tender.

Add garlic, potatoes, the other half of the green pepper and tomato. Add enough water, if needed, to cover the meat and vegetables. Bring to a boil, and then simmer for 30 minutes.

In the last 10 minutes add the pinched noodles.

Serve hot in individual soup bowl or from a soup tureen. Garnish with green pepper rings.

Notes
If you can't tolerate onions and garlic, try using ⅛ teaspoon asafoetida powder instead (may contain Gluten and is a strong spice, so only use the specified amount).

Fructose in potatoes can range anything between 582 mg – 989 mg depending on the size, type and skin colour. They also have FOS, PO and GOS. They can also be VHOX and MS again depending on the type of potatoes, colour of skin and how they are cooked.

Substitutions for green and bell peppers/capsicums in cooking include zucchini (HF, FOS, PO (sorbitol), VLOX and VHS) which is an ideal candidate for replacing because you can chop it or dice it into similar sizes, and unpeeled, it adds the same color as a pepper. You can use green or yellow zucchini, yellow summer squash (HF, PO (sorbitol) and HOX), carrots (HF, FOS (raffinose), PO (sorbitol), GOS, VHOX and HS) and celery (HF, FOS, PO (mannitol) and VHOX).

HUNGARIAN BAKED BLUEFISH

Ingredients

6 medium potatoes (see notes)
2½ lb or about 1kg large bluefish fillets (or substitute mackerel, trout or thin salmon fillets)
1 sliced green pepper/capsicum (HF, FOS, PO (sorbitol), MOX and VHS) (see notes for substitutions)
2 sliced tomatoes (HF, FOS, PO (mannitol), MOX and MS)
¼ lb or 250g bacon, in 1" strips
1 teaspoon paprika (F and VHS)
1 cup Lactose Free sour cream (at room temperature) or one to your liking

Directions

Preheat oven to 400°F / 200°C.

Peel and cut potatoes into ¼ inch slices. Boil them in salted water for 5 minutes; drain and scatter over bottom of large buttered baking dish.

Make slashes in fish about ¾ inch apart and insert in each one a slice of green pepper, tomato, and bacon.

Place fish over potatoes, sprinkle with paprika, and bake 20 minutes. Spread with sour cream and bake 5 minutes more. Serve.

Notes

Fructose in potatoes can range anything between 582 mg – 989 mg depending on the size, type and skin colour. They also have FOS, PO and GOS. They can also be VHOX and MS again depending on the type of potatoes, colour of skin and how they are cooked.

Substitutions for green and bell peppers/capsicums in cooking include Zucchini (HF, FOS, PO (sorbitol), VLOX and VHS) which is an ideal candidate for replacing because you can chop it or dice it into similar sizes, and unpeeled, it adds the same color as a pepper. You can use green or yellow zucchini, yellow summer squash (HF, PO (sorbitol) and HOX), carrots (HF, FOS (raffinose), PO (sorbitol), GOS, VHOX and HS) and celery (HF, FOS, PO (mannitol) and VHOX).

HUNGARIAN WALNUT PASTRIES OR KIFFLES

Ingredients to make about 48 pastries (these will take 2 days to make)
250g or 1 cup Lactose Free cream cheese or one to your liking (homemade recipe on page 38)
225g or 8oz or 1 cup Nuttelex Original or butter or one to your liking
3 egg yolks
1 teaspoon vanilla extract (F, VLOX and VHS)
310g or 2½ cups Gluten Free plain flour or one to your liking (see notes) (options on pages 13 & 14)
1 pinch salt
½ teaspoon baking powder (VLOX)
3 egg whites
225g or 1¾ cups ground walnuts (VHOX and HS) (see notes)
200g or 1 cup dextrose powder (Fructose Free and may contain Gluten) or caster sugar
40g or ⅓ cup of dextrose powder (Fructose Free and may contain Gluten) or icing sugar for decoration

Directions
Day 1
In a medium bowl, cream the butter and cream cheese. Stir in the egg yolks and vanilla.

Stir together the flour and baking powder.

Add the flour mixture a little at a time to the cream cheese mix until it is fully incorporated.

Divide dough into 5 parts, wrap in cling film and refrigerate overnight.

Day 2
Preheat oven to 180°C / 350°F.

In a medium bowl, beat egg whites to soft peaks. Add sugar a little at a time while continuing to beat to stiff peaks. Fold in ground walnuts and set aside.

On a lightly floured surface, roll the dough out to 3 - 5mm thickness. Cut into 7.5cm or 3" squares, place ½ teaspoon of filling in the centre of each square and roll up from corner to corner. Place on baking trays and chill until hardened.

Bake pastries for 10 - 12 minutes, until lightly browned. Roll in icing sugar when cool.

Variations
You could place ½ teaspoon of jam or another filling that you might prefer in the centre of each square and just pinch the two opposite corners together in the middle.

If you are not keen on walnuts, then try using a different type of nut instead. (Chestnuts are LOX)

Notes
Gluten Free flour is high in carbs and needs more liquid so you may need to add a touch of milk to bind.

HOMEMADE RECIPES FOR THE ABOVE RECIPES

HOMEMADE PINCHED NOODLES

Ingredients

¾ cup Gluten Free all-purpose flour or one to your liking (options on pages13 & 14)
½ teaspoon salt
1 tablespoon cream of wheat (substitute semolina flour or Farina baby cereal)
1 egg

Directions

Combine flour, salt and cream of wheat.

Break egg into center of the flour mixture. Stir to make a stiff dough.

Knead with your hands until smooth. Pinch off bits of the dough the size of hazelnuts and put them on a floured plate.

When all the noodles are ready: drop them into boiling soup/stock or salted boiling water.

Cook about 10 minutes or until tender. Test for doneness by cutting a noodle open; if it is not floury inside, it is done.

JAMAICA

The following recipes were kindly donated to me by the Jamaican Community.

The vegetables and fruit in these recipes will only make them Fructose Friendly. I have tried to source out whether they have Fructose, Fructans, Polyols or Galactans in them and have indicated this beside the ingredient plus a few ingredients have alternatives beside them or in the notes at the end of each recipe. I am hoping that this will help you as much as it has helped me. Salicylates and Oxalates may also be issues for some people so I have added them as well. They will all be noted in the code form below or mentioned in the notes. Please read these.

Low – L, Medium – M, High – H, Very High – VH, Salicylates – S, Oxalates – OX
Fructose – F, Fructans – FOS, Polyols – PO, Galactans – GOS

I have placed some homemade recipes for substituting the ingredients after the main recipes. These recipes will be for Gluten Free, Fructose Friendly, Lactose Free or Friendly, Diabetic Friendly and IBS Friendly depending on your sensitivity so that you can make your own if you want to. Please remember that Fructans, Polyols and Galactans can also come with Fructose.

Substituting ingredients will alter the original taste; however, it is a way to try different recipes from other countries and you can adjust the taste to your liking. Make these recipes your own and use your ingredients if you want to as you know what's best for you.

Australian tablespoons and cups measurements are used and they are: 1 teaspoon equals 5ml; 1 tablespoon equals 20ml; 1 cup equals 250ml. Oven temperatures are for conventional; if using fan-forced (convection), reduce the temperature by 20°C.

Corn Bread	175
Gluten Free Corn Bread	175
Curried Goat	176
Bammy Cakes	177
Jamaican Jerk Chicken Marinade	178
Mackerel Run Down	179
Jamaican Plantain Tarts	180
Homemade Recipes For The Above Recipes	
Jamaican Curry Powder	182
Homemade Balsamic Vinegar Substitute	182
Homemade Soy Sauce Substitute	183
Vegan Fish Sauce	183
Homemade Food Colouring	184

CORN BREAD

Ingredients
1 cup cornmeal (MOX and HS)
1 cup Gluten Free all-purpose flour or one to your liking (options on pages 13 & 14)
2 tablespoons dextrose powder (may contain Gluten) or sugar
4 tablespoons baking powder (VLOX)
½ teaspoon salt
½ cup Lactose Free milk or coconut milk (HF, FOS, PO (sorbitol), GOS and HS) or one to your liking
2 eggs beaten
¼ cup oil of your choosing

Directions
Preheat oven to 220°F / 105°C.

Grease baking pan.

Mix together cornmeal, flour, sugar and salt.

Whisk together the beaten eggs and coconut milk.

Add to this the dry ingredients and stir, blending well.

Add oil and bake for 25 minutes.

*   *   *   *   *

GLUTEN FREE CORNBREAD

Ingredients to serve 16
2 cups cornmeal (MOX and HS)
2 cups Lactose Free skim milk or one to your liking
½ cup dextrose powder (may contain Gluten) or sugar
2 tablespoons baking powder (VLOX)
See Notes for cooking pan options

Directions
Preheat oven to 350°F / 180°C and brush a cast iron skillet with a little oil preheat with the oven.

Mix all ingredients, adding baking powder last, and making sure to get out all the baking powder lumps you can.

Once the oven and skillet are preheated, pour batter into skillet and bake for 20 - 25 minutes.

Top of cornbread should be golden brown. Cut into 16 pieces.

Notes
A cast iron skillet will give you a crusty, crunchy cornbread.
A springform pan will not give a crust like a heavy skillet will.
Like a springform pan, a square cake pan will not give you a heavy crust
Cornbread molds are often cast iron and give a crunchy crust on all sides.

CURRIED GOAT

Curried Goat is one of the great dishes of Jamaica. If you cannot find goat: substitute lamb instead. Just have the butcher cut the meat, bones and all, into 1 or 2" pieces.

Ingredients
4 - 5 lbs about 2kg goat, sawed into 2" pieces, or lamb shoulder, cut up
2 large yellow onions, peeled and chopped (HF, HFOS, PO, (mannitol), LOX and LS) or 6 spring onions (green parts only) (white parts have M-HF, FOS, PO (mannitol) MOX and LS) (see notes)
1 medium green bell pepper, cored, seeded, and chopped (HF, FOS, PO (sorbitol), MOX and VHS) (see notes for substitute ideas)
4 scallions/spring onions, chopped (green parts only) (white parts have M-HF, FOS, PO (mannitol) and LS)
2 medium tomatoes, chopped (HF, FOS, PO (mannitol), MOX and MS)
4 tablespoons curry powder (homemade Jamaican country-style curry powder recipe after main recipes)
2 teaspoons paprika (F and VHS)
3 cloves garlic, peeled and crushed (F, FOS, GOS LOX and LS) (see notes)
2 tablespoons peanut oil (MS) or one to your liking
2 tablespoons Nuttelex Original or butter or one to your liking
4 cups water
Salt and freshly ground black pepper (HOX and VHS) to taste

Directions
In a large stainless steel bowl or pot, mix all of the ingredients except the oil, butter, water, salt, and pepper. Let marinate for ½ hour.

Separate the meat from the vegetable mixture, reserving the mixture. Heat a large frying pan and brown the meat, in small batches, in the oil and butter.

Place the browned goat in a 10 - 12 quart stove-top casserole and add the reserved vegetables from the marinade as well as any juice. Add 4 cups of water; cover and simmer until tender, about 3 hours for goat and 2½ hours for lamb.

Uncover the pot for the last hour or so in order to thicken the sauce a bit. Add the salt and pepper to taste.

Notes
If you can't tolerate onions and garlic, try using ⅛ teaspoon asafoetida powder (may contain Gluten) instead of both. DO NOT use any more than the amount specified as asafoetida is a strong spice.

Fructose in potatoes can range anything between 582 mg – 989 mg depending on the size, type and skin colour. They also have FOS, PO and GOS. They can also be VHOX and MS again depending on the type of potatoes, colour of skin and how they are cooked.

Substitutions for green and bell peppers/capsicums in cooking include zucchini (HF, FOS, PO (sorbitol), VLOX and VHS) which is an ideal candidate for replacing because you can chop it or dice it into similar sizes, and unpeeled, it adds the same color as a pepper. You can use green or yellow zucchini, yellow summer squash (HF, PO (sorbitol) and HOX), carrots (HF, FOS (raffinose), PO (sorbitol), GOS, VHOX and HS) and celery (HF, FOS, PO (mannitol) and VHOX).

BAMMY CAKES

Ingredients to serve 4-6 people
2 lbs frozen grated cassava defrosted (substitute yuca or potatoes (see notes))
¾ - 1teaspoon salt
1 cup coconut milk (HF, FOS, PO (sorbitol), GOS and HS) or Lactose Free milk or one of your choosing or water
1 tablespoon dextrose powder (may contain Gluten) or sugar (optional)
2 - 3 tablespoon ghee or vegetable oil to your liking

Directions
Depending on your frozen cassava you may have to use a cheesecloth or kitchen cloth and squeeze the grated cassava to get as much liquid out as possible. Use this method to remove all the liquid if using potato or yuca.

Place in large bowl, add salt and sugar. Mix well and then divide mixture into 8 and form circles or patties.

Heat up a fry pan or skillet on medium heat.

Oil the fry pan and add cassava mixture in the fry pan, then begin to flatten dough and form in a circular motion using the back of a spoon. Make sure all the parts of the mixture are oiled.

Cook for about 3 - 4 minutes on each side until lightly brown. You may have to do so in batches.

Submerge the Bammy in coconut milk for about 15 - 20 minutes.

Remove and lightly pat dry using a clean cloth or paper napkin Refry or grill on both sides for another 4 - 5 minutes until golden brown or according to your preference.

Serve Warm.

Notes
Fructose in potatoes can range anything between 582 mg – 989 mg depending on the size, type and skin colour. They also have FOS, PO, and GOS. They can also be VHOX and MS again depending on the type of potatoes, colour of skin and how they are cooked.

JAMAICAN JERK CHICKEN MARINADE

Ingredients to make about 3 cups
5 scallions (green onions/spring onions) (green parts only) (white parts have M-HF, FOS, PO (mannitol) MOX and LS)
1 onion (HF, HFOS, PO, (mannitol), LOX and LS) or 3 spring onions/scallions (green parts only) (white parts have M-HF, FOS, PO (mannitol) MOX and LS) (see notes)
2 cloves garlic (F, FOS, GOS, LOX and LS) (see notes) (omit if you can't tolerate)
5 sprigs of fresh thyme (about 1 tablespoon chopped) (LOX and VHS) or about ½ tablespoon dried thyme
2 teaspoons salt
½ teaspoon black pepper (HOX and VHS)
4 - 5 tablespoon brown sugar (Fructose Friendly) or for Fructose Free use dextrose powder (may contain Gluten)
2 teaspoons ground allspice (VHS)
1 teaspoon nutmeg (VLOX and VHS)
1 teaspoon cinnamon (F, HOX and VHS)
2 - 4 hot chili peppers (see notes)
⅓ cup soy sauce (FOS) (homemade substitute recipe after main recipes)
2 tablespoons vegetable oil or one to your liking
¼ cup vinegar (L-MOX and VHS)
½ cup orange juice (HF, PO (sorbitol), VLOX and MS)
1 teaspoon grated ginger (F, FOS, LOX and MS)
1 lime squeezed (F, PO and LOX)

Directions
Place all ingredients into a blender and process into a smooth paste. For best results use this sauce immediately; but marinate your chicken, pork, or fish for at least 2 hours before grilling or roasting in the oven.

Preheat the oven to 375°F / 190°C. Line a baking dish with aluminium foil to make the clean-up after easier.

Place your meat/chicken in a zip lock bag or bowl with a lid, pour the jerk marinade and mix everything well. Now seal and place in the fridge for at least 2 hours. (Tofu and veggies don't need to marinate since they absorb marinades really quickly).

Place the baking dish with the meat/chicken on the middle rack and allow this to cook for about 1 hour.

After about 45 minutes, turn your meat/chicken to the other side, coat it with more sauce and cook it for another 10 minutes. If you want to add some rich color to the finished dish, you can pop it under your broiler/grill for a few minutes.

Notes
In Jamaica scotch bonnet peppers are used and they are the hottest Chilis that you can get. To substitute try using ¼ teaspoon of cayenne pepper (LOX and VHS) to start with. I would start with a little less and keep tasting and adding more cayenne until I reached the right heat.

If you can't tolerate onions and garlic: try using ⅛ teaspoon asafoetida powder (may contain Gluten) instead of both. DO NOT use any more than the amount specified as asafoetida is a very strong spice. Personally I would omit the garlic and just use all the green parts of the spring onion/scallions even though the taste would be different.

MACKEREL RUN DOWN

Mackerel Run Down - salted mackerel, is call "pickled mackerel" in Jamaica. It is cooked in coconut milk and is another all-time favourite Jamaican dish, and it is great served with Bammy, Yam or Hard Dough Bread. It is commonly eaten for Breakfast or Brunch, but is good at any time of the day, and it is very quick and easy to make.

Ingredients
2 lbs or 900gm of salt mackerel (see alternative)
1 sweet pepper or capsicum (see notes)
1 hot chili pepper (see notes)
2 large or 3 small tomatoes (HF, FOS, PO (mannitol), MOX and MS)
6 stalks scallion or spring onions (green parts only) diced (white part has M-HF, FOS, PO (mannitol) MOX and LS)
1 large or 2 small onions (HF, HFOS, PO (mannitol), LOX and LS) or 6 spring onions (green parts only) diced (white part has M-HF, FOS, PO (mannitol) MOX and LS)
3 - 4 sprigs fresh thyme (LOX and VHS)
1 clove chopped garlic or a little garlic powder (F, FOS, GOS, LOX and LS)
3 cups of coconut milk (freshly made, or tinned, or made from powder) (HF, FOS, PO (sorbitol), GOS and HS) or one to your liking
Black pepper to taste (HOX and VHS)

Directions
Soak the mackerel in a large pot of cold water overnight. Change the water, bring to the boil and simmer for 20 mins. When done flake the fish off the bones and discard the bones and head.

Cut up the sweet pepper or capsicum, the chili pepper, the tomatoes, the scallion and the onions into strips or bite size pieces and stir fry. Add the fresh thyme and stir fry. Add the flaked mackerel and the coconut milk and simmer for another 5 minutes, remove sprigs of thyme.

You can serve Mackerel Run Down with anything you wish.

Alternative
If you can't find salt mackerel where you are, buy some fresh mackerel, fillet it, sprinkle it with salt and lime or lemon, and leave overnight in the fridge.

Next day the mackerel will already look cooked. Rinse and cut the fillets in to bite-sized pieces. Add stir-fried ingredients, fish and coconut milk to a frying pan and simmer for about 10 minutes until hot right through.

This will be an equally delicious and close substitute for the real thing.

Notes
In Jamaica Scotch Bonnet peppers are used and they are the hottest Chilis that you can get (F, PO (mannitol), HOX and HS).

Peppers, Green has HF, PO (sorbitol), MOX and VHS
Peppers, Red has HF, PO (sorbitol), VLOX and VHS
Capsicum, Red has HF, FOS, PO (sorbitol), LOX and VHS
Capsicum, Green has HF, FOS, PO (sorbitol), MOX and VHS
Capsicum, Yellow has HF, FOS, PO (sorbitol) MOX and VHS

JAMAICAN PLANTAIN TARTS

The Jamaican Plantain Tart is true island food. The luscious ripe plantain filling is sweet, flavorful and bright red in color.

Ingredients
For the filling
1 medium very ripe plantain, peeled and diced (high Carbs) (banana has a different texture but you can substitute with an unripened banana) (Bananas have F, FOS (inulin) PO (sorbitol), GOS and MOX. No info on Plantains found)
2 - 4 tablespoons dextrose powder (may contain Gluten) or sugar or sweetener to your liking
¼ cup orange juice (HF, PO (sorbitol), VLOX and MS)
1 teaspoon nutmeg (VLOX and VHS)
1 tablespoon Nuttelex Original or butter or one to your liking
2 teaspoons vanilla essence (F, VLOX and VHS)
Red food coloring (optional) (homemade after main recipes)

For the pastry
1⅓ cups Gluten Free flour or one to your liking (see notes) (options on pages 13 & 14)
½ teaspoons salt
¾ cup ice cold Nuttelex Original or butter or one to your liking
3 tablespoons Lactose Free sour cream or one to your liking
Ice cold water as needed

Directions
For the Filling
Place orange juice and plantain/banana into a small saucepan and cook over low heat for about 5 minutes. Add butter, vanilla and spices and cook until plantain/banana is soft and begins to break apart. Crush plantain/banana to get a smooth filling that is not too runny or too dry.

Set the mixture to cool to room temperature. Add sugar to taste as the sweetness of the plantain/banana affects how much sugar you need.

For the Pastry
Sift the flour and salt into a large mixing bowl. Combine the cold butter and flour mix together until the mixture resembles wet sand with only a few larger pieces.

Add the sour cream and a tablespoonful of water at a time, mixing until the dough binds together without getting sticky.

Use your hands to pat the dough into a ball and place on parchment paper on a flat surface.

Roll the dough to a rectangular shape, about 10" or 25cm long.

Fold dough over in thirds, like you would if you were folding a letter. Rotate the folded dough and roll out again.

Repeat at least twice. The dough will come together more cohesively with each turn and roll.

Place the folded dough in the fridge for minimum of 30 minutes. Once removed from the fridge, roll out to about ⅛" or 3cm thick.

Use an inverted bowl to cut 4" or 10cm circles from your dough and use a spoon to add some of the filling.

Fold over and seal using a fork to crimp the edges together. Use the fork to prick holes in the top of each tart.

Pop the tarts back in the fridge for about 5 minutes before baking.

Bake at 400°F / 200°C in a preheated oven for 10 minutes and then 12 - 15 minutes at 350°F / 180°C.

Tarts are done when they are golden brown and flaky.

Notes
Use a sheet of parchment paper on top of the dough and use the rolling pin over that. It makes the job of rolling much easier. Do not knead the dough as it makes the dough overworked. Handle as little as possible.

Gluten Free flour has a higher carb count so be mindful of this if you are watching your carbs or Diabetic. You may need to adjust the liquid if using Gluten Free flour as it tends to need a little bit more.

HOMEMADE RECIPES FOR THE ABOVE RECIPES

As I never had a recipe for Jamaican Curry Powder, I got this one from http://www.spice-mixes.com/jamaican-curry-powder.html. It is different from the Indian Curry Powder that is normally used for curries.

JAMAICAN CURRY POWDER

Ingredients (makes about 10 tablespoons)
4 tablespoons coriander seeds (MOX and HS)
1 tablespoon turmeric (F, VHOX and VHS)
1 tablespoon fenugreek seeds (PO, MOX and VHS)
1 tablespoon ground ginger (F, FOS, LOX and MS)
1 tablespoon dried thyme (LOX and VHS)
1 tablespoon dried oregano (F, HOX and VHS)
4 teaspoons garlic powder (F, FOS, GOS and LS)
4 teaspoons allspice berries (VHS)
4 teaspoons black peppercorns (HOX and VHS)
3 - 4 teaspoons cayenne pepper (or chili) (LOX and VHS)
2 inch piece cinnamon (F, HOX and VHS)
10 cloves (F VHOX and HS)
2 teaspoons sea salt

Directions
Break up the cinnamon.

Grind the cinnamon pieces with the salt, coriander, peppercorns, cloves, fenugreek and allspice berries and sieve into a bowl.

Add the pre-ground ingredients and combine.

Finally, crumble in the dried thyme and oregano and combine again.

Store your Jamaican curry seasoning in a cool place in a sealed jar out of direct sunlight. Use within 3 months before making more.

Note
To extract even more flavour you can dry toast the coriander, peppercorns, cloves, fenugreek and allspice berries before grinding and combining with the other ingredients.

*   *   *   *   *

HOMEMADE BALSAMIC VINEGAR SUBSTITUTE

For about 1 tablespoon of balsamic vinegar (F, VLOX and HS), combine 1 tablespoon red wine vinegar (L-MOX and VHS) and ½ teaspoon sugar

For Fructose friendly, substitute the sugar for dextrose.

HOMEMADE SOY SAUCE SUBSTITUTE

Ingredients for about ⅔ cup
1 cup beef broth (Gluten Free and minus the garlic and onion)
2 tablespoons balsamic vinegar (F, VLOX and HS) (substitute recipe in this section)
2 teaspoons white wine vinegar (L-MOX and VHS) or rice wine vinegar
3 teaspoons rice malt syrup (Fructose Free)
⅛ teaspoon ground black pepper (HOX and VHS)
A pinch of asafoetida powder (may contain Gluten and is a strong spice)
⅛ teaspoon ground ginger (F, FOS, LOX and MS)
¼ teaspoon salt or to taste
½ teaspoon fish sauce (optional) (homemade Vegan substitute in this section)

Directions
Place the following in a small saucepan: broth, both of the vinegars, rice malt syrups, black pepper, asafoetida and ground ginger. Bring to a brief boil over medium-high heat, and then reduce heat to a gentle simmer - small bubbles should just break on the surface. Cook until reduced to about ⅔ cup - this takes about 7 - 10 minutes. (NOTE: If you accidentally cook it longer, the flavors of the vinegar and syrup will be concentrated, and it becomes quite sweet. Keep an eye on the clock and don't miss that 10 minute max).

Remove the pan from the heat. Add the salt and fish sauce; stir to combine and taste to make sure it's salty enough for you. Pour into a glass container and allow to cool. Store it in the refrigerator for up to 10 days.

This sauce can be used in any recipe that calls for soy sauce.

Notes
⅛ teaspoon coarse (granulated) garlic powder can replace the asafoetida powder.
2 teaspoons cider vinegar (F, L-MOX and VHS) can replace white wine vinegar or rice wine vinegar.
Molasses (F and MOX) will replace rice malt syrup for a stronger flavour.

*   *   *   *   *

VEGAN FISH SAUCE

Ingredients for about ½ cup or 125 ml
¼ cup warm filtered or spring water
2 tablespoons raw turbinado sugar (for Fructose Friendly use dextrose powder instead and may contain Gluten)
¼ cup fresh or canned 100% pineapple juice (HF, PO (mannitol), VLOX and MS)
2 tablespoons light soy sauce (FOS) or tamari (homemade substitute in this section)

Directions
Stir the water and sugar together in a bowl until sugar dissolves. Add the pineapple juice and light soy sauce and mix well. Refrigerate in a glass container or jar with a lid for an hour or so. This may last up to 3 - 4 days.

Notes
This version is intended to make it saltier like 'light soy sauce': Alternatively instead of 2 tablespoons light soy sauce, use 1 tablespoon Gluten Free tamari and 1 tablespoon Gluten Free chicken free broth. You want it to be slightly saltier and lighter.

HOMEMADE FOOD COLOURING

And as an alternative, you can use natural food dye in a savory recipe. Remember, food dye isn't reserved just for sweets and treats. Remember that working with natural coloring will be different than the artificially amplified colors you're probably used to. In general you can expect a paler, more pastel-type of result. It is best if you experiment, play around with quantities and combinations, add a little at a time, and always taste as you go. Most importantly, let your creative juices flow, and have fun with it.

Pink and Red

You can use any number of options, but for a ton of color with almost no flavor, beets (HF, FOS, PO (mannitol), GOS, VHOX and MS) are your best bet. Use the juice from the canned kind, or make your own by either boiling or juicing the raw vegetable. Alternately, you can also use any red fruit, like red raspberries (F, PO (xylitol), HOX and VHS) or pomegranate (HF, MFOS, PO (sorbitol), GOS, MOX and HS). Just know that these may change the flavor – which can be a great thing. To procure your dye, pulverize the berries in a food processor or blender, then strain out the colored liquid using a mesh sieve or cheesecloth.

Pink/Red/Magenta: Juiced berries, Juiced cranberries, Juiced beetroot Juiced red capsicum, Juiced tomato, choose dark red tomatoes, rhubarb juiced or boiled, pomegranate juice, chili powder or paprika powder. The juicing of some vegetables and fruits can change the composition in them, especially where OX and S stand, so I will leave this one in your hands if you want to try them.

SWITZERLAND

The following recipes were kindly donated to me by the Swiss Community.

The vegetables and fruit in these recipes will only make them Fructose Friendly. I have tried to source out whether they have Fructose, Fructans, Polyols or Galactans in them and have indicated this beside the ingredient plus a few ingredients have alternatives beside them or in the notes at the end of each recipe. I am hoping that this will help you as much as it has helped me. Salicylates and Oxalates may also be issues for some people so I have added them as well. They will all be noted in the code form below or mentioned in the notes. Please read these.

Low – L, Medium – M, High – H, Very High – VH, Salicylates – S, Oxalates – OX
Fructose – F, Fructans – FOS, Polyols – PO, Galactans – GOS

I have placed some homemade recipes for substituting the ingredients after the main recipes. These recipes will be for Gluten Free, Fructose Friendly, Lactose Free or Friendly, Diabetic Friendly and IBS Friendly depending on your sensitivity so that you can make your own if you want to. Please remember that Fructans, Polyols and Galactans can also come with Fructose. Make these recipes your own and use your ingredients if you want to as you know what's best for you.

Substituting ingredients will alter the original taste; however, it is a way to try different recipes from other countries and you can adjust the taste to your liking. Make these recipes your own and use your ingredients if you want to as you know what's best for you.

Australian tablespoons and cups measurements are used and they are: 1 teaspoon equals 5ml; 1 tablespoon equals 20ml; 1 cup equals 250ml. Oven temperatures are for conventional; if using fan-forced (convection), reduce the temperature by 20°C.

Pastetli (Meat Pie)	186
Le Papet Vaudois	187
Veau Sauté Aux Champignons et Rösti (Veal and Mushroom Sauce and Rösti)	188
Chocolate Fondue	189
Easy Cheese Fondue	190
Zopf (Bread)	191
Carac (Green Chocolate Tart)	192
Zürcher Eintopf (Hot-pot Zürich style)	193
Homemade Recipes For The Above Recipes	
Homemade Worcestershire Sauce	194
Homemade Curry powder	194
Homemade Mustard Powder	194
Homemade Soy Sauce Substitute	195
Homemade Alternative Ideas For Food Colourings	195
Homemade Gluten Free Rough Puff Pastry	196
Homemade Lactose-Free Buttermilk	197
Dairy Free, Soy Free White Chocolate	198
Homemade Dark Chocolate	198
Homemade White Chocolate	199
Homemade Creme Fraiche	199

PASTETLI (MEAT PIE)

Ingredients for 6 pies
450g or 1lb puff-pastry (homemade Gluten Free Rough Puff Pastry recipe after main recipes) or one to your liking
2 tablespoons Nuttelex Original or margarine or butter or one to your liking
1 shallot, hacked (green parts only) diced (white part has M-HF, FOS, PO (mannitol) MOX and LS) (see notes)
1 clove of garlic, pressed (F, FOS, GOS, LOX and LS) (see notes)
800g (1.75 lbs) small mushrooms cut into four pieces each (see notes)
100ml (3.4 fl. oz) white wine (varies in OX and S) (see notes for substitutes)
180g (6.3oz) half and half sour (see notes)
100ml (3.4 fl. oz) Lactose Free cream or one to your liking
1 teaspoon curry powder (F and VHS) (homemade recipe after main recipes)
1 tablespoon Worcestershire sauce (HS) (homemade recipe after main recipes)
½ teaspoon paprika (F and VHS), a small amount of nutmeg (VLOX and VHS) and cayenne pepper (LOX and VHS)
Salt and pepper (black - HOX and VHS, white - VLOX and VHS)

Directions
Bake 6 large pies made out of the puff-paste for about 15 - 20 minutes.

Heat margarine or butter in a pot and add shallot and clove of garlic, and cook until softened. Add white wine and mushrooms, mix, cover and cook for about 5 minutes.

Increase heat, cook in open pot until half of the fluid has gone. Add half and half and cream, curry, Worcestershire sauce, paprika, nutmeg, pepper and salt.

Distribute the filling into the heated pies, serve immediately.

Notes
You can replace part of the mushrooms with small pieces of veal.
OR
Try substituting normal mushrooms (HF, FOS (raffinose), PO (mannitol and xylitol), GOS, VLOX and MS) for the gourmet style. It has been stated that Shiitake, Enoki, Oyster have low to no Polyols and information for Fructose, Fructans, Oxalates and Salicylates could not be found at all. Usually only "Mushrooms" in general comes up when researching so this ingredient will be your call as what you want to use. I don't have any issues when eating the Gourmet Style mushrooms.

You may want to prepare the pies in advance, but they have to be heated in the oven before the filling gets added.

HALF AND HALF

These recipes can be made by using any ingredient that you use.

2 cups whole Lactose Free milk + 1½ teaspoon butter/Nuttelex OR
½ cup whole Lactose Free milk + ½ cup light Lactose Free cream OR
¾ cup whole Lactose Free milk, ¼ cup heavy cream OR
⅔ cup Lactose Free low-fat or skim milk + ⅓ cup heavy cream.

Just stir in about 1 tablespoon of lemon juice (F, PO (sorbitol), LOX and L-HS) or vinegar (L-MOX and VHS) to mixture and let it sit for 5 minutes. This will make it sour and look curdled.

White wine substitute
Can substitute; white grape juice (F, PO (sorbitol), LOX and MS), apple cider (F), apple juice (F, PO (sorbitol), VLOX and MS), vegetable stock (minus onion and garlic) or water. For ¼ cup or more white wine, substitute the following: equal measure of white grape juice (F, PO (sorbitol), LOX and MS), chicken broth, vegetable broth, or non-alcoholic wine (no info on OX and S). If you use a non-alcoholic wine, add a tablespoon of vinegar to cut the sweetness.

*   *   *   *   *

LE PAPET VAUDOIS

Ingredients to serve 4 people
1 onion finely chopped (HF, HFOS, PO (mannitol), LOX and LS) or 6 spring onions (green parts only) diced (white part has M-HF, FOS, PO (mannitol) MOX and LS)
1¾ lbs or 800g leeks cut into 1" or 2½ cm pieces (F, FOS, PO (mannitol), GOS, MOX and LS) (Try using the green parts only as it is stated that they are safe for people who Malabsorb)
18oz or 510g potatoes sliced (see notes)
⅞ cup or 210ml dry white wine (see notes for substitute)
⅞ cup or 210ml vegetable stock (minus garlic and onion)
½ cup or 120ml evaporated skim milk (homemade recipe after main recipes)
Salt and pepper (black - HOX and VHS, white - VLOX and VHS) to taste
Pinch of nutmeg (VLOX and VHS)

Directions
Sauté the onion in your favorite liquid and then add the leeks and sauté a little more.

Add the white wine and broth, and cook covered for 15 minutes.

Add the potatoes, season with salt, pepper, and nutmeg, and cook another 10 - 15 minutes.

When the potatoes and leeks are tender, add the milk and adjust the seasoning.

Notes
This is traditionally served with sausage on top; if you have a favourite vegetable or two, try them instead of or with the ones suggested.

Very fresh crusty bread is good with this too.

Fructose in potatoes can range anything between 582 mg – 989 mg depending on the size, type and skin colour. They also have FOS, PO and GOS. They can also be VHOX and MS again depending on the type of potatoes, colour of skin and how they are cooked.

Dry white wine substitute
Water, chicken broth (minus onion and garlic), ginger ale (HF and LOX), white grape juice (F, PO (sorbitol), LOX and MS), diluted cider vinegar (F, L-MOX and VHS) or white wine vinegar (L-MOX and VHS).

VEAU SAUTÉ AUX CHAMPIGNONS ET RÖSTI (VEAL AND MUSHROOM SAUCE AND RÖSTI)

Ingredients
2 medium potatoes, boiled in the skin until par cooked, drained (see notes)
1 brown onion, finely chopped (HF, HFOS, PO (mannitol), LOX and LS) or 3 spring onions (green parts only) diced (white part has M-HF, FOS, PO (mannitol) MOX and LS)
Salt and freshly ground black pepper (HOX and VHS)
2 tablespoons vegetable oil or one to your liking
60g Nuttelex Original or butter or one to your liking
450g veal tenderloin, well-trimmed, finely sliced
250g Swiss brown mushrooms (HF, FOS, PO (mannitol and xylitol), GOS, VLOX and MS), sliced (see notes)
50ml dry white wine (varies in Oxalates and Salicylates) (see notes for substitutes)
125ml (½ cup) Lactose Free cream or one to your liking
3 tablespoons chopped parsley (F, PO (mannitol), LOX and LS)

Directions
Peel and grate the potatoes. Place in a bowl with half the onion and season with salt and pepper. Toss until well combined.

Heat half the oil and butter in a large non-stick frypan over a medium-high heat. Divide the potato mixture into thirds and place each portion in a mound in the pan, pressing down firmly with a fish slice to form discs about 1 cm thick. Cook on both sides for 3 - 4 minutes or until golden and crisp. Drain on paper towel and keep warm.

Heat the remaining oil and butter in a large non-stick frying pan over high heat and cook the veal, in batches if necessary just until browned on both sides. (Just sear the veal and don't overcook it).

Add the remaining chopped onion to the pan and stir for 1 minute. Add the mushrooms and cook for a few minutes.

Add the white wine, bring to the boil and evaporate the wine a little. Stir in the cream, bring to the boil and simmer for 1 minute.

Season well with salt and pepper and add the veal to the pan and reheat briefly.

Place the Rösti in the centre of 3 plates and serve the veal and sauce around. Sprinkle with parsley and serve.

Notes
Fructose in potatoes can range anything between 582 mg – 989 mg depending on the size, type and skin colour. They also have FOS, PO and GOS They can also be VHOX and MS again depending on the type of potatoes, colour of skin and how they are cooked.

Try substituting normal mushrooms (HF, FOS (raffinose), PO (mannitol and xylitol), GOS, VLOX and MS) for the gourmet style. It has been stated that Shiitake, Enoki, Oyster have low to no Polyols and information for Fructose, Fructans, Oxalates and Salicylates could not be found at all. Usually only "Mushrooms" in general comes up when researching so this ingredient will be your call as what you want to use. I don't have any issues when eating the Gourmet Style mushrooms.

Dry white wine substitute
Water, chicken broth (minus onion and garlic), ginger ale (HF and LOX), white grape juice (F, PO (sorbitol), LOX and MS), diluted cider vinegar (F, L-MOX and VHS) or white wine vinegar (L-MOX and VHS).

* * * * *

CHOCOLATE FONDUE

Ingredients (Full cream milk is preferred whether it be Lactose Free or another kind)
10oz / 280g bittersweet chocolate or 10oz / 280g semisweet chocolate, chopped into small pieces (F and VHOX) (homemade chocolate recipes after main recipes)
½ - ¾ cup milk (or ½ - ¾ cup milk plus 2 tablespoons unsalted butter) or ½ - ¾ cup half-and-half (or ½ - ¾ cup milk plus 2 tablespoons unsalted butter) or ½ - ¾ cup heavy cream (or ½ - ¾ cup milk plus 2 tablespoons unsalted butter) (see notes)
½ teaspoon vanilla extract (VLOX and VHS)

Directions
To make the sauce, in a small bowl, combine the chocolate and ½ cup milk or cream and melt gently in a barely simmering water bath or microwave on Medium (50%) power for about 2 minutes. Stir until smooth.

Add more liquid if the sauce seems too thick or look curdled.

Remove from the heat and stir in the vanilla.

Use warm fondue immediately or set aside until needed and rewarm briefly.

Have forks, skewers, or pretty (or goofy) swizzle sticks available for guests to dip with.

If the fondue gets too thick or cool, reheat gently (without boiling) for 1 minute in the microwave on Medium (50%) power or set in a pan of barely simmering water.

Leftover sauce keeps several days in the refrigerator.

It is a prefect topping for ice cream.

Note
This is a versatile recipe that can be tailored to your taste and the type of chocolate you are using. I have also placed 2 white chocolate recipes in the section after the main recipes.

For the most intense chocolate fondue, use milk, rather than half-and-half or cream, and omit the butter.

For even greater intensity, choose a bittersweet chocolate labelled anywhere from 66% - 70% and use the greater amount of liquid called for.

Butter or cream results in a softer, mellower chocolate flavor.

EASY CHEESE FONDUE

Ingredients
For the fondue
2 tablespoons cider vinegar (F, L-MOX and VHS) or one to your liking
1 teaspoon cornflour (MOX and HS)
250g cheddar, grated (Lactose Friendly) (other options on page 38)
250g Gruyère, grated (Lactose Friendly) (other options on page 38)
3 tablespoons crème fraîche (see notes for substitute) (homemade recipes after main recipes)

Suggestions for dipping
4 thick slices bread, such as sourdough, chopped into chunks
2 tablespoons olive oil (LOX and HS) or one to your liking
2 carrots cut into batons (HF, FOS (raffinose), PO (sorbitol), GOS, VHOX and HS)
2 peppers/capsicums, deseeded and cut into strips (see notes)
2 celery sticks, thickly sliced (HF, FOS, PO (mannitol, VHOX and Neg S)
200g pack mini salami or 1 thin salami stick cut into bite-size chunks

Directions
Preheat oven to 200°C / 400°F.

Mix the vinegar with the cornflour and place in a heatproof bowl with the cheeses. Set over a pan of boiling water and slowly melt the cheese, stirring occasionally.

When it's nearly melted, add the crème fraîche and a little black pepper, if you like. Lower the heat and keep warm.

To make croutons, toss the bread in the oil and a little seasoning on a baking sheet, then bake for 10 - 15 mins until golden and crisp.

To serve, put the cheese fondue on a large platter and arrange the croutons, veg and salamis alongside it.

Notes
To Replace Crème Fraiche
½ cup soy sour cream processed with ½ cup soy cream cheese
½ cup plain soy yogurt processed with ½ cup soy cream cheese
⅔ cup extra firm silken tofu processed with ⅓ cup soy yogurt or soy sour cream

Peppers, Green has HF, PO (sorbitol), MOX and VHS
Peppers, Red has HF, PO (sorbitol), VLOX and VHS
Peppers yellow has HF, PO (sorbitol), MOX and VHS
Pepper Aleppo pul biber has HF, PO (sorbitol), VLOX and LS
Capsicum red has HF, FOS, PO (sorbitol), LOX and VHS
Capsicum green has HF, FOS, PO (sorbitol), MOX and VHS
Capsicum yellow has HF, FOS, PO (sorbitol), MOX and VHS

ZOPF (BREAD)

Ingredients for 2 breads, about 800g (1.76 lbs) each
1 kg (2.2 lbs) Gluten Free white flour or one to your liking (options on pages 13 & 14) (see notes)
1 tablespoon salt
20 - 30g (0.7 - 1oz) yeast, broken in small pieces (bakers - MOX and LS and non- bakers - MOX and VHS)
1 teaspoon dextrose powder (may contain Gluten) or sugar
125g (4.4oz) Nuttelex Original or butter or margarine or one to your liking, soft
3 cups Lactose Free milk or one to your liking
1 egg yolk, diluted

Directions
Mix flour and salt in a bowl, add yeast, sugar, butter and milk, knead to a soft dough. It will take about 10 minutes by hand, 4 - 5 minutes when using a machine. Cover and let rise for about one hour until size has doubled.

Cut dough in two, three or four pieces of the same size. Roll into even length sausage rolls and weave. (3 weave instructions in notes).

Place bread on baking trays, covered with baking paper, brush with water. Let rise again for about 30 - 60 minutes.

Before baking, brush with the diluted egg yolk.

Bake for about 45 - 55 minutes in the lower part of the pre-heated oven at about 200°C / 400°F.

Serve within 2 - 3 days.

Notes
Gluten Free flour is high in carbs so may not be Diabetic Friendly. You can use normal flour if you are not gluten intolerant but omit the gums as they are not needed and adjust liquids.

How to Make a Three Weave Braid
A three strand braid is typically the easiest braid to make because this braid is often used to braid hair, and is a pattern that most people are familiar with. For this braid, divide the dough into three strands and stretch them out carefully until they are of an even thickness all the way down. Start your braid from the center of the strands to give both ends of the loaf a finished look.

Take the left strand (1) and cross it over the middle strand (2).

Take the right strand (3) and cross it over the middle strand (2).

Repeat crossing left (1) over center (2), followed by right (3) over center (2) until you reach the end.

Pinch the ends together to seal the loaf, and then repeat the process going up the rest of the dough. There is no need to keep track of which strand was originally number 1, 2 or 3 as you go because the pattern is the same the entire time.

CARAC (GREEN CHOCOLATE TART)

Ingredients
Pastry
1 cup Gluten Free flour or one to your liking (options on pages 13 & 14) (see notes)
⅓ cup almond meal (Almonds have FOS, PO (xylitol), VHOX and VHS)
½ cup dextrose powder (may contain Gluten) or powdered sugar
8 tablespoons Nuttelex Original or butter or one to your liking, cut into small cubes
1 egg yolk
1 tablespoon cold water
Pinch of salt

Filling for Carac
7oz dark chocolate (F and VHOX) (homemade recipe after main recipes)
4 tablespoons Lactose Free milk or one to your liking
4 tablespoons Nuttelex Original or butter or one to your liking

Frosting for Carac
1 cup dextrose powder (may contain Gluten) or powdered sugar
2 - 3 drops green food coloring (see notes for substitute)
2 tablespoons cold water

Directions
Pastry
Combine flour and butter in a blender or food processor; mix until dough has a sandy consistency.

Add the almond meal, powdered dextrose/sugar, egg yolk, cold water and salt.

Mix until dough is smooth; place on a floured work surface and knead for several minutes. Be careful not to overwork dough as it might become brittle. Form dough into a ball; place in a greased bowl and cover.

Refrigerate for up to two hours or overnight.

Preheat oven to 350°F / 180°C.

Sprinkle flat work surface with flour; spread the dough and prick with a fork. Place dough in greased tart molds, forming to fit.

Cut off pastry overhand. Bake for fifteen to twenty minutes; set aside to cool.

Filling
Combine milk, chocolate and butter in a small saucepan. Warm over medium heat, stirring gently.

Remove from heat when chocolate is melted and smooth. Allow mixture to cool for about fifteen minutes.

Pour filling into baked and cooled tart shells; refrigerate for two hours.

Frosting
In a bowl, combine the powdered dextrose/sugar, food coloring and water. Stir until mixture becomes thick and fluffy.

Spread frosting on top of chocolate in tart molds and allow to harden at room temperature for about one hour before serving.

Notes

Gluten Free flour is high in carbs so it may not be suitable for Diabetics or people having to watch their carb count. You may also have to adjust the amount of liquid depending on your choice of flour.

*   *   *   *   *

ZÜRCHER EINTOPF (HOT-POT ZÜRICH STYLE)

Ingredients for 4 persons (This recipe may also be cooked in a slow cooker)
750g (1.65 lbs) of meat from pork's neck, cut into pieces of about 3cm (1.2") in size
1 tablespoon of Nuttelex Original or margarine or one to your liking
3 onions, cut in stripes (HF, HFOS, PO (mannitol), LOX and LS) or 9 spring onions (green parts only) diced (white part has M-HF, FOS, PO (mannitol) MOX and LS)
1 garlic, hacked (F, FOS, GOS, LOX and LS) (see notes)
1 teaspoon of caraway seeds (HS)
1 teaspoon of salt
1 savoy cabbage (medium size), cut in large pieces (HF, HFOS, PO (sorbitol), GOS, LOX and LS)
4 - 6 potatoes, peeled, cut in pieces of about 0.5 cm (0.2") (see notes)
2 - 3 carrots, peeled, cut in pieces of about 0.5 cm (0.2") (HF, FOS (raffinose), PO (sorbitol), GOS, VHOX and HS)
Spices of your choice
½ glass of white wine (varies in OX and S) (see notes for substitutions)
½ cup of water

Directions

Put margarine in a pot and heat, roast meat gently. Sauté the onions and garlic until glassy looking. Add caraway, salt and pepper.

Put half of the cabbage onto the meat, add some spices. Add potatoes and carrots, and then put the rest of the cabbage on top of it. Again add some spices.

Add white wine, cover and cook for about 5 minutes and then add water and cook for about 2 - 3hours on a low heat.

Notes

Fructose in potatoes can range anything between 582 mg – 989 mg depending on the size, type and skin colour. They also have FOS, PO and GOS. They can also be VHOX and MS again depending on the type of potatoes, colour of skin and how they are cooked.

White wine substitute

Can substitute; white grape juice (F, PO (sorbitol), LOX and MS), apple cider (F), apple juice (F, PO (sorbitol), VLOX and MS), vegetable stock (minus onion and garlic) or water. For ¼ cup or more white wine, substitute the following: equal measure of white grape juice (F, PO (sorbitol), LOX and MS), chicken broth, vegetable broth, or non-alcoholic wine (no info on OX and S). If you use a non-alcoholic wine, add a tablespoon of vinegar (L-MOX and VHS) to cut the sweetness.

HOMEMADE RECIPES FOR THE ABOVE RECIPES

HOMEMADE WORCESTERSHIRE SAUCE

Ingredients
½ cup white wine vinegar (L-MOX and VHS) or rice wine vinegar
2 tablespoons water
2 tablespoons coconut aminos, Tamarin or Soy Sauce substitute (next recipe)
¼ teaspoon ground ginger (F, FOS, LOX and MS)
¼ teaspoon mustard powder (VLOX and VHS) (homemade recipe below)
A pinch of asafoetida powder (may contain gluten and is a strong spice)
⅛ teaspoon cinnamon (F, HOX and VHS)
⅛ teaspoon freshly ground black pepper (HOX and VHS)

Directions
Combine all the ingredients in a saucepan and slowly bring to a boil while stirring frequently. Let simmer for about a minute for the flavors to develop. Cool and store in the refrigerator.

Notes
¼ teaspoon onion powder (HF, HFOS, PO (mannitol), LOX and LS) and ¼ teaspoon garlic powder (F, FOS, GOS, LOX and LS) will replace the asafoetida powder which is a strong spice.

* * * * *

HOMEMADE CURRY POWDER

Ingredients
2 tablespoons whole cumin seeds, toasted (HOX)
2 tablespoons whole cardamom seeds, toasted (LOX and HS)
2 tablespoons whole coriander seeds, toasted (MOX and HS)
¼ cup ground turmeric (F, VHOX and VHS)
1 tablespoon dry mustard powder (VLOX and VHS) (see homemade recipe next)

Directions
Grind the cumin seeds, cardamon seeds and coriander seeds to a powder. Add the turmeric and dry mustard and mix well. Store in an airtight container.

* * * * *

HOMEMADE MUSTARD POWDER

Ingredients
Mustard seeds to the amount you need (F, FOS, GOS, VLOX and VHS)
Turmeric (F, VHOX and VHS)

Directions
To make a powder, toast your mustard seeds for 20 seconds in a dry skillet. Cool the seeds, then transfer to a spice grinder and pulse until you have a powder.

Pass the powder through a sieve to remove the hulls.

Blend a pinch or two of turmeric with the mustard to create the bright yellow associated with the condiment.

HOMEMADE SOY SAUCE SUBSTITUTE

Ingredients for about ⅔ cup
1 cup beef broth (Gluten Free and minus the garlic and onion)
2 tablespoons balsamic vinegar (F, VLOX and HS) (substitute recipe in this section)
2 teaspoons white wine vinegar (L-MOX and VHS) or rice wine vinegar
3 teaspoons rice malt syrup (Fructose Free)
⅛ teaspoon ground black pepper (HOX and VHS)
A pinch of asafoetida powder (may contain Gluten and is a strong spice so only use specified amount)
⅛ teaspoon ground ginger (F, FOS, LOX and MS)
¼ teaspoon salt or to taste
½ teaspoon fish sauce (optional) (homemade Vegan substitute in this section)

Directions
Place the following in a small saucepan: broth, both of the vinegars, rice malt syrups, black pepper, asafoetida and ground ginger. Bring to a brief boil over medium-high heat, then reduce heat to a gentle simmer - small bubbles should just break on the surface.

Cook until reduced to about ⅔ cup - this takes about 7 - 10 minutes. (NOTE: If you accidentally cook it longer, the flavors of the vinegar and syrup will be concentrated, and it becomes quite sweet. Keep an eye on the clock and don't miss that 10 minute max).

Remove the pan from the heat. Add the salt and fish sauce; stir to combine and taste to make sure it's salty enough for you. Pour into a glass container and allow to cool and then store in the refrigerator for up to 10 days. This sauce can be used in any recipe that calls for soy sauce.

Notes
⅛ teaspoon coarse (granulated) garlic powder (F, FOS, GOS, LOX and LS) can replace the asafoetida powder which is a strong spice.

2 teaspoons cider vinegar (L-MOX and VHS) can replace white wine vinegar (L-MOX and VHS) or rice wine vinegar.

Molasses (F and MS) will replace rice malt syrup for a stronger flavour.

*   *   *   *   *

HOMEMADE ALTERNATIVE IDEAS FOR FOOD COLOURINGS

And as an alternative, you can use natural food dye in a savory recipe. Remember, food dye isn't reserved just for sweets and treats.

Green
A little spinach will work like a charm, and doesn't impart any flavor at all. You can use juice, or you can even use the whole leaves.

Green: Juiced: kale, parsley, spinach, romaine, cucumber, capsicum, watercress. Boiled green veggies, using the water/juice will give you a much lighter green color.

GLUTEN FREE ROUGH PUFF PASTRY

I have had this recipe for over a year now, so I forget where it came from, so thank you to the person who quoted from the adaptor "Bake by weight and you'll be able to play. Play and let it be imperfect. Don't expect to be good at this the first time. I promise you this is a project you will master eventually. Allow yourself time in front of the kitchen counter, more than just once". (I still use cup measures because it's easier for me).

It is very hard to find out whether the ingredients had Fructose, Fructans, Polyols, GOS, Oxalates or Salicylates in them so I'll leave the decision up to you if you want to try this recipe.

Ingredients
345g (¾ lb or 1½ cups or 3 sticks) unsalted butter Or Nuttelex Original
137g (4⅞ oz or ¾ cup) potato starch (or tapioca flour)
137g (4½ oz or 1 cup) cornstarch (or arrowroot powder)
52g (1⅞ oz or ⅓ cup) superfine brown rice flour (or sorghum)
52g (1⅞ oz or ⅓ cup) superfine sweet rice flour (or millet flour)
2 teaspoons xanthan gum (omit if you are not sure of this gum)
½ teaspoon guar gum (plus the amount of xanthan gum if you choose to omit it)
OR 2½ teaspoons chia seeds ground to a powder (FOS, OX and HS)
1 teaspoon fine sea salt
180ml (¾ cup) ice water

Directions
Prepping the butter
Cut the butter into ½ inch cubes and arrange them on a plate, making sure they are separated. Put the plate in the freezer until the butter is frozen, at least 1 hour.

Combining the flours
Mix the potato starch, cornstarch, brown rice flour, and superfine sweet rice flour together. Whisk the flours together to aerate them. (Whirl the flours in the food processor for a few moments, to fully combine them). Add the xanthan gum, guar gum or chia seed powder and salt. Stir to combine.

Making the rough dough
Put the combined flours in the bowl of a stand mixer. (This batch is too big for a standard size food processor, or you could have done it there. You can also do this by hand, with the help of a pastry scraper).

Add the frozen butter. When you turn on the mixer, on the lowest speed, the butter will fly and your stand mixer will sound like it is suffering. Keep going. Turn it off and on a few times until the edges of the butter pieces have started to soften.

Turn off the mixer. Pour in the ice water and turn on the mixer again. Let it run until the flours have absorbed the water. This dough is going to look crazy ragged and unfinished.

Rolling out and turning (see notes below about a Silpat)
Pour the dough onto a Silpat or piece of parchment paper about the same size as a Silpat. Knead it together with your hands for a moment or two, just enough to bring it together.

Put a piece of parchment paper on top and roll this out to a rough rectangle, with a rolling pin. (Aim for roughly the size of a piece of notebook paper, with just a bit more length). You might like to pat it down with your hands.

Roll from the center outward, going both ways. Take care not to roll over the edges. Go gently.

Gently, using the edges of the Silpat or parchment paper, fold the bottom third of the dough toward the middle, then fold the top third on top of it. Eventually, this will look like a book. Right now, it might be hard to distinguish the folds from each other.

Rotate the dough one-quarter turn to your right (clockwise). You have now completed one turn.

Again, roll out the dough to roughly the same size as a piece of notebook paper, with just a bit more length. Go gently. In these early turns, you're going to think this is impossible but keep going. With each turn, the dough will become smoother and more cohesive. Once you are done rolling, fold the bottom third up, and overlap the top third over it. Try as best you can to align the edges.

Rotate the dough one-quarter turn to your right (clockwise). You have now completed two turns.

Follow the same process, rolling carefully, then turning, until you have completed four turns. Wrap the folded dough in plastic wrap and let it chill in the refrigerator for 2 hours.

Finishing the dough
Pull the puff pastry dough out of the refrigerator and let it sit on the counter for about 20 minutes before working with it again, since it will be hard from the cold. Don't let it sit out too long; however, you want the dough to be cold but pliable.

Complete the fifth and sixth turns, following the same procedure as above. Wrap the dough in plastic again and refrigerate for at least another 2 hours.

And there you have it; rough puff pastry, gluten-free. This batch makes enough for 2 large tarts or whatever recipes that you have made it for.

This dough does well in the refrigerator for 3 days or in the freezer for 1 month.

Notes
Silpat baking sheets replace parchment paper, and are heat-resistant up to 480°F / 250°C. The Silpat makes any baking sheet non-stick so no greasing is necessary.

*   *   *   *   *

HOMEMADE LACTOSE-FREE BUTTERMILK

Ingredients
1 cup Lactose Free milk or whatever amount is needed (you can use any milk)
1 tablespoon lemon juice (F, PO (sorbitol) LOX and L-HS or white vinegar (L-MOX and VHS)

Directions
Stir the milk and lemon juice/vinegar together in a medium bowl. Let the mixture sit for five minutes until the milk looks like it has curdled. Use as needed in the recipe.

DAIRY FREE, SOY FREE WHITE CHOCOLATE

Ingredients
4oz (112gm) edible raw cacao butter roughly chopped
2 teaspoons vanilla paste or pure extract (F, VLOX and VHS)
⅔ cup dextrose powder (for Fructose Free and may contain Gluten) or confectioner sugar
1 teaspoon finely ground almond flour (Almonds have FOS, PO (xylitol), VHOX and VHS)
¼ teaspoon kosher salt (an edible salt with a much larger grain size to common table salt and use half the amount specified if using normal salt)

Directions
Place butter in microwave bowl and heat 70% for 1 minute 30 seconds. Remove and stir – keep repeating until the butter has melted to a thin liquid. Add other ingredients and stir till smooth. Mould and set till solid either in the fridge or at room temperature.

* * * * *

HOMEMADE DARK CHOCOLATE

Ingredients (Fructose Free)
50g (3.5 tablespoons) cacao butter
25g (3.5 tablespoons) dark cacao powder (FOS, GOS, VHOX and MS)
1 tablespoon rice malt syrup
½ teaspoon vanilla extract (F, VLOX and VHS)
Pinch of salt

Directions
Using the double boiler method is having a bowl sitting on top of a saucepan that has a small amount of water simmering in it. Don't allow the base of the bowl come in contact with the water as it will spoil the chocolate.

Place the cocoa butter in the bowl and using a metal or rubber spoon or whisk mix it until it has melted – do not use a wooden spoon for this recipe as the wooden spoon holds moisture and will ruin the chocolate.

Add the vanilla extract and the rice malt syrup and mix it around until it's well combined. Add in the dark cocoa powder and mix it through until it's well combined and completely dissolved.

Once it is nice and glossy take it off the heat and pour the chocolate in to your selected mould/moulds and give it a quick jiggle to remove the air.

Let it sit for about an hour or so just until it starts to harden up because we don't want it to harden up to fast then place it into the fridge for another hour to completely set.

Notes
Add 1 tablespoon of Lactose Free milk powder or one to your liking to make this into a milk chocolate. Make chocolate melts by dropping small amounts of chocolate on a tray and letting them set.

HOMEMADE WHITE CHOCOLATE

Ingredients
50g cacao butter
⅓ cup dextrose powder (for Fructose Free and may contain Gluten) or powder sugar to taste
½ teaspoon powdered milk (can use Lactose Free powdered milk)
½ teaspoon vanilla extract (F, VLOX and VHS)
Pinch of salt

Directions
Using the double boiler method; (a bowl sitting on top of a saucepan that has a small amount of water simmering in it). Don't allow the base of the bowl come in contact with the water as it will spoil the chocolate.

Place the cocoa butter into the bowl and using a metal or rubber spoon or whisk continue to stir it until it is completely melted.

Once the cocoa butter has melted, sift in dextrose and continue stirring whilst adding until thoroughly combined and then add in the milk powder and mix thoroughly again. Add the vanilla extract, again mix thoroughly and then add a pinch of salt and mix thoroughly to make sure everything is combined.

Pour your chocolate mixture in to your preferred mould or moulds. You can even pour it onto a baking tray lines with paper that has been lightly sprayed and then broken into pieces or shards when completely set.

Once moulded, leave it to set for two hours at room temperature because we don't want it to cool down to fast and after two hours place it in the fridge for another hour and it will completely set.

Notes
You can also use soy powder if you choose. Yes you do have to use milk powder so don't leave it out.

I use silicon moulds because the chocolate is easy to get out without spoiling.

*   *   *   *   *

HOMEMADE CREME FRAICHE

Heat buttermilk and heavy cream and allow the mixture to sit at room temperature for 24 hours or until the liquid becomes thick and creamy -- similar to a slightly thinned sour cream.

Creme fraiche thickens faster at room temperature, but once it's thickened you'll need to stir it, cover and refrigerate for at least 6 hours before using.

Store it in the refrigerator for up to 2 weeks in an airtight container. Homemade creme fraiche is thinner than store-bought, but still has the same flavor.

TURKEY

The following recipes were kindly donated to me by Muge.

The vegetables and fruit in these recipes will only make them Fructose Friendly. I have tried to source out whether they have Fructose, Fructans, Polyols or Galactans in them and have indicated this beside the ingredient plus a few ingredients have alternatives beside them or in the notes at the end of each recipe. I am hoping that this will help you as much as it has helped me. Salicylates and Oxalates may also be issues for some people so I have added them as well. They will all be noted in the code form below or mentioned in the notes. Please read these.

Low – L, Medium – M, High – H, Very High – VH, Salicylates – S, Oxalates – OX
Fructose – F, Fructans – FOS, Polyols – PO, Galactans – GOS

I have placed some homemade recipes for substituting the ingredients after the main recipes. These recipes will be for Gluten Free, Fructose Friendly, Lactose Free or Friendly, Diabetic Friendly and IBS Friendly depending on your sensitivity so that you can make your own if you want to. Please remember that Fructans, Polyols and Galactans can also come with Fructose.

Substituting ingredients will alter the original taste; however, it is a way to try different recipes from other countries and you can adjust the taste to your liking. Make these recipes your own and use your ingredients if you want to as you know what's best for you.

Australian tablespoons and cups measurements are used and they are: 1 teaspoon equals 5ml; 1 tablespoon equals 20ml; 1 cup equals 250ml. Oven temperatures are for conventional; if using fan-forced (convection), reduce the temperature by 20°C.

Sigara Böreği (Stuffed Pastries)	201
Philo Dough (Yufka)	202
Yufka (Turkish Flatbread)	203
Classic Moussaka	204
Homemade Turkish Pide Bread (Pide Ekmek)	205
Baked Prawns With Vegetables And Cheese (Karides Guvec)	206
Grilled Turkish Meat Balls (Izgara Kofte)	207
Kofte	208
Patlican Salatası (Aubergine/Eggplant Salad)	209
Homemade Recipes For The Above Recipes	
Gluten Free Filo Pastry Number 1	210
Filo Dough Number 2	210

SIGARA BÖREĞI (STUFFED PASTRIES)

Börek is one of THE great indulgences of Turkish cuisine. You can find specialist börek cafes in every town, with great metal trays heaving under rectangular slabs of the stuff. Essentially it's layer upon layer of filo pastry, filled with a range of delights - cheese, meat, spinach...some moist, some crispy, but there's one börek that you usually won't see in the börek cafes but that is served in almost all the restaurants in Turkey - Sigara Böreği . Small cylindrical rolls of filo pastry (shaped like cigarettes), stuffed with white cheese and parsley, and served hot and crispy as a mouth-watering meze. You can be as adventurous as you like with the fillings, but the traditional version is as follows:

Ingredients to serve 4 people
2 sheets of filo pastry (known as yufka in Turkish) (2 homemade recipes after main recipes)
250ml oil (Olive (LOX and HS) or Sunflower) for frying (or you can bake them, in which case you will need 50g of butter) (see notes)

Filling
200g of crumbled white cheese (Turkish white cheese, or feta cheese (VLOX)
1 egg yolk
¼ bunch parsley (F, PO (mannitol), LOX and LS) or coriander (MOX and HS)
¼ bunch dill (F, L-MOX and VHS) or tarragon (VLOX and VHS) or chives (F, FOS (raffinose), PO (mannitol), VLOX and LS)
Pinch of salt

Directions
Divide the filo pastry sheets into two semi circles, and then into four curved triangles. Cover any filo pastry you are not using with a towel to stop it drying out.

Place the filling at the wide end, fold up the long sides to hold in the filling and then roll it up like a small cigar. Wet the pointed end with a wet (use water/milk/egg) pastry brush and stick it down.

Fry in hot oil until golden, making sure you turn the cigars frequently, and serve piping hot.

Alternatively, you can brush them with melted butter and bake in a preheated oven 200°C / 400°F on a greased baking sheet until they are golden and crisp. This should take approx 15 minutes.

Other fillings suggestions for your Sigara Böreği
Sage (LOX and VHS) with the cheese instead of dill and parsley
Savoury lamb/beef (even chicken) mince filling (preferably cooked with some onions, tomato puree and herbs) (see notes)
Spinach (HF, FOS, PO (sorbitol), VHOX and HS) or Spinach and cheese
Pine nuts (FOS, VHOX and HS) make a crunchy and a tasty addition to any of the above

Notes
Onions have HF, HFOS, PO (mannitol), LOX and LS or substitute 3 spring onions (green parts only for each onion) diced (white part has M-HF, FOS, PO (mannitol) MOX and LS).
Tomato puree has HF, FOS, PO (mannitol), HOX and VHS.

PHILO DOUGH (YUFKA)

These are ready made, very thin, big and round sheets of dough used for various kinds of pastries (börek), baked of fried. If you have to prepare the dough yourself for some of the Turkish recipes, you'll need an 80cm or 32" long rolling pin as thin as a finger (oklava). This is the only way to roll out paper thin sheets of dough for the famous flaky pastries. But it takes a certain experience to obtain the desired thinness.

After rolling the dough with a large rolling-pin until it is as large as a plate Turkish cooks, then gently roll the dough with the "oklava" letting the entire surface of the dough wrap itself around the "oklava". Press the dough with your hands to spread it toward the ends of the "oklava". Now, unroll the dough from the "oklava" and repeat the operation from another edge of the dough. Continue until the dough is about 60cm in diameter.

Ingredients
2 cups Gluten Free flour or one to your liking (options on pages 13 & 14)
6½ soup spoons Nuttelex Original or butter or margarine to your liking
½ cup water (add more if needed)
2 eggs
Salt to taste

Directions
Sift the flour, keeping back 2 soup spoonsful. Pour the flour into a large salad bowl and make a hollow place in the center. Put an egg, ½ cup water, a ½ spoonful of melted butter and salt into the hollow. Make the dough by mixing and kneading these ingredients. Sprinkle the dough with flour and let stand 15 minutes, covered with a damp cloth.

With a rolling pin roll the dough to a thickness of 2cm. Spread on 3 soupspoons of softened butter. Cut the dough into 3 pieces, placing one on top of the other. Roll the 3 pieces. Spread on the remaining butter. Cut again into 3 pieces and place one of the other. Knead a few minutes and shape into a ball.

Divide the dough into balls, a little bigger then the size of a tennis ball, and roll out each of these balls to obtain the "yufka" - thin disks of dough approximately 60cm in diameter. Let dry a little before using.

YUFKA (TURKISH FLATBREAD)

This easy-to-make flatbread is sturdy enough to hold the filling for a shawarma (meat) sandwich, but thin enough that it doesn't overwhelm them.

Ingredients

7⅜ oz or 1⅔ cups Gluten Free unbleached all-purpose flour; more as needed or one to your liking (options on pages 13 & 14)
1 teaspoon kosher salt (an edible salt with a much larger grain size to common table salt so use only half the amount of common salt if substituting)
⅔ cup lukewarm (90°F - 100°F) water
2 tablespoons olive oil (LOX and HS); more as needed or one to your liking

Directions

In a medium bowl, whisk the flour and salt. Make a well in the center and pour in the water and oil. Using your fingers, draw the flour in from the sides, working the mixture into a sticky dough.

Turn the dough out onto a floured surface and knead, adding more flour as necessary to prevent sticking, until the dough is smooth and elastic, about 3 minutes.

Transfer to the mixing bowl, drizzle with a little bit of oil, and turn to coat. Cover the dough with plastic wrap and let rest at room temperature for 4 hours or refrigerate overnight.

On a floured surface, divide the dough into 6 equal pieces (about 2oz each). Roll each piece into a ball. Cover the dough balls with a clean kitchen towel and let rest at room temperature for 15 minutes.

Cut seven 10" squares of parchment. On a floured surface with a lightly floured rolling pin, roll the balls into very thin 9" rounds, using more flour as needed to prevent sticking. (If the dough resists rolling, let it rest for another 15 minutes.) Layer the rounds between pieces of parchment in a stack.

Heat an 11-12" non-stick or cast-iron skillet or griddle over medium heat. Lightly oil the skillet.

Peel a dough round from the parchment and drop it into the skillet, carefully using your fingertips to lay it flat, if necessary. Cook until light golden and puffed in spots, about 2 minutes.

Using your fingers or a spatula, flip and cook until the second side is light golden in spots, 1 - 2 minutes. Transfer to a plate. Repeat with the remaining dough, stacking the cooked flatbreads so they steam a bit and stay warm.

Make Ahead Tips

If not using immediately, transfer the warm yufka to a large zip-top plastic bag, close it, and store at room temperature overnight. You can also freeze the yufka for up to 2 weeks. Reheat briefly in a skillet over medium heat before using.

CLASSIC MOUSSAKA

Ingredients
2 large eggplant, thinly sliced (F, FOS, PO (xylitol), MOX and HS)
Olive oil cooking spray (LOX and HS) or one to your liking
1 tablespoon olive oil (LOX and HS) or one to your liking
1 medium brown onion, finely chopped (HF, HFOS, PO (mannitol), LOX and LS) or 3 spring onions (green parts only) diced (white part has M-HF, FOS, PO (mannitol) MOX and LS) (see notes)
2 garlic cloves, crushed (F, FOS, GOS, LOX and LS) (see notes)
800g or 28oz lamb mince or one to your liking
420g can or 2 x 14oz cans crushed tomatoes (HF, PO (aspartame), H-VHOX and LS?)
1 teaspoon ground cinnamon (F, HOX and VHS)
½ teaspoon ground allspice (VHS)
⅓ cup Lactose Free grated pizza cheese or one to your liking
Lemon wedges, to serve (F, PO (sorbitol), VLOX and MS)

White sauce
75g or ⅓ cup Nuttelex Original or butter or one to your liking
⅓ cup Gluten Free plain flour or one to your liking (options on pages 13 & 14)
2 cups Lactose Free milk or one to your liking

Directions
Spray eggplant with oil. Heat a large frying pan over medium-high heat. Cook eggplant, in batches, for 2 - 3 minutes each side or until browned and transfer to a large plate.

Heat oil in a large saucepan over medium-high heat and add onion and garlic. Cook, stirring, for 5 minutes or until onion has softened.

Add mince. Cook, stirring with a wooden spoon to break up mince, for 6 - 8 minutes or until browned.

Add tomatoes, cinnamon and allspice. Bring to the boil. Reduce heat to medium-low and simmer for 30 minutes or until sauce is thick and liquid has evaporated.

Meanwhile, make the sauce.

Melt butter in a saucepan over medium-high heat. Add flour and cook, stirring, for 1 minute or until bubbling and then gradually stir in milk. Bring to the boil.

Reduce heat to medium and cook, stirring, for 5 minutes or until mixture has thickened. Remove from heat.

Preheat oven to 180°C / 350°F. Grease an 8 cup capacity ovenproof dish.

Place ⅓ of the eggplant, slightly overlapping, over base of prepared dish. Spread half the meat sauce over eggplant. Repeat layers, ending with eggplant.

Spread white sauce over eggplant and sprinkle with cheese.

Bake for 45 minutes or until golden. Stand 15 minutes. Serve with lemon wedges.

Notes
A pinch of asafoetida powder (may contain Gluten) only can be substituted for both the onion and garlic. This is a strong spice so only use the specified amount.

HOMEMADE TURKISH PIDE BREAD (PIDE EKMEK)

Ingredients

1lb / 450g Gluten Free all-purpose plain flour or one to your liking (options on pages 13 & 14)
¼ oz or 7g dried yeast or ½ oz or 15g fresh yeast (bakers - MOX and LS, non-bakers - MOX and VHS)
½ teaspoon dextrose powder (may contain Gluten) or sugar
6 fl. oz or 175ml or ⅔ cup lukewarm water
5ml or 1 teaspoon salt
30ml or 2 tablespoons thick yoghurt (Commercial) VLOX and (homemade) Nil OX and S)
30ml or 2 tablespoons olive oil (LOX and HS) or one to your liking
1 egg beaten
30ml or 2 tablespoons nigella seeds or poppy seeds (L-Neg S)
30ml or 2 tablespoons sesame seeds (FOS, VHOX and HS)

Directions

Preheat oven to 400°F / 200°C.

Cream the yeast with sugar in half of the lukewarm water, leave to froth.

Sift the flour with the salt. Make a well in the middle and pour in the yeast, olive oil, yoghurt and the rest of the water.

Using your hands, draw in the flour from the sides and work the mixture into a sticky dough. Add a little more water if necessary. Knead until the dough is smooth and leaves the sides of the bowl (drizzle a little oil in your hands to help shape the dough, if needed too).

Continue to knead on a lightly floured surface until the dough is elastic and smooth. Roll it in the few drops of olive oil in the bowl, cover with a damp towel and leave to prove in a warm place for 1 - 1½ hours or until doubled in size.

Once doubled, punch the dough down, knead again and divide it into two pieces. Knead each piece well.

Flatten them out with the heel of your hand and stretch them into large, uneven rounds or ovals, creating thick lip around the edges. Indent the dough with your fingertips.

Lightly oil two hot baking sheets or trays and place them in the oven for 2 minutes. Place the Pide on them and brush the pides with the beaten egg. Then sprinkle the nigella (or poppy) seeds and sesame seeds over the top.

Bake the pides for 18 - 20 minutes, until lightly golden with a crisp crust around the edges. Transfer them to a wire rack. If you want them to retain their softness, wrap them in aluminium foil or in a dry towel while still warm.

Notes

To keep the pides soft and warm, place a dry towel over them when fresh out of the oven. You can also reheat them before eating; just sprinkle them with water and place in a hot oven (180°C / 350°F) for a few minutes.

KARIDES GUVEC (BAKED PRAWNS WITH VEGETABLES AND CHEESE)

Karides guvec is traditionally cooked in earthenware pot, though ramekin dish works well too. Traditionally, prawns are cooked here with plenty of vegetables in a one big earthenware pot (or in smaller individual ones), called guvec, which delivers a wonderful flavor. But no worries if you don't have one; a ramekin dish or a glass baking dish also works very well too.

Ingredients to serve 4
225g / 8oz fresh raw king prawns, shelled, cleaned and pat dried
225g / 8oz chestnut or white mushrooms, wiped cleaned, halved and sliced (see notes)
1 onion, quartered and thinly sliced (HF, HFOS, PO (mannitol), LOX and LS) or 3 spring onions (green parts only) diced (white part has M-HF, FOS, PO (mannitol) MOX and LS)
3 - 4 garlic cloves, chopped (F, FOS, GOS, LOX and LS)
1 green bell pepper (F, PO (sorbitol), MOX and VHS), seeded, quartered and thinly sliced or green capsicum (HF, FOS, PO (sorbitol), MOX and VHS) seeded, quartered and thinly sliced
2 bay leaves (optional) (VHS)
400g / 14oz good quality fresh tomatoes (HF, FOS, PO (mannitol), MOX and MS) or 1 can of chopped tomatoes (HF, PO (aspartame), H-VHOX and LS?)
120g / 4oz grated cheddar (kasar) or mozzarella, if you prefer a milder taste (Lactose Friendly)
3 tablespoons / 45ml olive oil (LOX and HS) or one to your liking
2 fl oz / ¼ cup water
Salt and freshly ground black pepper to taste (HOX and VHS)
10ml / 2 teaspoons red pepper flakes, (HF, PO (sorbitol), VLOX and VHS) Turkish pul biber (Aleppo pepper flakes) (HF, PO (sorbitol), VL and LS) or chili flakes (F and VHS)
Handful of chopped flat leaf parsley, for garnish (F, PO, (mannitol), LOX and LS)
Slices of fresh, crusty bread or Turkish flat breads, Pide to serve (homemade recipe above)

Directions
Preheat the oven to 180°C / 350°F.

Heat the olive oil in a wide, heavy pan over medium heat. Stir in the onion, peppers and mushrooms and cook for about 4 - 5 minutes, until they begin to soften.

Add the garlic, season with salt (mushrooms especially require generous seasoning) black pepper and red pepper flakes, pul biber.

Stir and cook over medium heat for another 4 - 5 minutes. Add the chopped tomatoes, bay leaves and ¼ cups water, combine well. Simmer over medium to low heat for about 10 minutes, until you get a nice chunky sauce.

Check the seasoning of your sauce and add more salt or spices to your taste.

Stir in the fresh, raw prawns to the sauce and mix well.

Spoon this mixture into individual or a one big earthenware pot or ramekin dish or any baking dish you have. Sprinkle the grated cheese over the top and bake in the preheated oven for about 10 minutes or until the prawns are just cooked through and the cheese is nicely golden brown on top.

Garnish with chopped parsley over the top and serve hot with slices of crusty bread or Turkish flat breads, pide by the side.

A refreshing, Coban Salatasi (Shepherd's Salad) of sliced onions, (HF, HFOS, PO (mannitol), LOX and LS) or spring onions (green parts only) diced (white part has M-HF, FOS, PO (mannitol) MOX and LS), cucumbers (HF, FOS, PO (sorbitol), VLOX and HS) and tomatoes, (HF, FOS, PO (mannitol), MOX and MS) complements this dish beautifully.

Notes
A Chestnut Mushroom is the same mushroom as White Button Mushrooms and normal mushrooms have HF, FOS (raffinose), PO (mannitol and xylitol) GOS, VLOX and MS). Try substituting Shitake, Enoki and Oyster mushroom as they contain little or no Fructose or Fructans or Polyols and are considered by some as safe to eat. Not too sure about the King Brown even though one site states that they are in the same category as the other Gourmet mushrooms.

The proper proportion for the best alternative to Aleppo pepper: Mix four parts sweet paprika to one part cayenne. Optional: Add a tiny pinch of salt.

*   *   *   *   *

IZGARA KOFTE (GRILLED TURKISH MEAT BALLS)

Ingredients
2 lb or 900g lean ground beef
1 big onion, grated or minced (HF, HFOS, PO (mannitol), LOX and LS) or 3 spring onions (green parts only) diced (white part has M-HF, FOS, PO (mannitol) MOX and LS) or a pinch of asafoetida powder (may contain Gluten) (this is a strong spice so you don't any more than what is specified)
1 teaspoon black pepper (HOX and VHS)
1 teaspoon baking soda
½ teaspoon cumin (VHOX) (optional)
1 egg
1 tablespoon salt to taste

Directions
Mix all the ingredients in a large bowl. Knead with your hands for about 5 - 10 minutes. Leave it in the fridge at least for 2 - 3 hours.

Grab egg size pieces and make round shaped thin meat balls. Repeat this until you use all the mixture. Then cook them over a barbecue or electric grill, till both sides get lightly brown. Serve them while still hot.

KOFTE

Kofte are Middle Eastern sausage-shaped meatballs. They're perfect for the barbecue, the pan or the oven

Ingredients to serve 6
500g or 1.1lb minced lamb
1 medium onion, grated (HF, HFOS, PO (mannitol), LOX and LS) or 6 spring onions (green parts only) diced (white part has M-HF, FOS, PO (mannitol) MOX and LS) (see notes)
2 garlic cloves, crushed (F, FOS, GOS, LOX and LS) (see notes)
Pinch of allspice (VHS)
Pinch of freshly ground black pepper (HOX and VHS)
Pinch of chilli flakes (F and VHS)
Pinch of sweet paprika (F and VHS)
Pinch of ground cumin (VHOX)
1 teaspoon salt
1 egg

Directions
Mix the ingredients together with your hands, kneading until smooth.

Wet your hands and roll walnut-sized pieces of mixture into balls. Flatten them slightly.

Fry the Kofte on a lightly oiled barbecue grill or in a chargrill pan, for about 1 minute on each side.

Notes
A good pinch of asafoetida powder (may contain Gluten) will replace both the onion and garlic. This is a strong spice so only use specified amount.

PATLICAN SALATASI (AUBERGINE/EGGPLANT SALAD)

This is a recipe that you can change to suit your own taste. You can either cook the onions and tomatoes, by putting them into the coals for 10 - 15 minutes until they become soft, or if you'd prefer, leave them raw and slice up into the salad as they are.

Ingredients

3 - 4 aubergines or eggplants (F, FOS, PO (xylitol) MOX and HS)
2 medium red peppers (HF, PO (sorbitol), VLOX and VHS) or red capsicum (HF, FOS, PO (sorbitol) LOX and VHS)
2 medium onions (HF, HFOS, PO (mannitol), LOX and LS) or 6 spring onions (green parts only) diced (white part has M-HF, FOS, PO (mannitol) MOX and LS)
2 medium tomatoes (HF, FOS, PO (mannitol), MOX and MS)
1 lemon (for the juice) (F, PO (sorbitol), LOX and L-HS)
1 - 2 tablespoons of olive oil (LOX and HS) or one to your liking
3 cloves of garlic (F, FOS, GOS, LOX and LS) (omit if you can't tolerate)
Salt to taste

Directions

Once the BBQ is lit and ready to grill on, put the aubergines/eggplant and peppers directly into the hot coals or plate. Turn them occasionally with a pair of tongs so that they cook evenly. They need to cook for around 15 minutes until they are soft and the skins are blackened. This is important, as this is what gives them the real smoky barbequed taste. Once they get to this point take them out and set them aside until cool enough to handle.

While they are cooling, peel the garlic cloves and chop into small thin pieces.

Once the aubergine/eggplant and peppers have cooled down a little (and the onion and tomatoes if you chose to cook them too) you need to peel the skins off (or just the outside few layers of the onion). If they have been sat in the coals long enough, the skins should peel off really easily. It's a messy job and be careful not to burn yourself as they will still be very hot inside.

Cut off the top/stalk end of the aubergines and peppers (some people like to remove the seeds too) then chop up everything into smaller pieces - the aubergines/eggplant, peppers, onions and tomatoes - and add them all into the same bowl.

Add the garlic (if using) into the bowl along with the olive oil and salt. Turkish people use a lot of oil and salt so they add a lot of both, but you can adapt it to your own taste.

Finally, cut the lemon in half and squeeze the juice of one half into the salad and toss to combine.

HOMEMADE RECIPES FOR THE ABOVE RECIPES

GLUTEN FREE FILO PASTRY NUMBER 1

Ingredients
¼ cup water
2 cups Gluten Free flour (probably use amaranth flour) (HOX)
4 teaspoons olive oil (LOX and HS) or one to your liking
¼ teaspoon salt

Directions
Sift flour and salt and make a well, then add the water and oil in it. Work the dough, and on a dusted board, knead it for about 5 minutes. It gets smooth. Roll it out in a huge rectangle, put a damp towel over it, and let it stay for about 15 minutes.

Work it out again so it's about 3 x 3 feet (92 x 92cm). Cut it with a knife to sheet size, and then use for your recipe.

* * * * *

FILO DOUGH NUMBER 2

Ingredients
1¾ cups fine white rice flour
¼ cup sweet rice flour
4 teaspoons of guar gum or xanthan gum or chia seed powder (FOS, OX and HS)
1 teaspoon gelatin (VLOX)
1 egg
¼ - ½ cup Lactose Free milk or one of choice
1 stick butter or ½ cup or 4oz or 113g Nuttelex Original, melted or margarine or oil
1 teaspoon rice malt syrup (Fructose Free)

Directions
Mix together rice flour, sweet rice flour, xanthan gum/guar gum/chia seed powder and gelatin. Make a well in dry ingredients large enough to hold the liquids.

Lightly beat egg with ¼ cup milk, butter and rice malt syrup. Pour this into well in dry ingredients. Mix everything together until you have a soft dough. (Depending on brand of rice flour, you may want to stir in more milk).

Wrap dough in plastic wrap until ready to use for your favorite holiday pastry. Store in refrigerator if not using immediately.

IRELAND

The following recipes were kindly donated to me by Kylie.
(My in-laws were from Ireland)

The vegetables and fruit in these recipes will only make them Fructose Friendly. I have tried to source out whether they have Fructose, Fructans, Polyols or Galactans in them and have indicated this beside the ingredient plus a few ingredients have alternatives beside them or in the notes at the end of each recipe. I am hoping that this will help you as much as it has helped me. Salicylates and Oxalates may also be issues for some people so I have added them as well. They will all be noted in the code form below or mentioned in the notes. Please read these.

Low – L, Medium – M, High – H, Very High – VH, Salicylates – S, Oxalates – OX
Fructose – F, Fructans – FOS, Polyols – PO, Galactans – GOS

I have placed some homemade recipes for substituting the ingredients after the main recipes. These recipes will be for Gluten Free, Fructose Friendly, Lactose Free or Friendly, Diabetic Friendly and IBS Friendly depending on your sensitivity so that you can make your own if you want to. Please remember that Fructans, Polyols and Galactans can also come with Fructose.

Substituting ingredients will alter the original taste; however, it is a way to try different recipes from other countries and you can adjust the taste to your liking. Make these recipes your own and use your ingredients if you want to as you know what's best for you.

Australian tablespoons and cups measurements are used and they are: 1 teaspoon equals 5ml; 1 tablespoon equals 20ml; 1 cup equals 250ml. Oven temperatures are for conventional; if using fan-forced (convection), reduce the temperature by 20°C.

Irish Roast Rabbit	212
Dublin Coddle	213
Pratie Oaten	214
Leek And Oatmeal Broth	214
Soda Bread	215
Urney Pudding	216
Cherry Dog	217
Belem tarts	218
Homemade Recipes For The Above Recipes	
Homemade Lactose-Free Buttermilk	221
Homemade Lactose Free And Fructose Friendly Custard	221
Homemade Mustard Powder	222

IRISH ROAST RABBIT

This rabbit is not roasted at all, but is casseroled in the oven.

Ingredients to serve 4 people
1 rabbit jointed (**see notes**)
Vinegar (L-MOX and VHS) and water mixed
2 tablespoons Gluten Free flour or one to your liking (see notes)
½ teaspoon dry mustard (VLOX and VHS) (homemade recipe after main recipes)
Salt and black pepper (HOX and VHS) to taste
2oz or ¼ cup or 4 tablespoons or 57g Nuttelex Original or butter or one to your liking
2 onions peeled and chopped (HF, HFOS, PO (mannitol), LOX and LS) or 6 spring onions (green parts only) diced (white part has M-HF, FOS, PO (mannitol) MOX and LS)
4 rashes of bacon, de-rinded and chopped
1 dessertspoon fresh chopped parsley (F, PO (mannitol), LOX and LS) or coriander (MOX and HS)
½ teaspoon fresh chopped thyme (LOX and VHS)
½ pint or 1 cup Lactose Free milk or one to your choosing
See notes on accompanying vegetables

Directions
Soak the rabbit joints in the vinegar and water for about 30 minutes. Drain and pat dry on kitchen paper.

Preheat oven to 375°F / 190°C.

Mix the flour, mustard and seasoning together and coat rabbit joints.

Melt butter in a frypan and lightly brown the rabbit joints on both sides. Place in an ovenproof dish.

Fry the onion in the remaining pan butter and cook until soft and then add to the casserole with bacon and herbs.

Heat the milk until just below boiling point and pour over the casserole contents. Cover and cook for 1 hour.

Serve with boiled potatoes, carrots (see notes) and a green vegetable of your choice.

Notes
Just covering the meat in cold water, adding a good splash of white wine vinegar, and leaving it for an hour at most helps to draw the blood out and 'sweetens' the meat.

You may want to substitute chicken pieces without soaking for the rabbit.

Fructose in potatoes can range anything between 582 mg – 989 mg depending on the size, type and skin colour. They also have FOS, PO and GOS. They can also be VHOX and MS again depending on the type of potatoes, colour of skin and how they are cooked.

Carrots have HF, FOS (raffinose), PO (sorbitol) GOS and Carrots-Boiled have MOX and HS and Carrots-Raw have VHOX and HS.

Some Gluten Free flours have a higher carb count and may affect people with Diabetes and those who have to watch their intake of carbohydrates.

DUBLIN CODDLE

To 'coddle' means to 'cook slowly or parboil' and this dish of ham, sausages, onions and potatoes dates back to the 18th century.

Ingredients to serve 4 to 6 people
1½ pints or 3 cups water
8 thick slices of ham cut into chunks
8 pork sausages cut into thick slices
2 large onions, peeled and sliced (HF, HFOS, PO (mannitol), LOX and LS) or 6 spring onions (green parts only) diced (white part has M-HF, FOS, PO (mannitol) MOX and LS)
1½ lbs or 700g potatoes peeled and sliced (see notes)
Salt and black pepper (HOX and VHS) to taste
2 heaped tablespoons fresh, chopped parsley (F, PO (mannitol), LOX and LS) or coriander (MOX and HS)
Fresh chopped parsley for garnish (optional)

Directions
Bring the water to the boil in a saucepan, then add the ham and sausages and cook for 5 minutes. Drain well, reserving the cooking liquid.

Preheat oven to 300°F / 150°C.

Place the ham and sausages in an ovenproof dish, add the onions, potatoes, seasoning and chopped parsley and pour over just enough liquid to cover.

Cover with a piece of buttered greaseproof paper, put on the lid and cook for 1 - 1½ hours or until the liquid is greatly reduced and the vegetables are cooked but not mushy.

Serve garnished with parsley and soda bread.

Notes
Fructose in potatoes can range anything between 582 mg – 989 mg depending on the size, type and skin colour. They also have FOS, PO and GOS. They can also be VHOX and MS again depending on the type of potatoes, colour of skin and how they are cooked.

PRATIE OATEN

'Pratie' is slang for potato in Ireland and these potato oatcakes are a popular teatime treat in County Antrim.

Ingredients
1lb or 450g cooked, well mashed potatoes (see notes)
8oz or 1½ cups fine oatmeal (MOX) (grind oats in a processor until it becomes a powder)
Salt and pepper to taste (black - HOX and VHS, white - VLOX and VHS)
Lactose Free milk or one to your liking

Directions
Mix the potatoes, oatmeal and seasoning well together in a bowl, then add sufficient milk to for a soft dough-like consistency. Turn out onto a surface lightly dusted with oatmeal and roll out until about 1" or 2½ cm thick and cut into triangles.

Heat an ungreased griddle or frypan and cook for about 4 - 5 minutes on each side until golden. Serve hot with butter.

Notes
Fructose in potatoes can range anything between 582 mg – 989 mg depending on the size, type and skin colour. They also have FOS, PO and GOS. They can also be VHOX and MS again depending on the type of potatoes, colour of skin and how they are cooked.

*   *   *   *   *

LEEK AND OATMEAL BROTH

Ingredients to serve 4 to 6 people
1 pint or 2 cups Lactose Free milk or one to your liking
1 pint or 2 cups chicken or vegetable stock (minus onion and garlic)
A walnut size or a heaping tablespoon Nuttelex Original or butter or one to your liking
3 rounded tablespoons oatmeal (MOX)
Salt and pepper to taste (black - HOX and VHS, white - VLOX and VHS)
4 leeks trimmed, washed well and cut into 1" rings (green parts only for Fructose Friendly (white parts have F, FOS, PO (mannitol), GOS and MOX)
2 tablespoons fresh chopped parsley (F, PO (mannitol), LOX and LS) or coriander (MOX and HS)
A single light Lactose Free cream or one to your liking for garnish (optional)

Directions
Mix the milk and stock together and pour into a large saucepan. Add the butter and bring to the boil and then add the oatmeal, stirring well. Return to the boil and simmer for 10 minutes, stirring occasionally.

Add the leeks and seasoning, return to the boil and then simmer for a further 15 - 20 minutes, stirring in parsley/coriander a few minutes before the end of the cooking times.

Serve in soup bowls, garnished with a swirl of cream if desired and Soda Bread.

Notes
You can puree this soup in a blender or using a stick blender before serving but it is usually served chunky.

SODA BREAD

Soda Bread should always be prepared quickly as possible and handled very lightly in the process. It is not a 'keeper' so by tradition, it should be fresh baked every morning or on the day you wish to use it.

This recipe would be better made accurately if you weigh all the ingredients on a scale.

Ingredients to make 1 loaf
1lb or 3¾ cups Gluten Free wholemeal flour or one to your liking (see notes)
8oz or 1¾ cups Gluten Free white flour (see notes)
1 teaspoon salt
1 teaspoon bicarbonate soda
1oz or ⅓ cup oats (optional)
Approximately ½ pint Lactose Free buttermilk or one to your liking (homemade recipes after main recipes)
A little beaten egg to glaze (optional)

Directions
Preheat oven to 425°F / 220°C.

Combine together in a bowl the flours, salt, bicarbonate soda and oats, if desired, then stir in sufficient buttermilk to make a soft dough.

Turn out on a lightly floured surface and knead **very** lightly before shaping into a round loaf.

Place on a buttered baking sheet or tray and using a loured knife, slash the top with a cross or markings for 8 sections. Glaze with beaten egg, if desired.

Bake for 20 - 30 minutes or until the loaf sounds hollow when tapped on the base.

Serve warm, cut into slices with butter.

Variation
You can make a White Soda Bread by replacing the wholemeal flour with white flour making 1½ lbs of white flour in all.

Notes
Gluten Free flour is higher in carbs so be mindful of this if you need to watch your carb count or diabetic (options on pages 13 & 14). Gluten Free flours tend to need more liquid so adjust accordingly.

URNEY PUDDING

This steamed pudding, flavoured with jam, comes from Northern Ireland

Ingredients
4oz or ½ cup Nuttelex Original or butter or one to your liking
3 tablespoons dextrose powder (may contain Gluten) or sugar or sweetener to your liking
2 eggs
A few drops vanilla essence (F, VLOX and VHS)
4oz or 1 cup Gluten Free flour or one to your liking (options pages 13 & 14) (see notes)
1 teaspoon baking powder (VLOX)
2 heaped tablespoons red jam: raspberry, strawberry etc. to your liking

Directions
Cream the butter and sugar together in a bowl.

Beat the eggs lightly and add to the mixture a little at a time, combining well between each addition. Stir in the vanilla essence.

Sift the flour and baking powder together and fold into the mixture.

Warm the jam slightly over a basin of hot water if at all stiff, and stir into the mixture.

Turn into a well buttered 1 - 1½ pint / 4 cup / 1.2 litre pudding basin, cover with a piece of buttered greaseproof paper and seal with kitchen foil.

Place in a steamer and steam over a saucepan of boiling water for 1½ hours, topping up the water if necessary.

Serve with a matching hot jam sauce.

Variations
If desired, apricot jam can be used, in which case substitute butterscotch essence or a little finely grated lemon rind for the vanilla and add a little lemon juice to the jam sauce.

Vanilla custard would also be something different to serve over the pudding (homemade recipe after main recipes).

Notes
Some Gluten Free flours have a higher carb count and may affect people with Diabetes and those who have to watch their intake of carbohydrates. Gluten Free flours tend to need more liquid so adjust accordingly.

CHERRY DOG

Ingredients
3oz or 10g glacé cherries (fresh cherries have F, PO (sorbitol), VLOX and HS)
8oz or 2 cups Gluten Free flour or one to your liking (options pages 13 & 14) (see notes)
2 level teaspoons cream of tartar (VLOX)
1 level teaspoon bicarbonate soda
Pinch of salt
2oz or 4 tablespoons Nuttelex Original or butter or one to your liking
2oz or ⅓ cup dextrose powder (may contain Gluten) or sugar or sweetener to your liking
1 egg beaten
Lactose Free milk or one to your liking
A little extra dextrose powder (may contain Gluten) or sugar for sprinkling

Directions
Preheat oven to 400°F / 200°C.

Cut cherries into halves or quarters, rinse in warm water to remove excess syrup, dry thoroughly and toss in a little flour.

Sift together into a bowl the flour, cream of tartar, bicarbonate soda and salt, rub in the butter until the mixture resembles breadcrumbs, then stir in the sugar and the prepared cherries.

Make a well in the centre of the dry mixture, drop in the egg and gradually work in the dry mixture from side to side, adding sufficient milk to produce a smooth, elastic dough.

Turn out onto a lightly floured surface, knead lightly and then, with the hands, form into a round or into a thick sausage shape.

Place on a greased baking sheet or tray, brush with milk to glaze then sprinkle with a little sugar.

Bake for about 30 minutes until golden. Cool on a wire rack and serve plain or spread with butter.

Notes
Some Gluten Free flours have a higher carb count and may affect people with Diabetes and those who have to watch their intake of carbohydrates. Gluten Free flours tend to need more liquid so adjust accordingly.

BELEM TARTS

I have placed a few pastry ideas for these tarts in the Variation section if you really want to try something different or make your own. You may wish to make 1 big tart instead of little ones. Please remember that if using Gluten Free flour you may need to adjust the liquid to suit.

Ingredients
Enough sheets of Flaky pastry to line 8 - 10 tartlet tins or 1 large pie tin (see variations)
5 egg yolks
4oz or ½ cup dextrose powder (may contain Gluten) or caster sugar or sweetener to your liking
½ pint or 1 cup Lactose Free double or heavy cream or one to your liking (see notes)
Pinch salt
Ground cinnamon (HOX and VHS) or ground nutmeg (VLOX and VHS)

Directions
Preheat oven to 400°F / 200°C.

Cut 8 - 10 pastry rings and line lightly buttered and floured tartlet tins.

Whisk the egg yolks together with the salt in a bowl and then beat in the cream and the sugar.

Spoon the filling into the pastry cases and sprinkle over the ground cinnamon or ground nutmeg.

Bake for about 20 minutes until the filling is set and golden. Cool on a wire rack.

Notes
You can also make your own heavy cream with ½ cup plain milk substitute and ½ cup canola oil (F, PO and LOX). Dairy and Lactose Free half-and-half substitutes work well in many recipes.

Variations

FLAKY VINEGAR PIE CRUST

Ingredients to make enough for 1 double crust pie or two 9" crusts
2¼ cups all-purpose Gluten Free flour of your liking (options on pages 13 & 14) (see notes)
1 cup butter, cold and cut into several large pieces (use Nuttelex Original for Lactose Free)
1 tablespoon of dextrose powder (for Fructose Friendly and may contain Gluten) or sugar
½ teaspoon salt
2 teaspoons vinegar (L-MOX and VHS) of your choice
6 - 10 tablespoons ice water

Directions
In a large bowl, stir together flour, dextrose and salt until combined. Add pieces of cold butter and toss to coat in the flour mixture.

Rub butter in with your fingertips until it is broken down into pieces about the size of an almond. Some pieces of butter may be slightly larger, some may be slightly smaller. (This can also be done by pulsing the ingredients in a food processor).

In a small bowl, combine vinegar and ice water.

While stirring your dough with a fork, gradually add in the water until the dough comes together into a slightly shaggy mass. If the dough becomes too sticky, add in an extra tablespoonful of flour.

Turn dough out onto a very lightly floured surface and press firmly until the dough comes together.

Cover with plastic wrap and refrigerate for 1 - 2 hours before rolling and using for your tart or tartlets.

Notes
Some Gluten Free flours have a higher carb count and may affect people with Diabetes and those who have to watch their intake of carbohydrates. Gluten Free flours tend to need more liquid so adjust accordingly.

* * * * *

COCOA CRUMB CRUST
Ingredients
1½ cups vanilla wafer crumbs or crumbs to your liking
¼ cup cocoa powder (FOS, GOS, VHOX and MS)
⅓ cup powdered dextrose (for Fructose Friendly and may contain Gluten) or sweetener of your choice
6 tablespoons melted Nuttelex Original or butter or oil of your choice

Directions
Mix thoroughly and press in 9" or 23cm pie plate. Bake at 350°F / 180°C for 8 minutes. Cool.

* * * * *

ALMOND TART CRUST
Ingredients
2½ cups almond flour (almonds have FOS, PO (xylitol) VHOX and VHS)
2½ tablespoons dextrose powder (for Fructose Friendly and may contain Gluten) (see notes) or sweetener of your choice
A pinch of salt
5 tablespoons (75g) of Nuttelex Original or butter, chilled and cubed or one to your liking
1 large egg white

Directions
In the bowl of a food processor, combine all the ingredients. Pulse until the dough resembles coarse meal.

Remove from the food processor and use your hands to form a dough.

Press evenly into the bottom and sides of a greased tart pan and place in the freezer while you preheat the oven to 400°F / 200°C.

Bake on the middle rack for about 15 - 20 minutes until it is light brown (do not over bake or the almonds will taste bitter). Let cool before filling.

Notes
Dextrose is not as sweet as sugar so use the same amount of sugar or for sweeter using recipe use more dextrose.

WHOLE GRAIN PIE CRUST

Ingredients
2 cups whole wheat Gluten Free flour of your choice (options on pages 13 & 14) (see notes)
1 cup ground oatmeal (MOX) (grind oats in a processor until it becomes a powder)
½ teaspoons salt
⅓ cup vegetable oil or one to your liking
½ cup water

Directions
Combine the flour, oatmeal and salt in a bowl. Blend in the oil, and then add the water. Bake as per your recipe.

Notes
Some Gluten Free flours have a higher carb count and may affect people with Diabetes and those who have to watch their intake of carbohydrates. You may also need to adjust the liquid to suit.

HOMEMADE RECIPES FOR THE ABOVE RECIPES

HOMEMADE LACTOSE-FREE BUTTERMILK

Ingredients
1 cup Lactose Free milk or whatever amount is needed (you can use any milk)
1 tablespoon lemon juice (F, PO (sorbitol), LOX and L-HS) or white vinegar (L-MOX and VHS)

Directions
Stir the milk and lemon juice/vinegar together in a medium bowl and let the mixture sit for five minutes until the milk looks like it has curdled.

Use as needed in the recipe.

*   *   *   *   *

HOMEMADE LACTOSE FREE AND FRUCTOSE FRIENDLY CUSTARD

Ingredients
2 cup (500mls) of Lactose Free milk or one of your choosing
2 tablespoons of cornflour (MOX and HS)
2 eggs
1 teaspoon of vanilla essence (VLOX and VHS) or ½ teaspoon of vanilla powder
¼ cup dextrose powder (for Fructose Friendly and may contain Gluten) or sweetener of your choice (or more or less to taste)

Directions
In a small bowl place ¼ cup of the milk and the cornflour. Mix the milk and cornflour until it forms a paste, using the back of a spoon to mash any cornflour lumps onto the bowl ensuring you get a smooth paste.

Place the rest of the milk, eggs, and cornflour paste in a medium saucepan and whisk together until smooth.

Place the saucepan on a medium heat on the stovetop and continue to whisk/stir until custard becomes creamy. Remove from heat, whisk in dextrose and vanilla.

Serve warm and flowing over your favourite pudding.

Notes
There are lots of different recipes and ways to make custard. This method as it is the simplest, less likely to burn, uses just milk and uses whole eggs. You can stir in ¼ cup of brandy at the end if brandy custard is a family favourite at Christmas time or anytime you feel like something different.

HOMEMADE MUSTARD POWDER

Ingredients
Mustard seeds to the amount you need (F, FOS, GOS, VLOX and VHS)
Turmeric (F, VHOX and VHS)

Directions
To make a powder, toast your mustard seeds for 20 seconds in a dry skillet. Cool the seeds, then transfer to a spice grinder and pulse until you have a powder.

Pass the powder through a sieve to remove the hulls.

Blend a pinch or two of turmeric with the mustard to create the bright yellow associated with the condiment.

ETHIOPIA

The following recipes were kindly donated to me by Tesfaye Teferq.

The vegetables and fruit in these recipes will only make them Fructose Friendly. I have tried to source out whether they have Fructose, Fructans, Polyols or Galactans in them and have indicated this beside the ingredient plus a few ingredients have alternatives beside them or in the notes at the end of each recipe. I am hoping that this will help you as much as it has helped me. Salicylates and Oxalates may also be issues for some people so I have added them as well. They will all be noted in the code form below or mentioned in the notes. Please read these.

Low – L, Medium – M, High – H, Very High – VH, Salicylates – S, Oxalates – OX
Fructose – F, Fructans – FOS, Polyols – PO, Galactans – GOS

I have placed some homemade recipes for substituting the ingredients after the main recipes. These recipes will be for Gluten Free, Fructose Friendly, Lactose Free or Friendly, Diabetic Friendly and IBS Friendly depending on your sensitivity so that you can make your own if you want to. Please remember that Fructans, Polyols and Galactans can also come with Fructose.

Substituting ingredients will alter the original taste; however, it is a way to try different recipes from other countries and you can adjust the taste to your liking. Make these recipes your own and use your ingredients if you want to as you know what's best for you.

Australian tablespoons and cups measurements are used and they are: 1 teaspoon equals 5ml; 1 tablespoon equals 20ml; 1 cup equals 250ml. Oven temperatures are for conventional; if using fan-forced (convection), reduce the temperature by 20°C.

Recipe	Page
Doro Wot (Chicken Stew)	224
Shiro (Chickpea Flour Or Besan Flour)	225
Tibs Wot (Ethiopian Lamb Stew)	226
YeBeg Wot (Ethiopian Spicy Lamb Stew)	227
Alicha Doro (Mild Ethiopian Chicken Stew)	228
Key Wot (Ethiopian Spicy Beef Stew)	229
Quick Injera	230
Gluten Free Injera	231
Homemade Recipes For The Above Recipes	
Berbere	232
Homemade Chili Powder	233
Niter Kibbeh	234
How To make Tomato Paste The Quick And Easy Way	235

DORO WOT (CHICKEN STEW)

Ingredients
2 large or 3 small chicken breast fillets
1 cup very finely chopped onions (HF, HFOS, PO (mannitol), LOX and LS) or 3 spring onions (green parts only) diced (white part has M-HF, FOS, PO (mannitol) MOX and LS)
¼ cup red wine (varies in both OX and S) or t'ej (honey wine) (homemade recipe in notes) or non-alcoholic red wine (see red wine substitutes in notes)
¾ - 1 tablespoon berbere, to taste (homemade recipes after main recipes)
2 jalapeños, seeded and cut into slices or chili to your liking (F, PO (mannitol), HOX and HS) (see notes for heat tip)
4 tablespoons niter kibbeh (spiced clarified butter) (homemade recipe after main recipes) or olive oil (LOX and HS) or one to your liking

Directions
Cut the chicken into bite-sized pieces.

In a hot frying pan over medium heat, cook the onions, turning and stirring them often, until they begin to lightly brown and caramelize. Don't let them burn.

When they seem like they might soon begin to burn if you cook them any longer, add the kibbeh or oil, and stir the mixture. If you use kibbeh, wait until it's all melted until you add the next ingredients.

Add the berbere, and stir it into the moist sizzling onions. Let it cook for a minute, stirring it constantly. Then add the wine, and mix the ingredients together well. The wine will begin to cook off almost immediately.

Add the chicken and stir the mixture, then let it cook for a few minutes until the chicken begins to turn white on the outside. Slowly add ½ - ¾ cups of water, bring it just to a boil, and reduce the heat. Finally, add the sliced jalapeños.

Let it all simmer until the liquid is almost cooked off and the chicken pieces remain in a thick red sauce, about 15 - 20 minutes.

Notes
Quick and easy T'ej - Ethiopian Honey Wine (no info available for anything)
Combine the following ingredients in a glass jug or pitcher and stir to combine. Serve chilled.
2 cups light, sweet white wine (varies in OX and S) or non-alcoholic white wine (see substitute recipes below)
2 cups water (reduce to 1 - 1½ cups if you'd like a stronger drink)
¼ cup honey (HF, FOS, VLOX and VHS) or rice malt syrup for Fructose Free

Red wine substitute
Non-alcoholic wine with a tablespoon of vinegar (L-MOX and VHS) added to cut the sweetness, grape juice (Purple has HF, FOS, PO (sorbitol) and S. Red has HF, FOS, PO (sorbitol), MOX and S. White has MF, FOS, PO (sorbitol), LOX and S), cranberry juice (LF, PO, VLOX and VHS), grape jelly (no info available), tomato juice (HF, PO (aspartame), MOX and MS), beef broth, liquid drained from vegetables, or water. Use equal amounts of liquid as called for in the recipe.

White wine substitute
Can substitute; white grape juice (F, PO (sorbitol), LOX and MS), apple cider (F, PO (sorbitol), LOX and L-MS), apple juice (F, PO (sorbitol), VLOX and MS), vegetable stock (minus onion and garlic) or water.

For ¼ cup or more white wine, substitute the following: equal measure of white grape juice (F, PO (sorbitol) LOX and MS), chicken broth, vegetable broth, or non-alcoholic wine (no info on OX and S). If you use a non-alcoholic wine, add a tablespoon of vinegar (L-MOX and VHS) to cut the sweetness.

Tip
I have read that if you completely de-vein and take every seed out of a chili, it helps to cut down on the heat.

*   *   *   *   *

SHIRO (CHICKPEA FLOUR OR BESAN FLOUR)

Ingredients
3 cups of mitten Shiro to your liking (see notes)
3 large onions fine chopped (HF, HFOS, PO (mannitol), LOX and LS) or 9 spring onions (green parts only) diced (white part has M-HF, FOS, PO (mannitol) MOX and LS) (see notes)
1 cup of vegetable oil or one to your liking
5 teaspoons minced garlic (F, FOS, GOS, LOX and LS) (see notes)
1 tablespoon Berbere (homemade recipe after main recipes)
2 teaspoons salt
10 cups of water
1 spoonful niter kibbeh or to your taste (homemade recipe after main recipes)

Directions
In your pot, simmer onion and garlic with vegetable oil. Add berbere and simmer for about 8 minutes at low heat while adding a dash of water to avoid sticking.

Add the remaining water and mix the Shiro by adding a small portion of the Shiro flour at a time and continuously stirring. Let it cook until it becomes thick, but runny for about 25 minutes at low heat. Finish off by adding a spoon of niter kibbe.

Notes
There are two types of Shiro:
Mitten Shiro: chickpeas flour mix with a small amount of berbere to bring in additional flavor.

Shiro: chickpeas flour mix WITHOUT berbere.

You could try using a good pinch of asafoetida powder instead of both the onion and garlic. This is a very strong spice so don't use more than the specified amount.

TIBS WOT (ETHIOPIAN LAMB STEW)

Ingredients to serve 4
2 lbs or 900g loin lamb, boneless cut into ½ inch cubes
1 red onion, minced (HF, HFOS, PO (mannitol), MOX and MS) or 3 spring onions (green parts only) finely diced (white part has M-HF, FOS, PO (mannitol) MOX and LS)
1 jalapeno pepper, seeded and minced or chili to your liking (F, PO (mannitol), HOX and HS) (see notes for heat tip)
1¼ cups dry red wine (varies in OX and S) or stock to your liking (minus onion and garlic) (see notes for red wine substitutes)
1½ cups sweet butter (unsalted butter) Nuttelex Original or one to your liking
½ tablespoon turmeric (F, VHOX and VHS)
1 garlic clove, crushed (F, FOS, GOS, LOX and LS) (see notes)
2 cardamom pods, crushed (LOX and HS)
2 tablespoons mild chili powder (F and VHS) (homemade recipe after main recipes)
Kosher salt (an edible salt with a much larger grain size to common table salt so use only half the amount of common salt if substituting)
Fresh ground pepper (black - HOX and VHS, white - VLOX and VHS) to taste
1 tablespoon fresh rosemary, chopped (LOX and VHS)

Directions
In a medium mixing bowl, combine lamb, onion and jalapeno and add ¾ cup of red wine and mix well. Cover and refrigerate for one to two hours.

In a small saucepan, combine butter, turmeric, garlic and cardamom and bring to a boil. With a skimmer or large spoon, remove any impurities which come to the surface. Carefully pour only the clarified butter into a clean container, discarding the rest.

In a small saucepan over low heat, combine one tablespoon of the clarified butter with the chili powder and stir for about one minute; do not allow the butter to burn. Add ½ cup of red wine and then remove from heat and pour chili sauce into serving bowl.

Using a slotted spoon; remove lamb from marinade and drain lamb on paper towels. Reserve the marinade.

Place a large iron skillet over medium-high heat until very hot and then add two tablespoons clarified butter and add lamb and sauté until lamb is seared on all sides.

Add marinade to pan and continue stirring until lamb is cooked through, about two to three minutes. Season with the salt, pepper and rosemary.

Allow liquid in pan to reduce slightly.

Serve lamb and pan juices in individual bowls, accompanied by chili dipping sauce and Injera, (homemade recipe further down) with which to scoop up the meat.

Notes
You could try using a pinch of asafoetida powder instead of both the onion and garlic. This is a very strong spice so don't use more than the specified amount.

Red wine substitute
Non-alcoholic wine with a tablespoon of vinegar (L-MOX and VHS) added to cut the sweetness, grape juice (Purple has HF, FOS, PO (sorbitol) and S. Red has HF, FOS, PO (sorbitol), MOX and S.

White has MF, FOS, PO (sorbitol), LOX and S), cranberry juice (LF, PO, VLOX and VHS), grape jelly (no info available), tomato juice (HF, PO (aspartame), MOX and MS), beef broth, liquid drained from vegetables, or water. Use equal amounts of liquid as called for in the recipe.

Tip
I have read that if you completely de-vein and take every seed out of a chili, it helps to cut down on the heat.

*   *   *   *   *

YEBEG WOT (ETHIOPIAN SPICY LAMB STEW)

Ingredients
1lb or 450g lamb chops or 2lb or 900g lamb leg meat and bone
1 cup purified butter or niter kibbeh (spiced clarified butter - homemade recipes after main recipes) ¼ cup extra-virgin olive oil (LOX and HS) or one to your liking
4 cups chopped red onion (HF, HFOS, PO (mannitol), MOX and MS) or shallots (green parts only) (white part has M-HF, FOS, PO (mannitol) MOX and LS) thinly chopped (see notes)
1 cup hot red chili powder (berbere homemade recipe after main recipes)
2 teaspoon fresh garlic or 2 teaspoon garlic powder (F, FOS, GOS, LOX and LS) (see notes)
1 tablespoon red wine (varies in OX and S) (if preferred) or beef stock (minus onion and garlic)
2 teaspoons finely chopped rosemary (LOX and VHS)
2 teaspoons finely chopped thyme (LOX and VHS)
OR
¼ teaspoon black cumin (VHS)
1 teaspoon cardamom (korerima) (LOX and HS)
5 cups boiled water
Salt and black pepper (HOX and VHS) to taste

Directions
Cut the ribs, chop the meat and bone from the legs in desired shapes; wash it with cold water.

Boil water in large pot and put in the cleaned ribs, bone and the meat. Cover and boil it for 10 minutes and then strain.

In medium pot cook the chopped onion until golden brown using one cup of water by adding two tablespoon at a time until the onion is golden brown and soft.

Add one cup of warm water to the cooked onion, berbere (red chili powder), garlic, black cumin, red wine or stock and stir it well; add the purified butter and mix it very well (10 minutes).

Add the ribs and bone; stir for 10 minutes. Add the meat. Stir five minutes and add three cups warm (or more as desired) Cook it for 20 - 25 minutes until it simmers.

Add cardamom (korerima), salt and black pepper to taste. Remove from heat. Serve it warm. Keep the leftovers (if any) in the fridge.

Notes
You could try using ⅛ teaspoon of asafoetida powder instead of both the onion and garlic. This is a very strong spice so don't use more than the specified amount.

ALICHA DORO (MILD ETHIOPIAN CHICKEN STEW)

Ingredients
6 onions (HF, HFOS, PO (mannitol), LOX and LS) or 12 spring onions (green parts only) diced (white part has M-HF, FOS, PO (mannitol) MOX and LS) (see notes)
1 chicken, cut in parts, without skin
2 cups clarified, spiced butter (recipe below)
¼ teaspoon black pepper (HOX and VHS)
¼ teaspoon garlic powder (F, FOS, GOS, LOX and LS) or a pinch of asafoetida powder (may contain Gluten) (see notes)
¼ teaspoon ginger (F, FOS, LOX and MS)
½ cup wine (varies in OX and S) or chicken stock (minus onion and garlic) (see substitutes in notes)
Salt to taste
About 4 cups of water
4 hard-boiled eggs
A lime, quartered (F, PO, MOX and LS)

Spice Butter
1 lb of butter or Nuttelex Original or store bought clarified butter or one to your liking
Small piece of chopped ginger (F, FOS, LOX and MS)
1 clove of garlic (minced) (F, FOS, GOS, LOX and LS) or a pinch of asafoetida powder (may contain Gluten and is a strong spice)
A couple of slices of chopped onion (HF, HFOS, PO (mannitol), LOX and LS) (don't use if using asafoetida powder)
1 teaspoon of fenugreek (PO, MOX and VHS)
¼ teaspoon cumin (VHS)
½ teaspoon basil (F, MOX and VHS)
¼ teaspoon cardamon seeds (LOX and HS)
1 teaspoon of oregano (F, HOX and VHS)
A pinch of turmeric (F, VHOX and VHS)

Directions
Wash the chicken parts and soak in water with the lime.

In a large pot, fry the onions without fat until tender. Add butter (and asafoetida powder if using) and stir.

Add about ½ cup of water and the wine or stock and add the spices and then add the chicken and cook for about 45 minutes.

Add more water if necessary, and cook until done, and until the sauce is reduced (though it'll have to cool down to solidify a little).

Add four eggs and serve.

To make the spiced butter
Melt the butter in a pot. Skim the foam as it forms, until the butter is pretty much clear or you can also use store bought clarified butter.

Mix chopped ginger, minced garlic and a couple of slices of chopped onion or asafoetida powder and add to the butter.

Add fenugreek, cumin, basil, cardamon seeds, oregano and a pinch of turmeric. Stir and simmer for about 15 minutes. Let the spices settle, and then drain.

Note

You could try using ⅛ teaspoon of asafoetida powder instead of both the onion and garlic in the man recipe. This is a very strong spice so don't use more than the specified amount.

You can make this dish into the much more delicious (and spicy) doro wat, chicken stew, by adding up to one cup of berbere.

White wine substitute

Can substitute; white grape juice (F, PO (sorbitol), LOX and MS), apple cider (F, PO (sorbitol), LOX and L-MS), apple juice (F, PO (sorbitol), VLOX and MS), vegetable stock (minus onion and garlic) or water. For ¼ cup or more white wine, substitute the following: equal measure of white grape juice (F, PO (sorbitol), LOX and MS), chicken broth (minus onion and garlic), vegetable broth (minus onion and garlic), or non-alcoholic wine (no info on OX and S). If you use a non-alcoholic wine, add a tablespoon of vinegar (L-MOX and VHS) to cut the sweetness.

*   *   *   *   *

KEY WOT (ETHIOPIAN SPICY BEEF STEW)

Ingredients

1½ lbs or 750g beef, cut into 1 inch cubes
3 tablespoons oil to your liking
2 tablespoons ghee or unsalted butter or niter kibbeh, (which is the real thing) (homemade recipe after main recipes)
1 onion, small, finely chopped (HF, HFOS, PO (mannitol), LOX and LS) or 3 spring onions (green parts only) diced (white part has M-HF, FOS, PO (mannitol) MOX and LS) (see notes)
2 garlic cloves, chopped and crushed (F, FOS, GOS, LOX and LS) (see notes)
2 teaspoons berbere spice powder (homemade recipe after main recipes)
2 tablespoons tomato paste (HF, FOS, PO (mannitol), HOX and VHS) (homemade recipe after main recipes)
½ teaspoon dextrose powder (may contain Gluten) or sugar
2 cups or 500ml beef stock (minus onion and garlic) or water
2 teaspoons sea salt or to taste

Directions

Add the oil and ghee or butter to a pan over medium heat and gently fry the onion until very soft and just about caramelised.

Add the garlic, berbere spice powder, tomato paste and dextrose powder or sugar, mix well, and cook until thick. Add a little of the stock (or water) to make a paste.

Add the remaining liquid and the meat cubes, season with salt, and cook gently for 1 hour or until the meat is tender and the sauce thickened and reduced.

Serve with Injera, the Ethiopian flatbread. (If correctly made and almost crispy, pieces can be used as eating utensils).

QUICK INJERA http://www.whats4eats.com/sauces/niter-kibbeh-recipe

For those craving Ethiopian food but short on time; this shortcut recipe approximates true Injera, which is a sourdough crepe made from a fermented sourdough batter. Most quick recipes don't call for the lemon juice, but I find it necessary to supply the essential sour flavor that real Injera adds to a meal. This recipe is for normal Injera.

Ingredients for 6 to 8 crepes
1½ cups all-purpose flour to your liking
½ cup whole wheat flour to your liking
1 tablespoon baking powder (VLOX)
½ teaspoon salt
2 - 2½ cups club soda
2 lemons, juice only (F, PO (sorbitol), LOX and L-HS)

Directions
Preheat a large cast-iron skillet over a medium flame. Mix the all-purpose flour, whole-wheat flour, baking powder and salt together in a large bowl.

Stir in the club soda and mix to a smooth batter. It should have the thin consistency of a pancake batter.

Wipe the skillet with a little oil using a paper towel. Ladle about ½ cup of the batter into the skillet and spread it with a spatula to make a large crepe.

Let bake in the skillet until all the bubbles on top burst and begin to dry out, about 2 - 3 minutes.

Carefully turn the Injera over and cook on second side another minute or two. Try not to brown it too much.

Remove the Injera to a warm platter and repeat with the rest of the batter, wiping the skillet clean with an oiled paper towel each time.

After the batter is used up, use a pastry brush to brush each Injera with the lemon juice. Serve immediately or hold covered in a warm oven.

Quick Injera Variations
You can substitute buckwheat flour for the whole wheat flour if you like, or just use all white flour. If you can find teff flour at a health food store, by all means use it.

GLUTEN FREE INJERA

Ingredients to make 4-6 Injera (Try to buy everything organic)
1½ cups teff flour
2 cups pure water
½ teaspoon baking powder (VLOX)
Coconut oil (HS) for pan or one to your liking
¼ teaspoon salt, or more to taste

Directions
Place Teff flour in a large glass bowl, add water and stir well.

Cover with a cheesecloth or towel and place on the counter and let it sit for 1 day / 24hrs. Do not agitate or stir the batter, just leave it be.

After 24 hours, you'll see that your batter is alive and fermenting. (Every batch you make may look a bit different from the one before).

Bring a pan to medium heat, and very lightly, coat the pan with coconut oil.

Stir in the salt and season with more taste if you like, until you can barely detect the saltiness and stir in the baking powder. Your batter will deflate when you stir it.

Now pour enough batter into the pan to fill entire surface and cover with a lid, or if you don't have a lid, use a cookie sheet. It's important to keep a lot of moisture in the pan or the Injera will crack.

You don't flip Injera, and you aren't supposed to brown its underside, but if you like the taste of it browned, then overcook it a bit. It takes about 5 - 7 minutes to cook Injera.

You'll see the top bubble like pancakes and start to dry out. When the top is dry, and the edges begin to curl/dry, use a spatula to remove the Injera from the pan.

Place on a plate and repeat, layering cooked Injera with parchment paper until you use up all the batter.

Notes
This recipe has been successfully prepared without fermentation many times - it's just not sour. If you want to prepare it this way, just skip the fermentation step, mix all ingredients in a bowl and cook. Store in an airtight glass container in the fridge.

HOMEMADE RECIPES FOR THE ABOVE RECIPES

BERBERE http://www.whats4eats.com/sauces/niter-kibbeh-recipe

Berbere, along with niter kibbeh, supplies one of the unique flavors of Ethiopian cuisine. There really is no substitute. Use as many of the spices as you can, but do try to use fenugreek and the dried peppers or paprika. They supply an essential flavor.

The recipe below makes a spice paste that is ready to use in Ethiopian dishes. If you prefer a longer shelf life, use the variation below that eliminates the moist ingredients and makes a dry spice mix.

Ingredients to make about 1½ cups
2 teaspoons whole cumin (VHS)
1 or 2 teaspoons red pepper flakes (HF, PO (sorbitol), VLOX and VHS)
1 teaspoon cardamom seeds (LOX and HS)
1 teaspoon Fenugreek seeds (PO, MOX and VHS)
8 whole peppercorns (HOX and VHS)
6 allspice berries (VHS)
4 whole cloves (F, VHOX and HS)
3 or 4 New Mexico dried chilies (F, PO (mannitol) HOX and HS) (**see notes**)
1 onion, chopped (HF, HFOS, PO (mannitol), LOX and LS) or 3 spring onions (green parts only) diced (white part has M-HF, FOS, PO (mannitol) MOX and LS) (see notes)
3 garlic cloves, crushed (F, FOS, GOS, LOX and LS) (see notes)
1 tablespoon paprika (F and VHS)
1 tablespoon salt
1 teaspoon ginger, ground (F, FOS, LOX and MS)
1 teaspoon turmeric (F, VHOX and VHS)
½ - 1 teaspoon cayenne pepper (LOX and VHS)
½ teaspoon nutmeg (VLOX and VHS)
½ cup oil to your liking
¼ cup water or red wine (varies in OX and S) (see notes for substitutions)

Directions
Heat a cast-iron skillet over medium flame. Add the whole spices and toast, stirring for about 2 - 3 minutes until they give off their aroma. Do not burn. Remove from heat.

Over an open flame, use a pair of tongs to lightly toast the New Mexico chilies, turning quickly from side to side until they soften and become flexible. Do not burn. Remove the stems and seeds and roughly chop.

Put the spices and dried peppers into a spice or coffee grinder and grind to a powder.

Put the ground toasted spices into a food processor or blender along with the remaining ingredients and process until smooth.

Store in the refrigerator for up to a week or freeze portions for later use.

Berbere Variations
Dry Berbere Spice Mix
Omit the onion, garlic, water and oil. Mix all the spices together and store in an airtight jar.

Add the powder when paste is called for in recipes. Stored in a cool, dark place, this spice mix should keep its flavor for about 4 - 6 months.

You can make berbere as spicy or as mild as you like. Just vary the amount of pepper flakes and cayenne in the recipe.

Notes

If you don't have all the whole spices, substitute an equivalent amount of ground. Eliminate the toasting step.

If New Mexico chilies are not available, substitute another Mexican-style dried chili: anchos, guajilla, etc. If no dried chilies are available, substitute 2 more tablespoons of paprika.

You may like to use a pinch of asafoetida powder (may contain Gluten) instead of the garlic and onion. This is a very strong spice so don't use more than the specified amount.

Red wine substitute

Non-alcoholic wine with a tablespoon of vinegar (L-MOX and VHS) added to cut the sweetness, grape juice (Purple has HF, FOS, PO (sorbitol) and S. Red has HF, FOS, PO (sorbitol), MOX and S. White has MF, FOS, PO (sorbitol), LOX and S), cranberry juice (LF, PO, VLOX and VHS), grape jelly (no info available), tomato juice (HF, PO (aspartame), MOX and MS), beef broth, liquid drained from vegetables, or water. Use equal amounts of liquid as called for in the recipe.

    *   *   *   *   *

HOMEMADE CHILI POWDER

Ingredients

2 tablespoons paprika (F and VHS)
2 teaspoons oregano (F, HOX and VHS)
1½ teaspoons cumin (VHS)
1½ teaspoons garlic powder (F, FOS, GOS, LOX and LS)
¾ teaspoon onion powder (HF, HFOS, PO (mannitol), LOX and LS)
½ teaspoon cayenne pepper (LOX and VHS) (omit or increase to taste)

Directions

Place all ingredients in a bowl and blend thoroughly.

Store in an airtight container in the refrigerator.

Paprika is a pepper and should be refrigerated for maximum shelf life and potency.

NITER KIBBEH http://www.whats4eats.com/sauces/niter-kibbeh-recipe

Niter kibbeh - a spice-infused, clarified butter - is a ubiquitous cooking medium in Ethiopian cuisine that adds an incomparable flavor to dishes. Plain butter or oil can be substituted in Ethiopian recipes if you don't have the time to make niter kibbeh, but something special will be missing.

Ingredients to make about 2 cups
1 lb or 450g unsalted butter or Nuttelex Original or one to your liking
½ onion, chopped (HF, HFOS, PO (mannitol), LOX and LS) or 2 spring onions (green parts only) diced (white part has M-HF, FOS, PO (mannitol) MOX and LS) (see notes)
2 or 3 cloves garlic, crushed (F, FOS, GOS, LOX and LS) (see notes)
2 or 3 pieces gingerroot, cut into ¼-inch or 6mm slices (F, FOS, LOX and MS)
3 or 4 cardamom pods (LOX and HS)
1 cinnamon stick (F, HOX and VHS)
3 or 4 whole cloves (F, VHOX and HS)
1 teaspoon fenugreek seeds (PO, MOX and VHS)
½ teaspoon turmeric (F, VHOX and VHS)

Directions
Place the butter in a small saucepan and melt over low heat. Add the remaining ingredients and simmer on the lowest possible heat for about 1 hour.

Pour the clear golden liquid off the top leaving all the solids in the bottom of the pan. Strain through cheesecloth if necessary. Discard solids.

Store in the refrigerator or freezer and use as needed.

Niter Kibbeh Variations
For a lower cholesterol version, substitute 2 cups of vegetable oil or a combination of oil and butter.

The spices and amounts are not set in stone, so don't worry if you don't have all of them.

Notes
As the garlic and onion are only used for flavouring, you may like to use a pinch of asafoetida powder (may contain Gluten) instead. This is a strong spice so don't use more than a pinch.

HOW TO MAKE TOMATO PASTE THE QUICK AND EASY WAY

This recipe makes about 5 heaped tablespoons.

Soak 2 kilos (4½ lbs) of tomatoes (HF, FOS, PO (mannitol), MOX and MS) in boiling water for five minutes or until the skins can be easily peeled off. Drain and carefully remove the tomato skin. The tomatoes may be hot to handle.

Carefully cut tomatoes in half or quarters longways and de-seed completely. Place tomato pieces in to processor and process to a very liquidy paste.

If you have a slow cooker, then place this liquid paste in it and leave it to reduce and thicken up. Stir occasionally. I left mine on all day and got a beautiful thick tomato paste to use in my recipes.

If you don't have a slow cooker you can cook the paste in a 350°F / 180°C preheated oven on shallow trays until it is reduced to a paste. Check the tomatoes every half hour, stirring the paste and switching the position of the trays so that they reduce evenly. Over time, the paste will start to reduce to the point where you can make one tray.

The paste is done when shiny and brick-colored, and it has reduced by more than half. There shouldn't be any remaining water or moisture separating from the paste at this point. This will take 3 - 4 hours, though exact baking/cooking times will depend on the juiciness of your tomatoes and your oven.

After the paste was cold; I put it in a container and kept it in the refrigerator or freezer.

Making small batches when you need it can be useful; however, if you use a lot of tomato paste then just double or triple the amount of tomatoes used. I made a very small batch using the same prep method but I cooked them down in my non-stick frypan over low heat and I continually stirred the mixture. I did not add anything to the paste because I can do that when I use it in a recipe.

ITALY

I would like to say Grazie to Nonna for kindly donating the following recipes to me.

The vegetables and fruit in these recipes will only make them Fructose Friendly. I have tried to source out whether they have Fructose, Fructans, Polyols or Galactans in them and have indicated this beside the ingredient plus a few ingredients have alternatives beside them or in the notes at the end of each recipe. I am hoping that this will help you as much as it has helped me. Salicylates and Oxalates may also be issues for some people so I have added them as well. They will all be noted in the code form below or mentioned in the notes. Please read these.

Low – L, Medium – M, High – H, Very High – VH, Salicylates – S, Oxalates – OX
Fructose – F, Fructans – FOS, Polyols – PO, Galactans – GOS

I have placed some homemade recipes for substituting the ingredients after the main recipes. These recipes will be for Gluten Free, Fructose Friendly, Lactose Free or Friendly, Diabetic Friendly and IBS Friendly depending on your sensitivity so that you can make your own if you want to. Please remember that Fructans, Polyols and Galactans can also come with Fructose.

Substituting ingredients will alter the original taste; however, it is a way to try different recipes from other countries and you can adjust the taste to your liking. Make these recipes your own and use your ingredients if you want to as you know what's best for you.

Australian tablespoons and cups measurements are used and they are: 1 teaspoon equals 5ml; 1 tablespoon equals 20ml; 1 cup equals 250ml. Oven temperatures are for conventional; if using fan-forced (convection), reduce the temperature by 20°C.

Amatrice Spaghetti	237
Minestrone Soup	238
Linguine With Porcini Mushrooms And Sausage	239
Vegetable Focaccia	240
Gluten Free Focaccia Bread 1	241
Gluten Free Focaccia Bread 2	242
Pizza Margherita	243
Gluten-Free Mini Pizzas And Bread Sticks	244
Savoiardi (Ladyfingers)	245
Gluten-Free Tiramisu Squares	246
Authentic Tiramisu	248
Homemade Recipes For The Above Recipes	
How To Make Tomato Paste The Quick And Easy Way	250
Homemade Tin/Can Tomatoes Substitute	251
Homemade Dairy Free, Soy Free White Chocolate	251
Homemade Dark Chocolate (Fructose Free)	252
Homemade Compound Chocolate	252
Homemade Lactose Free Mascarpone Cheese	253

AMATRICE SPAGHETTI

Ingredients to serve 4
200g (⅓ cup) of chopped guanciale (cured pork cheek) or pancetta
Extra virgin olive oil (LOX and HS) or one to your liking
Chopped dry chilli to your liking (F, PO (mannitol) HOX and HS)
A tablespoon of white wine vinegar (L-MOX and VHS)
¼ cup of dry white wine (varies in OX and S) (see notes for substitutions)
450g or 1lb of Gluten Free pasta or one to your liking
500g or 2 cups of peeled tomatoes (fresh HF, FOS, PO (mannitol), MOX and MS) (tinned tomatoes HF, PO (aspartame), H-VHOX and LS?) or passata (HF, FOS, PO (mannitol), HOX and VHS) (homemade recipes after main recipes)
Salt and pepper (black - HOX and VHS, white - VLOX and VHS) to taste
Freshly grated Pecorino cheese to serve (stated to be Lactose Free)

Directions
Fry the guanciale or pancetta in the oil keeping the flame low to allow the fat to render and the pork to develop a sweet flavour. When it's starting to get a nice sun-burnt colour, add a sprinkle of chopped dry chilli and glaze the pan with white wine vinegar and dry white wine. The acidity will balance the richness of the caramelized cured pork.

In the meantime, drop the pasta into salted boiling water.

Return to your sauce. When the alcohol has evaporated, add the tinned tomatoes (or passata) and allow to cook for 20 - 25 minutes over low heat. Taste for salt and adjust accordingly.

When the pasta is al dente, drop it into your sauce, with a couple of tablespoons of pasta cooking water. This will help to bind the sauce and achieve a creamy consistency.

Turn the heat off and mix through a very generous amount of pecorino and freshly ground black pepper, if liked. Let it rest for a few minutes before serving, to allow the pepperiness of the cheese to impregnate the pasta.

Notes
Dry white wine substitute
Water, chicken broth (minus onion and garlic), ginger ale (HF and LOX), white grape juice (F, PO (sorbitol), LOX and MS), diluted cider vinegar (F, L-MOX and VHS) or white wine vinegar (L-MOX and VHS).

MINESTRONE SOUP

Ingredients

2 tablespoons extra-virgin olive oil (LOX and HS) or one to your liking
1 large onion, diced (HF, HFOS, PO (mannitol), LOX and LS) or 3 spring onions (green parts only) diced (white part has M-HF, FOS, PO (mannitol) MOX and LS) (see notes)
4 cloves garlic, minced (F, FOS, GOS, LOX and LS) (see notes)
2 stalks celery, diced (HF, FOS, PO (mannitol) and VHOX) (try substituting ¾ cup of chopped celery leaves for the stalks)
1 large carrot, diced (HF, FOS (raffinose), PO (sorbitol), GOS, VHOX and HS)
⅓ lb or 150g green beans, trimmed and cut into ½" pieces (about 1½ cups) (HF, FOS, PO (sorbitol), VLOX and MS)
1 teaspoon dried oregano (F, HOX and VHS)
1 teaspoon dried basil (F, MOX and VHS)
Kosher salt (an edible salt with a much larger grain size to common table salt so use half the amount if substituting)
Freshly ground pepper (black - HOX and VHS, white - VLOX and VHS)
1 x 28oz can or 800g no-salt-added diced tomatoes (HF, PO (aspartame), H-VHOX and LS?) (homemade recipe after main recipes)
1 x 14oz or 400g can crushed tomatoes (HF, PO (aspartame), H-VHOX and LS?) (homemade recipe after main recipes)
6 cups low-sodium chicken broth (minus onion and garlic)
1 x 15oz or 420g can low-sodium kidney beans, drained and rinsed or 1½ cups cooked or 30g or 1oz dry kidney beans soaked overnight and then cooked (F, GOS and HOX) (see notes)
1 cup Gluten Free elbow pasta or one to your liking
⅓ cup finely grated parmesan cheese (stated to be Lactose Free)
2 tablespoons chopped fresh basil (F, MOX and VHS)

Directions

Heat the olive oil in a large pot over medium-high heat. Add the onion and cook until translucent, about 4 minutes. Add the garlic and cook 30 seconds. Add the celery and carrot and cook until they begin to soften, about 5 minutes. Stir in the green beans, dried oregano and basil, ¾ teaspoon salt, and pepper to taste; cook 3 more minutes.

Add the diced and crushed tomatoes and the chicken broth to the pot and bring to a boil. Reduce the heat to medium low and simmer 10 minutes. Stir in the kidney beans and pasta and cook until the pasta and vegetables are tender, about 10 minutes.

Season with more salt if needed and then ladle into bowls and top with the parmesan and chopped basil.

Notes

You could try using ⅛ teaspoon of asafoetida powder instead of both the onion and garlic. This is a very strong spice so don't use more than the specified amount.

Soaking the dried kidney beans overnight in warm water with a heaped teaspoon of bi-carb soda may help to reduce the gas effect. Change the water a few times and rinse well before cooking.

LINGUINE WITH PORCINI MUSHROOMS AND SAUSAGE

Ingredients for 4 people
350g or 11oz Gluten Free linguine or spaghetti or one to your liking
4 young porcini mushrooms (see notes) or ones to your liking
2 sausages flavored with fennel seeds (FOS and LS) or ones to your liking
1 clove of garlic crushed (F, FOS, GOS, LOX and LS) (see notes)
4 ripe tomatoes (HF, FOS, PO (mannitol), MOX and MS)
Olive oil (LOX and HS) or one to your liking
Salt and pepper (black - HOX and VHS, white - VLOX and VHS)
5 - 6 pieces dried or smoked herring (optional) (see notes)

Directions
Clean the mushrooms with a damp cloth to remove the remaining dirt and cut into small pieces. Crumble sausage removing the outer casing and set it aside.

In a saucepan, sauté the garlic along with olive oil and, soon is golden, remove it and add the mushrooms and sausage leaving them to cook over medium heat for about 15 minutes.

After this time, with the help of a wooden spoon, move mushrooms and sausage on the side edges of the pan and pour in the center the chopped tomatoes and cook over high heat for about 5 minutes and then mix well, season with salt and pepper and remove from the heat.

Separately, boil the linguine in plenty of boiling salted water and just cooked, drain briefly and add to the pan with the mushrooms and sausage. Mix well for a few moments and serve immediately.

Notes
Dried mushrooms usually require soaking in boiled water for an hour to return them to an edible state (the liquor they have been soaked in is a great addition to stocks and sauces or you can use the liquid but leave any sediment in the bottom of the bowl). Dried mushrooms usually have a stronger flavour than their fresh counterpart.

Substitute for Porcini mushrooms
Substitute reconstituted dry for fresh OR use Shiitake (less earthy but similar meaty texture)

Equivalents
1½ oz or 40g dried porcini mushrooms = 1lb or 450g fresh porcini mushrooms

Dried Herring
You can buy these dried herring in bottles in Asian stores or other stores, depending on where you live (preferred). Outside the Philippines, it is more common to find the dried herring that still need to be cooked. If you want to brave the smell, then grab a saucepan with oil and warm it up over medium heat.

When the oil is already hot, drop the dried herring and cook both sides. The scales should come out crispy (that you will scrape away when you are about to eat). This takes only about 5 - 8 minutes but you will have to open your windows the whole day to send the last of the dried herring smell. Don't say I didn't tell you to buy the bottled ones.

You can also crumble smoked kippers over pasta. A good smoked herring, especially the canned kippers, which are more satisfying than sardines (members of the herring family).

VEGETABLE FOCACCIA
Basic Normal Focaccia Recipe

Ingredients
5 cups all-purpose unbleached flour or one to your liking
2 teaspoons Instant yeast (baker's - MOX and LS, non- bakers - MOX and VHS)
2 - 3 tablespoons extra virgin olive oil (LOX and HS) (plus 2 extra tablespoons to oil the bowl) or one to your liking
1 teaspoon salt
2 cups warm water
Extra virgin olive oil (LOX and HS) for top
Coarse sea salt for top
Optional toppings of choice
Grated vegetables or cheese to add in to your dough (optional) (see notes)

Directions
Measure and assemble your flour, oil, salt, yeast, and water.

Add everything but the water into a large bowl and stir to combine well and then add half the water and stir.

Continue to add water until the dough begins to come together into a shaggy ball.

Dump the dough mixture onto a lightly floured surface and begin to knead with the heels of your hand.

Knead for about 5 minutes, or until the dough is smooth and pliant.

Add a little oil (2 tablespoons) to the bottom of a large bowl and place your ball of dough inside. Roll the ball around in the oil, ensuring the sides of the bowl, and ball of dough are both lightly oiled.

Cover your bowl with plastic wrap and place in a warm spot to rise.

Let the dough rise until it is doubled in size, about 1 - 1½ hours depending on the temperature.

You can see how pillowy and soft the dough becomes.

To make a large rectangular focaccia; lightly oil a 13 x 9" (23 x 33cm) baking sheet with sides.

Dump your risen dough into the pan punching it down to deflate it.

Use your fingers to push and press the dough evenly over the bottom of the pan. Cover with a kitchen towel and let rise for another 20 - 30 minutes or until the dough dimples when pushed with your fingertip.

Use the tips of your fingers to dimple the entire top of the focaccia.

Drizzle olive oil over the top turning the pan carefully to allow the oil to roll into the indentations.

Sprinkle coarse sea salt over the top of your focaccia and then let it sit and rise for another 15 minutes while you preheat your oven to 425°F / 220°C.

Bake for 20 - 25 minutes until golden brown. Cool to room temperature before slicing.

Notes
This is something different to try:
Finely grate vegetables and squeeze out as much liquid as possible and add to the flour mix and stir well to cover the vegetables with flour before adding any liquid. You could also finely grate cheese and add it or use a selection of your favourite herbs. This process of adding to the focaccia mix is similar to making a savoury or cheese loaf of bread. Imagine serving something like this to your friends or family for a change. Your imagination can go wild here.

*   *   *   *   *

GLUTEN FREE FOCACCIA BREAD 1

Ingredients to serve 6 - 8 people
1 cup sorghum flour (FOS)
1 cup yellow corn flour (MOX and HS) (organic if possible)
⅔ cup tapioca flour (FOS)
⅓ cup chickpea flour/besan flour (FOS, GOS and MOX)
1 teaspoon Instant dried yeast (bakers - MOX and LS, non- bakers - MOX and VHS)
300ml or 1¼ cups water room temperature

Directions
Add all of the dry bread mix ingredients to a large mixing bowl and stir well to combine.

Add water gradually and stir until it forms a dough ball. Don't add too much water or you could end up with pancake batter.

Once the mixture comes together into a ball, cover it with a tea towel and let it sit in a warm draft free area for at least one hour. You will feel that it becomes a little bit spongy.

Preheat oven to 210°C / 420°F.

Line a baking tray with some non-stick parchment paper and place the dough on top. Spread flat and into a rectangular shape. If you find the dough is too dry, just wet your hands slightly to help shape it.

Poke holes into the dough with your fingers to help the dough cook more evenly and to add the traditional focaccia look.

Top with your favourite topping and bake for 20 minutes or until top is browned to your liking.

Notes
Some Gluten Free flours have a higher carb count and may affect people with Diabetes and those who have to watch their intake of carbohydrates. You may also need to adjust the liquid to suit.

GLUTEN FREE FOCACCIA BREAD 2

Ingredients
3½ cups Gluten Free Bread Mix (options pages 13 & 14) (see notes)
1 package yeast (bakers - MOX and LS, non- bakers - MOX and VHS)
¼ cup olive oil (LOX and HS) or one to your liking
1½ cups warm water
2 teaspoons fresh rosemary, finely chopped (LOX and VHS)
1½ tablespoons dried chopped onion flakes (HF, HFOS, PO (mannitol), LOX and LS) or 3 single pieces of spring onions (green parts only) diced (white part has M-HF, FOS, PO (mannitol) MOX and LS)
½ teaspoon dried parsley flakes (F, PO (mannitol) LOX and LS)
½ teaspoon dried basil (F, MOX and VHS)
1 teaspoon salt or to taste

Directions
Preheat oven to 425°F / 220°C.

Using an electric stand mixer, place the bread mix, yeast, and rosemary in mixing bowl and stir or mix (use whisk) to combine. Then add the wet ingredients, the warm water and olive oil and mix on medium speed for 2 minutes.

OR

Add all of the dry bread mix ingredients to a large mixing bowl and mix well to combine. Add water gradually and stir until it forms a dough ball. Don't add too much water or you could end up with pancake batter.

Pour a tablespoon or two of oil into a baking dish (9 x 13" or 23 x 33cm) and rub the oil all over the dish. Place the dough into the baking dish and spread it to cover the entire bottom of dish, using a spreader and knife or your hands to get it to the sides.

Brush olive oil over the top of the focaccia bread and then use your fingers to press divots all over the dough. Sprinkle the onion, parsley, basil, and salt over the top. Cover with plastic wrap and place in a warm spot to rise for at least 1 hour.

Remove the plastic wrap and place in the center of the oven and bake for 12 minutes. Then check the bread to see how it's doing. Ovens vary so it's good to see how things are cooking.

Place back in the oven for an additional 10 minutes. You want the top of the bread to be a nice golden brown. Look at the bottom of the dish if using glass and see how golden that is.

If the dough is a little doughy after cutting into it, simply place it back in the oven for 3 minute and then check it again. Continue to do the checking every 3 minutes until done to your liking.

Focaccia bread is always best the day you make it. You can save it for the next day by placing it in a ziploc bag and reheating in a 375°F / 190°C oven.

Notes
Some Gluten Free flours have a higher carb count and may affect people with Diabetes and those who have to watch their intake of carbohydrates. You may also need to adjust the liquid to suit.

PIZZA MARGHERITA

Ingredients (normal pizza)
For base
2lb or 900g all-purpose flour
1oz or 9 teaspoons or 4 x 7g packets fresh or dried yeast (bakers - MOX and LS, non- bakers - MOX and VHS)
2 cups water
⅜ oz or 2¼ teaspoons salt

For dressing
½ cup extra virgin olive oil (LOX and HS) or one to your liking
1lb or 450g mozzarella cheese
Basil leaves to taste (F, MOX and VHS)
1lb or 2 cups canned tomatoes (HF, PO (aspartame), H-VHOX and LS?) (homemade recipe for passata/sauce after main recipes)
Salt to taste

Directions
On a wooden or marble or clean work surface, shape the flour into a well. Place the yeast, salt and warm water in the center. Be careful not to let the salt come in contact with the yeast.

Knead the dough vigorously with your hands for 15 - 20 minutes, or in a mixer, until the dough is soft and smooth. Once you have the right consistency, adding a bit of water or flour if necessary, shape the dough into a ball. Cover with a plastic bowl so that the dough is protected from the air. Let rise for 3 - 4 hours at room temperature or for about an hour in a warm place.

Once the dough will be doubled in volume, shape into spherical shapes, cover with a sheet of plastic wrap and let them rise at room temperature for a couple of hours or in a warm place for about 45 minutes.

As soon as the loaves have doubled in volume, prepare the tomato sauce and place it in a bowl. Add a pinch of salt and ⅓ of the olive oil. Knead the dough, then flattening them using your fingers.

Make the sauce
Cut the tomatoes into wedges and trim away the stem area. Gently squeeze the wedges over a bowl to remove the excess juices and seeds.

Combine the tomatoes with the garlic and half of the basil in the bowl of a food processor or blender. Process until the tomatoes break down into a sauce, scraping down the sides as needed. If desired, strain to make a thicker sauce.

Use a ladle or a spoon to spread a good amount of tomato sauce on the pizza. Then, cover with mozzarella, torn into pieces. Garnish with a couple leaves of basil and bake in a 480°F / 250°C oven for 5 - 6 minutes.

Once ready, remove the pizza from the oven. Garnish with more basil and a drizzle of oil and serve immediately.

Notes
These may not be Diabetic Friendly due to carbs in flour.

GLUTEN-FREE MINI PIZZAS AND BREAD STICKS

This recipes comes from my first cook book

Ingredients to make 4 (9") pizzas or about 30 bread sticks of varying lengths
150g (1⅔ cups) blanched almond meal (FOS, PO (xylitol), VHOX and VHS)
150g (1 cup + 1 tablespoon) brown rice flour (FOS)
63g (½ cup) tapioca flour (FOS)
63g (¼ cup + 2 tablespoons) potato starch (LOX)
2 teaspoons (10ml) baking powder (VLOX)
1 teaspoon (5ml) kosher salt (an edible salt with a much larger grain size to common table salt so half the amount if substituting)
1 cup (240ml) buttermilk or Lactose Free milk +1 tablespoon or 10ml lemon juice (F, PO (sorbitol), LOX and L-HS) or vinegar (L-MOX and VHS)
½ cup (120ml) water

Directions
Preheat a Panini press. (To me, it looks like a heavy based frypan with grill lines in it, and has a lid, which sits on the stove top. The electrical ones, to me, looks like a "George Foreman" style grill. A big sandwich press with grill lines).

Combine the almond flour, brown rice flour, tapioca flour, potato starch, baking powder and salt in a large bowl and whisk together.

Add the buttermilk and water, and then beat with an electric mixer until there is no dry flour and the batter is smooth.

Pour ¾ cup of batter on the center of the Panini press. Use a heat-resistant utensil to spread it across the widest part of the grill surface.

Quickly press the top down, holding firmly for a moment so that the dough spreads evenly.

Cook for 3 minutes if you're making pizzas. Cook for 5 minutes if you're making bread sticks. Remove the bread to a wire rack to cool and cook the remaining batter.

For bread sticks: while the bread is warm, use a serrated knife to cut it into narrow sticks.

Run the knife along a ridge to score the top, and then fold along the scored line to break the bread evenly. Try making your bread sticks two ridges wide. Cool on a wire rack.

For pizzas: you can finish the pizzas now or cool them and freeze for later.

Heat the oven to 500°F / 260°C.

Cover a cookie sheet with aluminium foil and put 2 of the flat breads on it. Add your choice of cheese and toppings to the flat breads.

Bake for 15 minutes, or till the cheese melts and begins to brown. Put toppings on the remaining pizzas while the first ones are in the oven. Remove from oven when done and serve.

Notes
These may not be Diabetic Friendly due to carbs in flour. Your choice of topping will determine if they are Fructose/Fructan/Polyol Friendly, IBS Friendly, Salicylate and Oxalate friendly.

These next 2 recipes I have had in my stock pile of recipes; however, they didn't make it into my first cook book so now I can use them in this one.

SAVOIARDI (LADYFINGERS)

Ingredients for normal recipes
3 eggs, separated
100g or ½ cup dextrose powder (may contain Gluten) or granulated sugar, divided
A pinch of salt
1 teaspoon vanilla extract (F, VLOX and VHS)
2 teaspoons freshly squeezed lemon juice, divided (F, PO (sorbitol), LOX and L-HS)
The zest of 1 lemon, grated (F, PO (sorbitol) and HOX)
65g or ½ cup Gluten Free cake flour, sifted or one to your liking (options on pages 13 & 14)
30g or 2 tablespoons potato starch (LOX)
Dextrose powder (may contain Gluten) or Icing sugar (powdered sugar) for dusting

Directions
Preheat the oven to 180°C / 350°F.

Line two baking sheets with parchment paper. Prepare a pastry bag fitted with a round 1.5 cm (½") tip.

In a medium bowl, beat the egg whites, 50g or ¼ cup of sugar and 1 teaspoon of lemon juice until stiff peaks form.

In another bowl, beat the egg yolks with the remaining sugar, lemon zest, vanilla extract, 1 teaspoon of lemon juice and salt until thick and light yellow.

Sift the flour and potato starch over the egg mixture and gently fold it in with a rubber spatula until smooth and well combined.

Gently fold in the egg whites.

Transfer half of the batter to the prepared piping bag. Pipe the batter into lines about 10 cm (4") long, keeping distance between them.

Repeat with the rest of the batter.

Sprinkle the cookies lightly with icing sugar. Let them rest for about 5 minutes and sprinkle again with icing sugar.

Place the baking sheet in the oven and bake for about 15 minutes until lightly golden.

Let the ladyfingers cool for a few minutes then release them from the parchment paper, with a flat spatula, while they are still warm.

Serve the Savoiardi immediately or store in an airtight container up to 2 weeks.

GLUTEN-FREE TIRAMISU SQUARES

Due to different weights in the flour blends, this recipe would be best cooked by weight rather than other measurements.

Ingredients

125g or ½ cup Nuttelex Original or butter or one to your liking
125g or ⅝ cup dextrose powder (may contain Gluten) or caster sugar
2 eggs
100g Gluten-Free self-raising flour blend of flours will work best (options on pages 13 & 14) or one to your liking
50g or ½ cup ground almonds (F, PO (xylitol), VHOX and VHS)
1 teaspoon vanilla sugar (F, VLOX and VHS)
125ml or ½ cup espresso (Coffee beans have F, FOS, PO (mannitol), GOS, VLOX and varies in S and Coffee (Instant) has F, FOS, PO (mannitol), GOS, VLOX and varies in S)
1½ tablespoons rum or brandy essence (both have HS but no info for OX)
4 egg yolks
100g or ½ cup dextrose powder (may contain Gluten) or sugar
450g or 2 cups mascarpone cheese (see notes or homemade Lactose Free recipe after main recipes)
250ml or 1 cup Lactose Free whipping cream or one to your liking
125ml or ½ cup fresh orange juice (HF, PO (sorbitol), VLOX and MS)

Directions

Beat the sugar and butter together. Add the eggs, one at a time. Mixing each time until well combined.

Sift the flour, ground almonds and vanilla sugar together and combine with the mixture until you have a smooth batter.

Transfer the mixture into a piping bag with a wide nozzle. Line a baking tray with baking paper.

Pipe out "fingers" about 3" / 10cm long until all the mixture is used up. Be sure not to pipe the lady fingers too close together, as they will spread out when they are baked.

Refrigerate for 15 minutes before baking to avoid them spreading out too much. Preheat oven to 180°C / 350°F.

Bake for 8-10 minutes until golden. Transfer to a wire rack and leave to cool completely.

Beat egg yolks in a bowl over a double boiler until light and fluffy. Add the sugar and sweet wine and continue beating until the mixture thickens (about 5 minutes). This is called a zabaglione.

Mash the mascarpone in a bowl until smooth. Add the zabaglione and mix well.

In another bowl, whip the cream until very light. Fold this into the zabaglione mixture.

Assembling the Tiramisu

In a small bowl, put the espresso and brandy/rum. Dip each ladyfinger into the liquid and place on the bottom of the serving dish.

Once the bottom layer is covered, spread half of the zabaglione mixture on top of the ladyfingers.

Start dipping and placing ladyfingers on top of this layer and finish it off with another layer of zabaglione mixture.

Dust a little cocoa powder on top of the entire dessert. Cover the finished dessert with cling film and refrigerate for at least 4 hours or overnight.

Notes
Mascarpone substitute
Mascarpone is a cream cheese with a high fat content and a slightly sweet taste. It is difficult to find a substitute and regular cream cheese has a lower fat content and a more acidic flavour. However you could try beating together 225g or 8oz full fat cream cheese with 60ml or 4 tablespoons or ¼ cup double or whipping cream and 30g or 1oz or 2 tablespoons softened unsalted butter until just blended. This will give the equivalent of around 300g or 10oz or 1¼ cups mascarpone.

AUTHENTIC TIRAMISU

Ingredients
7 egg yolks
½ cup dextrose powder (may contain Gluten) or sugar
⅓ cup + 2 tablespoons sweet marsala (see notes for substitute)
8oz or 225g or 1 cup mascarpone, softened to room temperature (see notes or homemade Lactose Free recipe after main recipes)
1 cup Lactose Free heavy cream or one to your liking
1 cup brewed espresso coffee (Coffee beans have F, FOS, PO (mannitol), GOS, VLOX and varies in S and Coffee (Instant) has F FOS, PO (mannitol), GOS, VLOX and varies in S)
1oz or 28g dark chocolate (HF and VHOX) (homemade Fructose Free recipes after main recipes)
¼ cup rum (see notes for substitute)
1 teaspoon natural vanilla extract (F, VLOX and VHS)
48 ladyfingers (2 homemade recipes follow)
¼ cup unsweetened cocoa powder (FOS, GOS, VHOX and MS)

Directions
Cream together egg yolks and sugar in a heatproof bowl set over a pot of simmering water. Add ⅓ cup of the Marsala and continue to whisk until mixture is thick and doubled in volume. This is basically a zabaglione. Remove from heat. Stir in the mascarpone until completely blended.

In a chilled bowl, whip the heavy cream to soft peaks. Fold the whipped cream into the mascarpone mixture, to lighten.

In a small saucepan, combine espresso, chocolate, rum, vanilla, and remaining 2 tablespoons Marsala. Heat gently, and stir to dissolve the chocolate.

Chill the mixture to cool it down, about 15 minutes.

Quickly dip each ladyfinger in the chilled coffee mixture and arrange in a single layer on a 9 x 13" (23 x 33cm) glass baking pan. Do not soak the cookies or they will become too moist.

Spread ½ the mascarpone cream evenly with a spatula on top of the dipped ladyfingers. Repeat with a second layer of dipped ladyfingers and remaining mascarpone cream.

Sprinkle top with cocoa powder. Refrigerate for 2 hours before serving.

Notes
Marsala Substitute
1) Mix together
¼ cup white grape juice (F, PO (sorbitol), LOX and MS) or ¼ cup non-alcoholic dry white wine (varies in both OX and S) (see substitutes below)
1 teaspoon brandy essence (HS but no info on OX)

2) Mix together
¼ cup white grape juice (F, PO (sorbitol), LOX and MS) or for optimal taste non-alcoholic wine
2 tablespoons sherry vinegar (Vinegar red/wine - L-MOX and VHS and Sherry - MOX)

(**Substitutes:** balsamic vinegar (F, VLOX and VHS) **OR** red wine vinegar (L-MOX and VHS) (Also add a little dextrose powder (may contain Gluten) or sugar if you wish.) **OR** rice vinegar)

1-tablespoon non-alcoholic vanilla extract (F, VLOX and VHS)

3) Mix together

¼ cup of dry white wine (varies in OX and S) with 1 teaspoon of brandy (HS)

Rum Substitute

If you have a recipe which calls for real rum and you want to use rum extract instead, you can convert the recipe. As a general rule, for every two tablespoons of dark rum in a recipe, one tablespoon of extract can be used. For every five tablespoons of light rum called for, one tablespoon of extract is usually sufficient. Because significant differences in liquid levels can emerge when doing these conversions, some cooks like to add water to make up for the missing liquid.

Rum substitute

¼ cup - 1 tablespoon rum extract +plus enough water to equal ¼ cup
OR - an equal amount of Pineapple Juice (F, PO (mannitol), VLOX and MS)
OR - an equal amount of Apple Cider (F, PO (sorbitol), LOX and L-MS)

Dry white wine substitute

Water, ginger ale (HF and LOX), white grape juice (F, PO (sorbitol), LOX and MS), diluted cider vinegar (F, L-MOX and VHS) or white wine vinegar (L-MOX and VHS)

Mascarpone substitute

Mascarpone is a cream cheese with a high fat content and a slightly sweet taste. It is difficult to find a substitute and regular cream cheese has a lower fat content and a more acidic flavour. However you could try beating together 225g or 8oz full fat cream cheese with 60ml or 4 tablespoons or ¼ cup double or whipping cream and 30g or 1oz or 2 tablespoons softened unsalted butter until just blended. This will give the equivalent of around 300g or 10oz or 1¼ cups mascarpone.

HOMEMADE RECIPES FOR THE ABOVE RECIPES
HOW TO MAKE TOMATO PASTE THE QUICK AND EASY WAY

This recipe makes about 5 heaped tablespoons of paste.

Directions

Soak 2 kilos (4½ lbs) of tomatoes (HF, FOS, PO (mannitol), MOX and MS) in boiling water for five minutes or until the skins can be easily peeled off. Drain and carefully remove the tomato skin. The tomatoes may be hot to handle.

Carefully cut tomatoes in half or quarters longways and de-seed completely. Place tomato pieces in to processor and process to a very liquidy paste.

If you have a slow cooker, then place this liquid paste in it and leave it to reduce and thicken up. Stir occasionally. I left mine on all day and got a beautiful thick tomato paste to use in my recipes.

If you don't have a slow cooker you can cook the paste in a 350°F / 180°C preheated oven on shallow trays until it is reduced to a paste. Check the tomatoes every half hour, stirring the paste and switching the position of the trays so that they reduce evenly. Over time, the paste will start to reduce to the point where you can make one tray.

The paste is done when shiny and brick-colored, and it has reduced by more than half. There shouldn't be any remaining water or moisture separating from the paste at this point. This will take 3 - 4 hours, though exact baking/cooking times will depend on the juiciness of your tomatoes and your oven. After the paste was cold; I put it in a container and kept it in the refrigerator or freezer.

Making small batches when you need it can be useful; however, if you use a lot of tomato paste then just double or triple the amount of tomatoes used.

I made a very small batch using the same prep method but I cooked them down in my non-stick frypan over low heat and I continually stirred the mixture. I did not add anything to the paste because I can do that when I use it in a recipe.

OR

Cut your tomatoes in half and put them all in a saucepan. Sprinkle with a pinch of salt, cover the saucepan and let the tomatoes simmer over moderate heat, stirring from time to time. After about 5 - 10 minutes, they should have softened and just begun to melt.

Pour the tomatoes into a food mill positioned over a large mixing bowl. Let the tomatoes cool off for a couple of minutes. By this time, depending on your tomatoes, there will be either a little or quite a bit of liquid that will have drained into the bowl. Discard it before proceeding.

Re-position the food mill on top of the bowl and rotate the handle until all you have left in the food mill are skins and seeds. You'll want to throw this stuff away, of course. What you'll have in the mixing bowl is your passata.

Transfer the purée into a mason jar or any other container you want. If you like, nestle a basil leaf or two (F, MOX and VHS) in the passata. Let it cool off completely before closing the container.

Notes

Use paste tomatoes, like Romas and San Marzanos, for the greatest yield. Juicy heirloom tomatoes can also be used, but will have a smaller yield.

You can also make a "tomato paste" by simply pureeing sun dried tomatoes. Add a little oil if necessary, or reconstitute the tomatoes a little bit, then if it's slightly too thin, bake it in your oven on 350°F / 180°C until the water evaporates and it makes a paste.

When de-seeding the tomatoes, place the seeds in a bowl along with the juice. If you strain this through a sieve, you can freeze the juice in ice cube trays and use as part of the flavouring when a recipe calls for stock and if you're really conservative, you could plant the seeds and grow your own tomato plants. The skins can be dried and crumbled and used as flavouring in many dishes without issues.

* * * * *

HOMEMADE TIN/CAN TOMATOES SUBSTITUTE

Place the weight amount of tomatoes needed in a bowl of boiling water for 5 minutes. Carefully remove and peel tomatoes; they will be hot. Place them in a saucepan and bring them to a boil. Cook until soft but not soggy. Follow the recipe as to their use. For crushed tomatoes, process by pulsing for a few seconds in your processor or chop finely.

* * * * *

HOMEMADE DAIRY FREE, SOY FREE WHITE CHOCOLATE

Ingredients
4oz (112g) edible raw cacao butter roughly chopped
2 teaspoons vanilla paste or pure extract (F, VLOX and VHS)
⅔ cup dextrose powder (for Fructose Free and may contain Gluten) or confectioner sugar
1 teaspoon finely ground almond flour (F, PO (xylitol), VHOX and VHS)
¼ teaspoon kosher salt (an edible salt with a much larger grain size to common table salt so use half the amount if substituting)

Directions
Place butter in microwave bowl and heat 70% for 1 minute 30 seconds. Remove and stir - keep repeating until the butter has melted to a thin liquid.

Add other ingredients and stir till smooth and then mould and set till solid either in the fridge or at room temperature.

Notes
A friend added some cocoa powder to make it into a darker chocolate. If you wish to do this, then you will have to be the judge to the amount you use.

HOMEMADE DARK CHOCOLATE (Fructose Free)

Ingredients
50g (3.5 tablespoons) cacao butter
25g (3.5 tablespoons) dark cacao powder (FOS, GOS, VHOX and MS)
1 tablespoon rice malt syrup
½ teaspoon vanilla extract (F, VLOX and VHS)
Pinch of salt

Directions
Using the double boiler method is having a bowl sitting on top of a saucepan that has a small amount of water simmering in it. Don't allow the base of the bowl come in contact with the water as it will spoil the chocolate.

Place the cocoa butter in the bowl and using a metal or rubber spoon or whisk mix it until it has melted - do not use a wooden spoon for this recipe as the wooden spoon holds moisture and will ruin the chocolate.

Add the vanilla extract and the rice malt syrup and mix it around until it's well combined.

Add in the dark cocoa powder and mix it through until it's well combined and completely dissolved.

Once it is nice and glossy take it off the heat and pour the chocolate in to your selected mould/moulds and give it a quick jiggle to remove the air.

Let it sit for about an hour or so just until it starts to harden up because we don't want it to harden up to fast then place it into the fridge for another hour to completely set.

Notes
Add 1 tablespoon of milk powder to make this into a milk chocolate. Make chocolate melts by dropping small amounts of chocolate on a tray and letting them set.

*   *   *   *   *

HOMEMADE COMPOUND CHOCOLATE

Ingredients
150g of dextrose powder (may contain Gluten) or sweetener of your choice but will not be Fructose Free
8 tablespoons of Lactose Free full cream milk powder (can use Lactose Free full cream powdered milk)
12 tablespoons about 250g of a vegetable shortening (copha is solid coconut oil (HS) and may cause issues) or one to your liking
12 tablespoons cocoa powder (FOS, GOS, VHOX and MS)
A pinch of salt

Directions
Melt the vegetable shortening (copha) over a medium heat.

Place the dextrose, full cream milk powder, cocoa powder and the pinch of salt into a bowl and mix it until combined.

Pour over the melted vegetable shortening and mix until well combined and smooth. Pour chocolate mixture in to a shallow baking dish lined with lightly sprayed baking paper or pour into moulds. Put it in the fridge for a few hours to let it set nice and hard.

Notes
Other ingredients you might like to add to your chocolate include:
Nuts, spices (chilli or cinnamon, for example), dried fruit, coffee, Liqueur, teas, sea salt, vanilla, flavour essences. (I have not included extra information as the extras are just general ingredients so I will leave this decision up to you as you know what you can have).

*   *   *   *   *

HOMEMADE LACTOSE FREE MASCARPONE CHEESE
http://lassothelactose.blogspot.com.au/2014/06/mascarpone-cheese.html

Mascarpone is most commonly known as the staple ingredient in tiramisu, but it can be used in a wide variety of recipes and is often used as a substitute for cream cheese due to its creamy texture. Since this recipe only calls for two ingredients, I knew it would be a basic yet versatile cheese to add to my lactose-free repertoire.

Ingredients
2 cups Lactose-Free heavy cream or one to your liking
1 tablespoon freshly squeezed lemon juice. (F, PO (sorbitol), LOX and L-HS)

Directions
In a medium sauce pan, heat two cups of heavy cream over medium heat to 190°F, stirring constantly. Once the temperature of the cream has reached 190° add the lemon juice. Continue stirring the mixture constantly at 190° for five minutes.

After the five minutes is over, allow the mixture to cool off the heat for 30 - 45 minutes.

Next set a strainer in a bowl, large enough to allow the excess liquid to drain and line the strainer with a cheese cloth. Fold the cheese cloth so it is about four layers thick.

After the lemon and cream mixture has cooled transfer to cheese lined strainer, cover with plastic wrap and allow the mixture to drain and set in the refrigerator for 8 - 12 hours.

Once chilled, discard the excess liquid and transfer the mascarpone cheese into an air tight container. Store mascarpone cheese in the refrigerator.

When the process was all said and done I was left with a little over a cup of mascarpone. With just two ingredients and a few simple steps you can create a delicious lactose free Italian cheese with an incredible creamy, light texture.

SOUTHERN AFRICA

The following recipes were kindly donated to me the Southern Africa community.

The vegetables and fruit in these recipes will only make them Fructose Friendly. I have tried to source out whether they have Fructose, Fructans, Polyols or Galactans in them and have indicated this beside the ingredient plus a few ingredients have alternatives beside them or in the notes at the end of each recipe. I am hoping that this will help you as much as it has helped me. Salicylates and Oxalates may also be issues for some people so I have added them as well. They will all be noted in the code form below or mentioned in the notes. Please read these.

Low – L, Medium – M, High – H, Very High – VH, Salicylates – S, Oxalates – OX
Fructose – F, Fructans – FOS, Polyols – PO, Galactans – GOS

Substituting ingredients will alter the original taste; however, it is a way to try different recipes from other countries and you can adjust the taste to your liking. I have placed some homemade recipes for substituting the ingredients after the main recipes. These recipes will be for Gluten Free, Fructose Friendly, Lactose Free or Friendly, Diabetic Friendly and IBS Friendly depending on your sensitivity so that you can make your own if you want to. Please remember that Fructans, Polyols and Galactans can also come with Fructose. Make these recipes your own and use your ingredients if you want to as you know what's best for you.

Australian tablespoons and cups measurements are used and they are: 1 teaspoon equals 5ml; 1 tablespoon equals 20ml; 1 cup equals 250ml. Oven temperatures are for conventional; if using fan-forced (convection), reduce the temperature by 20°C.

Nigeria
Ugali	255
Obe Eja Dindin (Nigerian Fish Stew)	256
Fufu (West African Mashed Yams)	257

Zimbabwe
Sadza Ne Nyama Ye Huku (Sadza With Chicken Stew)	258
Nyama (Zimbabwean Beef Stew)	260
Dovi (Peanut Butter Stew)	261

Congo
Saka-Saka (Cassava Leaves)	262
After Chop (Fruit Salad)	263
Akotonshi (Stuffed Crabs)	264

Kenya
Mshenye (Mashed Sweet Potatoes Mixed With Beans And Corn)	265
Chapati (whole Wheat Flatbread)	265
Easy Gluten-Free Flatbreads, Pita Or Naan Bread	266
Nyama Choma (Kenyan Grilled Meat)	267

Ghana
Ghana Meat Stew	268
Avocado And Crab	269
Potato Greens	270

Homemade Recipes For The Above Recipes
How To Make Tomato Paste The Quick And Easy Way	271
Homemade Curry Powder	271

NIGERIA

UGALI

Ugali (pronounced oo-ga-ly) is the staple starch component of many meals. Ugali is generally made from maize flour and water, which is cooked into a dough-like consistency and then used to dip into other dishes during a meal, such as greens or stew.

Ingredients
1 cup (or more) corn flour (MOX and HS) or maize flour (MOX and LS)
3 cups of boiling water
1 cup of cold water

Directions
You will need a saucepan big enough to hold the 6 cups of ingredients with room to vigorously stir them around.

Bring 3 cups of water to a boil in a kettle or other pan. You want the water to be very hot so that it keeps enough heat while you add the flour.

Combine cornmeal and cold water while other water is boiling. You want to do this gradually, sprinkling in a little at a time. Add 1 cup of boiling water at a time to avoid lumps.

Stir briskly with a wooden cooking spoon. You want to keep stirring constantly, making sure that the mixture is getting even heating and that you smooth out any lumps that develop.

You want to cook it to a very thick consistency. You may need to add more than 1 cup of flour to get your Ugali to the right texture. (Don't worry about staying strictly at 1 cup; instead pay more attention to the texture).

Cook to a firm texture. The texture is usually thicker than mashed potatoes and is best cooked until the dough pulls from the side of the pot. It may get difficult to stir and incorporate the flour by the end of cooking. However, you want to keep going, so that the finished product is pretty firm.

Turn the cooked Ugali onto a serving plate as one large mound. Use a wooden spoon to transfer it, taking care while you do it, as the Ugali can be very hot.

Cut the Ugali into pieces with a knife once it is on the serving plate. Simply cut across making a grid-like pattern, so that the pieces are easier to handle. You could also cut the Ugali into slices like a pie, cutting across the center in all directions. If you don't want to cut the Ugali, you can just keep it whole. During the meal allow people to simply pull chunks off with their fingers.

To eat it, you first want to roll a small piece into a ball, about the size of a golf ball or smaller. Then make an indentation in the middle of it with your thumb. You can then use this indentation to scoop up other foods served in the meal.

Pair the Ugali with another dish. It goes well with any kind of stew. Just use it as you would bread, for instance sopping up any delicious leftover sauce.

OBE EJA DINDIN (NIGERIAN FISH STEW)

Nigerian Fish Stew is a very popular Nigerian stew made with fish. It is made with either raw, steamed or fried/grilled fish. You can use any type of fish you desire for this recipe; Hake as part of the Cod family is the preferred fish.

Ingredients
8 cut pieces fresh fish fillets of your choice
Vegetable Oil or one to your liking
3 red capsicums (HF, FOS, PO (sorbitol), LOX and VHS) or bell peppers (HF, PO (sorbitol), LOX and VHS)
4 big tomatoes (HF, FOS, PO (mannitol), MOX and MS)
3½ tablespoons tomato puree (HF, FOS, PO (mannitol), HOX and VHS) (homemade recipe after main recipes)
1½ onions (HF, HFOS, PO (mannitol), LOX and LS) or 4 spring onions stems (green parts only) diced (white part has M-HF, FOS, PO (mannitol) MOX and LS) (see notes)
4 cloves garlic (F, FOS, GOS, LOX and LS) (see notes)
1 tablespoon minced ginger (F, FOS, LOX and MS)
2 lemons (F, PO (sorbitol) VLOX and MS)
1 tablespoon curry powder (F and VHS) (homemade recipe after main recipes)
1 teaspoon thyme (LOX and VHS)
1 teaspoon cumin powder (VHS) (Optional)
½ teaspoon garlic powder (F, FOS, GOS, LOX and LS) (see notes)
½ tablespoon any fish or chicken seasoning, (minus onion or garlic)
3 chicken cubes or your preferred stock cubes (minus onion and garlic)
Salt to taste

Directions
Clean the fish thoroughly with lemon.

Marinate with salt, 1 lemon, stock cubes, ½ of the curry, the cumin powder, garlic powder, 1 stock cube. Leave to marinate in a cool place for at least 30 minutes. You can leave it overnight, the longer the better.

Blend the capsicum/peppers, tomatoes, ginger and 1 onion till smooth and set aside.

Pour oil into a wok or frying pan, enough to deep fry the fish, place on the stove top on very medium heat, then fry the marinated fish till golden brown. You don't have to fry your fish, you can choose to grill them instead or just marinate and add to the stew.

Transfer the fried fish into a colander to drain the oil.

Next, add some of the oil used for frying into a big saucepan, 1 cup at least. You should sieve out the fish residue/particles first, then place on the stove top on medium heat. When it's hot, add the ½ onion, sauté for 3 minutes, then add the garlic, sauté till fragrant, be careful so you don't burn the garlic. (Stew fries better when deep fried in excess oil than little oil).

Now, add tomato puree, fry for 3 - 4 minutes, stirring occasionally. Then add the blended pepper, also add the remaining thyme, curry, stock cubes, seasoning and salt to taste, stir and combine, leave to fry for 18 - 20 minutes.

By this time, the oil would have settled on the top and the pepper reduced in quantity. Now, add the fried/grilled or marinated fish gently, stir and combine, turn the heat down to low, then leave to cook for a further 6 - 8 minutes. Now it's ready to serve with whatever you choose.

Notes
You may wish to substitute ⅛ teaspoon of asafoetida powder for the onion and garlic. This is a very strong spice so don't use more than the specified amount.

*   *   *   *   *

FUFU (WEST AFRICAN MASHED YAMS)

Fufu is a mash of yams or other starches that is served in West Africa as an accompaniment to meat or vegetable stews. To eat fufu, pull a small ball of mush off with your fingers, form an indentation with your thumb and use it to scoop up stews and other dishes. Or place large balls in individual serving bowls and spoon the stew around them. The East and Southern African counterpart is Ugali.

Ingredients to make 4 to 6 servings
2 lbs or 900g white yams (FOS, PO (mannitol), HOX and HS) or white sweet potatoes (HF, FOS, PO (mannitol) VHOX and HS)
2 tablespoons Nuttelex Original or butter or one to your liking
Salt and pepper (black - HOX and VHS, white - VLOX and VHS) to taste

Directions
Place the unpeeled yams or white sweet potatoes in a large pot, cover with cold water and bring to a boil over medium-high heat. Boil for 15 - 30 minutes, or until the yams/sweet potatoes are cooked through and tender. Drain and let cool somewhat.

Peel the yams/sweet potatoes, chop them into large pieces and place them into a large bowl with the butter, salt and pepper. Mash with a potato masher until very smooth. Alternatively, put the yams through a potato ricer and then mix with the butter, salt and pepper.

Place the fufu into a large serving bowl. Wet your hands with water, form into a large ball and serve.

Fufu Variations
Other options are semolina and ground rice.

ZIMBABWE

SADZA NE NYAMA YE HUKU (SADZA WITH CHICKEN STEW)

Chicken Stew
Ingredients to serve 5 adults
2lbs or 900g fresh boneless chicken breast
3 - 3½ lb or 1½ - 2kg of very ripe red tomatoes (HF, FOS, PO (mannitol), MOX and MS)
1 bunch scallions/spring onions (about 6 - 8 scallion plants) (green ends only. White part has M-HF, FOS, PO (mannitol) MOX and LS)
2 medium size onions (HF, HFOS, PO (mannitol), LOX and LS) or 6 spring onions (green parts only) diced (white part has M-HF, FOS, PO (mannitol) MOX and LS)
Ginger root 1 tablespoon of fresh ginger root is equal to ⅛ - ¼ teaspoon of ground ginger (F, FOS, LOX and MS)
Red pepper or mild paprika (F and VHS) or cayenne pepper (LOX and VHS) to taste
Black pepper to your taste (HOX and VHS)
Chili powder to your taste (F and VHS)
Parsley flakes to your taste (F, PO (mannitol), LOX and LS)
Salt to taste
Olive oil (LOX and HS) or one to your liking

Sadza Ingredients
Mealie Meal - white maize corn meal. Cornmeal comes in different colors: white, yellow, and blue. Yellow cornmeal has more beta carotene than the others, while blue cornmeal has more protein and turns baked goods purple. Larger supermarkets may also carry stone-ground cornmeal.

Substitutes: polenta (HS) OR corn flour (MOX and HS) (gives baked goods a lighter texture)

Directions
Preparing the Ingredients
Slice up two onions into small chunks and store in an air-tight container.

Cut up all tomatoes into ¼" or 6mm pieces and store in a large container.

Skin and finely cut about 3 ounces or 6 tablespoons of fresh ginger - and store in an air-tight container to maintain freshness.

Cut up the chicken into ¼" or 6mm cubes.

Cut up 1 bunch of scallions into ¼" or 6mm pieces and store in an air-tight container. Keep the leaves.

Preparing the Sauce
Cover the bottom of a large sauce-pan with olive oil and apply medium to high heat. When the oil is very hot (and thin), stir fry the ginger alone for ½ minute and then add the onions and continue to stir fry. (Leave a tiny bit of ginger and onions for next step).

Sprinkle enough chili powder to redden the onions and ginger and while stirring constantly also add a tinge of red pepper, a fair amount of black pepper.

Add 1 - 2 teaspoons of salt and continue to stir. Using your finger, grab a half teaspoon worth of dried parsley leaves and pulverize it with your fingers while sprinkling in the pan.

Continue to stir. The contents should shimmer from the heat and a spicy aroma should be evident.

Turn the heat to high. The heat will begin to brown/blacken the bottom of the pan and add the cut tomatoes in 4 - 5 portions at a time while stirring constantly. You aim to maintain boiling point while you add tomatoes.

When all the tomatoes are in, and the sauce has reached/maintained boiling point, turn the heat down to medium and let boil for 10 - 15 minutes. Stir and mash the tomatoes occasionally.

Re-sprinkle some more chili powder and stir. After five minutes turn the heat down to low to where the sauce is barely at boiling point. Cook for 10 - 20 minutes stirring and mashing the tomatoes as needed and then turn off the heat and allow to stand and cool slightly.

Preparing the Chicken
Cover the bottom of a frying sauce-pan with olive oil and apply medium to high heat. When the oil is very hot, carefully tilt the pan to spread the oil so as to cover the walls of the frying pan. Add the tiny amount of ginger and onions left from last step and stir fry for a couple of seconds.

Apply high heat. Add all the cut chicken into a large pile in the center of the frying pan and allow bottom pieces to cook and spread/stir the rest around the pan while stirring. Do not allow any of it to burn. After a while the water in the chicken will cover the bottom of the pan and boil. Continue to stir and add, chili powder, black pepper, red pepper, salt and parsley leaves.

Allow all the water to boil off and continue to stir until the bottom of the pan is dark brown from the heat and spices.

Mix the chicken with the tomato sauce in the tomato saucepan and stir to ensure an even mixture. Keep under low heat - barely boiling. Let simmer for 30 minutes or until done, stirring occasionally and then turn the heat off but keep saucepan on the hot burner to use the residual heat.

Cooking Sadza
Before you begin, bring to boil about one gallon or 3½ litres of water in a kettle.

Put 5 cups of mealie meal or whatever you are using in a 3 quart or 3.4lt saucepan. Add enough cold water to completely soak the mealie meal. Most of the water will be absorbed by the mealie meal.

Add little more water to allow you to stir with a wooden spoon into a very thick white mixture and place saucepan over medium high heat, and while stirring add boiling water slowly. Continue to stir evenly and constantly to prevent the mealie meal from settling and hardening at the bottom of the pan. (If this happens you end up with lumpy Sadza).

As the mixture heats up the texture changes from rough to smooth. Continue to add water to loosen the mixture and allow it boil with enough movement - some upward spattering will occur.

At this stage, the Sadza is in porridge state. If the water/mealie meal mixture is just right, the Sadza will boil without spilling over.

However if it is too thin it might spill over, especially if you put a saucepan lid on. Keep an eye on it. Allow the mixture to boil under medium high heat for about 5 minutes. At this point the Sadza requires relatively heavy stirring as it thickens.

Continue to add mealie meal ½ cup at a time and stir evenly until the Sadza takes on the appearance of mashed potatoes. Be careful not to make it too thick otherwise it becomes too hard (like a "brick") and not as enjoyable to eat. After the Sadza reaches the desired texture and is well mixed, turn heat off and cover and let it sit for a couple of minutes before serving.

Before serving, bring the chicken stew to a boil again. Turn heat off completely and add the cut scallions. Stir evenly to spread scallions in the stew. Let sit for 1 minute and serve while scallions are green and crunchy. Stew is served in a bowl and Sadza on a plate.

How to eat Sadza ne Nyama
Sadza is finger food. Wash your hand well in a bowl of clean water. Using your right hand partition a small chunk of Sadza and mold it into a little round or oval ball in your palm. Be careful not to burn yourself. Dip it in the soup and bite off and eat a sizable chunk. Re-mold the remainder of your Sadza in your palm and continue the process. Use your fingers to pick up and eat chunks of chicken.

*   *   *   *   *

NYAMA (ZIMBABWEAN BEEF STEW)

Ingredients for 4 people
2 lb or 900g beef, cut into medium sized chunks
4 garlic cloves, finely chopped (F, FOS, GOS LOX and LS) (see notes)
1 onion, finely chopped (HF, HFOS, PO (mannitol), LOX and LS) (see notes)
2 tomatoes, chopped (HF, FOS, PO (mannitol), MOX and MS)
1 bunch scallions/spring onions (about 6 - 8 scallion plants) (green ends only. White part has M-HF, FOS, PO (mannitol) MOX and LS)
1 teaspoon salt
½ teaspoon curry powder (F and VHS) (homemade recipe after main recipes)
2 carrots, diced (HF, FOF, PO (sorbitol), GOS, VHOX and HS)
1 cup fresh green beans, cut in 1" or 2½ cm sections (HF, FOS, PO (sorbitol), VLOX and MS)
1 tablespoon cornstarch (MOX) (optional) (see notes)
Oil for frying to your liking

Directions
Heat the oil in pot and add the beef, garlic and salt. Fry until the meat is a lovely brown color. Add enough water to just cover the meat and reduce heat. Allow to simmer gently and slowly uncovered until meat is tender.

When the water is entirely reduced, add the onions (or asafoetida powder) and curry powder. Fry for 2 minutes. Add the tomatoes and cook for another 3 - 4 minutes or until the tomatoes are tender and cooked through. Add a little bit of water, the carrots and green beans and simmer for another 5 minutes, stirring regularly. Thicken with cornstarch diluted in water if you wish.

Note
You may wish to substitute ⅛ teaspoon of asafoetida powder for the onion and garlic. This is a very strong spice so don't use more than the specified amount.

DOVI (PEANUT BUTTER STEW)

Ingredients

2 medium onions, finely chopped (HF, HFOS, PO (mannitol), LOX and LS) or 6 spring onions (green parts only) diced (white part has M-HF, FOS, PO (mannitol) MOX and LS) (see notes)
2 tablespoons Nuttelex Original or butter or one to your liking
2 cloves garlic, crushed (F, FOS, GOS, LOX and LS) (see notes)
1 teaspoon salt
½ teaspoon pepper (black - HOX and VHS, white - VLOX and VHS)
½ teaspoon cayenne pepper (LOX and VHS)
2 green bell peppers, chopped (HF, FOS, PO (sorbitol), GOS, MOX and VHS)
1 chicken, cut into pieces (may use skinless, boneless chicken if preferred)
3 or 4 tomatoes (HF, FOS, PO (mannitol), MOX and MS)
6 tablespoons creamy peanut butter (FOS, GOS, VHOX and VHS and may have Fructose depending on your selection) (Fructose Free homemade recipe in notes)
½ pound fresh spinach (HF, FOS, PO (sorbitol), VHOX and HS) or 1 package frozen spinach (HF, FOS, PO (sorbitol), VHOX and MS)

Directions

Cook onions (or asafoetida powder) with butter in a big stew pot until browned and then add the garlic, salt, and seasonings. Stir while adding the green peppers and chicken.

Once the chicken is browned, add the tomatoes and mash them with a fork and add 2 cups water and simmer for 5 - 10 minutes. Add half the peanut butter to the pot, lower heat, and continue to simmer.

In a separate pan, cook the spinach. If using fresh spinach, wash the leaves, add about 2 tablespoons of water to a saucepan with the spinach and heat over medium low until spinach leaves are limp and tender. If using frozen spinach, cook according to package directions and then add the rest of the peanut butter to the spinach and heat for 5 minutes.

Serve the stew and the greens together.

Notes

You may wish to substitute ⅛ teaspoon of asafoetida powder for the onion and garlic. This is a very strong spice so don't use more than the specified amount.

HOMEMADE FRUCTOSE FREE PEANUT BUTTER

Ingredients for 1½ cups

2 cups dry roasted peanuts (FOS, GOS, VHOX and VHS)
1 - 2 tablespoons rice malt syrup or dextrose powder (may contain Gluten)
Additional salt to taste if needed

Directions

Place peanuts in a food processor and turn it on and let it run for 4 - 5 minutes. During this time, you'll see the peanuts go in stages from crumbs to a dry ball to a smooth and creamy "liquid" peanut butter. (Stop occasionally to scrape down the sides). Stir in the rice malt syrup or dextrose powder or salt, if you want. (Maple syrup or honey or sugar can replace the rice malt syrup and dextrose powder).

Store in the fridge or at room temperature depending on how often you will use or eat it.

CONGO

SAKA-SAKA (CASSAVA LEAVES)

Ingredients
Lots of cassava greens or substitute kale (F, FOS, PO (sorbitol), GOS and MOX), collards (PO and raw has LOX, boiled has MOX), turnip greens (HF, PO, MOX and LS), spinach (HF, FOS, PO (sorbitol), VHOX and HS), or similar, stems removed, cleaned, and cut or torn into pieces (see notes)
A few spoonfuls of palm oil (LOX) or coconut oil (HS) or any oil of your choice
1 onion, chopped (HF, HFOS, PO (mannitol), LOX and LS) or 3 spring onions (green parts only) diced (white part has M-HF, FOS, PO (mannitol) MOX and LS) (see notes)
1 clove garlic, minced (F, FOS, GOS, LOX and LS) (see notes)
1 sweet green pepper or capsicum and/or sweet red pepper or capsicum, chopped (optional) (see notes)
1 eggplant (F, FOS, PO (xylitol), MOX and HS) (peeled, cubed, rinsed, and salted) or okra (HF, HFOS, PO, VHOX and HS), chopped (optional)
Salt, or baking soda, to taste
1 piece of dried, salted, or smoked fish; or one can of pilchards; or one can of sardines

Directions
Thoroughly crush, mash, or grind the greens in a mortar and pestle or with whatever you can improvise (roll them with a rolling pin, crush them in a heavy bowl with the bottom of a sturdy bottle, etc.).

Bring a large pot of water to a boil; add greens and cook for thirty minutes or more (much more if using cassava leaves).

Add all the remaining ingredients to the greens and bring to a boil, then reduce heat and simmer. Do not stir. Simmer until the water is mostly gone and the greens are cooked to a pulp.

Serve as a side with a chicken, meat, or fish main course.

Notes
Many Central African cooks use baking soda, or a piece of rough potash, to give a salty flavor to soups and sauces. This replicates the flavor of traditional salts which are obtained by burning the barks or leaves of certain plants. This was necessary because there is no other source of salt in much of Central Africa.

Notes
Peppers, Green has HF, FOS, PO (sorbitol), GOS, MOX and VHS
Peppers, Red has HF, FOS, PO (sorbitol), GOS, VLOX and VHS
Capsicum green has HF, FOS, PO (sorbitol), MOX and VHS
Capsicum red has HF, FOS, PO (sorbitol), LOX and VHS

You may wish to substitute a pinch of asafoetida powder for the onion and garlic. This is a very strong spice so don't use more than the specified amount.

AFTER CHOP (FRUIT SALAD)

A wide variety of tropical fruits, both native and non-native, are cultivated in Africa. One interesting thing about the African fruit salad is the use of the avocado. A perfectly fine fruit salad can be made from just three or four of the ingredients listed below. A fruit salad makes a fine dessert course for an African-style dinner.

Ingredients
Any of the following (fresh or canned)
Avocado has F, FOS, PO (sorbitol), VLOX and VHS
Banana has F, FOS (inulin) PO (sorbitol) and MOX
Grapefruit has F, PO (sorbitol) and HS
Guava has F, PO (sorbitol) and VHS
Mango has F, PO (sorbitol), LOX and MS
Melon to your liking (see notes)
Orange has F, PO (sorbitol), HOX and VHS)
Papaya has F, PO (sorbitol), MOX and LS
Peach has F, HFOS, HPO (sorbitol), VLOX and HS)
Pear has VHF, PO (sorbitol), MOX and HS
Pineapple has F, PO (mannitol), LOX and VHS
Tangerine has F, PO (sorbitol) and VHS
Juice of one lemon (F, PO (sorbitol), LOX and L-HS) or chopped, crushed mint leaves (VHS)
Grated coconut (F, FOS, PO (sorbitol), VLOX and MS) or chopped roasted peanuts (VHOX and VHS)
Dextrose powder (may contain Gluten) or sugar (optional) (rice malt syrup or honey can also be used)

Directions
If using canned fruits: drain and save the liquid. Peel and remove seeds from the fresh fruit as necessary, cut fruit into bite-sized pieces.

Combine all fruit in a glass bowl. Add the lemon juice (or mint leaves), some sugar water (water which has been boiled, mixed with sugar, and allowed to cool--or use some of the liquid from the canned fruits). Stir gently. There should only be enough liquid to coat the fruit; it does not have to be covered in liquid.

Cover the fruit salad and allow it to stand for a half hour before serving. The fruit salad may be refrigerated after it has stood for an hour. It should be eaten the same day it is made. It does not keep well overnight.

Top with grated coconut or chopped peanuts immediately before serving.

Variations
For a simple fruit snack or dessert: just cut up any of the fruit above and serve with rice malt syrup or honey dripped over it.

Notes
The watermelon and many other members of the gourd family (Cucurbitaceae, which includes gourds, melons, pumpkins, and squashes) are native to tropical Africa and widely cultivated there. Watermelons have been cultivated in the Eastern hemisphere for thousands of years; they appear in ancient Egyptian art and Sanskrit literature.

AKOTONSHI (STUFFED CRABS)

Ingredients
2 lbs or 900g fresh crab meat
1 teaspoon salt
1" or 2½ cm piece of fresh ginger (F, FOS, LOX and MS)
4 - 6 cloves (F, VHOX and HS)
4 tablespoons cooking oil to your liking
1 small onion, minced (HF, HFOS, PO (mannitol), LOX and LS) or 3 spring onions (green parts only) finely diced (white part has M-HF, FOS, PO (mannitol) MOX and LS) or a pinch of asafoetida powder (may contain Gluten) (this is a strong spice so don't use more than specified amount)
1 teaspoon ground ginger (F, FOS, LOX and MS)
2 tomatoes, finely chopped (HF, FOS, PO (mannitol) MOX and MS)
1 tablespoon tomato paste (HF, FOS, PO (mannitol), HOX and VHS) (homemade recipe after main recipes)
2 green bell peppers (HF, FOS, PO (sorbitol), GOS, MOX and VHS) or capsicums (HF, FOS, PO (sorbitol), MOX and VHS), finely chopped
Pinch of paprika (F and VHS)
1 teaspoon cayenne pepper (LOX and VHS)
½ cup Gluten Free whole-wheat bread crumbs or one to your liking
1 egg, hardboiled and finely chopped
1 sprig parsley (F, PO (mannitol), LOX and LS)

Directions
Put crab meat in boiling salted water along with ginger piece and cloves. Cook about 15 minutes, until meat is tender enough to flake with a fork. Drain, flake and set aside.

In a heavy pot, heat the oil to a moderate temperature and add other ingredients in the following sequence, stirring for a minute or so between each: onions, ground ginger, tomatoes, tomato paste, green pepper, paprika, and cayenne. Reduce heat and simmer for 4 - 5 minutes stirring constantly until vegetables are cooked.

Add crab meat and stir another couple of minutes to heat it through. Then spoon the mixture into clean crab shells or ramekins or small individual baking dishes.

Sprinkle bread crumbs on top of each crab and toast under an oven broiler/grill, being careful not to let the crumbs scorch.

Garnish with egg and parsley.

KENYA

MSHENYE (MASHED SWEET POTATOES MIXED WITH BEANS AND CORN)

Ingredients
12 pieces sweet potatoes boiled until cooked (Use the yellow ones because they are perfect for this recipe. Keep hot. (HF, FOS, PO (mannitol), VHOX and HS)
1 cup kidney beans (FOS, GOS and HOX) boiled until soft. Keep hot. (Soaking the beans in warm water for 12 hours lowers oxalates and adding a teaspoon of bi-carb soda may help to reduce gas. Change the water often and rinse well before cooking)
1 cup corn boiled until soft. Keep hot. (HF, FOS, PO (xylitol), LOX and MS)
Salt to taste

Directions
In a cooking pan, put in the hot sweet potatoes the hot corn and the hot kidney beans. Add salt and use a potato masher and start to mash thoroughly before serving.

* * * * *

CHAPATI (WHOLE WHEAT FLATBREAD)

Ingredients to make 12 Normal Chapatis
2 cups whole-wheat flour or one to your liking (see notes)
2 tablespoons ghee or oil to your choosing
¾ - 1 cup warm water
½ teaspoon salt

Directions
Mix the flour and oil or ghee together well using your hands or a food processor.

Stir the salt into the water and add the water, a little at a time, until you have a soft, kneadable ball. Remove to a floured work surface and knead for 8 - 10 minutes, or until smooth and elastic. If using a food processor, add water until the mass comes together and continue processing for 30 seconds more.

Remove the dough to a lightly greased bowl, cover and rest for at least 30 minutes and up to 2 hours.

Return the dough to a floured work surface. Roll the dough into a long log and cut it into 12 separate balls. Dust the dough balls with a little flour and roll each one out into a very thin round about 6 inches in diameter.

Heat an ungreased, heavy skillet or frypan over medium flame. Add a dough round and press down gently all over with a spatula or the back of a spoon to help make chapati puff up.

Bake until lightly browned, flip and brown on the second side. Repeat with all rounds. Brush each chapati with melted butter or ghee as it comes from the skillet if you like.

Notes
Airam says she uses a blend of wheat and malted barley flours used to make chapatis or she has bought it from shops that sell Indian supplies.

Substitute: Sift together equal parts whole wheat flour and all-purpose flour.

EASY GLUTEN-FREE FLATBREADS, PITA OR NAAN BREAD

THIS RECIPE IS FROM MY FIRST COOK BOOK.
These can also be made into Chapatis.

Ingredients for 5-6 flatbreads
2 cups (270g) all-purpose Gluten Free flour of your choosing (Gluten Free flour is high in carbs so may not be Diabetic Friendly) (options on pages 13 & 14)
2 teaspoons baking powder (VLOX)
½ teaspoon baking soda
½ teaspoon coarse sea salt
¼ teaspoon fine sea salt
¾ cup warm Lactose Free milk or one to your liking
¼ cup warm Lactose Free yogurt or one of your choice OR ¼ cup Lactose Free milk or one of your choice
1 tablespoon vegetable oil or one to your liking
Additional oil for hands

Directions
Preheat oven to 425°F / 220°C.

Whisk the dry ingredients together in a large bowl.

Warm milk and yogurt, then add with oil to the bowl and blend, just until integrated. Do not over-mix or the breads may become gummy when baked. The dough will hold together once mixed, and be slightly sticky. It should not be dry.

Sprinkle more flour onto a parchment-lined baking sheet and using a large spoon or ice cream scoop, place six balls of dough onto the prepared, lined pan.

Pour a teaspoon of oil into your hands and then press with your palms to spread each ball into a 5" (12½ cm) circle, flattening with your palms; add more oil to your hands as necessary. The dough should be approximately ⅛" thick. Repeat with other balls of dough.

If this is your first time making these, keep an eye on them so you can get an accurate time and temperatures for your oven for baking them again and to get the best result.

Bake for 10 minutes, OR until the breads are puffing up and browning slightly. Flip to the other side and bake for an additional 3 - 4 minutes. (To get a traditional naan baked in a tandoor oven look, lightly pan fry the breads to brown the high points).

These breads may appear slightly gummy when hot out of the oven; let them cool for at least 5 minutes before tearing or cutting open so the structure of the breads will set first. If you tear open one of the breads, it should be fully cooked and have some pockets of air; it should not be gummy or look uncooked inside. If it is gummy or not fully cooked, return to the oven and monitor until fully cooked.

Notes
You can also use this recipe for personal pizza crusts, naan, pita breads, chapatis or cut into triangles and toasted or broiled for crisp toast points.

NYAMA CHOMA (KENYAN GRILLED MEAT)

Ingredients to serve 4 to 6
2 lbs or 900g goat or beef meat, cut into bite-sized chunks (see notes)
3 tablespoons oil to your liking
2 cups warm water
2 tablespoons Kosher or sea salt (an edible salt with a much larger grain size to common table salt so use only half the amount if substituting)

Directions
Prepare your grill and have it hot. Toss the meat with the oil, then thread it on skewers. Stir the salt into the warm water until it is fully dissolved.

Grill the skewered meat, basting it occasionally with the salt water, until it is cooked to your liking.

Remove the meat from the skewers and serve with Kachumbari salad (tomato and onion) and Ugali.

Notes
The only seasoning used for authentic Nyama Choma is salt and pepper (black - HOX and VHS, white - VLOX and VHS), but you can marinate your meat first in a mixture of minced onions (HF, HFOS, PO (mannitol), LOX and LS), minced garlic (F, FOS, GOS, LOX and LS), ground ginger (F, FOS, LOX and MS), hot pepper flakes (F, VHS) and a little lemon juice (F, PO (sorbitol), LOX and L-HS). OR use a pinch of asafoetida powder (may contain Gluten) to replace the onion and garlic. This is a strong spice so don't use more than the amount specified.

GHANA
GHANA MEAT STEW

Ingredients
2 lbs or 900g beef
2½ onions (HF, HFOS, PO (mannitol), LOX and LS) or 6 spring onions (green parts only) diced (white part has M-HF, FOS, PO (mannitol) MOX and LS) (see notes)
12 small tomatoes (HF, FOS, PO (mannitol), MOX and MS)
2 cups brown rice (FOS and MOX) or one of your choosing
1 cup of cooking oil of your liking
1 large potato (see notes)
12 - 15 string beans (HF, FOS, PO (sorbitol), VLOX and MS)
3 small carrots (HF, FOS, PO (sorbitol), GOS, VHOX and HS)
8 hot green peppers (the larger type) or capsicums (see notes)
2 teaspoons of curry powder (F and VHS) (homemade recipe after main recipes)
2 bay leaves (VHS)
4 cloves of garlic (F, FOS, GOS, LOX and LS) (see notes)
1" piece of ginger (F, FOS, LOX and MS) or galangal (no info available) (see notes)
5 cloves (F, VHOX and HS)
A pinch of anise (VHS)
A pinch of dried rosemary (LOX and VHS)

Directions
Wash the meat, and then cut it up into 2" cubes. Try and make them as even as possible, so that they cook evenly.

Blend the ½ onion, garlic, ginger, anise, rosemary and cloves until very smooth.

Pour over the meat. Add 2 teaspoons of salt, the 2 bay leaves and 1 stock cube. Toss and make sure all pieces are covered well. Leave to marinate in the fridge for at least an hour or leave overnight in the fridge.

Place the meat in a pot and steam until it is tender. Add water when it runs low in the pot.

Heat the cooking oil in a pan and fry the meat. When it turns dark brown it is ready. Remove quickly so it doesn't burn. Fry in batches if necessary.

Pick and wash the rice and cook as you would regular rice or by instructions on the packet.

Blend the tomatoes and peppers/capsicums.

Peel the potato, scrape the carrots and remove strings from the beans.

Cut the string beans on a slant, about 1" or 2½ cm long pieces. Cut the carrots to match the shape of the beans. Bring a pot of water to the boil, then add the carrots and boil for about 3 minutes then add the string beans and boil for an additional 1 minute. Pour off the hot water, then run under cold water and drain in a colander (this stops further cooking of the vegetables).

Cube the potato into ½" or 12mm cubes. If they are too small, they tend to break up in the stew. You want to still have chunks you can bite on.

Slice the 2 onions.

Heat 2 tablespoons of the cooking oil and fry the onions. When they turn translucent, add the curry and fry until the edges begin to brown. Add the blended tomatoes.

Fry until almost sticking to the bottom of the pan.

Add the stock from the meat and simmer and then add the pieces of fried meat, and the cubed potatoes, plus 2 cups of water, cover and bring to the boil. Reduce the heat and let it simmer down until the stew thickens and the potatoes are cooked.

Serve with the brown rice and steamed vegetable.

Notes
You may wish to substitute ⅛ teaspoon of asafoetida powder for the onion and garlic. This is a very strong spice so don't use more than the specified amount.

Fructose in potatoes can range anything between 582 mg – 989 mg depending on the size, type and skin colour. They also have FOS, PO and GOS. They can also be VHOX and MS again depending on the type of potatoes, colour of skin and how they are cooked.

Chili Peppers has F, PO (mannitol), HOX and HS
Peppers, Green has HF, FOS, PO (sorbitol), GOS, MOX and VHS
Capsicum green has HF, FOS, PO (sorbitol), MOX and VHS

Ginger has a sweeter, spicy tone to it where galangal has more of a peppery tone to it.

*   *   *   *   *

AVOCADO AND CRAB

Ingredients
1 tablespoon lemon juice (F, PO (sorbitol), LOX and L-HS)
1 clove of garlic, crushed (F, FOS, GOS, LOX and LS) (see notes)
1 avocado (F, FOS, PO (sorbitol), VLOX and HS)
6oz or 170g cooked white crab meat
Pinch of salt
Freshly ground black pepper (HOX and VHS)
Pinch of paprika (F and VHS)
Spring onions (green parts only), to garnish (white part has M-HF, FOS, PO (mannitol) MOX and LS)

Directions
Mix together the lemon juice and the seasoning. Peel and remove the seed from the avocado and mash the flesh with the lemon mixture.

Mix in the flaked crabmeat with a fork. Garnish with spring onions.

Serve on fingers of toast.

POTATO GREENS

Potato greens are the young leaves of sweet potato and are consumed as a vegetable in many African countries. There are many ways to cook sweet potato leaves and this is just one way to cook and eat it.

Ingredients
300g or 10½ oz sweet potato leaves, finely chopped and washed (substitute spinach (HF, FOS, PO (sorbitol), VHOX and HS) or Swiss chard (F, FOS, PO (sorbitol) and VHOX)
250g or 9oz beef, cut into small pieces
1 fish whole or fillets to your liking
6 okras (HF, HFOS, PO, VHOX and VHS) cut finely (substitute green beans (HF, FOS, PO (sorbitol), VLOX and MS) or eggplant (F, FOS, PO, MOX and HS) and use cornstarch (MOX) or flour to thicken)
Hot pepper to your liking to taste
100ml of palm oil (LOX) or one to your liking
1 big onion, sliced (HF, HFOS, PO (mannitol), LOX and LS) or 3 spring onions (green parts only) diced (white part has M-HF, FOS, PO (mannitol) MOX and LS)
1 or 2 stock cubes (minus onion and garlic) or ones to your liking
Salt (to taste)
Spring onion, finely chopped (green parts only as white part has M-HF, FOS, PO (mannitol) MOX and LS) (optional)
Smoked fish (optional)
3 cups water

Directions
Note: If your potato greens are not fresh, soak them in water for 2 hours before the cooking time.

In the cooking pot, put the meat and fish. Then add 1 of water and salt. Bring it boil for 10 minutes.

Remove the fish from pot and set aside, let it cool down for few minutes, then remove the bones if using a whole fish.

Add the potato greens with the remaining water and simmer for 10 minutes.

Add the onion, spring onion, stock cubes and oil.

Add hot pepper and salt. Then return the fish in the pot and the sliced okra and simmer on medium heat for 20 minutes.

Stir the sauce regularly, the sauce is ready when all the liquid is totally absorb.

Serve it with rice.

HOMEMADE RECIPES FOR THE ABOVE RECIPES

HOW TO MAKE TOMATO PASTE THE QUICK AND EASY WAY

This recipe makes about 5 heaped tablespoons.

Soak 2 kilos (4½ lbs) of tomatoes (HF, FOS, PO (mannitol), MOX and MS) in boiling water for five minutes or until the skins can be easily peeled off. Drain and carefully remove the tomato skin. The tomatoes may be hot to handle.

Carefully cut tomatoes in half or quarters longways and de-seed completely. Place tomato pieces in to processor and process to a very liquidy paste.

If you have a slow cooker, then place this liquid paste in it and leave it to reduce and thicken up. Stir occasionally. I left mine on all day and got a beautiful thick tomato paste to use in my recipes.

If you don't have a slow cooker you can cook the paste in a 350°F / 180°C preheated oven on shallow trays until it is reduced to a paste. Check the tomatoes every half hour, stirring the paste and switching the position of the trays so that they reduce evenly. Over time, the paste will start to reduce to the point where you can make one tray.

The paste is done when shiny and brick-colored, and it has reduced by more than half. There shouldn't be any remaining water or moisture separating from the paste at this point. This will take 3 - 4 hours, though exact baking/cooking times will depend on the juiciness of your tomatoes and your oven.

After the paste was cold; I put it in a container and kept it in the refrigerator or freezer.

Making small batches when you need it can be useful; however, if you use a lot of tomato paste then just double or triple the amount of tomatoes used. I made a very small batch using the same prep method but I cooked them down in my non-stick frypan over low heat and I continually stirred the mixture. I did not add anything to the paste because I can do that when I use it in a recipe.

*   *   *   *   *

HOMEMADE CURRY POWDER

Ingredients to your needs
Mustard seeds (F, FOS, GOS, VLOX and VHS)
Turmeric (F, VHOX and VHS)

Directions
Toast your mustard seeds for 20 seconds in a dry skillet. Cool the seeds, then transfer to a spice grinder and pulse until you have a powder.

Pass the powder through a sieve to remove the hulls.

Blend a pinch or two of turmeric with the mustard to create the bright yellow associated with the condiment.

JAPAN

The following recipes were kindly donated to me by Allen.

The vegetables and fruit in these recipes will only make them Fructose Friendly. I have tried to source out whether they have Fructose, Fructans, Polyols or Galactans in them and have indicated this beside the ingredient plus a few ingredients have alternatives beside them or in the notes at the end of each recipe. I am hoping that this will help you as much as it has helped me. Salicylates and Oxalates may also be issues for some people so I have added them as well. They will all be noted in the code form below or mentioned in the notes. Please read these.

Low – L, Medium – M, High – H, Very High – VH, Salicylates – S, Oxalates – OX
Fructose – F, Fructans – FOS, Polyols – PO, Galactans – GOS

I have placed some homemade recipes for substituting the ingredients after the main recipes. These recipes will be for Gluten Free, Fructose Friendly, Lactose Free or Friendly, Diabetic Friendly and IBS Friendly depending on your sensitivity so that you can make your own if you want to. Please remember that Fructans, Polyols and Galactans can also come with Fructose.

Substituting ingredients will alter the original taste; however, it is a way to try different recipes from other countries and you can adjust the taste to your liking. Make these recipes your own and use your ingredients if you want to as you know what's best for you.

Australian tablespoons and cups measurements are used and they are: 1 teaspoon equals 5ml; 1 tablespoon equals 20ml; 1 cup equals 250ml. Oven temperatures are for conventional; if using fan-forced (convection), reduce the temperature by 20°C.

Teriyaki Chicken Rice	273
Teriyaki Beef Rice	274
Spicy Pork Rice	275
Fried Chicken Rice	276
Gyoza	278
Chicken Karaage (Japanese Fried Chicken)	280
Wonton Wrappers And Gyoza Wrapper	281
Easy Gluten Free Egg Roll Or Wonton Wrappers	281
Japanese Vegetarian Curry With Rice	282
Homemade Recipes For The Above Recipes	
Homemade Worcestershire Sauce	284
Homemade Ketchup	284
Homemade Soy Sauce Substitute	285
Homemade Garam Masala	285
Homemade Teriyaki Sauce	286
Homemade Hoisin Sauce	286
How To Make Tomato Paste The Quick And Easy Way	287
Homemade Almond Butter	287
Almond Butter	288

TERIYAKI CHICKEN RICE

Ingredients

1 onion, cut into wedges (HF, HFOS, PO (mannitol), LOX and LS) or 3 spring onions (green parts only) diced (white part has M-HF, FOS, PO (mannitol) MOX and LS)
2 broccoli heads (HF, FOS, PO (sorbitol), GOS, MOX and HS), cut into florets
1 green capsicum (HF, FOS, PO (sorbitol), MOX and VHS) or bell pepper (HF, FOS, PO (sorbitol), GOS, MOX and VHS), cut into wedges
1 cup sugar snap peas (HF, HFOS, PO (mannitol) GOS, HOX and MS) or snow peas (HF, HFOS, PO (mannitol), GOS, MOX and MS)
1 tablespoon sesame oil (VHOX and MS) or one to your liking
500g or 1lb chicken thigh fillets, skinless and boneless, cut into bite sized pieces
¼ cup soy sauce (FOS) (homemade recipe after main recipes)
¼ cup mirin (sweet rice wine) (homemade substitute recipe after main recipes)
¼ cup dextrose powder (may contain Gluten) or brown sugar
2 tablespoons sake (see notes for substitutes)
1 teaspoon minced garlic or 1 clove garlic minced (F, FOS, GOS, LOX and LS) (see notes)
1 shallot/green onion stem, sliced to garnish (HF, HFOS, PO (mannitol), LOX and LS) or 1 spring onions (green parts only) diced (white part has M-HF, FOS, PO (mannitol) MOX and LS)

Directions

Stir fry onion, broccoli, capsicum/peppers and sugar snap peas with cooking oil spray until just starting to turn vibrant in colour. Add 2 tablespoons of water, reduce heat to medium, and stir fry until cooked to your liking (crunchy or soft). Remove vegetables from pan and set aside. Alternatively, steam vegetables until cooked to your liking.

Add sesame oil into the same pan. Stir fry chicken over medium-high heat, stirring occasionally to prevent burning. When chicken is golden and crispy, remove from pan.

Lightly wipe pan over with a paper towel and add the soy sauce, Mirin, Sake (or vinegar), brown sugar and garlic. Stir sauces through together, reduce heat and allow to simmer until sauce thickens. Add the chicken and vegetables and stir through the sauce to evenly coat. (If the sauce is too thick for your liking, add a small amount of water, 1 tablespoon at a time, until desired consistency is achieved).

Garnish with green onion (or shallot) slices and serve over steamed rice.

Notes
Saki substitutes
Substitute rice wine vinegar mixed with water or white grape juice (F, PO (sorbitol), LOX and MS) for the sake at a 1 to 3 part ratio.

TERIYAKI BEEF RICE

Ingredients
For the stir fry
250g or 9oz beef fillet or sirloin tip steak sliced thinly against the grain
Black pepper, ground (HOX and VHS)
½ cup soy sauce (FOS) (homemade recipe after main recipes) or tamari
¼ cup rice syrup or honey (HF, FOS, VLOX and VHS)
4 - 6 tablespoons macadamia oil or sesame oil (VHOX and MS) or light olive oil (LOX and HS) for frying or one to your liking
1 Spanish onion, cut into quarters (HF, HFOS, PO (mannitol), LOX and LS) or 3 spring onions (green parts only) diced (white part has M-HF, FOS, PO (mannitol) MOX and LS)
2 sprigs of spring onions (green parts only) chopped, (white part has M-HF, FOS, PO (mannitol) MOX and LS)
300g green beans (HF, FOS, PO (sorbitol), VLOX and MS), cut in half or snow peas (HF, HFOS, PO (mannitol), GOS, MOX and MS) or both
10 small button mushrooms (HF, FOS (raffinose), PO (mannitol and xylitol), GOS, VLOX and MS), cut into quarters (see notes)
4 cloves of garlic, sliced thinly (F, FOS, GOS, LOX and LS) (see notes)
4 slices of fresh ginger, diced (F, FOS, LOX and MS)
1 cup carrots sliced very thin (HF, FOS (raffinose), PO (sorbitol), GOS, VHOX and HS)
4 ounces mixed sweet bell peppers or capsicum (red, yellow and/or orange) cut into strips (see notes)

Directions
Spread the sliced beef fillets on a cutting board and season well with freshly ground black pepper.

In a measuring jug mix the soy sauce or tamari with the rice syrup or honey.

Heat the oil in a wok (or a frypan) until just starting to smoke and fry beef slices in batches - only one layer should cover the pan at any time. The meat will only take about 10 seconds to brown on each side. Flip using tongs and brown the other side.

Place the meat in a bowl, set aside and repeat with the remaining slices.

Wipe down wok with paper towel. Add 1 tablespoon oil and return to heat.

Add the onion, spring onions and beans and stir fry until onion has separated and starts to caramelise. Add mushrooms and stir fry for another couple of minutes and then add the garlic and ginger. Stir to combine.

Return the beef to the wok and add soy sauce mixture and stir fry until the sauce thickens slightly and blends in with the meat and vegetables.

Notes
Try substituting normal mushrooms (HF, FOS (raffinose), PO (mannitol and xylitol), GOS, VLOX and MS) for the gourmet style. It has been stated that Shiitake, Enoki, Oyster have low to no Polyols and information for Fructose, Fructans, Oxalates and Salicylates could not be found at all. Usually only "Mushrooms" in general comes up when researching so this ingredient will be your call as what you want to use. I don't have any issues when eating the Gourmet Style mushrooms.

Peppers, red has HF, FOS, PO (sorbitol), GOS, VLOX and VHS
Peppers yellow has HF, FOS, PO (sorbitol), GOS, MOX and VHS
Capsicum red has HF, FOS, PO (sorbitol), LS and VHS
Capsicum yellow has HF, FOS, PO (sorbitol), MOX and VHS

*   *   *   *   *

SPICY PORK RICE

Ingredients (hard to convert weight due to size of vegetables needed)
150g or 5oz pork, cut thinly into bite sized pieces (can use other meat if preferred)
Olive oil spray (LOX and HS) or one to your liking
3 green onions/ spring onions (green parts only), sliced diagonally (white part has M-HF, FOS, PO (mannitol) MOX and LS)
1 fresh red chilli, chopped (F, PO (mannitol), HOX and HS)
100g (HF, FOS, PO (mannitol) and VHOX), sliced diagonally
150g carrots (HF, FOS (raffinose), PO (sorbitol), GOS, VHOX and HS), cut into matchsticks
100g broccoli florets (HF, FOS, PO (sorbitol), GOS, MOX and HS)
50g green capsicum (HF, FOS, PO (sorbitol), MOX and VHS)
300g bean sprouts (F, FOS and LS)
200ml stock of your choice (minus onion and garlic)
2 tablespoons soy sauce (FOS) (homemade recipe after main recipes)

Directions
Lightly spray a wok or large frying pan with olive oil and place on medium to high heat.

Cook pork for 2 minutes.

Add chilli and all vegetables except bean sprouts. Lower heat to medium and stir fry for 5 minutes.

Add stock, cover pan with a lid and cook on a low heat for 5 minutes.

Add bean sprouts, stir into other ingredients. Replace lid and cook for 2 minutes.

Add soy sauce and stir through.

Notes
To prevent bean sprouts becoming slimy, place them in a container lined with kitchen paper. Stored this way they will last up to 4 days.

FRIED CHICKEN RICE

Ingredients
4 cups cooked rice, cooled to room temperature (see notes)
4 tablespoons Nuttelex Original or sweet butter (unsalted) softened or one to your liking
2 garlic cloves, finely minced (use 1 if you want a lighter garlic flavor) (F, FOS, GOS, LOX and LS)
1 teaspoon sesame oil (VHOX and MS) or one to your liking
3 eggs, beaten
6 - 8oz boneless skinless chicken breasts, cubed
2 tablespoons sesame oil (VHOX and MS) or one to your liking
½ cup frozen peas, thawed (may omit) (HFOS, GOS, LOX and N-LS)
½ cup fresh carrot (HF, FOS (raffinose), PO (sorbitol), GOS, VHOX and HS), thinly sliced, or frozen carrots, thawed (HF, FOS (raffinose), PO (sorbitol), GOS, and no info on OX or S)
1 cup onion, diced (HF, HFOS, PO (mannitol), LOX and LS) or 3 spring onions (green parts only) diced (white part has M-HF, FOS, PO (mannitol) MOX and LS)
¼ cup green onion/spring onion (green parts only, white part has M-HF, FOS, PO (mannitol) MOX and LS)
½ teaspoon salt or to taste
½ teaspoon black pepper (HOX and VHS) to taste
2 tablespoons low sodium soy sauce (FOS) (homemade recipe after main recipes)
2 tablespoons toasted sesame seeds (FOS, VHOX and HS) (optional)

Directions
The rice could be pre-cooked the night before and stored in fridge or cook the rice using package directions - Note: double the water per each cup of uncooked rice.

For this recipe you would use 4 cups of water and 2 cups of uncooked rice, pinch of salt and once you bring it to a boil, turn the heat down and cook for 20 minutes covered. You must spread the rice out after it is cooked in a shallow pan and cool it off in the fridge (or freezer if you have room). It needs to be at room temperature or cooler.

Make your garlic butter
Put softened butter in a bowl large enough to allow you to mix the garlic into the butter. It needs to be well blended. Use a potato masher to mash the butter or use a hand mixer if you wish.

Peel garlic by hitting each clove with the side of a knife being careful and keep sharp end of knife away from you. It is now easy to peel and you will do this with both of the cloves (or 1 if you want less of a garlic flavor) and then finely mince.

After garlic is minced you will use the side of the knife and run the side of the blade in each direction to mash the garlic. You want to make a paste out of the garlic. Add the garlic to the butter and mix really well. Keep the bowl on the counter ready for use.

Wash and dry your chicken breast and cube it into small bite size pieces.

Dice your onion. Thinly cut the greens on the green onion.

Scramble the eggs in a frying pan with 1 teaspoon of sesame oil. Then cut the cooked eggs into small pieces and put aside.

In a large frying pan or a wok add 2 tablespoons of sesame oil and cook the onion on medium heat for 5 minutes stirring often. You just want it soft and don't burn it.

Now add your cubed chicken and stir often. You don't want to burn the chicken but a little color is fine. Add some salt and pepper to taste. Cook the chicken for about 5 - 7 minutes on medium heat. It will cook fast because it is cubed small.

Add 1 tablespoon of the garlic butter. Add the peas, carrots, and green onions and cook for 5 minutes or until just tender (you can taste a carrot to test for desired taste). Do not overcook but stir often. Leave it in the pan.

Add 2 tablespoons of garlic butter and add the rice a handful at a time. Carefully stir everything together and keep adding rice until all the rice is added and well mixed together.

At this time add 1 more tablespoons of the garlic butter. Cook rice for 5 - 7 minutes stirring often. Add the cooked eggs, stir well carefully and add your soy sauce and mix well to distribute evenly. Add remaining salt and pepper to taste.

If you wish to add the toasted sesame seeds do so now and stir and serve. Since sesame oil is used in the recipe the seeds are optional.

Notes
Basmati is low in carbs and has FOS, LOX and MS. Doongara is low in carbs and has FOS and LOX. Soaking rice and grains for 12 hours lowers oxalates.

GYOZA

Ingredients
1 package (or about 45) Gluten Free gyoza wrappers (2 homemade Gyoza Wrappers after next recipe)
1½ tablespoons oil for frying each batch of gyoza of your choice
¼ cup water for frying each batch of gyoza
1 tablespoon sesame oil (VHOX and MS) for frying each batch of gyoza

Filling
10oz or 290g ground pork
2 - 3 or 140g or 5oz cabbage leaves (HF, HFOS, PO (sorbitol), GOS, LOX and LS)
1 - 2 or 15g or 0.5oz green onion/scallion (green parts only) (HF, HFOS, PO (mannitol), LOX and LS) or 6 spring onions (green parts only) diced (white part has M-HF, FOS, PO (mannitol) MOX and LS)
2 shiitake mushrooms (no info for anything except they are Fructose Friendly)
1 clove garlic, minced (F, FOS, GOS, LOX and LS)
1 teaspoon grated ginger (F, FOS, LOX and MS)

Seasonings
½ tablespoon sake (see notes for substitutes)
½ tablespoon sesame oil (VHOX and MS) or one to your liking
1 teaspoon soy sauce (FOS) (homemade recipe after main recipes)
¼ teaspoon salt
Freshly ground black pepper (HOX and VHS)

Dipping Sauce
1 tablespoon rice vinegar
1 tablespoon soy sauce (FOS) (homemade recipe after main recipes)
⅛ teaspoon chili oil (La-Yu) (optional) or one to your liking (homemade recipe in notes)

Directions

Microwave cabbage leaves for 1 minute and chop into very small pieces. Mince green onion and shiitake mushrooms as well.

Combine the meat and seasonings and knead the mixture with hands until the texture becomes sticky. Add the rest of fillings and continue to knead.

Wrap the filling with gyoza wrappers. (2 homemade recipe next)

Heat the oil in a large non-stick frying pan over medium high heat and when the pan is hot, place the gyoza in a single layer, flat side down (in two rows or in a circular shape).

When the bottom of the gyoza turns golden brown, add ¼ cup of water to the pan.

Immediately cover with a lid and steam the gyoza for about 2 minutes or until most of the water evaporates.

Remove the lid to evaporate any remaining water. Add sesame oil and cook uncovered until the gyoza is nice and crisp on the bottom. Transfer to a plate. For the gyoza lined up in circular shape, place a serving plate on top of the pan and quickly flip.

For the dipping sauce
Combine the sauce ingredients in a small plate or shallow bowl and mix all together. Serve the gyoza with dipping sauce.

Notes

After you wrap gyoza, cook or freeze it right away; otherwise water from the ingredients will start to make the wrapper wet.

To save gyoza for later, put the gyoza on a baking sheet leaving some space between to keep them from sticking, and put it in freezer. Transfer frozen gyoza into a freezer bag and store in freezer up to a month. When you use frozen gyoza, do not defrost. Cook while they are frozen.

Saki substitutes

Substitute rice wine vinegar mixed with water or white grape juice (F, PO (sorbitol), LOX and MS) for the sake at a 1 to 3 part ratio.

HOMEMADE CHILI OIL (LA-YU)

Ingredients for 1 cup
1¼ cup canola (LOX) or peanut oil (MS) or one to your liking
¼ cup red chili flakes or coarse powder (F and VHS)
½ teaspoon minced garlic (F, FOS, GOS, LOX and LS)

Directions
Put the oil, chili flakes, and minced garlic in a pot and bring to a boil over medium heat. Keep stirring so the chili flakes don't burn. Let it bubble for about 30 seconds and turn off heat and keep stirring for a few seconds more. Use a strainer and discard the pepper flakes and garlic.

Let the oil cool down and pour it into a bottle. Store it in the refrigerator until ready to use.

HOMEMADE CHILI SAUCE SUBSTITUTE

Ingredients for about 1 cup
Mix together:
1 cup tomato sauce (HF, FOS, PO (aspartame), VLOX and VHS) / ketchup (HF, FOS, PO, VLOX and VHS) (homemade recipe after main recipes)
¼ cup brown sugar or rice malt syrup or dextrose powder (may contain Gluten) (all three are Fructose Friendly or Free)
2 tablespoons vinegar (L-MOX, and VHS)
¼ teaspoon cinnamon (F, HOX and VHS)
1 dash ground cloves (F, VHOX and HS)
1 dash allspice (VHS)

CHICKEN KARAAGE (JAPANESE FRIED CHICKEN)

Ingredients
1 portion chicken thigh meat
1 tablespoon soy sauce (FOS) (homemade recipe after main recipes)
1 tablespoon sake (see notes for substitutions)
A small amount of garlic to your taste (F, FOS, GOS, LOX and LS) (see notes)
A small amount of ginger (F, FOS, LOX and MS) to your liking
⅔ teaspoon chicken soup stock granules (minus onion or garlic)
1 teaspoon sesame oil (VHOX and MS) or one to your liking
Salt and pepper (black - HOX and VHS, white - VLOX and VHS) to taste
Potato starch (LOX) / flour (katakuriko) for coating

Directions
Cut the chicken into bite sized pieces. Add all the flavouring ingredients and mix well (leave to marinate for at least 10 minutes).

Coat with potato starch/flour (katakuriko).

Deep fry until a deep golden brown at 170°C or until it has a nice light and crispy finish.

For the salad use any or all of the following ingredients
1 head romaine lettuce (½ cup) (F, FOS, MOX and MS)
4 - 5 leaves kale, chopped (F, FOS, PO (sorbitol), GOS and MOX
¼ small head red cabbage, shredded (HF, HFOS, PO (sorbitol), GOS, LOX and LS)
1 carrot, peeled into ribbons (HF, FOS (raffinose), PO (sorbitol), GOS, VHOX and HS)
½ cup sugar snap peas, sliced (HF, HFOS, PO (mannitol) GOS, HOX and MS)
3 - 4 spring onions (green parts only), sliced (white part has M-HF, FOS, PO (mannitol) MOX and LS)
½ avocado per person (F, FOS, PO (sorbitol), VLOX and HS)

Notes
The light coating with potato starch/flour (katakuriko) makes the chicken juicy and crispy.

Saki substitutes
Substitute rice wine vinegar mixed with water or white grape juice (F, PO (sorbitol), LOX and MS) for the sake at a 1 to 3 part ratio.

HOMEMADE JAPANESE MAYONNAISE

Ingredients
1 egg yolk at room temperature
Pinch of salt
½ tablespoon rice wine vinegar
¾ cup salad oil or one to your liking

Directions
In a glass mixing bowl combine egg yolk, salt and vinegar and whisk very well.

Once the egg mixture is mixed up well, add the oil little by little. I emphasize little by little so that the oil incorporates very well with the egg mixture. The mixture should be thick.

Place in refrigerator for at least an hour before enjoying.

WONTON WRAPPERS AND GYOZA WRAPPER

Ingredients for Normal wrappers
1 egg
½ teaspoon salt
2 cups all-purpose flour of your choice
⅓ - ½ cup water as needed
Extra flour as needed

Directions
Lightly beat egg with salt and add ¼ cup of water.

Sift flour into a large bowl and make a well in the middle and add the egg and water mixture to mix in with the flour.

Add as much of the remaining water as necessary to form a dough (add more water than the recipe calls for, if the dough is too dry). Form the dough into a ball and knead for 5 mins or until it forms a smooth, workable dough.

Cover and let rest for 30 mins.

Turn out onto a lightly floured surface and roll out until very thin and cut into 3½" or 9cm squares. Store them in a plastic bag in the refrigerator or freezer until ready to use.

*   *   *   *   *

EASY GLUTEN FREE EGG ROLL OR WONTON WRAPPERS

Ingredients
½ cup cold water + ¼ cup cold water to be added tablespoon by tablespoon
1 egg
½ teaspoon salt
1⅓ cup rice flour or Gluten Free oat flour to your liking
⅔ cup corn starch (MOX)
1 tablespoon sugar or dextrose powder (for Fructose Friendly and may contain Gluten)
1 teaspoon xanthan/guar gum or chia seed powder (FOS, OX and HS)

Directions
Whisk together the egg and the first ½ cup of the cold water until thoroughly combined.

Meanwhile, place all the dry ingredients in a food processor, blender, or the bowl of your electric mixer. Blend with chosen device until combined.

Add the egg and cold water to the dry ingredients and blend until combined. If the dough feels a little dry, add some of the remaining ¼ cup cold water. You want a soft (not sticky at all) dough that can easily be shaped into a ball without getting dough all over your hands.

Add water until you have the right consistency.

Flour the table or counter top with cornstarch and place dough on it. Divide the dough into 2 inch round balls.

Taking one ball at a time, roll them out with a rolling pin to as thin as you can get them. Then place them on wax paper and under slightly damp paper towels until you are ready to cook them.

JAPANESE VEGETARIAN CURRY WITH RICE

Ingredients
For the roux
3 tablespoons Nuttelex Original or butter or one to your liking
¼ cup Gluten Free flour of your liking (options on pages 13 & 14) or one to your liking
2 tablespoons garam masala or curry powder (F and VHS) (homemade recipes for both after main recipes)
½ teaspoon cayenne pepper (LOX and VHS) (add less if you want it mild or more if you want it spicy)
Fresh ground black pepper (HOX and VHS)
1 tablespoons ketchup (HF, FOS, PO, VLOX and VHS) or tomato paste (HF, FOS, PO (mannitol), HOX and VHS) (homemade recipes for both are after main recipes)
1 tablespoons Worcestershire sauce (HS) (may have added anchovies) (homemade recipe after the main recipes

For the curry
2 teaspoon oil of your liking
2 large onions sliced thin (HF, HFOS, PO (mannitol), LOX and LS) or 6 spring onions (green parts only) diced (white part has M-HF, FOS, PO (mannitol) MOX and LS)
2 l or 900g of tofu (MOX) cut into chunks (you could also use beef, shrimp, or chicken thighs cleaned)
2 carrots cut into chunks (HF, FOS, PO (sorbitol), GOS, VHOX and HS)
4 cups water
2 large Yukon gold potatoes cut into large chunks or ones to your liking (see notes)
1 small apple peeled cored and pureed (all apples have F, FOS (raffinose) and PO (sorbitol) but they vary from VL-LOX and L-HS depending on the apple you use)
2 teaspoons kosher salt (an edible salt with a much larger grain size to common table salt so use only half the amount of common salt if substituting)
1 teaspoon garam masala (homemade recipe after main recipes)
½ cup peas (HFOS, GOS, LOX and N-LS)

Directions
Heat the oil in a large saucepan over medium low heat and add the onions. Sauté the onions until they are golden brown and caramelized (about 30 minutes). Turn up the heat to high, add the tofu or meat, and brown.

Add the carrots and the water, and then bring to a boil. Skim off any foam or oil that accumulates at the surface then lower heat to medium and add the potatoes, puréed apple, salt, and garam masala. Simmer for about 30 minutes or until you can pass a fork through the carrots and potatoes and the tofu or meat is tender.

For the roux
Melt the butter over medium low heat. Add the flour and garam masala, stirring until you have a thick paste. Add the cayenne pepper and some fresh ground black pepper and incorporate into the roux. Add the ketchup and Worcestershire sauce and combine. Continue to cook until the paste starts crumbling. Remove from heat and set aside until the meat and veggies are ready.

To make the curry
Just ladle about 2 cups of liquid into the roux then whisk until it is smooth. Pour this mixture back into the other pot and gently stir until thickened. Add the peas and heat through.

Serve over rice or noodles.

Notes

Fructose in potatoes can range anything between 582 mg – 989 mg depending on the size, type and skin colour. They also have FOS, PO and GOS. They can also be VHOX and MS again depending on the type of potatoes, colour of skin and how they are cooked.

HOMEMADE RECIPES FOR THE ABOVE RECIPES

HOMEMADE WORCESTERSHIRE SAUCE

Ingredients
½ cup white wine vinegar (L-MOX and VHS) or rice wine vinegar
2 tablespoons water
2 tablespoons coconut aminos, Tamarin or Soy Sauce (FOS) substitute (next recipe)
¼ teaspoon ground ginger (F, FOS, LOX and MS)
¼ teaspoon mustard powder (VLOX and VHS) (homemade recipe below)
A pinch of asafoetida powder (may contain gluten) (see notes)
⅛ teaspoon cinnamon (F, HOX and VHS)
⅛ teaspoon freshly ground black pepper (HOX and VHS)

Directions
Combine all the ingredients in a saucepan and slowly bring to a boil while stirring frequently.

Let simmer for about a minute for the flavors to develop.

Cool and store in the refrigerator.

Notes
¼ teaspoon onion powder (HF, HFOS, PO (mannitol), LOX and LS) and ¼ teaspoon garlic powder (F, FOS, GOS, LOX and LS) will replace the asafoetida powder which is a strong spice so only use the specified amount.

*   *   *   *   *

HOMEMADE KETCHUP

Ingredients
One 6oz can or ¾ cup or 10 tablespoons of tomato paste (HF, FOS, PO (mannitol), HOX and VHS) (homemade recipe in this section)
½ cup white vinegar (L-MOX and VHS)
½ cup + 2 tablespoons dextrose powder (may contain Gluten)
1 teaspoon salt
⅛ teaspoon ground celery (HF, FOS, PO (mannitol), and VHOX). Try using a few finely chopped leaves only) or omit
Pinch of ground cloves (F, VHOX and HS)

Directions
Put all ingredients into a saucepan and whisk together until smooth.

Heat on medium heat until just boiling; immediately reduce heat and simmer for 20 more minutes, stirring frequently.

Remove from heat and let cool on the counter or stove. Store in a covered container in the fridge.

HOMEMADE SOY SAUCE SUBSTITUTE

Ingredients for about ⅔ cup
1 cup beef broth (Gluten Free and minus the garlic and onion)
2 tablespoons balsamic vinegar (F, VLOX and HS) (substitute recipe in this section)
2 teaspoons white wine vinegar (L-MOX, and VHS) or rice wine vinegar
3 teaspoons rice malt syrup (Fructose Free)
⅛ teaspoon ground black pepper (HOX and VHS)
A pinch of asafoetida powder (may contain Gluten) (see notes)
⅛ teaspoon ground ginger (F, FOS, LOX and MS)
¼ teaspoon salt or to taste
½ teaspoon fish sauce (optional)

Directions
Place the following in a small saucepan: broth, both vinegars, rice malt syrup, black pepper, asafoetida and ground ginger. Bring to a brief boil over medium-high heat, and then reduce heat to a gentle simmer - small bubbles should just break on the surface. Cook until reduced to about ⅔ cup - this takes about 7 - 10 minutes. (NOTE: If you accidentally cook it longer, the flavors of the vinegar and syrup will be concentrated, and it becomes quite sweet. Keep an eye on the clock and don't miss that 10 minute max).

Remove the pan from the heat. Add the salt and fish sauce; stir to combine and taste to make sure it's salty enough for you. Pour into a glass container and allow to cool. Store in the refrigerator for up to 10 days. This sauce can be used in any recipe that calls for soy sauce.

Notes
⅛ teaspoon coarse (granulated) garlic powder (F, FOS, GOS, LOX and LS) can replace the asafoetida powder which is a strong spice so only use the specified amount.

2 teaspoons cider vinegar (F, L-MOX and VHS) can replace white wine vinegar or rice wine vinegar.

Molasses (F, MS) will replace rice malt syrup for a stronger flavour.

*   *   *   *   *

HOMEMADE GARAM MASALA

Ingredients
2 parts ground cardamom (LOX and HS)
5 parts ground coriander (MOX and HS)
4 parts ground cumin (VHS)
2 parts ground black pepper (HOX and VHS)
1 part ground cloves (F, VHOX and HS)
1 part ground cinnamon (F, HOX and VHS)
1 part ground nutmeg (VLOX and VHS)

Directions
Place all the in a screw top jar and shake to combine. Use in recipes.

Notes
I have left the recipes as is so that you can make the quantity that you want using either teaspoons or tablespoons.

HOMEMADE TERIYAKI SAUCE

Ingredients
Just mix together:
¼ cup vegetable oil or one to your liking
¼ cup soy sauce (FOS) (homemade in this section)
2 tablespoons ketchup (HF, FOS, PO, VLOX and VHS) (homemade recipe in this section)
1 tablespoon white vinegar (L-MOX and VHS)
¼ teaspoon pepper (black - HOX and VHS, white - VLOX and VHS)
2 cloves garlic, finely minced (F, FOS, GOS, LOX and LS)

    *   *   *   *   *

HOMEMADE HOISIN SAUCE

Ingredients for about 1 cup
Juice of 1 orange (HF, PO (sorbitol), VLOX and MS) (remove any pits) (may not make this Fructose Friendly depending on your tolerance)
2 tablespoon almond butter (FOX, PO (xylitol), VHOX and VHS) (2 homemade recipes in this section) or sunflower butter (FOS and HOX) or one to your liking
A pinch of asafoetida powder (may contain Gluten and also this is a strong spice so only use the specified amount) (see notes)
1 tablespoon grated ginger (thumb size knob of fresh ginger) or 1 teaspoon powdered ginger (F, FOS, LOX and MS)
1 teaspoon rice wine vinegar or white vinegar (L-MOX and VHS)
1 teaspoon rice malt syrup
5 tablespoons Gluten Free soy sauce (FOS) such as Tamari or coconut aminos or homemade substitute in this section
½ teaspoon Chinese Five Spice powder
1 teaspoon sesame oil (VHOX and MS) or one to your liking
½ teaspoon chilli flakes or powder (F and VHS) (omit if you can't tolerate) or substitute
½ teaspoon paprika (F and VHS)
1 teaspoon tomato paste (HF, FOS, PO (mannitol), HOX and VHS) (homemade recipe in this section)

Directions
Add all ingredients to a small saucepan and heat over medium heat to boil. Turn the heat down to very low, whisk and simmer gently for 3 - 5 minutes, stirring frequently to prevent sticking. The mixture will thicken and darken. Remove to a ramekin and set aside. Store the leftovers in an air-tight container in the refrigerator for up to two weeks.

Notes
For those who want to avoid soy all together, use coconut aminos or the substitute instead and it will still taste hoisin delicious.

1 teaspoon of grated garlic (about 1 large clove) (F, FOS, GOS, LOX and LS) will replace the asafoetida powder.

HOW TO MAKE TOMATO PASTE THE QUICK AND EASY WAY

This recipe makes about 5 heaped tablespoons.

Soak 2 kilos (4½ lbs) of tomatoes (HF, FOS, PO (mannitol), MOX and MS) in boiling water for five minutes or until the skins can be easily peeled off. Drain and carefully remove the tomato skin. The tomatoes may be hot to handle.

Carefully cut tomatoes in half or quarters longways and de-seed completely. Place tomato pieces in to processor and process to a very liquidy paste.

If you have a slow cooker, then place this liquid paste in it and leave it to reduce and thicken up. Stir occasionally. I left mine on all day and got a beautiful thick tomato paste to use in my recipes.

If you don't have a slow cooker you can cook the paste in a 350°F / 180°C preheated oven on shallow trays until it is reduced to a paste. Check the tomatoes every half hour, stirring the paste and switching the position of the trays so that they reduce evenly. Over time, the paste will start to reduce to the point where you can make one tray.

The paste is done when shiny and brick-colored, and it has reduced by more than half. There shouldn't be any remaining water or moisture separating from the paste at this point. This will take 3 - 4 hours, though exact baking/cooking times will depend on the juiciness of your tomatoes and your oven.

After the paste was cold; I put it in a container and kept it in the refrigerator or freezer.

Making small batches when you need it can be useful; however, if you use a lot of tomato paste then just double or triple the amount of tomatoes used. I made a very small batch using the same prep method but I cooked them down in my non-stick frypan over low heat and I continually stirred the mixture. I did not add anything to the paste because I can do that when I use it in a recipe.

*   *   *   *   *

HOMEMADE ALMOND BUTTER

Ingredients for about 1½ cups
3 cups almonds (preferably dry-roasted, unsalted) (FOS, PO (xylitol), VHOX and VHS)

Directions
Pour almonds into food processor. Pulse/process until the nuts go from coarsely chopped, to crumbly, to finely ground. Stop and scrape down the sides as needed.

Process again until the almonds resemble a thick and relatively smooth almond butter.

Notes
Add 1 - 2 tablespoons of a neutral tasting oil during the blending process to make the almond butter extra creamy.

You could stop processing when it reaches the finely ground Almond meal stage and use the meal for baking.

ALMOND BUTTER

Ingredients for about 1 cup
2 cups almonds (plain, raw, no salt) (FOS, PO (xylitol), VHOX and VHS)

Directions
Smooth Almond Butter
Preheat the oven to 350°F / 180°C.

Spread the almonds on a baking sheet and roast for 15 minutes. (NOTE: Check the almonds at 10 minutes. Some older ovens may be hotter than others).

Place the roasted almonds in a food processor and let it run for about 5 - 10 minutes until desired smoothness, stopping occasionally to scrape down the sides.

Be patient. It takes a few minutes for the almonds to release the oils for a creamy nut-butter.

Within the first few minutes, you'll notice a dry, meal-like consistency. The fibers will eventually break down. (NOTE: older food processors may require a bit more time).

Chunky Almond Butter
Roughly chop ¼ cup of roasted almonds (either with knife or a food processor). Set aside.

Follow the steps above to make a Smooth Almond Butter with the remaining almonds.

Once you reach a smooth, creamy texture, add the roughly chopped almonds and pulse for 10 seconds.

Store in a tightly sealed jar in the refrigerator for up to 3 months.

COLOMBIA

The following recipes were kindly donated to me by Maria.

The vegetables and fruit in these recipes will only make them Fructose Friendly. I have tried to source out whether they have Fructose, Fructans, Polyols or Galactans in them and have indicated this beside the ingredient plus a few ingredients have alternatives beside them or in the notes at the end of each recipe. I am hoping that this will help you as much as it has helped me. Salicylates and Oxalates may also be issues for some people so I have added them as well. They will all be noted in the code form below or mentioned in the notes. Please read these.

Low – L, Medium – M, High – H, Very High – VH, Salicylates – S, Oxalates – OX
Fructose – F, Fructans – FOS, Polyols – PO, Galactans – GOS

I have placed some homemade recipes for substituting the ingredients after the main recipes. These recipes will be for Gluten Free, Fructose Friendly, Lactose Free or Friendly, Diabetic Friendly and IBS Friendly depending on your sensitivity so that you can make your own if you want to. Please remember that Fructans, Polyols and Galactans can also come with Fructose.

Substituting ingredients will alter the original taste; however, it is a way to try different recipes from other countries and you can adjust the taste to your liking. Make these recipes your own and use your ingredients if you want to as you know what's best for you.

Australian tablespoons and cups measurements are used and they are: 1 teaspoon equals 5ml; 1 tablespoon equals 20ml; 1 cup equals 250ml. Oven temperatures are for conventional; if using fan-forced (convection), reduce the temperature by 20°C.

Meat Empanadas	290
Sancocho (Colombian Soup)	291
Traditional Tamales (Pork)	292
Sancocho De Gallina (Chicken Or Hen Soup)	294
Homemade Guacamole	295
Hogao Sauce	295
Bandeja Paisa With Arepas And Hogao Sauce	296
Frijoles Paisas (Pinto Beans)	298
Homemade Recipes For The Above Recipes	
Homemade All-Purpose Seasoning Substitute	299

MEAT EMPANADAS

Ingredients to suit your family
Yellow cornflour (MOX and HS) (not polenta - HS)
Potatoes (see notes)
Whole piece of Skirt steak
Capsicum (any colour) finely diced (see notes)
Tomatoes finely diced (HF, FOS, PO (mannitol), MOX and MS)
Green parts only of the spring onion diced (white part has M-HF, FOS, PO (mannitol) MOX and LS)
Garlic to taste (F, FOS, GOS, LOX and LS) (omit if you can't tolerate)
Coriander to taste (MOX and HS)
Salt to taste
Oil of your liking for frying

Directions
Slow cook the whole piece of steak in a little water until it is tender. Allow it to cool a little before cutting it in to large pieces. Rip or shred the pieces and set aside. Reserve the cooking water.

Cook the potatoes with their skins on until done and then peel.

Heat the oil in a saucepan over medium heat and put in the capsicum, tomatoes, onion, garlic and coriander and sauté for 4 minutes.

Add the cooked meat to the vegetables and add the potatoes, squashing them slightly between fingers when adding (the potatoes should be still be chunky but slightly mashed).

Mix gently and adjust seasoning.

Add enough warm meat juice or seasoned warm water to the cornflour to make a soft dough for rolling.

Serve with Guacamole. (Recipe in this section)

Notes
Fructose in potatoes can range anything between 582 mg – 989 mg depending on the size, type and skin colour. They also have FOS, PO and GOS. They can also be VHOX and MS again depending on the type of potatoes, colour of skin and how they are cooked.

Capsicum red has HF, FOS, PO (sorbitol), LOX and VHS
Capsicum green has HF, FOS, PO (sorbitol), MOX and VHS
Capsicum yellow has HF, FOS, PO (sorbitol), MOX and VHS

SANCOCHO (COLOMBIAN SOUP)

Ingredients

Meat soup bone or desired meat (beef stew meat or ox tail or chicken wings, or breast, peel skin)

6 red radishes sliced thin (HF, PO and VHS)

4 celery sticks, chopped (HF, FOS, PO (mannitol) and VHOX) or try using 1 cups celery leaves

½ onion, chopped (HF, HFOS, PO (mannitol), LOX and LS) or 3 spring onions sprigs (green parts only) diced (white part has M-HF, FOS, PO (mannitol) MOX and LS)

½ bell pepper, chopped or capsicum (see notes)

¼ cup cilantro (VLOX) chopped, if desired (can substitute with coriander (MOX and HS)

2 plantains (no info available) peeled and cut at angle or green bananas (F, FOS (inulin), PO (sorbitol), GOS and HOX)

1 yuca (F, FOS, GOS and HOX) peeled and cut into strips or sweet potato (HF, FOS, PO (mannitol), VHOX and HS) (you may use corn on the cob (HF, FOS, PO (xylitol), LOX and MS) and potatoes (see notes) in place of plantain and yuca)

Directions

In a Dutch oven or large saucepan, add meat and vegetables and fill with water to ¾ full and then add garlic, salt and pepper to taste. Boil for 30 minutes.

After meat is tender add plantains and yuca. Boil for 20 - 30 minutes more.

Follow same if corn on the cob and potatoes are added. This should take 1½ hours; the secret to good soup is the more you boil the better the taste.

Serve with Colombian white rice on a side dish.

Notes

Peppers, Green has HF, FOS, PO (sorbitol), GOS, MOX and VHS
Peppers, Red has HF, FOS, PO (sorbitol), GOS, VLOX and VHS
Peppers yellow has HF, FOS, PO (sorbitol), GOS, MOX and VHS
Capsicum red has HF, FOS, PO (sorbitol), GOS, LOX and VHS
Capsicum green has HF, FOS, PO (sorbitol), GOS, MOX and VHS
Capsicum yellow has HF, FOS, PO (sorbitol), GOS, MOX and VHS

Fructose in potatoes can range anything between 582 mg – 989 mg depending on the size, type and skin colour. They also have FOS, PO and GOS. They can also be VHOX and MS again depending on the type of potatoes, colour of skin and how they are cooked.

TRADITIONAL TAMALES (PORK)

Ingredients

3½ lbs or just over 1½ kg pork shoulder or 3½ lbs or just over 1½ kg pork butt, trimmed of fat and cut up
10 cups water
1 medium onion, quartered (HF, HFOS, PO (mannitol), LOX and LS) or 3 spring onions (green parts only) diced (white part has M-HF, FOS, PO (mannitol) MOX and LS) (see notes)
3 garlic cloves, minced (F, FOS, GOS, LOX and LS) (see notes)
3½ teaspoons salt
4 cups red chili sauce (F and VHS) (see recipe below)
¾ cup shortening to your liking
6 cups masa harina (see notes) or cornflour (MOX and HS)
1½ teaspoons baking powder (VLOX)
50 dried corn husks (about 8 inches long) most tamales are wrapped in corn husks, but parchment paper or even cotton bed-sheet material can also be used.

Directions

In a 5 quart Dutch oven or saucepan, bring pork, water, onion, garlic and 1½ teaspoon salt to boil. Simmer covered, about 2½ hours or until meat is very tender.

Remove meat from broth and allow both meat and broth to cool. (Chilling the broth will allow you to easily remove the fat if you desire to do so).

Shred the meat using 2 forks, discarding fat.

Strain the broth and reserve 6 cups.

In a large sauce pan, heat the red chili sauce and add meat; simmer, covered for 10 minutes.

To make masa beat shortening on medium speed in a large bowl for 1 minute.

In a separate bowl, stir together masa harina, baking powder and 2 teaspoons salt.

Alternately add masa harina mixture and broth to shortening, beating well after each addition. (Add just enough broth to make a thick, creamy paste).

In the meantime, soak corn husks in warm water for at least 20 minutes; rinse to remove any corn silk and drain well.

To assemble each tamale; spread 2 tablespoons of the masa mixture on the center of the corn husk (each husk should be 8" (20cm) long and 6" (15cm) wide at the top. If husks are small, overlap 2 small ones to form one. If it is large, tear a strip from the side).

Place about 1 tablespoon meat and sauce mixture in the middle of the masa. Fold in sides of husk and fold up the bottom.

Place a mound of extra husks or a foil ball in the center of a steamer basket placed in a Dutch oven. Lean the tamales in the basket, open side up.

Add water to Dutch oven just below the basket. Bring water to boil and reduce heat.

Cover and steam 40 minutes, adding water when necessary.

To freeze these for future meals, leave them in the husks and place them in freezer bags. To reheat, thaw and wrap in a wet paper towel and reheat in the microwave for 2 minutes for one or two or re-steam them just until hot.

RED CHILI SAUCE

Ingredients

15 large dried chilies (F, PO (mannitol), HOX and HS) of your liking **(see notes)**
4 - 5 garlic cloves (F, FOS, GOS, LOX and LS) (see notes)
2 teaspoons ground cumin (VHS)
1 teaspoon salt
2 teaspoons Gluten Free all-purpose flour or one to your liking
2 teaspoons olive oil (LOX and HS) or 2 teaspoons melted shortening or one to your liking

Directions

Remove stems and seeds from dried chili peppers.

Place peppers in a single layer on a baking sheet and roast in 350°F / 180°C oven for 2 - 5 minutes or until you smell a sweet roasted aroma, checking often to avoid burning.

Remove from oven and soak in enough hot water to cover for about 30 minutes or until cool.

Put peppers and 2½ cups of the soaking water (save the remaining soaking water), garlic, cumin and salt into a blender. Cover and blend until smooth.

In a 2 quart sauce pan, stir flour into oil or melted shortening over med heat until browned.

Carefully stir in blended chili mixture.

Simmer uncovered for 5 - 10 minutes or until slightly thickened. (If sauce gets too thick, stir in up to 1 cup of the remaining soaking water until you reach the desired thickness).

Notes

When working with chilies, use rubber gloves to protect your skin, and avoid contact with your eyes. Wash hands thoroughly with soap and water to remove all of the chili oils.

Masa harina is a very finely ground corn flour made from corn that's dried, cooked in water with slaked lime (which gives it distinctive flavor), ground, and dried again. Mixed with water (or sometimes oil), it forms the dough called "masa" that is used to make corn tortillas.

To get that distinctive flavor, try grinding stale or dry corn tortillas in a food processor until you get a fine powder. If the masa harina is used as a thickener (such as in chili), regular flour or cornmeal will give you the right texture, though the flavor won't be quite the same.

⅛ teaspoon asafoetida powder (may contain Gluten) can replace the minced garlic and onion. This is a strong spice so don't go over the specified amount.

SANCOCHO DE GALLINA (CHICKEN OR HEN SOUP)

Ingredients
3 ears fresh corn, cut into 3 pieces (HF, FOS, PO (xylitol), LOX and MS)
12 cups of water
½ cup aliños seasoning (see notes)
1 big whole chicken
1 teaspoon salt
2 green plantains (no info available), peeled and cut crosswise into 2" (5cm) pieces or green bananas (F, FOS (inulin), PO (sorbitol), GOS and MOX)
2 chicken bouillon/stock cubes (minus onion and garlic)
6 medium white potatoes, peeled and cut in half (see notes)
1 lb frozen yuca cut into big pieces (F, FOS, GOS and HOX) peeled and cut into strips or sweet potato (HF, FOS, PO (mannitol), VHOX and HS)
¼ cup chopped fresh cilantro (VLOX) or coriander (MOX and HS)
¼ teaspoon ground pepper (black - HOX and VHS, white - VLOX and VH)

Directions
In a large pot, place the chicken, corn, aliños seasoning, chicken bouillon/stock cube, salt and green plantain. Add the water and bring to a boil, then cover and reduce heat to medium and cook for about 30 - 35 minutes.

Add the potatoes, yuca and pepper and continue cooking for 30 more minutes or until the yuca and potatoes are fork tender. Stir in the cilantro.

Taste and adjust the seasoning. Serve in large soup bowls, dividing the chicken and vegetables evenly.

Notes
Fructose in potatoes can range anything between 582 mg – 989 mg depending on the size, type and skin colour. They also have FOS, PO and GOS. They can also be VHOX and MS again depending on the type of potatoes, colour of skin and how they are cooked

COLOMBIAN ALIÑOS (SEASONING)

Ingredients to make 2 cups
1 medium tomato, chopped (HF, FOS, PO (mannitol), MOX and MS)
½ cup red pepper, chopped (HF, FOS, PO (sorbitol), GOS, VLOX and VHS)
½ cup green pepper, chopped (HF, FOS, PO (sorbitol), GOS, MOX and VHS)
½ cup white onion, chopped (HF, HFOS, PO (mannitol), LOX and LS) or spring onions strips (green parts only) diced (white part has M-HF, FOS, PO (mannitol) MOX and LS)
2 garlic cloves, chopped (F, FOS, GOS, LOX and LS) (see notes)
1 teaspoon ground cumin (VHS)
1½ teaspoon of all-purpose seasoning (homemade recipe for substitution after main recipes)
¼ teaspoon ground black pepper (HOX and VHS)
1 cup cilantro, chopped (VLOX) or coriander (MOX and HS)
¼ cup olive oil (LOX and HS) or one to your liking
½ cup water

Directions
Put all ingredients in a blender and blend until smooth.

You can store this sauce in an airtight container in the refrigerator up to one week. You can also freeze it using an ice cube tray and then putting the cubes in a Zip Loc bag to store in the freezer.

Notes
A good pinch of asafoetida powder (may contain Gluten) can replace the minced garlic and onion. This is a strong spice so don't go over the specified amount.

*   *   *   *   *

HOMEMADE GUACAMOLE

There are many ways that people make Guacamole but this is the way that it was given to me.

Ingredients
1 avocado mashed or purée (F, FOS, PO (sorbitol), VLOX and HS)
Green parts only of a spring onion cut very fine (white part has M-HF, FOS, PO (mannitol) MOX and LS)
Dash lemon juice (F, PO (sorbitol), LOX and L-HS)
Water
Pinch salt

Direction
Mix all the ingredients together adding just enough water to make it thick and soft.

*   *   *   *   *

HOGAO SAUCE

Ingredients
3 tablespoons vegetable oil or one to your liking
1 cup green parts of the spring onions finely chopped (white part has M-HF, FOS, PO (mannitol) MOX and LS)
2 cups chopped tomatoes (HF, FOS, PO (mannitol), MOX and MS)
1 clove garlic minced (F, FOS, GOS, LOX and LS) or a small pinch of asafoetida powder (may contain Gluten. This is a strong spice so only use specified amount)
1 teaspoon ground cumin (VHS)
¼ teaspoon salt
¼ teaspoon black pepper (HOX and VHS)

Directions
In a saucepan, heat the oil and then add the spring onion, chopped tomatoes, garlic and cumin. Cook this on medium heat for about 10 minutes.

Lower the heat and add the salt and pepper and cook for a further 10 minutes until thick and then adjust the seasoning to your taste.

BANDEJA PAISA WITH AREPAS AND HOGAO SAUCE

Ingredients for 4 people
500g or 2¾ cups of white rice (F, FOS and VLOX) to your liking
4 Arepas or Corn dumplings (see recipe below)
4 slice of ripe plantains (no info available) (see notes)
½ cup of Hogao Sauce (see recipe prior to this recipe)
4 cans of pinto beans in water or 3 cups of dried pinto beans cooked (see notes) (FOS, GOS and VHOX)
1 large or 2 medium avocado (F, FOS, PO (sorbitol), VLOX and HS)
500g or 1lb of belly pork
4 Chorizos or sausages to your liking
4 eggs
500g or 1lb of beef whole piece
1 teaspoon of garlic paste (F, FOS, GOS, LOX and LS)
1 teaspoon of all-purpose seasoning (homemade recipe for substitution after main recipes)
Salt and black pepper (HOX and VHS)

Directions
Cook the white rice according to directions (see notes)

Make 4 Arepas or Corn cakes (see recipe below)

Cook 4 slices of fried plantain.

Prepare the Hogao sauce (see recipe above).

In a saucepan cook the beans, with the Hogao sauce and the all-purpose seasoning and let them to cook until they get a little bit thick.

Separately cook the meat with 4 cups of water, garlic, salt and pepper to taste.

Remove the meat and let it drain for a few minutes and grate it in a food processor or shred it.

Cut the belly pork into four portions and cook in salted water for several minutes. Then fry in a little bit of oil.

Fry the eggs separately.

Divide the avocado into 4 portions.

Cook the Chorizos or sausages in water and then fry in a little oil as well.

Plate up and serve immediately.

Note
This is a delicious dish and complex, but you can omit ingredients and or can be made with substitutions, like green bananas (F, FOS (inulin), PO (sorbitol), GOS and MOX) and the seasoning below. Some ingredients can be cooked in advance.

Pinto beans: soaking the beans for 12 hours or longer lowers oxalates and if you use warm water with a good teaspoon of bi-carb soda, may also lower the "gas" issue. Change water at regular intervals.

Plain white rice: soaking the rice for 12 hours lowers oxalates.

AREPAS

Ingredients
2 cups or 235g maize flour or cornmeal/cornflour (MOX and HS)
2 cups or 250ml water
A pinch of salt
Oil or Nuttelex Original or butter melted or one to your liking

Directions
Place the maize flour and a pinch of salt in a large mixing bowl. Use your fingers or a whisk to thoroughly combine them. Measure warm water and slowly pour it over the flour.

Use your hands to knead the flour and water together to create a soft pliable dough. Continue kneading until the dough has no more grainy lumps and can be rolled into a ball without falling apart. (If the dough seems too wet, add a few tablespoons of flour and continue kneading. If the dough falls apart easily, add a tablespoon or two of warm water. Continue adding water until the dough has reached the correct texture).

Take a handful of dough in your hands and shape it into a ball, then press it with your palms to form a large patty shape. It should be about ½" or 2½ cm thick and 3 - 4" or 7 - 10cm across, depending on how large you want your arepas to be.

Place the first arepa on a baking sheet and continue shaping arepas until you run out of dough or Place each ball between 2 plastic bags and with a flat pot cover flatten to ½" or 2½ cm.

(If you want to save the arepas to be cooked later, cover the baking sheet with plastic wrap and place it in the refrigerator for 3 - 4 days. You can freeze uncooked arepas, too. Wrap each one in plastic wrap and place them in a seal-able freezer container. They will keep this way for several months).

Add the oil or butter to a non-stick pan over medium heat. Place the arepas in the pan, and cook about 3 minutes on each side, until a crust forms or they are golden brown.

OR

After frying them place them in a preheated the oven to 250°C / 480°F for 10 minutes.

Variations
Add ⅓ cup white or mozzarella cheese, grated to dry ingredients OR Add 2 tablespoons sugar and 1 teaspoon toasted, crushed anise seeds OR Use shredded meat instead of the mince.

Serve with Hogao sauce (recipe prior to this one)

FRIJOLES PAISAS (PINTO BEANS)

Ingredients
3 cups pinto beans (FOS, GOS and VHOX) (see notes)
1 or 2 pork hock (about ½ lb or 225g)
6 cups water
1 cup shredded carrot (HF, FOS (raffinose), PO (sorbitol), GOS, VHOX and HS)
½ teaspoon salt
½ green plantain, (no info available) cut into ¼" pieces or green banana (F, FOS (inulin), PO (sorbitol), GOS and MOX)

Sauce Mix
1 tablespoon chopped onion (HF, HFOS, PO (mannitol), LOX and LS) or spring onions (green parts only) diced (white part has M-HF, FOS, PO (mannitol) MOX and LS) (see notes)
2 cups diced tomatoes (HF, FOS, PO (mannitol), MOX and MS)
3 tablespoons vegetable oil or one to your liking
¼ teaspoon salt
1 garlic clove, minced (F, FOS, GOS, LOX and LS) (see notes)
¼ cup chopped fresh cilantro (VLOX) or coriander (MOX and HS)
¼ teaspoon ground cumin (VHS)

Directions
Stove Top
Wash the beans and soak overnight in warm/cold water. Drain the beans and rinse well and place in a large pot and add the water and pork hocks. Over medium-high heat, bring the beans to a boil, then cover the pot and reduce the heat to medium-low. Allow the beans to cook until almost tender, approximately 2 hours.

When the beans are cooking, prepare the sauce mix. In a large skillet, heat the vegetable oil over medium heat, add the tomatoes, onions, salt, garlic or asafoetida powder, cilantro or coriander and ground cumin and cook for 10 - 15 minutes.

When the beans are almost tender, add the sauce mix, plantains/green bananas, carrots and salt. Cover and cook for another hour or until the beans are fully cooked.

Slow Cooker
Use the same ingredients except use just 4 cups of water instead of 6.

Wash the beans and soak overnight in cold water. Drain the beans and place in a slow cooker, add 4 cups water and pork hocks and cook on high for about 2 hours.

Follow step 2 in the regular pot recipe.

Add the condiment mix, plantains, carrots and salt then cover and cook for another 3 hours. Taste for salt and serve.

Notes
Soaking the beans for 12 hours or longer lowers oxalates and if you use warm water with a good teaspoon of bi-carb soda, may also lower the "gas" issue. Change the water regularly.

A pinch of asafoetida powder (may contain Gluten) can replace the minced garlic (F, FOS, GOS, LOX and LS). This is a strong spice so don't use more than the specified amount.

HOMEMADE RECIPES FOR THE ABOVE RECIPES

HOMEMADE ALL-PURPOSE SEASONING SUBSTITUTE

Ingredients to make approx. ½ cup (4 oz)
1 tablespoon paprika (F and VHS) or turmeric (F, VHOX and VHS)
1 tablespoon ground cumin (VHS)
1 tablespoon ground coriander (MOX and HS)
1 tablespoon oregano powder (F, HOX and VHS)
1 tablespoon salt or adjust to your liking
½ tablespoon black ground pepper (HOX and VHS) or adjust to your liking
A pinch asafoetida powder (may contain Gluten) (see notes)

Directions
Mix all ingredients in a small bowl and store in a spice jar or air tight container.

Note
If you can't find these ingredients in powdered form, you can buy them whole and blend them in a food processor.

1 tablespoon garlic powder will replace the asafoetida powder or omit if you can't tolerate garlic. Asafoetida powder is a strong spice so only use the specified amount.

CYPRUS

The following recipes were kindly donated to me by Sylvia.

The vegetables and fruit in these recipes will only make them Fructose Friendly. I have tried to source out whether they have Fructose, Fructans, Polyols or Galactans in them and have indicated this beside the ingredient plus a few ingredients have alternatives beside them or in the notes at the end of each recipe. I am hoping that this will help you as much as it has helped me. Salicylates and Oxalates may also be issues for some people so I have added them as well. They will all be noted in the code form below or mentioned in the notes. Please read these.

Low – L, Medium – M, High – H, Very High – VH, Salicylates – S, Oxalates – OX
Fructose – F, Fructans – FOS, Polyols – PO, Galactans – GOS

I have placed some homemade recipes for substituting the ingredients after the main recipes. These recipes will be for Gluten Free, Fructose Friendly, Lactose Free or Friendly, Diabetic Friendly and IBS Friendly depending on your sensitivity so that you can make your own if you want to. Please remember that Fructans, Polyols and Galactans can also come with Fructose.

Substituting ingredients will alter the original taste; however, it is a way to try different recipes from other countries and you can adjust the taste to your liking. Make these recipes your own and use your ingredients if you want to as you know what's best for you.

Australian tablespoons and cups measurements are used and they are: 1 teaspoon equals 5ml; 1 tablespoon equals 20ml; 1 cup equals 250ml. Oven temperatures are for conventional; if using fan-forced (convection), reduce the temperature by 20°C.

Moussaka (Eggplant And Mince With Béchamel)	301
Spanokopita (Spinach Pie)	302
Anginares me Koukia Stifatho (Broad Bean And Artichoke Casserole)	303
Psari Plaki (Baked Fish)	304
Baklava (Almond Pastry Roll)	305
Galaktoboureko (Semolina Custard Pastry)	306
Homemade Recipes For The Above Recipes	
Gluten Free Filo Pastry Number 1	307
Filo Dough Number 2	307
Homemade Tin/Can Tomatoes Substitute	307
How To Make Tomato Paste The Quick And Easy Way	308
Homemade Béchamel Sauce	309

MOUSSAKA (EGGPLANT AND MINCE WITH BÉCHAMEL)

Ingredients
Eggplant and mince
2 eggplants sliced (F, FOS, PO (xylitol), MOX and HS)
600g or 1lb 2oz extra lean minced beef
1 kg or about 2.2 lbs potatoes peeled and sliced (see notes)
2 medium onions grated (HF, HFOS, PO (mannitol), LOX and LS) or spring onions (green parts only) diced (white part has M-HF, FOS, PO (mannitol) MOX and LS) (see notes)
4 garlic cloves crushed (F, FOS, GOS, LOX and LS) (see notes)
2 tablespoons extra virgin olive oil (LOX and HS) or one to your liking
½ cup white wine (substitutes water, white grape juice (F, PO (sorbitol), LOX and MS), diluted cider vinegar (F, L-MOX and VHS) or white wine vinegar (L-MOX and VHS))
400g or 14oz tin diced tomatoes (F, PO (aspartame), H-VHOX and LS?) (homemade recipe after main recipes)
2 tablespoons tomato paste (HF, FOS, PO (mannitol), HOX and VHS) (homemade recipe after main recipes)
2 bay leaves (VHS)
1 cinnamon stick (F, HOX and VHS)
1 teaspoon allspice (VHS)
1 teaspoon beef stock powder (salt reduced and minus onion and garlic)
Pinch of pepper (black - HOX and VHS, white - VLOX and VHS)

Béchamel Sauce
4 cups of prepared Béchamel Sauce (homemade recipe after main recipes)
⅓ cup Lactose Free light grated cheese or one to your liking
⅓ cup kefalotyri cheese or Romano or Parmesan grated
2 eggs

Directions
Preheat the oven to 180°C / 350°F and thinly slice the potatoes and dry bake on a baking paper until tender and then set aside. Thinly slice the eggplant and place on a baking tray. Sprinkle with a pinch of salt and brush the tops with the rest of the oil. Bake in the preheated oven for 10 minutes or until brown.

In a large saucepan, sauté the onion and garlic in 1 tablespoon of oil until softened. Add the mince and brown all over. Once mince is brown, add the wine, tomatoes, tomato paste, bay leaves, cinnamon stick, allspice, stock powder and pepper and simmer for a further
10 minutes. Remove the bay leaves and cinnamon stick.

In a baking dish, cover the bottom with sliced potato, layer with eggplant and then mince. Continue to layer in order until all ingredients are used.

Prepare béchamel sauce and remove from heat before stirring in the eggs and cheese and getting an even smooth consistency. Pour over the top layer of eggplant in the dish. Return to the oven and bake for 40 - 45 minutes or until golden.

Notes
Only use ⅛ teaspoon of asafoetida powder which is a strong spice to replace onion and garlic.

Fructose in potatoes can range anything between 582 mg – 989 mg depending on the size, type and skin colour. They also have FOS, PO and GOS. They can also be VHOX and MS again depending on the type of potatoes, colour of skin and how they are cooked.

SPANOKOPITA (SPINACH PIE)

Ingredients
Pastry
2 cups Gluten Free plain flour or one to your liking (see notes)
1 cup Gluten Free self-raising flour or one to your liking (see notes)
½ cup extra virgin olive oil (LOX and HS) or one to your liking
1 cup warm water
Pinch of salt and pepper (black - HOX and VHS, white - VLOX and VHS)

Spinach Filling
2 bunches of silverbeet (F, FOS, GOS, HOX and HS) or spinach (HF, FOS, PO (sorbitol), (fresh) VHOX and HS and (frozen) VHOX and MS) washed and stems removed
¼ cup extra virgin olive oil (LOX and HS) or one to your liking
2 tablespoons uncooked rice or one to your liking (see notes)
5 eggs
500g or 4 cups Mizithra cheese or Mascarpone, Ricotta, Pecorino Romano, Parmesan or Nutritional yeast (see notes)
100g or 1 cup crumbled reduced fat Feta cheese
½ cup Kefalotyri cheese or Romano or Parmesan grated
1½ cups reduced fat cheddar cheese grated (see notes for all cheeses)
Pinch of salt and pepper (black - HOX and VHS, white - VLOX and VHS)
1 egg whisked for glazing

Directions
Pastry
Place flours in a large bowl and blend together. Add in the olive oil and water and season with salt and pepper.

Mix to form a dough and then knead on a floured board until well combined.

Cover dough and allow to rest in the fridge for about an hour.

Spinach Filling
Roughly chop silverbeet or spinach, squeeze the leaves over the sink to remove excess water.

Whisk the eggs and combine with the silverbeet or spinach, cheeses and rice in a large bowl. Season with salt and pepper.

Mix with hands thoroughly until eggs and cheeses are evenly distributed over the silverbeet or spinach.

Assembly
Preheat oven to 180°C / 350°F. Lightly oil a baking tray (15" x 10" / 38cm x 25cm) with oil.

Divide pastry into 2 portions and roll out one half until big enough to line the tray.

Pour in the filling and distribute evenly over the pastry.

Roll out the other half and place on top and then pinch edges closed to seal well.

With a fork evenly pierce the top pastry layer about 6 – 8 time and then brush the top with the whisked egg.

Bake until golden brown and then cut into squares. It can be served warm or cold.

Notes

Gluten Free flour is high in carbs so be mindful if you are Diabetic or have to watch your carb count. You may need to adjust the liquid to suit the flour you are using. Optional flour mixes on pages 13 & 14.

There is a Lactose Free or Friendly cheese chart on page 36 followed by some homemade cheese alternatives.

Basmati is low in carbs and has FOS, LOX and MS. Doongara is low in carbs and has FOS and LOX. Soaking rice and grains for 12 hours lowers oxalates.

Nutritional yeast is sold in the flake form or yellow powder, which is used by vegans as a substitute for dairy products. It is high in vitamins and proteins, and most importantly, it is low in fat. This substitute can be used when you just have to sprinkle the cheese as it has a cheesy and creamy flavor.

*   *   *   *   *

ANGINARES ME KOUKIA STIFATHO (BROAD BEAN AND ARTICHOKE CASSEROLE)

Ingredients
500g packet or 2 cups frozen broad beans or fresh cooked (F, FOS, PO, GOS, HOX and S)
400g or 14oz tinned artichoke hearts in brine drained (F, FOS, MOX and HS)
400g or 14oz tin diced tomatoes (F, PO (aspartame), H-VHOX and LS?) (homemade recipe after main recipes)
1 large onion (HF, HFOS, PO (mannitol), LOX and LS) or spring onions (green parts only) diced (white part has M-HF, FOS, PO (mannitol) MOX and LS) or a pinch of asafoetida powder which is a strong spice so only use the specified amount.
1 cup fresh or frozen peas (FOS, GOS, LOX and N-LS)
2 medium potatoes (see notes)
⅓ cup extra virgin olive oil (LOX and HS) or one to your liking
⅓ cup chopped dill (F, L-MOX and VHS) or tarragon (VLOX and VHS)
1 cup low salt vegetable stock (minus onion and garlic) (see notes)

Directions
In a large pan heat the oil and the sauté onion. Add the tomatoes and stock and then bring the mixture to the boil before reducing the heat to a simmer.

Cut potatoes into small pieces and add to the tomato sauce and simmer until soft.

Add the broad beans and peas and simmer until the liquid has reduced by about half.

Add artichoke hearts and dill and serve when the artichoke hearts are hot.

Notes
Fructose in potatoes can range anything between 582 mg – 989 mg depending on the size, type and skin colour. They also have FOS, PO and GOS. They can also be VHOX and MS again depending on the type of potatoes, colour of skin and how they are cooked.

In Australia Massel's make a liquid vegetable stock minus onion and garlic.

PSARI PLAKI

Ingredients
1kg or 2lb 3oz white fish fillet (snapper or Cod) or one to your liking
2 lemons juiced (F, PO (sorbitol), LOX and L-HS)
Pinch of salt and pepper (black - HOX and VHS, white - VLOX and VHS)
2 onions finely chopped (HF, HFOS, PO (mannitol), LOX and LS) or spring onions (green parts only) diced (white part has M-HF, FOS, PO (mannitol) MOX and LS) (see notes)
1 carrot finely chopped (HF, FOS (raffinose) PO (sorbitol), GOS, VHOX and HS)
2 celery sticks finely chopped (HF, FOS, PO (mannitol) and VHOX) try using ½ cup celery leaves instead
¼ cup extra virgin olive oil (LOX and HS) or one to your liking
Dash of water
2 garlic cloves crushed (F, FOS, GOS, LOX and LS) (see notes)
400g or 14oz tin diced tomatoes (F, PO (aspartame), H-VHOX and LS?) (homemade recipe after main recipes)
1 tablespoons tomato paste (HF, FOS, PO (mannitol), HOX and VHS) (homemade recipe after main recipes)
¾ cup white wine (substitutes water, white grape juice (F, PO (sorbitol), LOX and MS), diluted cider vinegar (F, L-MOX and VHS) or white wine vinegar (L-MOX and VHS))
¼ teaspoon dried oregano (F, HOX and VHS)
1 tomato sliced (HF, FOS, PO (mannitol), MOX and MS)
3 tablespoons parsley (F, PO (mannitol), LOX and LS) or coriander (MOX and MS) finely chopped

Directions
Preheat the oven to 180°C / 350°F.

Put the fish in an oiled baking pan and cover with lemon juice, salt and pepper and set aside.

In a saucepan, sauté onions in 2 tablespoons of oil and a dash of water until softened and then add the carrot and celery/leaves and cook until the carrot is soft.

Add the garlic, oregano, tinned tomatoes, tomato paste and wine and simmer for 10 minutes or until the wine has evaporated.

Cover the fish with the vegetable mixture and arrange the tomato slices on top and then sprinkle with parsley/coriander and remaining oil.

Bake for about 45 minutes.

Notes
A good pinch of asafoetida powder can be used to replace the onion and garlic. This is a strong spice so only use the specified amount.

BAKLAVA (ALMOND PASTRY ROLL)

Ingredients
1 packet filo pastry (2 homemade recipes after main recipes)
250g or 1 cup Nuttelex Original or unsalted butter or one to your liking
250g or 2 cups almonds (FOS, PO (xylitol), VHOX and VHS) (see variations)
½ teaspoon cinnamon powder (F, HOX and VHS)
1 teaspoon dextrose powder (may contain Gluten) or sugar

Syrup
3 cups dextrose powder (may contain Gluten) or sugar or sweetener to your liking
1½ cups of water
1 cinnamon stick (F, HOX and VHS)
2 cloves (F, VHOX and HS)
½ a lemon juiced (F, PO (sorbitol), LOX and L-HS)
1 slice of lemon (F, PO (sorbitol), VLOX and MS)

Directions
Syrup
Combine water, sugar, cinnamon stick and cloves in a saucepan and then add the lemon slice and juice.

Boil on high heat for 6 minutes continuing to stir as sugar dissolves and then remove from heat and set aside.

Preheat oven to 200°C / 390°F.

Blend almonds, cinnamon powder and sugar together and set aside.

Divide filo pastry into 4 even bundles (about 5 sheets per bundle). Pull out 1 bundle and cover remaining bundles with a cloth so they don't dry out.

Melt butter in the microwave and brush melted butter over each layer of filo, stacking each layer together.

Sprinkle ¾ cup of almond mixture over the filo, leaving 10cm (4") from short end with just butter.

Start rolling baklava from the short edge that has nuts on it and make sure it stays firm. Continue rolling until you reach the end of filo. The buttered edge will make it all stick together.

Place baklava roll onto a cutting board and make 1cm deep diagonal cuts to create 6 even pieces. This will make it easier to cut the baklava when baked. Hold ends tightly so nuts don't fall out and place into a 30 x 25cm (12" x 10") baking dish or tray.

Repeat with the remaining bundles and placing them next to each other closely in the baking dish or tray and bake for 1 hour or until golden.

Once baklava has cooled, evenly pour 500ml or 2 cups of the syrup over the top and leave for 1 hour to allow the baklava to soak up the syrup before serving.

Variations
For people who can't eat almonds nuts, try making these with another nut, dates (Deglet Noor F, PO, HOX and VHS. Medjool HF, PO, HOX and VHS) or a filling to your liking.

GALAKTOBOUREKO (SEMOLINA CUSTARD PASTRY)

Ingredients
1 packet filo pastry (2 homemade recipes after main recipes)
1lt or 4 cups Lactose Free full cream milk or one to your liking
¾ cup semolina (only info I could find that it has Gluten. Substitution ideas in notes) (**NOT POLENTA**)
1 teaspoon vanilla sugar or vanilla extract (F, VLOX and VHS)
4 eggs
1 cup dextrose powder (may contain Gluten) or sugar or sweetener to your liking
75g or ⅓ cup Nuttelex Original or butter or one to your liking
1 teaspoon grated lemon rind (F, PO (sorbitol) and HOX)

Syrup
3 cups dextrose powder (may contain Gluten) or sugar or sweetener to your liking
1½ cups water
1 cinnamon stick (F, HOX and VHS)
2 cloves (F, VHOX and HS)
½ a lemon juiced (F, PO (sorbitol), LOX and L-HS)
1 slice of lemon (F, PO (sorbitol), VLOX and MS)

Directions
Syrup
Combine water, sugar, cinnamon stick and cloves in a saucepan and then add the lemon slice and juice. Boil on high heat for 6 minutes continuing to stir as sugar dissolves and then remove from heat and set aside.

Custard
In a large saucepan add eggs, dextrose powder/sugar, vanilla sugar/extract and semolina and mix with a whisk. Add the milk slowly and continuing whisking.

Place the saucepan onto a medium heat and bring to the boil and keep stirring the mixture to avoid it curdling. Once the mixture has started to thicken, add the butter and continue stirring until it boils and then take the custard off the heat and mix in the lemon rind before setting aside.

Assembly
Preheat oven to 200°C / 390°F.

Divide filo pastry into 2 even bundles (about 10 sheets per bundle). Pull out 1 bundle and cover remaining bundles with a cloth so they don't dry out.

Melt butter in the microwave and brush melted butter over each layer of filo, stacking each layer together. Fold filo stack in half then place into a 30 x 25cm (12" x 10") oven proof baking dish. Pour over the custard mixture forming an even layer.

Butter remaining bundle and fold in half and place on top of custard mix. Cut filo into 9 pieces (3 rows x 3 columns) and then each rectangle diagonally in half. Bake for 1 hour and 15 minutes or until golden.

Notes
Semolina Substitutions
Kamut Flour, Spelt Flour, All-Purpose Flour, Rice Flour, Amaranth Flour, Quinoa Flour, Garbanzo Flour

HOMEMADE RECIPES FOR THE ABOVE RECIPES

GLUTEN FREE FILO PASTRY NUMBER 1

Ingredients
¼ cup water
2 cups Gluten Free flour (probably use amaranth flour) (HOX) (options pages 13 & 14)
4 teaspoons olive oil (LOX and HS) or one to your liking
¼ teaspoon salt

Directions
Sift flour and salt and make a well, then add the water and oil in it. Work the dough, and on a dusted board, knead it for about 5 minutes. It gets smooth. Roll it out in a huge rectangle, put a damp towel over it, and let it stay for about 15 minutes.

Work it out again so it's about 3 x 3 feet (92 x 92cm). Cut it with a knife to sheet size, and then use for your recipe.

* * * * *

FILO DOUGH NUMBER 2

Ingredients
1¾ cups fine white rice flour
¼ cup sweet rice flour
4 teaspoons of guar gum or xanthan gum or chia seed powder (FOS, OX and HS)
1 teaspoon gelatin (VLOX)
1 egg
¼ - ½ cup Lactose Free milk or one of choice
1 stick butter or ½ cup or 4oz or 113g Nuttelex Original, melted or margarine or oil
1 teaspoon rice malt syrup (Fructose Free)

Directions
Mix together rice flour, sweet rice flour, xanthan gum/guar gum/chia seed powder and gelatin. Make a well in dry ingredients large enough to hold the liquids.

Lightly beat egg with ¼ cup milk, butter and rice malt syrup. Pour this into well in dry ingredients. Mix everything together until you have a soft dough. (Depending on brand of rice flour, you may want to stir in more milk).

Wrap dough in plastic wrap until ready to use for your favorite holiday pastry. Store in refrigerator if not using immediately.

* * * * *

HOMEMADE TIN/CAN TOMATOES SUBSTITUTE

Place the weight amount of tomatoes needed in a bowl of boiling water for 5 minutes. Carefully remove and peel tomatoes; they will be hot. Place them in a saucepan and bring them to a boil. Cook until soft but not soggy. Follow the recipe as to their use. For crushed tomatoes, process by pulsing for a few seconds in your processor or chop finely.

HOW TO MAKE TOMATO PASTE THE QUICK AND EASY WAY

This recipe makes about 5 heaped tablespoons of paste.

Directions

Soak 2 kilos (4½ lbs) of tomatoes (HF, FOS, PO (mannitol), MOX and MS) in boiling water for five minutes or until the skins can be easily peeled off. Drain and carefully remove the tomato skin. The tomatoes may be hot to handle.

Carefully cut tomatoes in half or quarters longways and de-seed completely. Place tomato pieces in to processor and process to a very liquidy paste.

If you have a slow cooker, then place this liquid paste in it and leave it to reduce and thicken up. Stir occasionally. I left mine on all day and got a beautiful thick tomato paste to use in my recipes.

If you don't have a slow cooker you can cook the paste in a 350°F / 180°C preheated oven on shallow trays until it is reduced to a paste. Check the tomatoes every half hour, stirring the paste and switching the position of the trays so that they reduce evenly. Over time, the paste will start to reduce to the point where you can make one tray.

The paste is done when shiny and brick-colored, and it has reduced by more than half. There shouldn't be any remaining water or moisture separating from the paste at this point. This will take 3 - 4 hours, though exact baking/cooking times will depend on the juiciness of your tomatoes and your oven. After the paste was cold; I put it in a container and kept it in the refrigerator or freezer.

Making small batches when you need it can be useful; however, if you use a lot of tomato paste then just double or triple the amount of tomatoes used.

I made a very small batch using the same prep method but I cooked them down in my non-stick frypan over low heat and I continually stirred the mixture. I did not add anything to the paste because I can do that when I use it in a recipe.

Notes

Use paste tomatoes, like Romas and San Marzanos, for the greatest yield. Juicy heirloom tomatoes can also be used, but will have a smaller yield.

You can also make a "tomato paste" by simply pureeing sun dried tomatoes. Add a little oil if necessary, or reconstitute the tomatoes a little bit, then if it's slightly too thin, bake it in your oven on 350°F / 180°C until the water evaporates and it makes a paste.

When de-seeding the tomatoes, place the seeds in a bowl along with the juice. If you strain this through a sieve, you can freeze the juice in ice cube trays and use as part of the flavouring when a recipe calls for stock and if you're really conservative, you could plant the seeds and grow your own tomato plants.

If you are intolerant to all FODMAPs then the skins can be dried and used crumbled, chopper or minced in any dish that calls for tomato flavouring. Only a small amount needs to be used.

HOMEMADE BÉCHAMEL SAUCE

This creamy sauce and is the basis for many pasta dishes and there is more butter than flour used in this recipe and the flour needs to cook for 2 - 3 minutes before adding the milk.

Ingredients to make approx. 500 ml or 2 cups
75g or ⅓ cup butter or Nuttelex Original for Lactose Free or one to your liking
50g or ⅓ cup Gluten Free plain flour (wheat free) to your liking
About 500ml or 2 cups Lactose Free milk or one to your liking
Salt to taste

Directions
Melt the butter in a medium saucepan. When it begins to foam, add the flour and cook for 2-3 minutes. Remove from the heat and add all the milk, whisking well.

When the flour and butter have blended well into the milk, return the pan to the heat and bring to the boil. Add a little salt and simmer for a further 2 - 3 minutes. Use immediately.

Notes
To make this sauce slightly different, you can add some chopped parsley and some Lactose Free grated cheese. A dash of cayenne pepper will give this sauce a little kick if you would like it that way.